Women and Indians on the Frontier

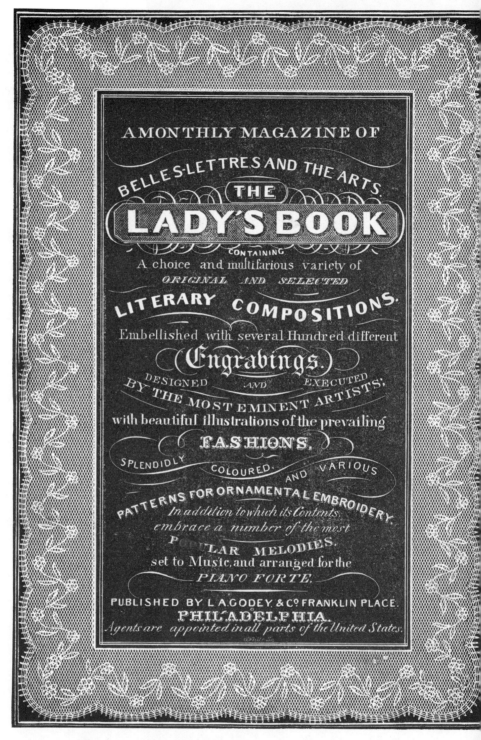

Godey's Lady's Book, 1833. The popular magazine influenced women's views of their abilities and prerogatives as well as their fashions.

Women and Indians on the Frontier
1825–1915

Glenda Riley

University of New Mexico Press
Albuquerque

Portions of Chapter 2 appeared as two articles: "European Views of White Women in the American West," *Journal of the West* 21 No. 2 (April 1982): 71–81, copyrighted by the Journal of the West, Inc., and reprinted by permission; and "Some European (Mis)Perceptions of American Indian Women," *New Mexico Historical Review* 59 (July 1984): 237–66, reprinted by permission of the regents of the University of New Mexico and the editor of the *New Mexico Historical Review*.

Portions of Chapter 3 appeared as "The Specter of a Savage: Rumors and Alarmism on the Overland Trail," *Western Historical Quarterly* XV (October 1984), 427–44, reprinted by permission.

Portions of Chapters 4 and 5 appeared as "Frontierswomen's Changing Views of Indians in the Trans-Mississippi West," *Montana, The Magazine of Western History* 34 No. 1 (Winter 1984): 20–35, reprinted by permission.

Library of Congress Cataloging in Publication Data

Riley, Glenda, 1938–
    Women and Indians on the frontier, 1825–1915.

    Bibliography: p.
    Includes index.
    1. Women pioneers—West (U.S.)—Attitudes—History—19th century. 2. Women pioneers—West (U.S.)—Attitudes—History—20th century. 3. Indians of North America—West (U.S.)—History. 4. West (U.S.)—Race relations. 5. Frontier and pioneer life—West (U.S.) I. Title.
    F596.R56   1984   978'.02   84-13235
    ISBN 0-8263-0778-7
    ISBN 0-8263-0780-9 (pbk.)

Design by Milenda Nan Ok Lee

Fifth paperbound printing, 1993

For my mother
Friend, confidante, supporter, proofreader, and critic

Contents

Illustrations

Acknowledgments

As is always the case with historical studies of this size and complexity, its development and completion owes much to the energies of many people.

The efficient and uncomplaining staffs of many libraries and archives aided me in the research stage, including the Newberry Library in Chicago, the Huntington Library in San Marino, California, the Bancroft Library in Berkeley, California, the California State Library in Sacramento, California, and my own institution's library, The University of Northern Iowa in Cedar Falls, Iowa. Special thanks go to Daryl Morrison and Jack Haley at the University of Oklahoma Library's Western History Collections in Norman, Oklahoma and to Bill Richter and Ralph Elder at the University of Texas's Eugene C. Barker Texas History Center in Austin, Texas. The patience and persistence of the many dedicated librarians and archivists who cheerfully answered questions, checked citations, ran photocopies, and retrieved endless manuscripts and documents for me cannot be adequately described.

In addition, three student assistants at the University of Northern Iowa deserve mention for their diligence as "gophers," typists, and general helpers. They are Kimberly Keiser, now an archivist herself,

Tara B. Whitnah, and Karmen Berger. All three are to be commended for the many library hours they logged during the course of the project.

The single greatest contribution to my research came from the late Ray Allen Billington, who graciously shared his own research notes on European images of western Americans with me during the summer of 1980. Having just completed his monumental *Land of Savagery, Land of Promise,* Ray was convinced that something more should be done with the resources he had collected on images of white and Indian women in the course of writing that book. Consequently, I spent hours listening to his thoughts and encouraging words, days sorting materials in his office, and months working through the many items he allowed me to haul home to Iowa. His generosity resulted in several scholarly papers, two journal articles, and a chapter in this book.

I was also fortunate to receive various grants to do research and writing for portions of the project. The Newberry Library provided fellowship support during the summers of 1978 and 1979; the National Endowment for the Humanities funded my participation in a seminar on "The New West" under the distinguished direction of W. Turrentine Jackson at the University of California, Davis, during the summer of 1980; and The University of Northern Iowa underwrote the completion of the manuscript with a Summer Research Fellowship during the summer of 1982. UNI also contributed various travel monies as well as the assistance of two fine typists, Judy Dohlman and Patricia Murphy.

As the writing of the manuscript proceeded, several readers contributed their time, energy, and expertise to its refinement. Richard S. Kirkendall, Henry A. Wallace Professor of Agricultural History at Iowa State University in Ames; Sandra L. Myres, Professor of History at the University of Texas at Arlington; and David A. Walker, Professor of History at the University of Northern Iowa; all have my everlasting appreciation for their many helpful comments and suggestions.

And finally, I would be remiss if I did not thank my mother Lillian Gates and son, Sean Riley, for their willingness to put up with the general chaos created by the writing of a book. They became skilled at running an unending variety of errands and otherwise filling in the gaps created by my seeming fixation to my typewriter. For this, and the general cheerfulness that they maintained, I am grateful.

Introduction

During the past decade, awareness of minority group issues prompted contemporary historians to explore white perceptions of American Indians. They have been particularly interested in the ways in which contact, interaction, and policy developed between the two populations in the American West in the nineteenth century. In discussing what images and stereotypes whites held toward Indian peoples, it has generally been assumed that these attitudes were adopted and applied in an identical manner by both white men and women.[1] While many argue that white women often shared the prejudices of the men with whom they lived, the major finding of this study is that women's perceptions of minority groups were modified by their perceptions of themselves and their distinct place in American society.

As women moved westward they, like whites in general, did carry with them certain deeply ingrained images and preconceptions of the native groups they would meet. But, as women, they also labored under a set of images and preconceptions of females in the nineteenth century that influenced and shaped their views of American Indians. As a result, they emphasized and reacted to particular aspects of Indian culture, society, and value systems. They responded, at least initially, in exactly the ways expected of properly indoctrinated white women of the nineteenth century.

A crucial change in this pattern of response appeared frequently as frontierswomen came into contact with various types of American

Indians, while at the same time discovering their own resilience in the face of the harsh demands imposed on them by the western environment. The effect of both experiences was quite often a revision of commonly held beliefs regarding what constituted "real" Indians and "true" women. Many frontierswomen began to reject such stereotypes in favor of a more authentic relationship between themselves and Indians. They started to trade and mix socially with natives and sometimes even expressed affection for and sympathy toward certain individuals.

This picture of white women's relations with American Indians was not reflected in contemporary American or European media. Journalists and novelists fed the anti-Indian prejudices of their reading public with fictionalized accounts of brutal and primitive savages who preyed especially upon the women who dared to venture into their domain. When women's own sources were printed, they were usually "penny dreadfuls" or captivity narratives that further inflamed white hatred of Indians.[2] Encouraged by profitable sales and enthusiastic readers, authors willingly responded with increasingly dramatic accounts of what were termed Indian depredations, particularly those perpetrated upon pure and passive womenfolk. One anthology of women's horror stories, for example, waxed eloquent on the subject:

> The very sight of Indians were terrible to many women on the frontier. The savages could not be looked upon without calling to mind the horrid work of the tomahawk and the scalping-knife—the desolated home and the butchered relatives.[3]

Undoubtedly, much can be learned about the tastes and prejudices of the nineteenth-century reading public from the captivity segments in James Fenimore Cooper's *Last of the Mohicans* or a captivity tale such as Abbie Gardner-Sharp's *Spirit Lake Massacre*, an inflammatory account of an attack on her own family.[4] But the only valid way to learn what average frontierswomen really felt about their associations with natives is to examine their own diaries, journals, letters, memoirs, and reminiscences. While these may not satisfy people of the late twentieth century accustomed to so-called scientific reports of public opinion, they are useful and valid sources of nineteenth-century opinions.

Introduction

Women's personal documents were seldom written for publication. Rather, they were usually a daily record of events of significance to a particular woman or perhaps to her family "back East" or in Europe. She had no reading public to please other than herself or her immediate family and friends. Except for memoirs and reminiscences, her writings mirrored her immediate feelings and reactions. The specific women's documents utilized here encompass diaries kept by trail women, journals and daybooks of women settlers, accounts by army wives, records of female missionaries, and several unpublished statements of women who were involved in violent white-Indian conflicts. They primarily represent the trans-Mississippi West, ranging from Iowa and Kansas to California and Oregon between the mid-1820s and the early decades of the twentieth century.

The one characteristic that these documents share is that they were not usually written as treatments of American Indians. They had no particular vested interest to promote, nor were they efforts to influence public opinion regarding Indians. They were generally reflections of the attitudes and feelings of a cross-section of western women who experienced the casual, intermittent contact with natives that was typical of most frontierswomen, rather than those of women such as missionaries and teachers who had more prolonged, intense intercourse with native groups. Trail diaries were particularly useful because they often revealed changes in women's reactions to Indians as they moved westward. Documents such as missionaries' accounts were less helpful because those women frequently held deeply ingrained and fairly inflexible perceptions of American Indians peculiar to their own sense of mission and not representative of frontierswomen in general.

Another salient feature of these women's documents is that they were not accurate sources of information regarding American Indian peoples and their customs, beliefs, and practices. Derived in large part from their own preconceptions, prejudices, and cultural values, these women's observations of Indians embodied their own perceptions of, and ethnocentric biases toward Indian societies rather than the realities of native cultures. The images and ideas that emerge from frontierswomen's writings in these pages are presented as illustrations of the ways in which frontierswomen saw events and people. No claim is made that these women's views were either accurate representations of American Indians or examples of defensible view-points and interpretations.[5] Consequently, the perspective of this study is that of white history rather than white-Indian or Indian history.[6]

The primary objective of this study is to examine the ways in which frontierswomen reacted to their initial contact and subsequent relations with American Indians. Rather than holding to the dark and dramatic picture presented them by myth and media, the women who went west frequently changed their minds to a more positive view of Indians. The study also attempts to contrast women's and men's exchanges with Indians, thus introducing the subject of gender into the study of white-native relations. And it offers several hypotheses intended to enlarge understanding of why the interplay between white women and American Indians developed a pattern that contradicted the accepted image, remained distinct from that established between white men and Indians, and that has received little, if any, scholarly attention.

In pursuing these goals, other larger questions are left unattended. There is no effort to resolve the long-standing controversy revolving around the definitions of the terms *frontier* and *West*. They are used interchangeably and are intended to denote regions in the trans-Mississippi United States existing into the early twentieth century, rather than to suggest a state of settlement or actual population figures as assessed and defined by the United States Census Bureau. In addition, minimal space is devoted to a defense and explanation of native cultural practices. Although a revision of the usual white conceptions of American Indians is both crucial and necessary to achieve further progress in the study of white-native relations, it is such an enormous task that it is introduced only occasionally to remind the reader that the women's views presented here expose much about white views and prejudices, but little about the reality of native life and culture.

Thus, the revisionist approach incorporated in this investigation of women's views of Indians in the trans-Mississippi West focuses neither on white males nor on natives, but on white frontierswomen themselves. By examining and elucidating women's westering experiences in relation to American Indians, I have tried to enhance awareness and understanding of the roles and relationships between women and Indians as well as to provide a model for the study of many other peoples in the American West.

American Influences upon
Frontierswomen's Ideas

In 1843 a popular American ladies' magazine exhorted its readers that women's "more delicate sensibility is the unseen power which is ever at work to purify and refine society."[1] This was hardly a novel sentiment. Ever since the first women migrated to the shores of British North America they had frequently been portrayed as purveyors of culture, inculcators of virtue and piety, and guardians of home and family. As early as 1692 the noted minister Cotton Mather summarized and idealized such thinking in his widely read *Ornaments for the Daughters of Zion*.[2] Although numerous other writers reiterated and enlarged upon Mather's view of American womanhood, not until the mid-nineteenth century did this image achieve the status of a cult.

Paradoxically, acceptance of the significance of women's passivity, domesticity, and moral guardianship peaked at about the same time that many American women were radically disrupting their domestic situations to transplant their homes, their families, and themselves to the vast and promising region that lay west of the Mississippi River. Whatever the social class or geographical location of these soon-to-be emigrants, they, like virtually all American women, were thoroughly indoctrinated into the ideals of true womanhood. But would

1

these westering women carry these values with them, or would they leave them behind like so much refuse as they crossed over the threshold of the old homestead for the last time? How would such ideas and aspirations serve them as they became frontierswomen? Would they discover that their customary ways of looking at women's roles were inappropriate in the less structured world of the West?

Several recent studies have argued persuasively that women migrants did indeed carry feminine value systems with them to their new homes. How they adapted these feminine ideals in practice to their new life-styles is as yet unclear, but apparently they did not shun the ideology of domesticity or the tenets of the moral guardian theory in favor of a more flexible, liberating set of ideals spawned by a frontier environment.[3] Since most of these women had been exposed throughout their lives to assertions and pronouncements regarding female qualities, it is not surprising that many women carried this dogma westward as an integral part of their cultural baggage.

The doctrine was purveyed through a rapidly proliferating, prescriptive literature that received impetus during the early 1800s from current religious revivalism stressing a return to fundamentalism. Vague fears about the role of women were also created by the first stirrings of industrialization, which compelled people to seek security by reaffirming old beliefs. Indeed, the very volume of ladies' periodicals, domestic novels, epistolary guidebooks, annuals, and gift books that appeared in the middle decades of the nineteenth century—all attempting to imbue women with the precepts of "true womanhood" and to guide them into customary female functions—suggests in itself society's need to allay a growing dissatisfaction with, and questioning of, traditional gender roles by a great many women. Even though its purpose was largely didactic, this literature still attracted a widespread and devoted readership among American women. Although now forgotten and gathering dust on library shelves, many domestic novels were runaway best-sellers in their own eras. And many ladies' periodicals enjoyed varying degrees of success in the new market created by the increased leisure, money, and education associated with the Industrial Revolution. While some of these publications vanished within a few years, others, such as *Godey's Lady's Book*, developed established reputations and extensive circulation that lasted from several decades to over half a century. In addition, the readership of such literature increasingly encompassed larger numbers of people, representatives from more social classes, and members of more age groups. All this was a result of rising literacy rate, decreasing costs of books and journals, and the introduction of a specialized literature for children.[4]

After examining numerous examples of such "domestic" writing (as it was called) from the mid-nineteenth century, one scholar stated conclusively:

> The greater part of our literary output has been created and conditioned principally by a feminine reading public. . . . This is particularly true of literature intended for popular consumption. . . . The women's magazines in America have always been those of widest circulation.[5]

Another writer has argued that these prescriptive outpourings actually did foster the development of a "sentimental" society in nineteenth-century America that is still reflected in modern mass culture.[6]

Advocates of these "domestic" or "sentimental" doctrines preached passive, or "feminine," ideals in opposition to the capitalistic or "male" standards that were allied with economic growth, industrial and territorial expansion, and urban development. Partially designed to lend larger meaning to the lives of the newly leisured middle and upper class women, sentimentalism (or domesticity, as some of its proponents labeled it) argued that such women had not become superfluous. Instead, it maintained that these women were absolutely crucial as guardians of morality and virtue for an increasingly capitalistic society. As defenders of home and hearth, women would protect traditional values, but they should not interfere in any essential way with the developments that were catapulting America toward prosperity and power.

Such teachings offered these women the hope of finding meaning and goals in a world radically altered from that of their grandmothers—or even of their mothers—where a woman's labor had been often critical to family survival. Devoid of real purpose and trapped in their homes while the menfolk left to labor in another part of the city, these middle and upper class women could not reasonably reject an ideology that justified their very existence. Consequently, even "intellectual" women who railed against the obvious limitations of women's "sphere" (as it was termed in the nineteenth century) could also see potential usefulness in the concept of separate spheres for men and women.[7] In 1814, Abigail Adams, long-time advocate of expanded roles for women in the new United States of America, wrote: "I believe nature has assigned to each sex its particular duties and sphere of action, and to act well your part, 'there all the honor lies.'"[8] And Margaret Fuller Ossoli, outspoken editor of the Transcendentalist journal *The Dial* and author of *Women in the Nineteenth Century,* declared in her 1852 memoirs, "I do think that the vocations of men and women differ, and that those who are forced to act out of their sphere are shorn of inward and outward brightness."[9]

Since even progressive thinkers concerning women's roles, such as Adams and Fuller, accepted the importance of the idea of a women's sphere, it is not surprising to discover that many other American women also adopted the notion. Evidently, women were beginning to see that the philosophy to be known as domesticity held out certain attractions to all women, not just the middle and upper class "ladies" to whom it was initially addressed. Even those women who intended to move westward were still very much members of the larger community of American women. Like their sisters, they too were increasingly vulnerable to the possibility that their otherwise subordinate female roles would earn status, respect, and esteem as women's moral impact upon society was amplified and idealized.

Supporters of domesticity and its associated values routinely proclaimed the idea that a woman's influence was "the all-mighty principle in order of social economy." Women, they maintained, were not only to "refine the tastes, ennoble the principles, and soften the asperities of man," but were also to pursue the "noble charge of training the youthful mind in the paths of virtue and true happiness."[10] These lofty and somewhat abstract pronouncements were intended to answer the issue of women's inequality in an era that was becoming increasingly committed to a democratic ideology of equal rights. Women could hardly help but notice that as opportunities for white males increased, their own roles became more circumscribed. They were reassured that equality was a moot issue because men and women operated in different spheres, each gender being equally important within its prescribed sphere. These spheres were supposedly determined by the unique physiology and intellect of men and women. According to male novelist T. S. Arthur's 1848 guidebook, *Advice to Young Ladies,* the very shape of women's heads indicated the development of brains and minds different from men's. Because of these obvious differences Arthur believed that men acted by intellect and women by love. It followed then that men and women were in a strange sense equal because each acted within their own capabilities, limitations, and of course, spheres.[11]

Other writers, who agreed that women exercised within their sphere a set of mental characteristics different from men's, stressed that women were particularly susceptible to religious feelings. "But where, let me ask," Reverend J. Adams queried in 1841, does religion "bloom with more grace than in the female heart?"[12] Author Hester Chapone also claimed that religion was the guiding principle for women and their sphere. She advised women that they would not only have an easier time with religious duties than men because of their natural softness and sensibility, but that they would need religion because women had to bear their sufferings in silence.[13] And in Stowe's 1859 novel, *The Minister's Wooing*, James admonished Mary, "You girls and women don't know your own power. . . . you are a living Gospel."[14]

The implications of these ideas for women's roles and status were enormous. If women developed feminine ideals based upon what one scholar has termed the "four cardinal virtues—piety, purity, submissiveness, and domesticity," while refusing to sully themselves by entering into the male sphere of business and politics, their salutary influence could be virtually unlimited.[15] A spate of domestic novels moralized that any problems within home and family could be effectively resolved by such women. The heroine of Caroline Lee Hentz's *Ernest Linwood*, published in 1856, reformed a maliciously jealous husband through her constancy and fortitude.[16] The heroine of another 1850s novel, *The Lamplighter* by Maria Cummins, was even more an epitome of the reforming female. Morally flawless, Gerty not only inspired every man who was fortunate enough to come into contact with her, but saved her sinning father by simply letting a tear fall on his sleeping face.[17] In 1855, in *Alone*, Ida could also reform those around her just by her own perfect example. Despite the disadvantages of being orphaned, young, and unmarried, she developed such moral strength that when her invalid guardian heaped abuse on her for trying to cheer him, she smiled and "bore up bravely until God gave her strength."[18]

The larger world of a woman's community could also benefit from her moral prowess.[19] According to Elizabeth Sandford's 1842 epistle titled *Woman, in Her Social and Domestic Character*, society received

5

its "balance and its tone" from women. "She may be here a corrective of what is wrong, a moderator of what is unruly, a restraint on what is indecorous," Sandford asserted. "Her presence will be a pledge against impropriety and excess, a check on vice, and a protection to virtue."[20] In 1839, a Dr. Blair, writing in the *Ladies Companion*, agreed that "the prevailing manners of an age depend, more than we are aware of, or are willing to allow, on the conduct of women: this is one of the principal things on which the great machine of human society turns."[21]

Even the country as a whole could be affected by women's behavior. They were therefore counseled that they should be interested in the affairs of their country, but not in a partisan way.[22] Rather, by acting as nurterers, teachers, and moral exemplars to young men, who comprised the future citizens of America, women could be "allies of legislators" and even "have agency in the prevention of crime."[23] And by training both female and male children to cherish their country and its government, women could affect America as well as its impact on the world. "Mothers of America!" the *Ladies Repository* reminded women in 1848, "the destiny of this mighty republic is under your control, and hence the consequent freedom and the political and moral elevation of humanity throughout the world."[24]

Catharine Beecher, women's educator and leading theorist of domestic philosophy, was particularly interested in the link between women and the well being of the country. She worked tirelessly to remedy "the fact that the honor and duties of the family state are not duly appreciated, that women are not trained for these duties as men are trained for their trades and professions, and that, as the consequence, family labor is poorly done, poorly paid, and regarded as menial and disgraceful." She believed that if schools were established to train women in their profession, appreciation of "the science and training which its high and sacred duties require" would develop.[25] She also sought a larger field of influence for women in her quest to bring them status and respect. She envisioned domesticity not just as professionalism in duties, but as social theory. Women were, Beecher argued, not only the protectors of home and family, but the saviors of democracy in America.[26] In her view, women filled a subordinate position in American society in order to promote the general good of society as a whole. In 1837, she explained that while woman holds a subordinate relation in society to the other sex, it is not because it was designed that her duties or her influence should be any the less important, or all-pervading. But it was designed that the mode of gaining influence and of exercising power should be altogether different and peculiar.[27]

Thus, to Beecher, women preserved the virtuous qualities of life that provided the very underpinning of the American democratic system.

Beecher did not stand alone in making such claims for the national influence of women. In 1854, author Lydia Maria Child drew upon world history to prove that "even under the most barbarous and tyrannical forms of society, the salutary influence of good and sensible women is felt and acknowledged."[28] A decade earlier another writer had insisted that it was only during the periods of history in which women had "proper influence" that any notable progress in science and literature was achieved.[29] Predictably, some commentators eventually portrayed women as the archetype for all humankind. "Let her stand forth as the model of humanity to the race," the *Ladies Repository* declared in 1846, "and let philosophy itself retire abashed in the presence of its long-sought idol, the restored image of the Good, the Beautiful, and True."[30]

Such inflated rhetoric, and the prominence it attempted to extend to women's roles, strongly appealed to many mid-nineteenth-century women. Blocked from exercising the right of suffrage and holding pubic office, unable to own property or control their wages, and certain to lose their children in a divorce action, these women understandably adopted many aspects of domestic philosophy. Through the arguments of domesticity, women's subordination and imputed inferiority served lofty purposes, including the redemption of all humankind. Moreover, its tenets even implied superiority for women, at least in the realm of morality. If women were the moral guardians of American society, the argument went, then the "other sex" must be lacking in this area.

But appeals to women were usually based on feminine ideals rather than on status and implied superiority. Some women quickly saw that their moral powers might be the very lever that would considerably widen women's sphere, while they coyly pleaded innocent to having entertained thoughts of even considering the possibility of leaving that sphere.[31] One of the most articulate of these women was Sarah Josepha Hale, who became editor of the much beloved *Godey's Lady's Book* in 1837. As early as 1827, Hale made it clear in her first novel, *Northwood,* that she believed that "'constitutions' and 'compromises' are the appropriate work of men: women are conservators of moral power, which, eventually . . . preserves or destroys the work of the warrior, the statesman, and the patriot."[32] In the many novels, articles, editorial comments, and personal crusades that followed, she demanded that women, in order to exercise fully their morality, be given access to improved education.[33] Maintaining all the while that she firmly believed in women acting only within their sphere, Hale frequently urged that morally uplifting domestic novels be written by women to fulfill their role as the moral shapers of society, that impressionable children be taught only by women rather than by the "other sex," that the poor and destitute be aided by women through charity organizations, and that the heathen of the world be rescued by women serving as missionaries.[34]

Although she aided in widening women's sphere, Hale never suggested that women leave it in order to enter into male affairs. On the contrary, "while the ocean of political life is heaving and raging with the storm of partisan passions among the men of America," she warned women in 1857, they, as "the true conservators of peace and goodwill, should be careful to cultivate every gentle feeling, and give prominence to every noble exhibition of patriotism."[35] Other domestic theorists of the era agreed that "the proper dignity of woman consists not in aspiring to direct the affairs of state, or to wield the reforms of the day."[36]

Yet a general consensus did exist that women's efforts were indispensable to the moral movements of the day, despite the fact that it would be clearly improper for them to lead such movements. During the Jackson years, an emphasis on reforming a variety of evils that had crept into American life developed, and women were called upon to exert their influence in every one of these movements. Temperance seemed a natural cause for women to support since so many of them were dependent economically on alcoholic husbands and fathers. To avoid this fate, young women were advised to shun the "society" and to refuse to "accept the addresses" of men who drank. Since men could not do without the society of women, they would naturally "take the jewel and throw away that which makes so many miserable outcasts."[37] If a woman found herself the wife or daughter of an alcoholic, she was to fight his perversity with all the moral power at her command. In one of the most popular novels of the time, *Ten Nights in a Barroom,* published in 1854, male novelist T. S. Arthur explored this approach by characterizing the drunkard as a pawn between the moral powers of his wife and daugher and those of evil, symbolized in this case by a rum seller.[38] To combat the problem of alcoholism on a larger social level, women formed temperance societies, held temperance conventions, and encouraged other women to desert alcoholic husbands.[39]

Whether there would be peace or strife in the country also seemed to depend on women.[40] They not only formed peace societies, but attempted to display peaceful behavior in their own lives as examples to society in general.[41] Charitable work outside of the home became part of women's province as well. In 1842 Margaret Coxe insisted that one of the claims that America could reasonably place upon its women would be for them to undertake the care of the sick and the needy.[42] Some years earlier, Elizabeth Sandford had argued that such demands upon women were justifiable because they had more leisure time than men in which to perform such duties, and they were also particularly suited to the care of the destitute and ill.[43] Throughout the 1840s and 1850s, Hale encouraged Ladies' Fairs for charitable purposes, supported the establishment of institutions to train female nurses and "visitors of the sick and the poor," and even suggested that the care of sick women and children become the responsibility of female physicians.[44]

Although the medical profession did not throw open its doors to interested women, the foreign mission field did. By mid-century it was firmly believed that women should extend their efforts to help the "poor and ignorant" by carrying the message of Christianity throughout the world.[45] According to poet Lydia Sigourney, women missionaries were the "stewards of God," and she immortalized them in many of her works.[46] Other writers also frequently eulogized women missionaries, emphasizing the talents and virtues displayed by such women and even lauding them as more courageous than medieval knights.[47] Young women were urged by an 1848 issue of the *Ladies Repository* to plan futures as female missionaries, and thereby "picture forth in their own lives, all that is lovely in woman's character, or sanctified and ennobling in woman's high ambition."[48] Another typical appeal from the 1840s maintained that Christianity "opens a wide field for the exercise of those peculiar talents and virtues which under the influence of a pure religion are resplendent" in woman's character.[49]

In addition to charity and missionary work, women also became Sunday school teachers. Women's morality earmarked them as the obvious inculcators of religious virtues, and many a young lady came to include a Sunday school class among her other good deeds. They were represented by Ida, who, in *Alone*, believed that the Sabbath was a "season of delight" due to the "band of little girls" who eagerly awaited her teachings.[50] Hale, immensely pleased by women's progress in these areas, asserted in 1846 that America owed "much of her glory to the character of her women" who supported the "cause of Christian mission, Sabbath schools, and charities of every kind."[51]

Of all the reform movements in which they participated, abolitionism involved the largest number of women reformers. As early as 1836, Angelina Grimke pointed out that women could aid the abolitionist cause, for although they did not make laws, they could read, pray, speak, and even act on the subject. Grimke explained that women could speak to relatives, friends, and acquaintances, while acting by educating or even freeing their own slaves.[52] In the same year, Elizabeth Chandler appealed to women to aid the abolitionist cause by boycotting slave-made goods and by forming societies to protest the injustice of slavery.[53] By 1860, Lydia Maria Child, author of several abolitionist tracts, took the position that while the issue of slavery must finally be decided by male legislators, women could employ their energies in creating the will to abolish the institution.[54] And Harriet Beecher Stowe offered many specific suggestions to women regarding their possible involvement in the abolitionist movement.

The first duty of every American woman at this time is to thoroughly understand the subject for herself and to feel that she is bound to use her influence for the right. Then they can obtain signatures to petitions to our national legislature. They can spread information upon this vital topic through their neighborhoods. They can employ lecturers to lay the subject before the people. They can circulate the speeches of their members of Congress that bear upon the subject, and in many other ways they can secure to all a full understanding of the present position of our country.[55]

One of the lessons women learned from their involvement in the various reform movements was that they lacked power. Unable to own property, to vote, to hold office, or even to speak in public without censure, women rapidly became disillusioned by their own ineffectiveness in achieving reform. As a result, many women reformers became advocates of yet another kind of reform, that of women's rights. Married women's property rights was a pressing issue in the 1830s, but it was not until 1848 that the New York legislature finally passed the first American law securing equal property rights for wives. Judging public sentiment as becoming increasingly sympathetic to women's issues, Lucretia Mott and Elizabeth Cady Stanton put a notice in the *Seneca County Courier* of July 14, 1848, announcing that "a Convention to discuss the social, civil, and religious condition and rights of woman" would be held at Seneca Falls, New York. This meeting was originally intended only for women, but it attracted many men as well. This group adopted a "Declaration of Sentiments," based in form and style on the Declaration of Independence, that demanded more personal liberty, control of their own property, and increased participation in government for women.[56]

Although, in closing, the declaration stated, "In entering upon the great work before us, we anticipate no small amount of misconception, misrepresentation, and ridicule," its signers seemed unprepared for the unmitigated derision that met the convention's efforts. According to Stanton and Anthony,

> The proceedings were extensively published, unsparingly ridiculed by the press, and denounced by the pulpit, much to the surprise and chagrin of the leaders. Being deeply in earnest, and believing their demands pre-eminently wise and just, they were wholly unprepared to find themselves the target for the jibes and jeers of the nation.[57]

Such caustic responses were to plague the women's rights movement throughout the years. In 1859, the *New York Times* reported a women's rights meeting held in New York City, during which those in the capacity crowd who had come to scoff and sneer interrupted such speakers as Lucretia Mott, Antoinette Blackwell, Ernestine Rose, and Wendell Phillips. Pleas from chairperson Susan B. Anthony were of little avail in quieting the crowd, and the confusion that prevailed seemed, to the *Times*, to be an embarrassment to the entire city of

11

New York. The *Times* lamented the absence of police, sarcastically remarking that police protection was lacking because "women have no rights in public that men are found to maintain."[58]

It was also disillusioning to the movement's leaders to discover that a large number of American women reacted in shock and horror to the concept of women's rights. Even as early as 1844, when *Yankee* editor and reformer John Neal gave a public lecture supporting extended rights for women, some of his most vehement critics were women. One woman called his ideas "insane crudities" and found it "gratifying to remark that *women* themselves have been the prominent satirists of the characteristic absurdities put forth on the occasion alluded to."[59] Another negative response to the idea of women's rights was the frequent appearance of fictional heroines, usually created by women authors, who lost their lovers, received rebukes from relatives, hastened parents' deaths, and ended their lives in insane asylums because they had worked for women's rights and equality with men.[60]

This controversy concerning women's rights, and indeed the whole notion of moral guardianship by women, was resolved for many women by Hale when she maintained that if women faithfully discharged their duties, they need not worry about women's rights. In 1841 Hale reasoned,

> Will a good son consent that his mother—that any mother should be wronged or oppressed? Let all mothers train up their sons to be good men, and we should have good legislators, who would speedily reform what is now unjust and injurious in our laws. And remember that good sons will make good husbands and fathers, thus securing and perpetuating the happiness, and improvement of social and domestic life.[61]

Hale's sentiments were expressed by many other self-appointed theorists of womens' roles. Typical of such statements, a lyric from the 1850s defined women's rights as follows:

> It is her right to watch beside
> The bed of sickness and pain;
> . . . to train her sons
> So they may Senate chambers grace—
> . . . to be admired
> By every generous, manly heart,

> What would she more, than to perform,
> On earth, life's holiest, sweetest tasks?
> When you a perfect woman find,
> No other rights than these, she asks.[62]

Similarly, Catharine Beecher remained conservative in her view of women's rights, and especially in suffrage for women. Even in the 1870s, Beecher was still advising women to concentrate on establishing their economic independence and to insist upon dignity for domestic labor rather than campaigning for the right to vote.[63]

As a result of this divisiveness in thinking regarding women's issues, those nineteenth-century women who were turning their faces toward the trans-Mississippi West heard as much or more about their moral powers and responsibilities as they did about their rights. Rather than being widely encouraged to seize their rights in the unsettled, flexible milieu of the West, women were generally told that there was much work for them to do there as the carriers of Christian civilization.[64] In an 1854 verse, Sigourney pointed out that it was in the nature of woman's character to take on courageously such a challenge.

> How beautiful is woman's love!
> That from the play-place of its birth . . .
> To stranger-bands, to stranger-home . . .
> Goes forth in perfect trust, to prove
> The untried toil, the burdening care,
> The peril and the pang to dare.[65]

Of course, women were in demand to become wives in western regions. With males greatly outnumbering females and with much work to be done, there was an almost constant campaign by westerners to attract women settlers.[66] But women were also greatly in demand as civilizers. In 1837 a western newspaper emphasized that "every respectable young woman who goes to the west, is almost sure of an advantageous marriage." The same newspaper noted in another issue that "whatever may be the customs of a country, the women of it decide the morals."[67] In an 1846 plea to eastern women to come to the lead mining region of Wisconsin, the *Wisconsin Herald* also pointed out that "the influence of one virtuous and refined woman will subdue more ferocity than half a dozen male missionaries."[68]

Many other types of media preached similar messages to women

13

who were about to become westward migrants. George Caleb Bingham's renowned painting of the early 1850s, *Daniel Boone Escorting Settlers through the Cumberland Gap,* was dominated by an archetypal woman mounted on a snow-white horse, suggesting clearly that woman was the respository of civilization.[69] An 1860 poem titled "Idyl of a Western Wife" also insisted that the rustic "housewife merry" marked the advance of civilization into the West.[70]

By 1880 these ideas reached their zenith in a popular work titled *Woman on the Frontier.* Its author, William Fowler, counseled women that it was as "pioneer and colonizer" that their life stories were the most "potent . . . and interesting." As humanizing, refining, and civilizing agents of the frontier, women were truly the "founders of the Republic." Indeed, according to Fowler, "the household, the hamlet, the village, the town, the city, the state" rise out of their "homely toils, and destiny obscure." He observed that women must execute their usual moral functions in the West—including inaugurating Sunday schools, introducing religion into the "frontier home," and serving as "unconscious legislators"—since their very presence rendered "more desirable life, property, and the other objects for which laws are made." He added that women as a group must also serve as the "great educator of the frontier" and should work with Indians to soften the "fierce temper of the pagan tribes."[71]

Fowler's point regarding women as frontier educators had long been argued by Catharine Beecher, who believed that it was women's mission to go to the West as teachers of children, immigrants, and the unschooled lower classes. To this end, she conducted many fundraising and promotional tours in western areas and attempted to found seminaries for the training of women teachers.[72] In her opinion, teaching was the only acceptable paid profession for women and would provide them with "honourable independence and extensive usefulness."[73] She was also committed to the idea that inhabitants of western regions were particularly in need of women's ministrations in the classroom. In promoting her scheme to send women teachers to the West in the 1840s, Beecher explained that:

> It is the immediate object of this enterprise now presented, to engage American women to exert the great power and influence put into their hands, to remedy the evils which now oppress their countrywomen, and thus, at the same time, and by the same method, to secure a

proper education to the vast multitude of neglected American children all over our land.[74]

One effect of such sermonizing on westering women was to implant firmly the notion in their minds that they were migrating not just as settlers, but as desperately needed moral missionaries. After hearing so much of this, some women must have begun to wonder how the inhabitants of the West would get along should they *not* decide to migrate. Certainly, it softened the blow of migration for those women who were not enthusiastic about their impending move if they could believe that the cause of morality would at least be served by their relocation. One can almost imagine many of these women heaving a sigh and determining to perform their moral duty in the West whether they liked it or not, while other women were envisioning the West as a vast moral wasteland that they would redeem.

As Fowler also suggested, in the eyes of most white Americans the western population most in need of such redemption was the Indians. Therefore, women migrants were thoroughly indoctrinated with the need to exert their moral powers on behalf of native peoples. In 1849, for example, Mary Eastman published a book intended "to excite attention to the moral wants of the Dahcotahs." In her foreword to Eastman's book, author Caroline Kirkland noted that "sympathy— feminine and religious—breathes through these pages, and the un- affected desire of the writer to awaken a kindly interest in the poor souls who have so twined themselves about her own best feelings, may be said to consecrate the work." In a similar vein, frontier editor Jane Swisshelm admonished her female readers not to let themselves become bored with the oft-discussed cause of the American Indian or to have their attention diverted from Indian problems by the more immediate cause of the Civil War.[75]

The novels of the period reinforced this message regarding women's particular responsibilities toward Indians. Such novels circulated widely among middle and upper class women, who drew upon them for both guidance and entertainment. They also trickled down to working class and homebound women through excerpts in newspapers, tracts, pam- phlets, sermons, speeches, street plays, their children's school and personal books and periodicals, chapbooks, jokes, folklore, and other manifestations of popular thought. In one representative novel, the young heroine, Natalie, displayed laudable talent in saving the souls of both Indians and blacks. She was duly praised, in dialect that most whites thought appropriate to natives, by an Indian convert on his deathbed: "Me love Great Spirit; Great Spirit so good to send his little white-face to tell me how to get home."[76] This trend of depicting women as the special liberators of American Indians was so accepted that it continued well into the twentieth century. In a 1911 dime novel, for instance, the only apologist for and defender of what the author described as "fanatical and cruel redskins" was a woman. She explained plaintively that "there are some good Indians that are not yet dead."[77]

These direct and indirect exhortations to women to provide moral direction for, and to otherwise aid, American Indians have caused several scholars to conclude that on the frontier women represented the world of civilization as opposed to the natural, free world of the Indians. According to Leslie A. Fiedler in *The Return of the Vanishing American*, the American Indian was the natural opponent of women in their attempts to civilize the West.[78] Another writer has argued that the two groups were at odds because women envisioned them- selves as harbingers of civilization while natives were representatives of "an alien and depraved culture, decidedly inferior to their own." Convinced of one basic fact, that the American Indian was a savage, women tended to see Indians as contemptible objects, salvageable only through women's civilizing influence.[79] That many women be- lieved they indeed could overcome the supposedly savage nature of Indians was demonstrated by the avowed eagerness of so many of them to venture into western areas as missionaries to American Indians.[80]

How many other women set out with a less well-articulated plan to save what Mary Austin's 1932 autobiography referred to as "savage hordes" is impossible to judge.[81] It is clear, however, that women were inadvertently predisposed to view the Indians they encountered in the worst possible light. As moral missionaries embarking on a crusade to the West in general and to American Indians in particular, women had prejudice toward Indians firmly in mind before they even set foot upon the westward trail. To heighten and enhance the nobility of their own powers to civilize, women generally were ready to be assailed and shocked by the primitivism of the natives they would soon confront.

If women had any doubts regarding the brutal natures of the American Indian populations, they were quickly dissipated by the climate of prejudicial opinion that enveloped women throughout the nineteenth century. The anti-Indian sentiment that characterized the era was developed during the American colonial period by the many settlers who eagerly attempted to enslave, civilize, assimilate, or reshape into agrarians the original inhabitants of the New World. When their various attempts to elevate and reform native peoples met with difficulties and resistance, many early Americans concluded that the only alternative for American Indians was eventual extermination.[82] Later generations of Americans elaborated upon that theme. They created the stereotype of the *Indian*—lumping together more than two thousand native cultures—under terms such as *savage, infidel, heathen,* and *barbarian.* These peoples were "bad"—naked, dirty, mean, rapacious, and hostile—fully deserving of removal or destruction by a progressive and civilized white society.[83] During the nineteenth century, these views of American Indians were translated into accepted public policy under the charismatic and often short-sighted leadership of Presidents Thomas Jefferson and Andrew Jackson.[84]

Throughout the nineteenth century, accounts depicting American Indians as savage barbarians were becoming a well-developed art in the literary genres of captivity narratives and "penny dreadfuls." These chronicles of brutal treatment inflicted upon white captives by Indians at once appealed to and reinforced the anti-native prejudices of their vast reading audience. Appearing first during the colonial period, captivity narratives clearly manifested the fear and hatred of colonists toward the native peoples of North America. In one of the most well-known captivity narratives, *The Narrative of the Captivity and Restoration of Mrs. Mary Rowlandson,* written in 1682, the author described her captors as "murderous wretches" and a "barbarous enemy."[85] This theme was reiterated again and again throughout the colonial period by both male and female captives of American Indians. Interestingly enough, during the American Revolution the captivity format was turned briefly against the British, who were villified in such well-known works as *A Narrative of Col. Ethan Allens's Captivity, and Treatment by the British, from 1775 to 1778.*[86]

As the nation continued its westward expansion into the Ohio Valley during the post-Revolution years, captivity narratives featuring American Indians quickly reclaimed readers' attention. The story of Mary Jemison, taken prisoner by Indians in 1758, was released in 1824 and republished some thirty times.[87] Cooper also contributed some captivity segments to the growing tradition, particularly in *The Deerslayer* and in *The Last of the Mohicans*.[88] By the mid-nineteenth century, the prairie region of the trans-Mississippi West had become the most prevalent setting for these horrifying dramas. The story of the Spirit Lake Massacre of 1857 in Iowa was not only written by survivor Abbie Gardner-Sharp, but was sold in a souvenir shop that she established in the very cabin where the "depredations" occurred.[89] The New Ulm Massacre of 1862 also received its share of the attention from Mary Renville in her *Thrilling Narrative of Indian Captivity*.[90] Emeline Fuller, attacked by American Indians in 1860, published her story in 1892 under the title *Left by the Indians*. She recalled that the unburied bodies she witnessed bore "marks of torture too devilish for any human beings to inflict except Indians." But she concluded her story on a charitable note: "Let those who have never suffered as I have pity the fate of the noble red man of the forest."[91]

Grim tales of captivity were also reported at length throughout these years by newspaper reporters who liberally laced their accounts with invective. In relating the return of two female captives to their family in 1866, the *Leavenworth Daily Times* noted that "they were in captivity about ten weeks, and in that time suffered all the cruelties that the fiend-like malignity and heartlessness of their cowardly captors could invent." A few years later a correspondent for the *Kansas Daily Tribune* presented readers with an account of a Mrs. White who had lost a daughter to the "hands of merciless savages."[92] Eastern newspapers also eagerly picked up news of captivities and their attendant "outrages" upon whites, especially upon white women and children. In 1859, the *New York Times* reported the cases of seventeen children retrieved by the Commissioner of Indian Affairs from the Indians involved in the Utah Massacres of 1857. In 1868, the *Times* offered its readers a detailed account of the execution of thirty-nine Indians in Minnesota for various crimes: "capture of women and children," "took a white woman and ravished her," "murder of a white woman and of design to ravish her daughter," and "shooting and cutting open a woman who was with child."[93] In addition, the *New York Times* routinely informed its readers of Indian "uprisings," "atrocities," drunkenness, and continued captivities of whites.[94]

In addition to fictional and nonfictional accounts, some nineteenth-century artists chose to dramatize in their works the horror of capture by the American Indians. German artist Carl Wimar's 1851 painting *The Abduction of Boone's Daugher by the Indians* presented a dark and murky scene filled with terror for Jemima Boone. In an 1851 American lithograph, Jemima's honor was vindicated and her captors punished, for here her rescuer, her father Daniel Boone, stood with rifle in hand and foot firmly planted on the back of a fallen native.[95] Similar themes were common in the widely reprinted illustrations from contemporary captivity narratives.[96]

In whatever media they appeared, these captivity narratives fulfilled various functions throughout the nearly three centuries of their existence. During the colonial period they were largely religious documents concerned with the issue of salvation for those who had escaped the savagery and debasement of their lives as captives. By the end of the eighteenth century, they became more strongly an expression of anti-Indian sentiment and as such began to deviate increasingly from factual accounts.[97] In focusing on the brutality of Indians they also served as a convenient vehicle to rationalize the extermination of American Indians and the taking of their lands. But as one researcher has pointed out, as American Indians became less of a threat, "captivity narratives were written for historical rather than propagandistic reasons." Valued as evidence of the courage and fortitude of frontiersmen and women, nineteenth-century captivity narratives thus became lore and tall tales that "often exaggerated the exploits of famous Indian captives to emphasize the heroic character" of American settlers. Consequently, they were sensationalized, fictionalized, and even revised for use as school texts in moral values.[98]

Throughout their history, captivity narratives deviated little in form. The unifying pattern was that of an odyssey. Whether male or female, the captive followed a sequence of separation from family and civilization, detention by the savage captors, and eventual reunion with white society. Yet the return to their former civilization was not always a happy one.[99] Some women experienced particular difficulties in adjustment because they missed their native children, because they found themselves rejected by white society due to their "contamination" by their Indian captors, or because they lacked financial means to support themselves. This loss of economic resources motivated many women to turn to the Congress of the United States to seek "memorials," requests for financial compensation for their trials as captives. In the mid-1860s, Fannie Kelly of Kansas approached Congress for aid after her five-month captivity. In her appeal she wrote that after being severely injured in an Indian raid, "your memorialist was then taken into captivity, and was forced to become the squaw of one of the O-gal-lal-lah Chiefs, who treated her in a manner too horrible to mention, and during her captivity was passed from Chief to Chief, and treated in a similar manner." Because she had relayed Indian attack plans to emigrant trains and to troops and was now a destitute widow without any means of support, she argued that she deserved remuneration from Congress for her services.[100] Other female captives, like Abbie Gardner-Sharp, resorted to titillating the public with dramatized versions of their ordeals in order to support themselves.

While former captives such as Kelly and Gardner-Sharp kept the image of the bad Indian very much alive in the minds of many Americans, this stereotypical figure was also becoming a pervasive presence in other nineteenth-century media.[101] In 1835, William Gilmore Simms's novel *The Yemassee* presented Americans with one type of ignoble savage, and in 1837 Robert Montgomery Bird's *Nick of the Woods* created another kind of Indian. During this period James Fenimore Cooper's *Leatherstocking Tales* frequently supplied yet another version of the American savage. At the same time, the Romantic historians George Bancroft and Francis Parkman produced widely read histories peopled by barbaric American Indians who deserved to be exterminated by more progressive white civilizations. Convinced of the natives' inherent savagery, Parkman particularly believed that "with every disposition to do justice to their good qualities," whites "must be conscious that an impassable gulf lies" between them and American Indians.[102] Indians were depicted in a similar way in many popular Currier and Ives prints, such as the 1813 *Death of Tecumseh at the Battle of the Thames.* Renowned artist Frederic Remington depicted so-called savages as skulking through his engravings, paintings, and sculptures. According to Remington's portrayals, such as those in *Sign Language* (1889), and in *The Luckless Hunter* (1910), the native was definitely an inferior being and obviously destined for extinction.[103]

Of course, the figure of the fierce savage, a caricature almost bordering upon buffoonery, had long been a staple of the many circuses that crisscrossed the United States.[104] By the latter part of the nineteenth century and the early years of the twentieth, Indians toured not only America, but a good part of the world. They appeared in

Buffalo Bill's and other Wild West shows, as well as in innumerable Indian "congresses" and "expositions."[105] They were also featured in the dime novels that were so immensely popular both at home and abroad. These dime novels and other pulp literature at once reflected and shamelessly exploited the anti-native sentiment that had been growing among white people almost from the moment of America's inception.[106] Their authors routinely referred to American Indians as "pesky redskins," "red skunks," "bloodthirsty wretches," and, of course, "savages."[107] In 1907 one author even put the following words into the mouth of one of his American Indian characters: "You may not know it, but the wild blood that flows in an Indian's veins craves for the excitement of the torture stake if that Indian be a bad one."[108]

American Indian women also received their share of defilement at the hands of white observers. The predominant image of the Indian woman was the squaw: an unfortunate, inferior, exploited female who carried out all the essential work while the males of her family played at fishing, hunting, and war games. This largely inaccurate view of the degraded, slavelike squaw was the result of ethnocentrism on the part of whites who often saw hunting and fishing only as sport. Many white commentators also frequently transferred their own view of white women as inferior beings to their perceptions of native societies, thus managing to ignore matrilineal Indian groups, the status granted Indian women due to their share in production, and the native women who served as warriors, shamans, healers, and religious leaders.[109]

In an 1830 story, one writer described the squaw: "In the opinion of the Indian, a woman was but a kind of slave, or beast of burthen [sic]."[110] In *The Pathfinder*, Cooper's Dew-of-June, wife of the Indian Arrowhead, was a typical representation of this kind of woman. Like all Indian women she exhibited "meek humility," "submissive quiet," and silent compliance with her "tyrant's" orders and wishes. Discussing her own husband's brutality, she said, "Arrowhead no feel for any wife—no feel for his own." And when asked by a friend to intercede with the men of the tribe, she replied plaintively, "June poor squaw. What warrior t'ink of what she say?"[111] In *The Prairie*, Cooper maintained that Indian men and women were bred from the day of birth for their respective roles of dominance and passivity. According to him, young native girls stole from their labors to admire the fierce and daring activities of young men who were already "making themselves distinguished for that species of domination which, in after life, was to mark the vast distinction between the sexes."[112] In 1868 a correspondent for the *New York Times*, traveling among the Navajos in New Mexico, offered a similar and somewhat patronizing view of the roles of American Indian women. After watching women moving their villages and families "on horseback and on foot," the reporter declared it was a "funny and interesting scene." The correspondent also included an account of "squaws" picking vermin from their mates' heads, as well as a story about a woman "who gave birth while walking, picked up her child, and traveled on."[113]

It wasn't simply this apparent exploitation of Indian women as domestic laborers that interested whites. Many commentators seemed fascinated with the plurality of wives among some American Indian groups, as well as with the question of sexual relations and inter-marriage between white men and native women.[114] Such practices suggested to many whites that American Indian women were squaws who were taken advantage of not only in terms of labor, but who were also sexually misused. Traded for the price of a pony or for trinkets to both tribal and white men, Indian women seemed to many whites to be little more than chattel to be bought and sold at the whim of their men.[115] In *The Trapper's Bride*, artist Alfred Jacob Miller de-picted a lovely young native woman being sold to a white trapper by Indian men for six hundred dollars' worth of guns, tobacco, alcohol, and beads.[116] And in *Joseph Walker and His Squaw*, Miller portrayed the Indian wife as a shadowy, inconsequential figure on a small pony following a respectful distance behind her strong, dominant, well-equipped, and well-mounted trapper husband.[117]

In 1841, Caroline Kirkland presented a comparable version of an American Indian woman married to a white man. In *A New Home*, Kirkland depicted the wife of a French trader as a withdrawn woman who refused to talk with white visitors, conversed only with "some wretched looking Indians who were hanging about the house," and seemed very pleased when her white guests departed. As for the children of this union, Kirkland noted that although they had "bright, gazelle-like eyes" they too showed little interest in their white visitors and kept to themselves.[118] Kirkland, like most nineteenth-century commentators, evidently saw the native woman as a pathetic, de-pressed figure who had little control, if any, over her own marital and sexual destiny. She could submit passively to poor treatment or escape it entirely by taking her own life, as James Hall, Kirkland's contemporary had his heroine do in his 1853 poem, "The Indian Wife's Lament."[119]

Clearly, for many whites the squaw was an inferior and abused creature who earned little esteem among even her own people. Developing from this image of the squaw was a curious and widespread assumption that native men could be insulted by accusing them of acting like women. In *The Last of the Mohicans*, one of Cooper's characters derided an enemy by saying, "your nation is a race of women, and the hoe is better fitted to your hands than the gun."[120] Historian Richard Drinnon has pointed out that this "gratuitous assumption, lifted almost directly from Jefferson's *Notes on Virginia*," was so common that it even found its way into the policy of governmental officials attempting to subdue their native charges. According to Drinnon, these whites, unaware of Indian laughter at their ignorance, revealed more about white misperceptions than they did about the actual state of native women.[121] However, despite the fact that patriarchal white attitudes may have frequently provided the basis for misunderstandings of native women's roles, the resulting views achieved the status of truth in the minds of many nineteenth-century Americans.[122]

Frequently, the brutalized and degraded image of American Indian women perceived by so many whites manifested itself in descriptions of the brutality of Indian women toward both Indian and white captives. As withered hags, hideous crones, and in a variety of similar characterizations, fictional American Indian women perpetrated outrages consonant with their own barbarous state. In *The Prairie*, Cooper's "crones" heaped verbal abuse upon their unfortunate victim. In Cooper's words, "they lavished upon their unmoved captive a torrent of that vindictive abuse, in which the women of the savages are so well known to excel, but which has been too often described to need a repetition here."[123] In *The Last of the Mohicans*, Cooper's squalid and crafty women added their piercing shrieks and derisive powers to the torment of captives.[124] In other fictional accounts, women were capable of physically attacking their captives. In an 1830 story titled "The Bois Brule," native women "unsheathed their knives and would have immolated the prisoner on the spot had they not been restrained by their men."[125] In 1835, William Gilmore Simms in *The Yemassee*, described Indian women as directing not only piercing shrieks and indecent gestures but also frequent blows toward a captive. He explained that these women had "reached a condition, in which they possessed all the passions of the one sex, without the possession of their powers;—to have lost the gentle nature of the woman without acquiring the magnanimity of the man, which is the result of his consciousness of strength."[126] And in one dime novel the women "began mouthing and gibbering maliciously" at their prisoner, and then they "proceeded to fling mud and filth into his face." As their fury rose, one or another of the women darted forward to "spit in his face, or strike him viciously with her open hand."[127]

This image of the cruel American squaw, like the image of the bad Indian in general, did little to reassure timorous white women already intimidated by frightening stories about the western regions where they intended to make their new homes. If white women did look to Indian women for possible deliverance from the ravages of Indian men, the squaw stereotype hardly encouraged such faint hopes. Because pejorative interpretations of both American Indian men and women have persisted through twentieth-century "western" films, we can understand from our own experience just how pernicious and damaging such media treatments can be.[128] Could we expect nineteenth-century women to have been any less gullible than ourselves? Given the fact that these women continually heard their own moral powers touted, it is understandable that many of them would come to accept themselves as civilizing forces.

Yet this was not the only message that assailed women regarding their potential interaction with Indians. At the same time that women were constantly reminded of the strength of their moral powers, they were also lectured on the weakness of their physical powers. In fact, one of the key characteristics of nineteenth-century "true womanhood," submissiveness, derived from women's physical inferiority. Because men were physically strong, they were the doers, but because women were physically weak, they had to seek protectors. Women naturally turned to the stronger sex, men, for such protection. Women's dependence upon men was thus seen as a product of their own physical inferiority.[129]

Almira Phelps emphasized this point in a series of lectures to Emma Willard's Troy Seminary students in the mid-1830s. The "delicacy" of women's nervous systems, she warned them, "subjects her to agitations to which man, favored by greater physical strength and more firmness of nerve, is exempt."[130] In an 1836 tract titled *Female Im-*

24

provement, Elizabeth Sandford added that there was "something un-feminine in independence." Women, she continued, are "conscious of inferiority, and therefore grateful for support" from men. To encourage the protective instinct in men, who "are themselves superior," women should show their dependence upon men's strength in all things.[131] In 1848, a male guidebook writer further explained that men and women resembled two halves of a circle: the man possessed physical strength, while the woman possessed sensibility and patience. As a result of this dichotomy, women clearly needed to seek out male protectors, upon whom they must be dependent. In such relationships, women had to strive continually to preserve their health because of problems inherent in their weaker constitutions.[132]

Godey's also frequently reiterated such interpretations of women's "natures" to their readers. In the "Editor's Table" in 1851, Hale declared that women were not mechanical, inventive, or strong because God had endowed men with these characteristics. Instead, God had granted women "moral insight or instinct, and the patience that endures physical suffering." Thus, Hale reasoned, the elevation of women "will not consist in becoming like man, in doing man's work, or striving for the dominion of the world. . . . she works in the elements of human nature . . . obedience, temperance, truth, love, piety."[133] Domestic novelists also stressed the idea of women's inferiority, particularly in the physical realm. E. D. E. N. Southworth's 1856 novel *Retribution* presented a heroine who firmly believed in "woman's subordination of love." She exclaimed, "Talk of woman's rights, woman's rights live in the instincts of her protector—man."[134]

It was not only women's, or domestic, literature that advocated these views of women. Popular novelists such as Cooper also regularly characterized women as weak, passive, docile, and submissive. A heroine who personified these feminine virtues was always rewarded in the end by the predictable prize of a hero, tailor-made to her needs and desires.[135] Cooper summarized these beliefs in *The Sea Lions,* where he admonished women that if they "thoroughly understand how much of their real power and influence with men arises from their seeming dependence there would be very little tolerance in their own circles for those among them who are for proclaiming their independence and their right to equality in all things."[136] Cooper also occasionally created an unfeminine heroine who inevitably demonstrated that independence could only reap unhappiness. The most ludicrous of these appeared in *Jack Tier,* written in 1848, the year of the first women's rights convention at Seneca Falls. *Jack Tier*'s heroine, deserted by her husband, disguised herself as a man and followed him to sea for several years. She was totally "unsexed" by the experience even when later her own clothing and identity were restored to her. The moral Cooper clearly intended was that Molly Swash desexed herself because she chose to act aggressively on her own behalf rather than "suffer" in the customary sentimental style by accepting the actions and decisions of the male.[137]

These injunctions were filtered from Cooper and appeared in diluted form in newspaper and periodical articles; wherever these views appeared they must have raised many questions in the minds of women who were about to become westward migrants. How would they survive in the arduous environment of the West? Would their limited physical prowess be sufficient to its demands? Could they survive in the West only under the vigilance of physically superior male protectors? Would the physical capabilities of these male protectors be sufficient? Could males protect females not only against their own weaknesses, but against threats from such frightening phenomena as wild animals and "savage" natives? And the most crucial question of all: Would male strength prove equal to that of the American Indian "barbarians" who attempted to assault and rape white women?

The fears that arose from conceptions of limited female strength must have dampened the enthusiasm of many women about becoming moral missionaries to the West. Although women had been told many times that female morality would triumph over all evil, the "land of savagery" awaiting them in the West seemed less than an ideal arena in which to test that particular thesis. Perhaps a woman's only option, when threatened with actual Indian assault, was the one suggested by a self-proclaimed expert on the "true character of women," John Frost, in 1875:

> when danger threatens the household, when the lurking savage is seen near the dwelling, or the war-whoop is heard in the surrounding woods, the matron becomes a heroine, and is ready to peril life, without a moment's hesitation, in the approaching conflict . . . when the life of husband or child is menaced, she throws herself beneath the threat-

ening tomahawk, and is ready to receive the threatening blow to save the loved one.[138]

At the same time, however, women's actual acceptance of these stereotypes was eroded by a countercurrent in the literature—works emerged showing a woman's ability to survive harsh physical demands through means other than her own sacrificial destruction. Even as the purported truth of female physical inferiority was heralded across the land, the capable woman was making her literary debut. Because women were touted as being morally adept, if not indeed morally superior, the capable woman exhibited signs that she could not only care for herself in certain situations, but that occasionally she could also aid a man. A close reading of Catherine Sedgwick's popular 1836 novel, *A Poor Rich Man and a Rich Poor Man*, provides a case in point. It reveals not a submissive, male-dominated female, but a militantly optimistic heroine who supported a large family and engaged in charitable pursuits including the educating of children while supported by an impossibly small income.[139] In the following year, the heroine of the novel *Elinor Fulton*, supporting her entire family after its bankruptcy, provided a constant inspiration for her family until her father finally was able to work his way back to solvency.[140] This is not to suggest that these earliest incarnations of the efficient and effective heroines won over American readers completely. According to book sales, the public still seemed to prefer the flighty, squandering Jane of *Three Experiments of Living*.[141]

The development of the capable woman was stimulated by the women's rights conventions of the 1850s and by the literating effects of the Civil War upon women's roles in the 1860s. It was epitomized in 1865 by Southworth's beloved heroine Capitola. Young, beautiful, and daring, Capitola entered the story disguised as a boy. After flouting her guardian, fighting a duel, outwitting her kidnappers, and generally romping through other people's lives as well as her own, she received the supreme compliment when her guardian commented that she deserved to be a man![142] That many readers loved and possibly imitated Capitola was proven by the book's sales, for it joined Dickens, Thackeray, and George Eliot on the best-seller list and was republished several times in later years. Even Cooper contributed his ideas regarding the capable woman to the genre. Cooper's capable heroine was both independent and successful, for she operated as an effective individual in a primarily male environment, often a frontier area, and thus she was less bound by female standards of delicacy. Elizabeth Temple in Cooper's *Pioneers* defended herself and her friend against a panther, helped Natty Bumppo break out of jail, and managed to obtain the gunpowder she needed without its owner's knowledge.[143]

Despite constant declarations of adherence to purely traditional feminine values, *Godey's* also began to include the capable woman among its other features. In the mid-1840s the journal started to publish on a regular basis sketches of heroic women of the American Revolution. "The women of that era were equal to the crisis," one of the authors wrote, for they contributed "active assistance, by the labor of their hands; by the sacrifice of their luxuries; by the surrender of what had been deemed necessaries."[144] In other *Godey's* stories more contemporary examples of female heroism were cited. In 1845, one long tale related how an explorer's life had been saved innumerable times by women. Another story celebrated the wife who realized that a robber was hiding under the bed and bravely detained him by staying in the room for two hours until help arrived.[145]

The emergence of the capable woman also manifested itself in *Godey's* through an increased emphasis on exercise, diet, health, beauty, and fashion. The basis for this trend was the argument that women could perform their moral duties and responsibilities effectively only if they were healthy and strong.[146] Women therefore needed to learn the laws of health and how to take proper care of themselves.[147] "Let the lady who expects to be or to make others happy," *Godey's* cautioned women in 1848, "cultivate high health by out-door exercise."[148] During the 1840s the delicate young lady was becoming quickly passé, as was the sedentary life of confinement that had produced her. A new standard of beauty based on health now appeared, and young women were advised to "go forth into the fields and woods, if you live in the country,—take long walks in the cool morning and evening hour, if you are in 'populous cities pent'—let the minimum of these daily excursions average at least two miles."[149] When indoors, dancing was now considered excellent exercise, as was the practice of the more modest calisthenics.[150]

Even a revision of *Godey's* fashion plates was justified by the increasing acceptance of the concept of the capable woman. These illustrations were no longer to amuse the idle and inactive housewife;

they were now meant to contribute to her "moral improvement." In the early 1840s, *Godey's* launched a campaign to do away with its formerly stiff and pudgy fashion figures, and to replace them with healthy, graceful figures.[151] *Godey's* told its readers that the new models were to be responsible for everything from taste and rationality to economy, grace, charm, health, and beauty.[152]

This apparent contradiction in mid-nineteenth-century thinking concerning women's physical inferiority as opposed to her ability to learn to cope reached its zenith in the dime novels of the latter part of the nineteenth century and the early twentieth century. On the one hand, women were characterized as "maidens" of beauty and gentleness who required protection from men. When one such heroine of the 1890s was accosted by a bully in quest of a kiss from her, she cried out, "Are there no *men* among you who will help me?" She was saved by a stalwart hero who proclaimed that he "never hesitated to face death in defense of a woman."[153] In another tale, "white maidens" were placed in a grotto by their protectors, who fought off approaching "savages" on their behalf. By the end of the story, the maidens were assured of perpetual care, through marriage to worthy men who would continue to protect them. One of them, "beautiful Maria," passed from the protection of her brother to that of her new husband. "Having seen his sister so happily united to so worthy a man" and his own responsibilities toward her ended, the brother felt free to pursue adventure. He thus "yielded to Red Cloud's importunities, and the two started off on a grand hunt on the prairies."[154]

On the other hand, the capable woman also abounded. In one popular novel of the 1890s, a stereotype male—Deadwood Dick—was threatened at gunpoint by a woman who insisted that he marry her. He was saved by his wife, who, although believed to be dead, appeared at the crucial moment to challenge Dick's tormentor to a duel. The resulting fight, a "strange, exciting combat between two infuriated women," was calmly observed by Dick, who had faith in his wife's abilities. Justifying his optimism, she lunged at her opponent who "fell back, with a blade run through her heart—dead!"[155] In another thrilling narrative from 1908, a madwoman and a young girl rescued the male hero from a band of "red devils" and "cussed redskins." The hero admiringly commented, "what a head piece yer have got, old gal." The author explained that "notwithstanding her demented condition, she was a woman of iron constitution and will."[156]

Yet another of the dime novel's capable women threw sandbags out of a hot air balloon on the heads of Sioux Indians, used the revolver she always carried to further discourage her pursuers, and then capped her unladylike performance by returning to camp where "with several of the females of the settlement," she "engaged in making coffee for the men."[157]

Apparently some hope existed for the survival of white women in the West. Male protectors did exist. In fact, the security of white women, who were a scarce commodity throughout much of the West, became almost legendary by the end of the nineteenth century. In a popular 1890s novel, a female stagecoach passenger was gallantly assured by a highwayman robbing the coach that she would not have to surrender her valuables. "We don't rob ladies, they're too scarce in this part of the Union," he told her, so "give yourself no uneasiness." The stagecoach driver confirmed her safety when he added, "I've never met a road agent yet that was mean enough to rob a lady."[158] Should male strength falter, however, the existence of the capable woman suggested to women migrants that by developing their own latent strengths they would be able to meet adequately the strenuous physical challenges involved in pioneering western regions.[159]

In addition, frontierswomen did not have to rely exclusively on their own or on men's efforts for their safety. Paradoxically, women could also look to their potential oppressors, the Indians, for aid. In nineteenth-century America the conception of the bad Indian was not an unrelieved image, for it was offset in most people's minds by the countervailing picture of the Noble Savage. While the primitive state of American Indians caused them to be cruel, rapacious, and savage, it was also believed that it compelled them to be pure, virtuous, and gentle. It was to this streak of natural nobility in American Indians that women could turn for protection from elements of the western environment that included those ruthless and rapacious Indians they might encounter.

The good Indian exhibited a panoply of attractive qualities. Courteous, friendly, brave, and courageous, these natives could be counted upon to respond favorably to the hordes of white invaders who were seizing their lands, destroying their food supplies, and murdering their numbers.[160] The good Indian was, in part, a product of European writers of the seventeenth and eighteenth centuries who envisioned American natives as "noble savages" possessing ingenuousness and "natural naiveté."[161] European Romantics of the eighteenth century, such as Jean Jacques Rousseau and François René de Chateaubriand, emphasized the inherent moral nature of Indians. It was, they declared, a result of living in "harmony with beneficient nature."[162]

It was in this tradition that Cooper created the character of Chingachgook, the brave and trusty right hand of Natty Bumppo in his 1826 novel, *The Last of the Mohicans*.[163] The tradition also spawned sympathetic treatments of American Indians in poems such as Lydia Sigourney's "Last Words of an Indian Chief," Philip Freneau's "Indian Burying Ground," and particularly Henry Wadsworth Longfellow's "Song of Hiawatha." In his 1855 poem, Longfellow wrote:

> Every human heart is human
> That in even savage bosoms
> There are longings, yearnings, strivings
> For the good they comprehend not.[164]

The same idealized Indian frequented the American stage throughout much of the nineteenth century. In plays such as *The Indian Princess, or, La Belle Sauvage*, first presented in 1808, and *Metamora, or, The Last of the Wampanoags*, originally staged in 1829, American Indians were melancholy, admirable figures who delivered their messages in the best Shakespearean style.[165]

On canvas these "quintessential" Indians, as historian Robert F. Berkhofer, Jr. has termed them, received ennoblement from the Romantic style of painting. Artists such as Captain Seth Eastman and particularly George Catlin reinforced the view that American Indians were indeed Noble Savages. In 1841, Catlin declared: "Nature has nowhere presented more beautiful and lovely scenes, than those of the vast prairies of the West and of *man* and *beast* no nobler specimens than those who inhabit them—the *Indian* and the *buffalo*."[166] In 1872, *Frank Leslie's Illustrated Newspaper* ran a front-page engraving of Catlin's proposed monument to natives, to be constructed in New York's new Central Park. The structure, which would have contained six hundred of Catlin's Indian paintings, plus Indian artifacts he had collected, engendered a good deal of enthusiasm but was never constructed.[167]

Other eastern newspapers, such as the *New York Times*, also supported the concept of the good Indian. In 1865 a *Times* correspondent, reporting on Seneca Indian relics unearthed in Ohio, rhapsodized that although the Senecas themselves were gone there still existed many "interesting remains of that noblest tribe of the Six Nations."[168] In other articles and editorials, the *Times* variously blamed the United States government, plundering Indian agents, and "abominable treatment" by Americans in general for the hapless condition of native peoples who really desired nothing more than peace.[169] In 1887 a *Times* correspondent described admiringly the incredible equestrian feats he had witnessed in an Indian camp. He was thrilled because he doubted "if anything outside of a circus ring ever equaled it."[170]

During these years, the good Indian received support from writer and reformer Helen Hunt Jackson, while the exciting, daring Indian became a stock character in dime novels. A typical male manifestation of the phenomenon was Gray Feather, who "had a reputation among the cow-punchers of being a good Indian, for they had always found him truthful and reliable." Like many of his forerunners in the theater, Gray Feather spoke beautiful and correct English, always referring to himself in the second person. "Gray Feather is pleased to see you, White Chief," he greeted one of his white acquaintances.[171]

One 1890s Indian heroine of this ilk was described as "fully cultured, and of fair education." A young woman, she was "the princess of her tribe, and the recipient of many valuable lands and money gifts from both the settlers and the Indian agents, because of the peaceful influence she exerted among the tribes."[172] This character embodied the image of the Indian princess. As the female good Indian, the princess was at the other end of the continuum from the squaw. She was beautiful, kind, pure, and like Pocahontas, frequently amenable to aiding whites in their campaign to overwhelm her people and seize their lands. She appeared in many guises, as Magawisca in Catherine Maria Sedgwick's *Hope Leslie* (1827), as Little Deer in Robert Strange's *Eoneguski; or, the Cherokee Chief* (1839), as Moinoona in Osgood Bradbury's *Peripold the Avenger* (1848), and as the Indian princess Winona in an Isabel Moore Kimball statue (1902).[173] Always the paragon of Indian beauty, and usually the daughter of a chieftain as well, the character of the Indian princess often seemed to be an embodiment of national pride in things and people uniquely American.[174]

These characters were clearly modeled on the prototypical Indian princess, Pocahontas, who was saved from savagery largely through her own personal relationship with an Englishman. This union demonstrated that "savages" could be Christianized and at the same time provided a rationalization for encouraging white man–native woman relationships in the name of such salvation.[175] Elevated to the status of a princess through her marriage to an English gentleman, Pocahontas adopted a white name, and white styles in clothing, and allowed herself to be presented to the English court. It is not surprising then that a seventeenth-century portrait of her, titled simply *Pocahontas*, depicted a fair-skinned woman with a ruff around her neck and a fan in her gloved hand. An eighteenth-century painting by Mary Woodbury, also titled *Pocahontas*, showed a woman with her dark hair pulled back neatly, her fair skin set off by a ribbon around her neck, her sloping shoulders and narrow waist accented by a lace-trimmed dress with voluminous skirts, and her delicate hand holding a single flower. In the nineteenth-century portrait by Robert Matthew Sully, also called *Pocahontas*, there was slightly more suggestion of naturalness in the subject's flowing hair and in the outdoor background. Yet here too was the face of a white woman with Cupid's bow lips, soulful eyes, and bejeweled ears, displayed above an elaborate gown.[176]

White eyes obviously saw the Pocahontas they wanted to see. She was to reappear in many other guises throughout the nineteenth century. Introduced on the stage first in 1808, through James Nelson Barker's play *The Indian Princess; or, La Belle Sauvage*, she, or her derivative, flitted over many other stages, often rescuing the white hero at some time during the course of the performance.[177] She was also the subject of countless numbers of poems, such as Lydia Sigourney's 1841 *Pocahontas*. To Sigourney, Pocahontas was "a forest-child" with "raven locks in strange profusion flowing" whose "spirit-glance bespoke the daugher of a king." After many stanzas recounting Pocahontas's story, Sigourney concluded that although her brave people were gone, her memory should never be assigned to oblivion. Regarding this female Noble Savage, Sigourney proclaimed:

> King, stately chief, and warrior-host are dead,
> Nor remnant nor memorial left behind:
> But thou, O forest-princess, true of heart,
> When o'er our fathers waved destruction's dart,
> Shalt in their children's loving hearts be shrined;

Pure, lonely star, o'er dark oblivion's waves,
It is not meet thy name should moulder in the grave.[178]

Part of this nineteenth-century idealization of Pocahontas came from an acceptance of her marriage to John Rolfe and the presumable introduction of native American blood into old-line American families. Families who would have considered the existence of a male Indian in a branch of their family tree as an occasion for mortification rushed to document the existence of an Indian princess perched in another branch of that family tree. This double standard regarding intermarriage was portrayed clearly in a mid-nineteenth-century love story in *The Ladies' Companion.* In "Malaeska; the Indian Wife of the White Hunter," author Ann Sophia Winterbotham Stephens presented the unfortunate tale of an Indian princess married to a white man. Over her husband's deathbed the protagonist promised to raise their son in the manner of a white person, but the boy was soon torn from her by whites who wanted to ensure his "proper" upbringing. Bereft of both husband and child, she returned to her tribe only to be condemned to death, a sentence she escaped with the aid of a former suitor. The story ended tragically with her death as well as the death of her son just as he was about to marry a white woman.[179] Judging from the dime novels, this double standard continued into the twentieth century. In one representative story, a young white woman was appalled and insulted by a marriage proposal from an Indian chief, yet the same woman graciously accepted her brother's impending marriage to a young native "belle" living among whites in St. Louis.[180]

Evidently, many nineteenth-century white Americans could accept that extenuating circumstances occasionally made a marriage between a white male and a native female acceptable and perhaps even desirable. This was not the case, however, with all Americans. Cooper, for example, objected to any pattern of intermarriage between Indians and whites. In *The Prairie*, he contrived to have a naturalist refuse vehemently the offer of a native wife, whether she be princess or common maiden. Cooper's character asserted that he was against the "admixture of the varieties of species, which only tend to tarnish the beauty and to interrupt the harmony of nature."[181] Later in the same novel, a female character excoriated her husband for even listening to an American Indian who had offered him a young woman as wife.

"Would ye disgrace color, and family, and nation," Cooper had her exclaim, "by mixing white blood with red, and would ye be the parent of a race of mules!"[182] When Cooper dealt with the question of native males proposing marriage to a white woman, he could not even bear to have his protagonist translate the Indian's proposal to the woman. Instead, the possibility of a translation was aborted by another figure who stated resolutely, "all that a savage says is not to be repeated before a Christian lady."[183]

Even though Cooper believed that intermarriage between American Indian and white was reprehensible, he still accepted the general concept of the Indian princess. Standing in dramatic contrast to the harsh picture of the squaw, the image of the princess demonstrated that some Indian women were in reality human, sensitive, and warm-hearted individuals. They too were worthy of love and esteem by their husbands.[184] Perhaps most significantly, they were frequently sympathetic to whites, often helping them escape their native American captors, even their own husbands.[185] Cooper characterized this type of native woman in *The Pathfinder* in the figure of Dew-of-June, who proved to be not only a warm and affectionate friend to the white heroine, Mabel, but her savior as well. Rebelling against the autocracy of her own husband and tribe, the formerly submissive June protected Mabel on several occasions and saved her life on another.[186]

The existence of an Indian woman like June held out a shred of hope to westering women who could cling to the idea that they too might be fortunate enough to encounter a princess who would rush to their aid, even if it meant turning against her own people. The ramifications of Pocahontas's early perfidy were indeed long-lived, especially to white women anxiously scrutinizing natives for evidence of one or two redeeming qualities.

As women's attentions swiveled from Pocahontas and other good Indians to representatives of bad Indians, and back again, they must have become aware of the incongruities between the two images. This contradictory manner of thinking about Indians by white Americans must have created in the minds of women migrants a good deal of confusion and perhaps even misgivings about their western venture. By the time they struck out for the West, they had to choose between apparitions of inferior native peoples who were bad, hostile, and vicious, interspersed with enigmatic visions of superior native beings who were friendly, kind, and courageous. Combined with the uncertainty created in their thinking by the mixed messages they had been receiving about their own natures, roles, and responsibilities, the equally mixed messages concerning American Indians created a tremendous potential for misunderstanding and misinterpretation.

As complex as this situation was for westering women, it was to be complicated even further by a steady influx of European ideas about women, American Indians, and the great American West that poured into the United States with increasing regularity throughout the nineteenth century.

⚜{ 2 }⚜

European Influences upon
Frontierswomen's Ideas

It is highly probable that American beliefs about the nature of women and of American Indians reached many Europeans. Ideas regarding concepts of domesticity and the moral guardianship of women were surely not restricted to the United States. Nor was curiosity regarding the American Indian confined to North American boundary lines. North American views of both women and Indians were widely published throughout European countries, where they were read by people anxious to learn more about the "promised land" in the New World. One novel of the 1850s that discussed both of these topics, Elizabeth Wetherell's *Wide, Wide World*, sold more copies in England than had any other American novel to that date, and it was also translated into French, German, Swedish, and Italian.[1]

Clearly, American ideas regarding these subjects received wide circulation and elicited much interest throughout nineteenth-century Europe. Yet at the same time, Europeans were developing their own views of frontierswomen and Indians. Although Europeans probably were not as schooled in the philosophy of domesticity as Americans, they did have a long-standing fascination with the American West. Writers and commentators frequently lavished extravagant numbers of pages of imaginative prose upon the question of how the white women and American Indians who inhabited the American frontier looked, acted, and thought.

These European attempts toward interpretation contributed significantly to the body of information about American westerners that engulfed both European and American female migrants prior to their departure for the frontier. Undaunted by their lack of firsthand personal contact with frontierswomen and American Indians, European writers did not hesitate to inform their readers—an audience expanded by improved education, increased leisure time, and decreased costs of books and periodicals—about the nature of these inhabitants of the western United States.

By the 1840s, European women of all social classes were avid readers of novels and periodicals.[2] As one scholar has noted, even untutored domestic servants became part of the rapidly growing mass reading public, due to the increasing availability of print media entering their employers' homes. Laborers, too, were urged to read by evangelists, Mechanic's Institutes, and purveyors of sensationalistic literature. Those who withstood such blandishments were exposed in other ways to ideas concerning America—through street theater, sermons, speeches, folklore, jokes, and other forms of popular culture.[3] Consequently, the minds of most European women migrants were well stocked with detailed, if somewhat inaccurate, preconceptions of the women and native Americans whom they would encounter in their western hegira.

These European images and interpretations of frontierswomen and American Indians reached American women primarily through the print media. European novels about the American West and excerpts from them, newspaper articles, tracts, pamphlets, humorous pieces, plays, and particularly the commentaries of travelers in the United States had long inundated American readers. Immensely curious to know what others thought of their fledgling country, many Americans consumed virtually everything they could lay their hands on that provided an image through European eyes of themselves and their nation. Although they were not always pleased with what they read or heard, as was the case with the writings of Charles Dickens or Harriet Martineau, their attitudes and prejudices about themselves were determined to some extent by European thinking.[4]

European observers and commentators who enthralled Europeans and Americans alike with portrayals of the American frontier were legion in number; a complete collection of their works would consume incalculable feet of library shelf space. Yet, despite the torrent of words that these spectators expended upon describing, analyzing, and criticizing the American peoples who so fascinated them, it is impossible to derive a clear picture of western Americans from European writings. Rather, the portrait that Europeans drew tended to be one of extremes, truisms, and wish fulfillment. Whether they realized it or not, these European commentators derived their views of western Americans through a complex filter that shaped and often distorted the end result. Thus, frontier people, as seen through European eyes, frequently loomed larger than life. As inhabitants of a strange new region characterized by both danger and opportunity, they often seemed to Europeans to be highly unusual specimens of humanity. The vices as well as the virtues of western Americans were therefore magnified by the many curious Europeans who attempted to fathom the reality and the meaning of their lives.

European visitors to America often blamed inaccurate notions of American frontier people on Americans themselves. In 1831, traveler and commentator Mary Austin Holley accused the Spanish government in Texas of deliberately exaggerating the cannibalism and ferocity of Indians in order to discourage adventurers and settlers from proceeding into the area.[5] In 1845, observer Frederick von Raumer complained that it was virtually impossible to become acquainted with American women because they were customarily segregated in ladies' parlors on steamboats and in hotels, thus effectively preventing anything but superficial conversations with European travelers.[6] And in 1856, writer Isabella Bird lamented that an English person in America asking questions with a notebook in hand heard the same stories over and over again, including the tale of the petticoated piano legs found in American parlors to avoid shocking the sensibility of ladies who had a universal aversion to "legs."[7]

Certainly, the work of American novelists did little to lend accuracy to European views of western Americans. James Fenimore Cooper's Leatherstocking Tales not only provided the medium whereby many Europeans formed their ideas about American Indians and frontier people; Cooper's work also opened a vast market for many other types of frontier literature, including the widely read dime novel.[8] By the late years of the nineteenth century, these formula novels regaled European audiences with Indians who were called "savages," "pesky redskins," "red devils," "cussed redskins," and "blood-thirsty wretches." Typically, Indians could speak only broken English: "Me see um. . . . But me no sabe somet'ing."[9] Western women, on the other hand, ran the gamut from damsels being rescued from various perils by heroes named Flying Floyd and Deadwood Dick to heroines waging sword duels, shooting Indians, rescuing in a hot air balloon a lover appropriately named Young Wild West, and thrashing an amorous young man for impertinence.[10]

It is little wonder that many European visitors carried romantic expectations with them as they embarked upon their expeditions to the American West. Bird, for example, as she approached Rock Island, rhapsodized, "On we flew to the West, the land of Wild Indians and Buffaloes."[11] Similarly, in the 1850s, Swedish observer Fredrika Bremer waxed eloquent: "the West is the garden where the rivers carry along with them gold . . . this enigmatic, promised land of the future, I shall now behold!"[12]

Of course, visitors with such preconceptions usually tended to see what they expected to see, even when the scene before them might actually contradict their own notions.[13] The popular French writer François René de Chateaubriand provided an example of such blurred vision. Although he derived most of his ideas about the American West from other authors and traveled in the United States only briefly during 1791, he proceeded nonetheless to write a series of highly stereotyped "Indian" novels as well as a detailed commentary on his American experiences.[14] Like so many of his contemporaries, Chateaubriand responded more to his own needs and to those of his audience than to the realities of western American life.[15] Despite the fact that he had ventured only as far west as upstate New York, he did not hesitate to generalize about all western peoples.[16] Similarly, in 1818 the "West" of William Cobbett was Indiana; in the 1830s Alexis de Tocqueville's West was New York and Michigan; in the 1840s Albert Koch's West was the Keokuk-Burlington region of the Iowa Territory; and in the early 1850s Moritz Busch's West was Ohio and Kentucky.[17] In the mid-1850s Bird was convinced that she had arrived in the "far West" when she reached Davenport, Iowa.[18]

Yet Americans were not totally responsible for creating these mistaken European conceptions of the American West. Most Europeans labored under their own unrealistic view of America. Increasingly, during the nineteenth century, they tended to view the American frontier as the child who would fulfill their own thwarted wishes and dreams. Literary scholar Jerzy Jedlicki has suggested that the Polish fascination with America began as compensation for things missing at home—including conceptions and realities of space, freedom, human rights, land, abundant food, and progress. The result, according to Jedlicki, was that the heroes of authors such as Henryk Sienkiewicz "vied with those of James Fennimore Cooper and his successors in rousing the imagination and dreams of derring-do among Polish adolescents."[19]

Discontented Germans also looked across the ocean for relief and hope. When many Germans migrated to America after 1817, German literature began to focus upon Indians and frontier people, who were now the symbols of the land of the future.[20] Many popular German novelists developed a deep and continuing interest in frontier motifs including wilderness, violence, and American Indian themes. Authors such as Charles Sealsfield, Friedrich Gerstacker, Friedrich Armand Strubberg, and Balduin Möllhausen presented their adventure novels, which regularly featured German-born heroes, as authentic accounts of life on the American frontier.[21] But German enthusiasm for the American West reached its height with the writings of Karl May, often called Germany's Cooper, who did not visit the United States until nearly all of his western American adventures had been written. He was an expert, as indeed were many of those Europeans who did visit America, at combining his own imagined "facts" with bits and pieces of information to produce the tales that served his readers' wishes and needs so well.[22]

Of course Poland and Germany were not alone in these hopeful and inaccurate interpretations of the American frontier. The pervasiveness of such thinking can be seen in the work of many European artists who also exhibited an inability to divorce themselves from European dreams and fears in their representation of western American peoples. From the 1570s to the early nineteenth century, artists depicted American Indians largely as fantasy figures whose primitive nudity was only partially disguised by feathered ornaments. Presented as simple and pure people, these stylized American Indians reflected Renaissance traditions by taking on, in most drawings and paintings, the proportions and classical lines of Greek and Roman figures.[23] By the late eighteenth century, artists such as Benjamin West had refined the use of these neoclassical, didactic Indian figures in paintings commemorating historical events that were so popular during that era.[24]

By the early nineteenth century, European artists began to reflect the Romantic view of the world, and the image of the American frontier changed accordingly. Painters such as Goya, Gerodet, Delacroix, and Doré frequently represented the personification of the West, the Indian, as a romantic hero in their works.[25] Although many European artists never saw the American West, they nevertheless believed themselves to be well qualified to purvey its image to Europeans who were anxious for a confirmation of their own preconceptions. Swiss artist Karl Bodmer, a member of German explorer Prince Maximilian's 1833 expedition to the West, was one of the few European artists who attempted to bring ethnic accuracy and anthropological clarity to his drawings of native Americans. Other artist-explorers, such as Charles Bird King, continued to produce highly idealized portraits of Indians that represented more hyperbole than truth.[26]

This European tendency toward wish fulfillment was encouraged by the continuous frontier emerging in America. Each successive frontier appeared to be one more promise, one more opportunity for the eventual redemption of the decayed world inhabited by Europeans. Many commentators thus reached new heights of exaggeration and inaccuracy in their analysis of frontier America. This willingness on the part of Europeans to perceive the American frontier in terms of their own needs and wishes still exists in the twentieth century. Wild West novels, poems, and movies are still best-sellers throughout Europe, where western wear and country music are popular consumer items. Cowboys and Indians is a game widely played by European children. And adult Western cultists and buffs throughout Europe continue to breathe life into a colorful but inaccurate image of the American West.[27]

How then could European interpreters of the American frontier possibly write with objectivity and impartiality while such complex pressures toward misrepresentation swirled around them? Largely middle- and upper-class, well-educated, and usually male, they were unprepared by virtue of either their background or experience to serve as accurate reporters of the western American scene. Whether they analyzed the New England frontier of the 1600s, the midwestern frontier of the early nineteenth century, the Far West of the late nineteenth century, or vestiges of the frontier that continued to exist into the twentieth century, European observations were permeated with image and myth. Factual reporting was elusive at best and impossible at worst. Yet European views of western Americans are well worth exploring: they not only interpreted frontier people for generations of Europeans who were extremely curious about the New World of the American West, but comments that filtered into American newspapers, periodicals, and popular culture helped shape the ways in which westering women thought about themselves and about the native populations they were about to encounter.

It quickly becomes clear, when one examines European interpretations of western women, that confusion was generated in many Europeans' minds when their traditional values clashed with the new, liberal, and innovative ideas demonstrated by frontierswomen. Given their customary and conservative notions about women's "place," what could Europeans possibly think when they confronted relatively independent, free, and sometimes even gun-toting western white women? Yet, in light of their belief that the God-given superiority of white people was destined to triumph over the West and its native populations, Europeans were also committed to perceiving western women as heroic conquerors.

This ambivalent mode of thinking by Europeans resulted in complex judgments regarding western women that were often contradictory, ranging from shock and outrage, on the one hand, to praise, on the other. The single view upon which European observers generally agreed was that frontierswomen, shaped by the crucible of the western environment, were unique among women. Seemingly liberated and freed by the frontier setting, these women were considered by many Europeans as a distinct and even superior breed of female.

While many Europeans were imputing almost saintlike proportions to white women on the frontier, they were also reacting to the hardworking, domestically oriented, and occasionally polygamous American Indian women. Because Europeans generally believed that the frontier's native population was doomed by its own primitive nature to eventual extinction, they tended to assign Indian females a place on the other end of the continuum from white frontierswomen; that is, Indian women were also viewed as savages. To most Europeans it was clear that the saints would triumph, while the savages would

43

disappear; the fate of each would be justifiable in relation to the clearly discernible characteristics of white and Indian women. In other words, saints *deserved* to survive, and savages *deserved* to disappear.

These biases resulted in images of white and Indian women that were derived, like so many other European judgments regarding the frontier, from what they wished to see rather than from what they actually saw. This is not to suggest that European comments upon white and native American women amounted to nothing more than pure fantasy. They were indeed based on a certain amount of factual observation, but the results were shaded, colored, and limned until the portrait of white women became slightly larger than life while that of American Indian women grew slightly less so.

Of course, many Europeans completely neglected to mention white frontierswomen as a separate category in their commentaries. In the fashion of the era, many onlookers, both male and female, either subsumed women under the category of "men" or ignored them entirely. Thus, when Francis Grund stated in 1837 that nine-tenths of the emigrants to the West were farmers or planters, one might reasonably have assumed that he actually meant that women were also engaged in agrarian-related pursuits.[28] But when Charles Dickens noted in the 1850s that western men of any grade could climb the social ladder, when Brissot de Warville declared in the 1780s that frontiersmen were brave and aggressive, and when W. Faux announced in the 1820s that nine-tenths of the adult population in the West owned land, it is likely that these writers literally meant "men." They tended to disregard women because they did not visualize females as having social status of their own, as possessing the innate ability to be brave and aggressive, or as being personally or legally qualified to own land.[29] It is unfortunate that such assumptions were unilaterally extended to all white frontierswomen, for these beliefs perpetuated a myth that the experiences of many women in the West were disproving. Indeed, one of the tasks of western women's history today is to demonstrate that some western women did have a type of social status of their own, that they were capable of being brave and aggressive, and that they did occasionally own land.

On the other hand, some Europeans may have ignored white frontierswomen simply because they were relatively few in number, at least in certain regions or during the early years of settlement. It might be argued, however, that a scarcity of women was remarkable in itself. Certainly, those Europeans who did comment upon western women frequently mentioned the dearth of women in relation to men.[30] An Italian traveler estimated the ratio of men to women in Colorado in the 1870s as 15 to 1, while one British traveler placed it as high as 20 to 1. "The cry is everywhere for girls; girls; and more girls," he wrote in 1869.[31] Another British traveler wrote that a Denver man was willing to pay "a ten-dollar piece to have seen the skirt of a servant-girl a mile off." In 1881, a British newspaper, the *American Settler,* cited a Durango newspaper's claim that the greatest want in Colorado was women, especially those "who can wait at table" and "above all . . . for sweethearts."[32]

Other western areas were also reportedly short of sufficient numbers of women. One British traveler who visited Texas in 1841 collected a variety of responses on the topic from Texas men: "a maid is hardly to be met with in a day's march"; any woman "has only to go to Texas to charm and fascinate at least one-half of a town's bachelor population"; and "Wimmen was powerful scarce in these diggins, and almost any sort of one was looked on as a reglar *find.*"[33] The *American Settler* frequently noted similar problems in other western areas. During the 1880s the newspaper claimed that only one unmarried woman lived in the town of Delta in Washington Territory and that in Modoc County, California, "ladies are rare birds."[34]

Despite this reported scarcity of white frontierswomen during the early settlement period in most areas, some Europeans did focus directly upon women in their commentaries. In the manner of their time, they often looked upon women as sexual and ornamental beings, concentrating their remarks on factors such as physical appearance, beauty, and dress. A few were unusually graphic in their descriptions. A Frenchman, Edouard de Montule, declared that western women were "on the whole very pretty and shapely" but that he had only encountered one woman who in his opinion had "truly lovely breasts (which American women rarely have)." Frontierswomen were, he wrote in 1821, "generally pleasing; and, with due respect to the amiable ladies of Philadelphia, they are much more attractive in the West than in the regions bordering the coast."[35]

Some Europeans concurred with Montule in his assessment of western women. In 1828, Charles Sealsfield asserted that they were "considered very handsome," and Fredrika Bremer said that in the American West "one seems to meet nothing but handsome faces, scarcely a countenance . . . may be called ugly."[36] Others, however, disputed these judgments. Some thought that few frontierswomen were beautiful, but rather that they grew old prematurely, with their beauty fading and their health disintegrating. They attributed this to a variety of factors, including climate, heavy labor, and poor diet.[37] One British traveler, William Shepard, thought that women all over the West displayed dull, expressionless faces due to hard work, poverty, and cheerless lives.[38] Tocqueville, however, believed that despite "fever, solitude, and a tedious life" in a "comfortless home" in the "Western wilds," most frontierswomen had not lost "the springs of their courage." To him,

> their features were impaired and faded, but their looks were firm: they appeared to be at once sad and resolute. I do not doubt that these young American women had amassed, in the education of their early years, that inward strength which they displayed under these circumstances.[39]

European observers also showed great interest in frontierswomen's dress. In the 1840s, Friedrich Gerstacker stated that women "even of the lowest classes . . . were simply but tastefully dressed." During a Fourth of July celebration, he was startled to learn that the women changed their dresses four or five times between noon and the following morning, but he concluded that since they had little chance to display their wardrobes they had to seize any opportunity to do so.[40] Some commentators mentioned Sunday church services as the occasion on which most frontierswomen flaunted their apparel. According to English traveler Frances Trollope, women attended church in "full costume" in 1832. Montule explained that "confined within the small, cleared spaces in the midst of this wilderness, they impatiently await Sunday, the only day when they can see each other, and be seen; therefore, they make the most of the occasion."[41] Some recalled having seen stylish women in other circumstances as well. Tocqueville considered the women walking along the streets of Albany to be "well turned out"; Busch thought that Kentucky horsewomen dressed "in modish costume"; and Hungarian traveler Theresa Pulszky judged women standing at the doors of loghouses in the Alleghenies of the 1850s to be elegantly dressed.[42]

Although many Europeans concerned themselves with physical aspects of western women, some did turn their attention to other aspects of these women's lives. Some were curious about the treatment received by women at the hands of reputedly rough and unpolished western men and what such treatment might indicate about the position of frontierswomen in society. They were generally impressed that western women were extended a great deal of courtesy and respect by men, but this state of affairs was usually attributed to the efforts of the women themselves. Charles Sealsfield believed that western women were "well entitled" to the chivalrous attention they received, and Gerstacker thought that women inspired such respect by their energy and grace.[43] Many others agreed that women's moral standards were very high and that they exhibited a certain delicacy in their manners which elicited esteem from men.[44]

Several Europeans explained that the apparent coolness and indifference of many frontiersmen toward other women was actually an attempt to maintain privacy and dignity rather than a way of showing a lack of affection.[45] Others argued that the true feelings of western men toward women were well demonstrated by the women's freedom to appear anywhere without fear of insult or injury.[46] One even asserted that the three outstanding qualities of character in western men were self-reliance, common sense, and "the manliness that under all circumstances does honour to itself by the uniform respect paid to woman."[47]

Yet others felt that chivalry on the part of frontiersmen was a sham in its intent as well as limited in nature. In 1838 Harriet Martineau, an English author and traveler, derided chivalry as a poor substitute for justice. In her eyes, these "ungentle, tyrannical" men fell far below their own democratic principles in the treatment of their women.[48] Another Englishwoman, Frances Trollope, also doubted the value that western men placed upon their women. As she watched women "amusing" themselves by engaging in strange religious exercises at a frontier revival, she wondered if "the men of America value their women as men ought to value their wives and daughters, would such scenes be permitted among them?"[49] Other dissenting notes came from Gerstacker, who disliked the frontier custom which decreed that women could eat only after the men had finished, and from Henryk Sienkiewicz, who thought it grossly uncultured for men to talk with ladies without wearing their coats or even their boots.[50]

But many others offered alternative views. In the 1820s, German traveler Gottfried Duden said that women were always served before the men. In 1842, English author Charles Dickens noted that "no man sat down until the ladies were seated." And in 1845, naturalist Charles Lyell stated that women always seated themselves at the table before men.[51] In 1849, Englishman Alexander Mackay was astounded to discover that men were willing to forego spitting and hewing in the presence of women; in his view, this constituted a "gallant self-denial."[52] And during the 1890s, Norwegian Eilert Storm marveled that "in this country where a woman has all rights over against a man, while the latter has none over against her, a judge finds it very difficult to sentence a woman, and for a jury that is even more difficult."[53]

Clearly, these onlookers were not really grappling with the issue, raised by Martineau and Trollope, of whether men's chivalry toward women stemmed from a deeper, more lasting esteem. Instead, most observers tended to assume that polite treatment automatically connoted respect. Consequently, many travelers, men and women alike, were very impressed by the safety with which a woman could travel over all parts of the West.[54] In 1845, Prussian traveler Friedrich von Raumer emphasized that women could travel alone through the "whole country" because even those men who were rough in their relations with other men extended courtesy to women. Gerstacker similarly maintained that "often one will see young girls and women undertake long journeys alone without protection, for they find in every companion a protector and friend. . . . we know here in the forest of nothing more cowardly and mean than the mistreatment of a woman."[55]

Since most European travelers toured America for only a short time and derived many of their opinions regarding women from limited contact on steamboats and stagecoaches, it is perhaps understandable that they drew conclusions from superficial evidence rather than, as Martineau might have preferred, delving deeper into women's situations. Consequently, steamboat and stagecoach stories regarding the preferential treatment of women almost assumed the proportions of legends. A Norwegian traveler of the 1840s described one captain's table as having empty chairs separating the ladies and the captain from the rest of the male passengers.[56] A French traveler related the tale of a steamboat captain madly brandishing a kitchen knife in pursuit of a passenger who had directed a mild swear word toward a lady.[57] Another Frenchman narrated a telling episode in which two steamboat gamblers, having decided to fight out their dispute with only gun butts in deference to the ladies present, were closely observed by these "ladies" who climbed upon the tables to get a closer view of the proceedings.[58]

On stagecoaches gentlemanly behavior also repeatedly assumed extreme proportions. In 1857, Hungarian traveler John Xantus seemed amazed that often in the West when a stagecoach was filled and a lady wanted to board,

> the last gentleman who got on will give his seat, get off and wait for the next coach, which sometimes may take a week; or he may have to proceed on foot or horseback. This happens so many times that it does not even occur to the party involved to grumble about it, even though it may be raining hard when he casually gives up his seat as if it were the most natural thing in the world.[59]

Another male traveler told of a stage journey through a heavy rain, during which a Houston merchant held an umbrella over a woman, protecting her but drenching the other passengers. "The water fell like a cascade over unfortunate me," he wryly noted.[60]

A female traveler, Lady Duffus Hardy, presented a similar, if slightly more romanticized, picture of a man's response to a woman traveling alone.

> To her the manly heart yields his interest in car or stage, gives her the best seat, that she might be screened and curtained, while he broils in the sun; for her he fights a way to the front ranks of refreshment rooms, skirmishes with the coffee pot, and bears triumphant ices aloft.[61]

While many European spectators of the western scene seemed concerned only with such superficial appearances, there were some who attempted to examine other less obvious aspects of western women's lives. These Europeans were particularly interested in educational opportunities offered to women on the frontier. They generally agreed that education was widely available and of high quality. Pulszky pointed out that schools for young women were common and that home education was rarer in the West than in the East.[62] Busch, upon viewing a Cincinnati ladies' school, was pleased to learn that such "an offspring of fashionable refinement does exist and is flourishing," while Trollope was interested in the fact that it actually had "higher branches of science."[63] Ranging a little farther afield, Bremer visited a ladies' school in Wisconsin, whereupon she remarked that "an important reformation in female schools is taking place in these Western States at the present time under the guidance of a Miss Beecher."[64]

Other visitors were struck by the westerner's acceptance of co-education. During the 1890s, French author Charles Varigny wrote that it was "strange instruction that, and strange schools, those, in which girls and boys sat together." Yet he eventually concluded that it was such schools that produced women who were "sure of themselves, able to compete with men, and capable of eliciting respect from men."[65] In 1869, Englishman William Bell had expressed a similar response to the strong coeducational movement in Kansas. To him, it was little wonder that political contests in Kansas were marked by "petticoats . . . well to the front," and that "woman's suffrage and equal rights form part of each platform in every election." He added that it would take a particularly bold Kansas man to oppose "openly the phalanx of political Amazons" that the Kansas educational system produced.[66]

But were these observers impressed by the mere existence of these schools for western women, or were they struck by their true quality? Several remarks suggest that some commentators may have confused academic education in subjects such as Engish, history, and science with the "female accomplishments," such as doing fancy needlework, playing the pianoforte, and cultivating an interest in literature. For instance, Sealsfield stated that women in Cincinnati evinced "a high taste for literary and mental accomplishments" and thus originated the *Literary Gazette*.[67] Another traveler noted that the many women living in boardinghouses in western towns filled their hours with a great deal of reading and with their attendance at public lectures.[68] Yet another explained that women, encouraged to develop their minds, were given more time to cultivate accomplishments, and as a result, they were more civilized than western men.[69]

Several female critics of frontier schools for women strongly believed that a confusion did exist in many people's minds between the existence of ladies' schools, coeducation, a superficial cultivation of accomplishments, and the existence of any meaningful education for women. After visiting upstate New York in 1818, Frances Wright, a Scottish reformer, decided that although there had been strides in women's education it was still puerile. Until it became "the concern of the state," she argued, women's education would offer little of real use of women.[70] Martineau believed that women's education tended to settle for rote methods rather than emphasize any real intellectual activity.[71] She was especially incensed by a young ladies' school that she visited in New Madrid, Missouri, in the late 1830s. "There are public exhibitions of their [the pupils] proficiency, and the poor ignorant little girls take degrees," she wrote scathingly. "Their heads must be so stuffed with vainglory that there can be little room for anything else."[72] Fredrika Bremer was even more vitriolic than Martineau on the subject of western women's education. Visiting St. Louis in 1850, she stated disgustedly that women were physically weak due to their "effeminate education" and that they lived a constricted "harem life" in which they were the pampered sultanas and men their subjects. "The harems of the West," she continued, "no less than those of the East, degrade the life and the consciousness of women."[73]

Martineau complained that the only possible life course open to women educated in this manner was marriage.[74] Of course, this direction was not totally inappropriate because on the frontier women *were* in demand as wives. European analysts of the western scene carried on at great length regarding the need for women to become the wives of male settlers. Assuming, as did most people of the era, that all women desired matrimony as soon as possible, one Norwegian declared that the West was an "El Dorado" for women. Another advised his hometown paper in Norway to publish the advice, "Go west, young woman."[75] Yet another insisted that even those women who "crossed the line"—a Norwegian folk expression for those who strayed from the straight and narrow—would be marriageable on the frontier.[76]

Other writers described locales where women could not only make good matches, but where they would have "mountains of gold dust" laid at their feet "in exchange for their hands."[77] Conservative voices were in a definite minority; one writer, in an 1884 issue of the *American Settler,* urged caution in case an ardent California swain already had "a surplus wife or two in the East."[78]

Many Europeans were also interested in the early marriages that such a population imbalance between men and women seemed to encourage. As early as 1698, an English farmer stated that the American woman usually married before twenty, and soon she "hath a child in her Belly, or one upon her Lap."[79] In the following year, another Englishman claimed that American women, who thought they were ready for husbands by age thirteen, were "very Fruitful, which shows that Men are Industrious in Bed, tho' Idle up."[80] This proclivity of some Americans toward early marriage seemed to move westward with the frontier, for brides of ages thirteen to fifteen were frequently remarked upon in traveler's journals, in immigrant's accounts, and in western novels. Although recent studies suggest that both early marriage and immediate remarriage were more apparent than real in the West, onlookers maintained that not only did women marry young on the frontier but they immediately remarried after the death of a spouse.[81] "Matrimony, like death," charged one English writer, "spares neither age nor condition. I have seen young girls of thirteen and hideous old girls of fifty snapped up eagerly as soon as they arrived in the country."[82]

Europeans often thought it unusual that young men and women chose their own mates, decided on marriage before consulting their parents, and ignored the tradition of a dowry.[83] A few disapproved of the freedom given frontierswomen to marry without parental consent or without even the usual formalities. One traveler was particularly horrified when he saw a young couple meet on a riverboat, decide to marry within fifteen days, and, when the minister they asked to meet their boat could not reach them due to ice, kneel on the deck to be married despite the distance between themselves and the shore-bound minister.[84]

Travelers were also amazed that so little time was spent courting on the frontier. According to Pulszky, a pioneer man simply paid a couple of taciturn calls to a neighbor's eligible daughter, during which he "places himself in a chair before the chimney, chews, spits in the fire," and eventually offered an equally taciturn proposal of marriage.[85] A German traveler of the 1850s described the process in a similar way:

> The American is abrupt; he has no time to beat around the bush. He meets a girl in a shop, in the theater, at a ball, or in her parents' home. He needs a wife, thinks this one will do. He asks the question, she answers. The next day they are married and then proceed to inform the parents.[86]

Many Europeans believed that these frontier marriage practices created a number of problems such as the breakdown of the family due to the early departure of the children to form their own family units.[87] Many felt that the greatest ill that resulted was the increased power that accrued to wives. A husband could go nowhere without his wife, the *American Settler* reported in 1892.[88] Worse yet, wives expected their husbands to be extremely affable, for, as one young western woman quipped in 1876, "if he don't there's plenty will."[89] Such wives purportedly refused to do barn work, legally protected their property before marriage, and even ordered servants to flog an errant husband.[90] If women were displeased with the course of their marriage, they reportedly sought divorce with little hesitation. In 1830, English traveler Simon O'Ferrall noted that three divorces were granted during his brief stay in Marion, Ohio. All three were initiated by women: one for desertion, one for physical abuse, and one for general neglect. O'Ferrall added that a woman was seldom refused a divorce in the West because her dislike of a husband was generally considered a sufficient reason for granting her freedom.[91]

Stories of such wifely misbehavior caused many immigrants to conclude that western women were so spoiled that a proper wife could be found only by importing one.[92] This reputation for brattiness was perhaps undeserved, for when critics turned their attention to frontierswomen's domestic labors they were usually complimentary in tone. Although an occasional visitor depicted the wives of settlers as living in "sloth and inactivity," others were pleased to learn that all women were not as lazy as rumored.[93] Still others represented western women as very diligent indeed. According to Sealsfield, a farm family was "in motion from morning till evening."[94] Englishman William Blane was even more laudatory. In his view, women in the backwoods of the 1820s were "the most industrious females" he had ever seen in any country.[95]

These women were said to perform all of their own domestic tasks, since young women preferred to marry rather than to work as servants and domestics.[96] But although they labored assiduously within their homes, frontierswomen reportedly never worked in the fields. As early as 1656, an English farmer pointed out that "the women are not (as is reported) put into the ground to worke, but occupie such domestique employments as in England."[97] Similar accounts followed as the frontier spread across the continent. British travelers consistently characterized frontierswomen as hard workers in the home but protected from "unwomanly employment" in the fields.[98] In 1841, one

Englishman emphasized that "every man here, rich or poor, seems on all occasions sedulously to give place and precedence to females, and the meanest of them are exempt, or I might rather say debarred, from those masculine or laborious tasks which are commonly enough assigned the sex, or assumed by them, in our country."[99] Other European observers confirmed these reports. In the 1820s, a German traveler said that "not even the poorest farmer allows his wife or daughter to work in the fields"; in 1860, a Swedish immigrant wrote home that "the women never work in the fields—not even milking cows."[100]

Various reasons were offered for women's exemption from field work. Most analysts believed that the generally high regard paid western women explained the situation. At least one writer suggested, however, that the high cost of imported British goods caused women to be "chiefly employed in making articles of domestic clothing."[101] It is interesting that many observers assumed that the restriction of frontierswomen to domestic labor meant a relatively easy life for them. They often characterized settlers' wives and daughters as "ladies" who would not even condescend to draw their own water from a well.[102] In 1848, a Swedish farmer in Illinois wrote home that "women do not have to do any other work here but wash clothes and cups and keep the house tidied up and at some places also cook food."[103] A Frenchman traveling in Kansas during the 1870s also presented a woman's life as one of ease. "An American woman's only job is to make a home and to make little Americans; we were never able to make the women there understand that country women in France work on the land and know how to do it almost as well as their husbands."[104]

Yet some nineteenth-century European women, who had themselves recently chosen to become frontierswomen, presented another side to the picture. A Norwegian woman, Elisabeth Koren, felt that frontierswomen did nothing but cook, thus leaving them little time for other chores, much less for leisure.[105] Another Norwegian settler, Gro Svendsen, pointed out that although frontierswomen were supposed to have much leisure time, she had not met any who actually thought so.[106] And Englishwoman Rebecca Burlend said that she did indeed work in the fields because her husband was unable to find a hired hand.[107]

These comments by women demonstrate, despite reports to the

contrary, that frontierswomen not only worked long and hard hours within their homes but that they also labored in the fields whenever necessary. Other accounts indicate that they also frequently refused to limit themselves to women's traditional tasks and responsibilities. For example, women did not hesitate to take up arms in their own defense. Busch remarked that in the early years of settlement "everyone was a soldier, and even the women knew how to handle a rifle." In 1840, French novelist Gustave Aimard said that women often "take a rifle in their delicate hands, and fight boldly in defence of the community." He added that "women fight by the side of the men, and forgetting the weakness of their sex, they can, on occasion, prove themselves as brave as their husbands and brothers."[108] Other tales told of western women moving into many customarily male areas. Women in business, as judges, and as university professors were among some of the cases mentioned.[109] Because they were not constrained as European women were, western women apparently achieved some latitude in their roles.[110]

European responses to such liberated western women ranged from shock and surprise to dismay and puzzlement. Most observers appeared to feel more comfortable with women who used their talents in accepted female ways, and particularly as civilizing forces in the newly settled regions. Most Europeans could understand and applaud women who exercised their moral powers. British visitors seemed delighted to observe that many frontierswomen seemingly exerted a stabilizing force in the West.[111] According to one, women were second only to churches in helping to refine the new society.[112] Another was positively enthusiastic in his description of women's salutary influence on the frontier:

> A lady is a power in this country. From the day when a silk dress and lace shawl were seen on Main Street, that thoroughfare became passably clean and quiet; oaths were less frequently heard; knives were less frequently drawn; pistols were less frequently fired.[113]

Other spectators went on to say that women were the judges of decency, the guardians of humanity, and the very cement of a society which, "without woman, is like an edifice built on sand."[114] Sienkiewicz insisted that women so softened the brutal habits of one frontier town of the 1870s that the men argued still, but quietly. Bowie knives remained in their sheaths and revolvers in the pocket. Cards were not played so fiercely and only cocktails were drunk, instead of the usual enormous draughts of whiskey.[115]

If these descriptions of western women seem to embody a superior type of being, it is perhaps because so many Europeans believed that frontierswomen were indeed unusual people. Despite the contradictions and disagreements regarding specific aspects of frontierswomen's lives, roles, and actions in the writings of Europeans, the overall assessment was in general agreement that frontierswomen had the best situation of any women in the world. To demonstrate this point, Europeans were very fond of favorably comparing American women's lives with those of women in other countries.[116] Europeans stressed again and again that western American women received more respect from men than did women anywhere else in the world. They also emphasized that frontierswomen wielded more power in both their homes and society than did women in other regions of the world.[117] As a case in point, one Dutch traveler, Tutein Nolthenius, wrote that western American women "are different from our womenfolk, who are kept inferior female animals from force of habit and superstition."[118] Moreover, Europeans often pointed out that western women faced more opportunities than other women within the institution of marriage, in the schools and colleges, and in employment.

Perhaps more importantly, many Europeans credited frontierswomen for taking the fullest possible advantage of such opportune conditions. In 1885, the *American Settler* emphasized the ability of frontierswomen to make "good use" of the "free field" they found opening before them in the West.[119] Others maintained that frontierswomen's opportunities resulted from a combination of environmental factors and the women's own abilities. Some argued that such abilities included strengths and skills that proved women to be the equals of men in almost every way.[120] As Varigny explained it, a frontierswoman was relieved of her "chains" by the environment, but she won equality with men through her own talents.[121]

Despite these many glowing statements by Europeans about western American women's supposed equality with men, there was little agreement among them on the actual status of women's legal and political rights in the West. Except for a few, such as Harriet Martineau and Fredrika Bremer, they did not seem to see any discrepancy between their view of western women's "equality" and the women's lack of actual rights. As a result, their descriptions of the women's rights movement in the nineteenth-century West were contradictory and confusing. One, for instance, claimed that frontierswomen did not "clamour" for their rights, but the writer did not explain why this was so.[122] Another, however, castigated frontierswomen who pushed to become more than the equals of their husbands.[123] Yet another lectured aggressive western women by reminding them that women had a "providential mission in this world" and should adhere to it.[124] And another patronizingly argued that western women who exercised the right of suffrage were acceptable because they were not creating social upheaval.[125]

In light of their own conservative ideas regarding women's rights, it is not difficult to understand why many Europeans would be confused and concerned about American women's political situation in the West. Because of their own traditional background and values, most European commentators were not yet ready to grapple with the many realities involved in issues such as women's actual equality and rights. Most were more interested in molding the myth of the American frontierswoman to meet their own needs and expectations.

When European observers turned their attention to American Indians the resulting images were as complex as those of frontierswomen. It was problematic for most Europeans to approach the topic of native Americans with any degree of objectivity. Caught between opposing interpretations of the "good" Indian, who was simple, pure, and virtuous, and the "bad" Indian, who was cruel, rapacious, and predatory, Europeans tended to reflect one view or the other. Seldom did they attempt to blend the two images into a composite portrait of Indians which combined both "good" or "bad."

One of the staunchest defenders of the "good" Indian was a German physician, Johann Schopf, who traveled through frontier America in the early 1870s. From his observations, he maintained that the moral character of American Indians was not nearly as black as it had been painted. He also argued that many of their endeavors demonstrated patience and invention and that their medical competence was particularly high.[126] Chateaubriand was also sympathetic to Indians. He believed that it was unfair to show only the unattractive characteristics of Indians because in reality their "laws . . . are grave and their manners often charming."[127]

Some novelists took similar positions. Norwegian novelist Jens Tvedt created a Dakota woman who, as a child of a trapper, grew up among Indians and married a native man. Tvedt put these words into her mouth:

> There are Indians who possess just as many good qualities as any white person. Although you may find some of the worst scum among them, I think that you will find quite as many bad specimens among our own people. You will seldom find such a degree of vile coarseness among the Indians as exists among the whites—at least as long as they have not been corrupted by contact with the whites.[128]

In the 1830s, author Charles Sealsfield decried the injustices perpetrated on Indians who were the legitimate owners of the lands that the whites were so ruthlessly seizing.[129] But the greatest supporter of the American Indian was Karl May, a German novelist famous for his 1892 novel *Winnetou*. May deplored the fact that Indians had not been granted adequate time to evolve from hunter to farmer to city dweller. Instead, May argued, Indians had been expected to make one great leap, and when unable to do so, they were killed off by whites. "What could the race have achieved given a chance?" he asked.[130]

Other sympathetic observers challenged the widespread use of the term "savage" to describe native Americans. In the 1790s, Louis Philippe of France said that he preferred to call natives "Indians" rather than "savages." He did not believe "that these people merit that epithet in any way."[131] Others suggested that white settlers deserved the term "savage" more than did Indians. Half-civilized and brutal in their actions toward American Indians, they were often considered less desirable acquaintances than "the genuine *uncontaminated* Indian."[132]

Significantly, portrayals of "bad" Indians seemed to far outnumber those of "good" Indians. As early as 1628, a Dutch minister described native Americans as "entirely savage and wild . . . uncivil and stupid as garden poles."[133] This theme was to be repeated many times throughout the following years. A French pianist called Indians in his audience "a delegation of savages." A Hungarian naturalist declared Indians to be "completely savage and far, far removed from civilization." And a Prussian traveler insisted that they were "corporeally and mentally so very different" from whites.[134] In 1913, English writer and social critic Rupert Brooke epitomized this line of thought when he proclaimed his own final judgment on American Indians in the *Westminster Gazette*. "The Indians have passed," he proclaimed. "They left no arts, no tradition, no buildings or roads or laws; only a story or two, and a few names, strange and beautiful."[135]

Some Europeans reacted negatively to the Indians they met because they had been led by writers such as Chateaubriand and Cooper to expect romantic, colorful figures. Like Tocqueville, many Europeans were disappointed and disillusioned to find small, wiry folk who could have come "from the lowest mob of our great European cities."[136] Comparisons of native Americans with peasants, Arabian bedouins, and gypsies were common.[137] One disenchanted Englishman concluded that "they are a dirty vagabond lot, not unlike our gipsies," while another stated that they "appeared like the lowest and worst of our gipsies."[138] Given the popularity of such unflattering assessment, it is little wonder that many authors increasingly judged Indians as having "snakes" in the "bosom of their race" and as people capable of anything from violently attacking an infant colony to harboring white murderers, robbers, and rapists.[139]

Even more than their dirty and ragged appearance, the drunkenness of some American Indians disgusted Europeans. Tocqueville, for example, recounted several instances of drunken native men and women. To him they were brutalized like wild beasts, and they were to be feared when in a drunken state.[140] Other writers ranged in their remarks from extending sympathy to "poor corrupted frontier Indians" to concluding that Indians would go to any lengths, including selling a wife or child, to obtain liquor.[141] However, many of these European spectators felt that they were seeing the worst representations of American Indians. They believed that the most visible Indians were often those whose culture had been destroyed, and who had now been transformed into lazy, dirty beggars hanging around towns and railroad depots in hopes of a handout.[142] In the 1820s, Paul Wilhelm, Duke of Württemberg, pointed out that it was highly unfair and inaccurate to extrapolate from the examples of a few drunken Indians to construct an image of all Indians, while Tocqueville searched in vain for the unspoiled native American tribes that he was convinced had retreated into the wilds.[143]

This degradation and destruction of America's native peoples so outraged many Europeans that they seemed to feel compelled to lay the blame for it on someone. Arguing that Indians were basically good, Chateaubriand placed the responsibility on Europeans for debasing and destroying Indian culture and society. According to him, "the right of force took independence" from America's original inhabitants.[144] Pulszky similarly condemned Anglo-Saxons for being great colonizers but ineffective civilizers, who routinely swept native races away in their settlement process.[145] Others indicted arrogant American frontier people for decimating "unhappy savages" and for driving them across the land.[146] Still others blamed the United States government for the harm done to American Indians by its unenlightened policies.[147]

The feeling that whites were in some way accountable for the plight of the American Indian was far from unanimous. Von Raumer charged that the Indians themselves were at fault. Their own idleness, he said, had made their assimilation into an industrious white society impossible; and not only was their degeneration inevitable due to their own habits, but their claim to land simply because they hunted on it was invalid.[148] In 1837, English observer Francis Grund supported von Raumer on both counts. Since they possessed little in the way of tradition or moral character, Indians could never be civilized, and because they had not cultivated the land, they had no "distinct title to it arising from actual labor." Although Grund regretted "the fate of the doomed people," he too could "hardly think of rescuing them from it, without being guilty of the most flagrant injustice to the rest of Mankind," who could use the land much more efficiently.[149] Other travelers agreed that the advance of the whites across the continent was grand and solemn. To them, rescuing the land from "savages" and "wild beasts" in order to turn it to industry was a progressive change, and they found it difficult to contemplate America's "growing wealth and strength without rejoicing."[150]

With so many countervailing and often less-than enlightened conceptions of Indians swirling through their minds, many Europeans reacted by simply giving the topic short shrift. It seems that many Europeans who remained in Europe were more enamored by the subject of the American Indian than those who traveled in America.

Alexis de Tocqueville, author of *Democracy in America* (1835). His observations of American life influenced Americans' perceptions of themselves. [John Graham Brooks, *As Others See Us* (New York: The Macmillan Co., 1908).]

Frances Trollope, author of *Domestic Manners of the Americans* (1832). A prolific English writer, she doubted that American women were truly valued by American men. [From Frances Trollope, *Domestic Manners of the Americans* (New York: Dodd, Mead and Co., 1927).]

Fredrika Bremer, author of *The Homes of the New World: Impressions of America* (1853). Her romantic expectations shaped her impressions of America. [From Adolph B. Benson, ed., *America of the Fifties: Letters of Fredrika Bremer* (New York: The Am.-Scan. Fdn., 1924).]

Harriet Martineau, author of *Society in America* (1837). The English novelist and feminist saw a contrast between the apparent physical freedom of American women and their actual legal status. [From John Graham Brooks, *As Others See Us* (New York: The Macmillan Co., 1908).]

Sarah Josepha Hale, editor of *Godey's Lady's Book*. Although she cam-
paigned for better education for women, Hale restricted their proper sphere
of activity to the moral and emotional. (Painted by W. B. Chambers and
engraved expressly for *Godey's Lady's Book* by W. G. Armstrong.)

"Heroism of Woman of the Nez Perces" from a drawing by F. S. Church (1898), from *The Adventures of Captain Bonneville, U.S.A.* The noble woman warrior represented one stereotypical, romantic image of American Indian women. (Courtesy Museum of New Mexico, neg. no. 107725.)

Blackfoot camp, circa 1910. Reflecting their incomplete knowledge of American Indian culture, many whites saw Indian women as little more than beasts of burden. (H. F. Robinson, courtesy Museum of New Mexico, neg. no. 36829.)

Typical pioneer wagon. White women learned new skills and often changed their view of womanhood through their experiences on the trail. (T. Harmon Parkhurst, courtesy Museum of New Mexico, neg. no. 8191.)

Others offered inaccurate accounts of native peoples, perhaps because they did not venture far enough west to actually encounter many native Americans. Still others allowed their own shock and disillusionment to interfere with objective and fair reporting. Whatever the cause, the result was often a disappointingly superficial and biased description of Indian society, customs, and culture.

Indian women received even less attention from observers than did Indians generally. Of course, as was the case with white women, writers often simply subsumed native women under the generic label of "Indian." When they did refer specifically to Indian women, Europeans tended to call them "squaws" rather than use more dignified terms comparable to "Indian," "brave," or "chief," which referred to Indian men. Given the historically harsh connotation of the term "squaw," this European usage suggests not only careless ignorance about the term's actual meaning but the existence of a negative pre-judgment of Indian women.[151] When they encountered female Indians, Europeans apparently were determined to see what they expected to see.

However, while Europeans categorized Indian women as Indians and as squaws, they also recognized them as women. Thus, although these observers clearly viewed Indian women as inferior females, they were still interested in some of the same issues that had concerned them regarding white women. As a result, many of the Europeans who mentioned Indian women at all paid inordinate attention to questions of physical appearance, beauty, and dress.

Some visitors characterized Indian women as "seldom ugly."[152] Others described native women as "quite lovely."[153] Still others noted beautiful women in certain tribes. A French naval officer thought that Louisiana Indians had "beautiful wives"; a German novelist said that Choctaw women had "beautiful figures"; and a French traveler declared that Lake Erie Indian women were "the most comely savages I had yet seen."[154] In the 1840s, the English author, Frederick Marryat, represented Comanche women as "exquisitely clean, good-looking, and but slightly bronzed." Marryat also compared favorably Shoshone women to graceful Arabian women.[155]

Such comments do not fit well with the accepted image of the squaw and were indeed an expression of a minority viewpoint. Most Europeans seemed quite convinced that American Indian women were generally dirty, ugly, and unattractive creatures. They shared

Tocqueville's view that there were no "passable" Indian women, and they offered a variety of explanations for the situation.[156] The hard work performed by women was frequently offered as the cause of early aging and ugliness.[157] Uncleanliness and extreme filth were also suggested as reasons for what seemed to some viewers the disgusting appearance of Indian women.[158] In the 1790s, an Englishman, Isaac Weld, set forth in no uncertain terms his own judgment of Indian women.

> I never saw an Indian woman of the age of thirty, but what her eyes were sunk, her forehead wrinkled, her skin loose and shrivelled, and her whole person, in short, forbidding; yet, when young, their faces and persons are really pleasing, not to say sometimes very captivating. . . . This sudden change is chiefly owning to the drudgery imposed on them by the men after a certain age; to their exposing themselves so much to the burning rays of the sun; sitting so continually in the smoke of wood fires; and, above all, to the general custom of prostituting themselves at a very early age.[159]

In the 1830s a German scientist, Prince Maximilian of Wied, consistently characterized women of various tribes in the upper Missouri River region as ugly, plain in appearance, and unappealing in manner of their dress and personal hygiene. Another early nineteenth-century traveler summarized his reaction to native American women more succinctly. "As to personal appearance, with very few exceptions, I can only specify three degrees—horrible, more horrible—most horrible."[160]

Yet when they turned their attention to the matter of women's dress, most Europeans did not seem to be describing ugly, filthy women. After a vehemently negative statement about Indian women, Isaac Weld went on to recount the many ribbons, jewelry, and profusion of ornaments with which they adorned themselves.[161] Others also spoke of the ribbons, shells, feathers, beautiful dresses, delicate moccasins, and ornaments favored by Indian women.[162] In addition, there were frequent comments regarding carefully arranged hair-dos.[163] "Their hair is very beautiful," Xantus wrote of native women in Missouri, "always dressed with great care and falling softly on the shoulders."[164]

Even those who encountered poor Indians generally were pleased by the women's dress. In 1898, according to English observer Charles

Trevelyan they were dressed "like shabby American."[165] Harriet Martineau was impressed by native women in Oneida, New York, who were neatly dressed and wrapped in clean blankets.[166] And Fredrika Bremer complimented Indian women in St. Paul for being "less painted, and with better taste than the men."[167]

Oddly enough, this was not the way American Indian women appeared in most European novels, where they were more often presented as lovely young maidens or as princesses in exotic garb. In the 1840s, Marryat characterized them as adorned in doeskin shirts, embroidered moccasins, ankle and wrist bracelets, and with valuable jewels in their luxuriant raven hair.[168] In 1845, another writer visualized his heroine in an elegant sheepskin cloak, porcupine-quill work, and elks' teeth ornaments.[169] Beads, tinkling silver bells, scarlet leggings, partially nude bosoms, hair that reached almost to the ground, and even wampum belts were also regularly mentioned by many authors.[170] In 1878, Gustave Aimard created a prototype of these maidens when he introduced Ova, the daughter of a chief, who wore "a tunic of water-green colour, fastened around her waist by a wampum-belt, with a large golden buckle." According to Aimard, she was much loved by all; when she danced for her father, "the old man's forehead became unwrinkled," while her ardent lover was moved to bring her "perfumes of grizzly bears' grease, necklaces of alligator's teeth, and wampum girdles."[171]

Clearly the contradiction between the "good" Indian and the "bad" Indian affected Europeans' interpretations of native American women. Were they pure, simple, lovely princesses clothed in exotic attire, or were they ugly, filthy, ragged squaws who deserved extermination? It seemed easier for Europeans to adopt the first view while reading a romanticized novel, sitting by a warm fire somewhere on the continent, than when they were traveling through America and observing real women. Arriving as they did with specific ideas about how women, even those of a supposedly inferior race, should act and be treated, Europeans were troubled by what they saw. Superficial topics, such as physical appearance and dress, obviously created problems for them; but when they moved on to a consideration of deeper issues, such as sexual behavior and marriage customs among Indian groups, their responses ranged from rationalization to acrimony.

Sexual relations between American Indian women and white men particularly evoked a complex spectrum of reactions from Europeans.

From the time of John Rolfe and Pocahontas, Europeans preferred to believe that European men were sent by Providence to guide and fulfill American Indian women in a way that Indian men were incapable of doing.[172] In 1837, Marryat noted in his diary that the daughter of a native American chief had brought heraldry into a white family and that the Randolphs of Virginia still boasted of their association with Pocahontas.[173] Marryat also pointed out that there were many practical reasons for an alliance between a white man and a native woman. "They labour hard, never complain," he stated, "are always faithful and devoted, and very sparing of their talk."[174] A German traveler of the 1820s stated that an Indian wife ensured a white man's safety while he was among the Indians; thus, she was only temporary, to be discarded when her usefulness came to an end.[175] Other factors that reportedly made native women attractive to white men were their lands or other kinds of income. According to von Raumer, "many improvident or dissolute whites marry Indian girls in order to share their income, the amount of which to their joy increases, as intemperance diminishes the number of the Indians."[176] And when a white man found it impossible to obtain a mistress or a wife in any other way, he supposedly could always purchase a native woman with ponies, liquor, or baubles.[177]

Despite the many reasons that were proffered for establishing liaisons with American Indian women, many European men rejected the practice. Some felt that it was detrimental to the Indians themselves. Weld believed that prostitution among native women caused sterility and therefore a decline in the Indian population. In the 1820s, Englishman Adam Hodgson expressed concern that intermarriage between Indians and whites undermined native American customs.[178]

Most Europeans who opposed Indian-white relationships did so on the basis of traditional white attitudes. A Hungarian traveler rejected miscegenation because he thought Indian women were unattractive.[179] The protagonist of a Hungarian novel refused the offer of an Indian bride because he believed that these women became dirty and untidy wives.[180] And the hero of a Polish story fled an impending marriage with a native woman because he thought her customs repulsive. He decided to ask his commanding officer for a distant mission, as he watched his bride-to-be presiding at a prenuptial banquet.

She sat there disembowelling the ox. She would plunge her round arms deep into the interior of the beast and then pull them out, dripping with gore and warm fat that she would offer to the whole company. . . . My betrothed greeted me with a smile, as she put a warm, raw bite to her lips, and swallowed it almost without chewing at all. Her eyes glistened with pleasure, as if she were eating caramels.[181]

Other Europeans were repelled by what they deemed a lack of morality in Indian-white relationships.[182] "The child of man in natural surroundings," one German traveler wrote in the 1850s, "knows little of the pure feelings of shame and love."[183] Others claimed that they pointed to their wedding rings or distributed presents widely among the Indians in order to avoid insulting them while rejecting one of their women.[184] Even Karl May, who was very partial to American Indians, had trouble dealing with this issue. In one of his works, he had an Indian character declare: "The great Spirit has cursed every red woman who loves a white man; therefore, the children of such a woman are like the worm." In another story, May went to the extreme length of killing Winnetou's sister to prevent further embarrassing affection between her and the hero, Shatterhand.[185]

It is significant that few, if any, European observers analyzed *why* native women became involved with white men. They not only failed to consider either political or economic motivations on the part of American Indians, but they also ignored the possible legitimacy of Indian customs that proscribed certain sexual and marital behavior for women. Instead, Europeans were quick to justify their own actions while condemning those of the Indian. Few voices challenged prevalent assumptions that white behavior toward Indians was justifiable while Indian behavior toward whites was immoral. One of the few who did speak out to the contrary in 1845 deserves to be quoted in full.

It is no new feature in the terrible history of slavery that we are giving publicity to. Certainly on all occasions when a white man honoured a red-skin girl with his affection, the parents or guardians fixed a price upon her possessions, which price paid, the woman was ever after the property of the purchaser. But is it alone amid the wild Indians of the American prairies that this custom prevails? If we look around, we shall find the fair daughters of Europe brought to market not so universally, neither so openly and avowedly, but still bought and sold as nakedly and as foully as any poor Comanche or Eutaw maiden ever was.[186]

Even if European critics actually considered the point raised here, they were faced with other evidence that seemed to assure them of their own moral righteousness and of the Indians' depravity.

Polygamy was especially shocking to Europeans. Because it was not part of their own cultural background, they were unprepared to find any possible validity in such an institution. Travelers frequently commented upon it at length, and many novelists incorporated it into their works as a commonplace of American Indian life.[187] The usual interpretation was that polygamy implied disdain for Indian women by their men. Louis Philippe claimed that polygamy rendered women contemptible in men's eyes. Von Raumer took the position that the treatment of women that resulted from polygamy did not reflect the mild and happy relationships that were assumed to exist among native Americans.[188] Other travelers recounted dramatic tales of women's responses to what Europeans saw as reprehensible treatment. These included stories of wives who fought violently the admittance of another wife into their home or who took their own lives and those of their children rather than tolerate such an indignity.[189]

The apparent liberality of premarital sexual practices among American Indian groups also upset many Europeans. "When an unmarried brave passes through a village, he hires a girl for a night or two, as he pleases, and her parents find nothing wrong with this," puzzled French naval officer Jean Bernard Bossu in the 1860s. He seemed less perplexed that chiefs would harangue young girls to offer their bodies to white men, for there was an advantage to be gained: women would then bear a white man's child, who would have white intelligence and would thus compel whites to fear rather than abuse it.[190] Paul Wilhelm, however, assumed that native women entered involvements with white men and often bore a child out of wedlock because they were outgoing, kind, and overly fond of ornaments.[191]

To European eyes such freedom appeared not only immoral and dangerous, but it seemed to contradict the fact that women in many Indian groups had little voice in the selection of a marriage partner. Observers were often as shocked by the extreme rigidity of this system as they were by the total lack of forethought that seemed to characterize white marriages on the frontier. Fredrika Bremer thought one of the worst features of Indian women's lives was that they were seldom able to choose their own mates.[192] The practice of arranged marriages also provided the raw material for hundreds of nineteenth-century fictionalized stories of true love sometimes eventually fulfilled but more often thwarted and ending with one or both lovers committing suicide.[193] Only a few analysts looked more deeply into the situation—as did one Polish writer in the 1870s—to see that women's lack of choice was perhaps not as absolute as it had first appeared.

> For you see that while Indian maidens appear to have no will of their own in choosing a husband, that is really not the case at all. The father sells you a young squaw and you take her from his wigwam to your tent or hut. But if you take her against her will, you are brewing yourself a whole pot of trouble. The maiden will sulk, bite, throw herself on you with a knife, hide away, malinger, and after a few days will flee back to her father, or at worst, with some other lover.[194]

It was also curious to many observers that women who were so sexually free before marriage were expected to be absolutely chaste after marriage.[195] One eighteenth-century author explained that it was only in the bud that these "wild roses" were accessible. "Liberal to profusion of their charms before marriage," he elucidated, "they are chastity itself after."[196] If they violated these standards of matrimonial fidelity, women in many tribes were harshly punished, even by physical disfigurement such as having an ear or nose cut off.[197] In the 1760s, Bossu concluded that such punishment was a practical matter because, according to him, "all the Indians trace their ancestry from their mother's family, since they are sure that they are her children but cannot be certain of the male parent."[198]

These high expectations of women's chastity in marriage did not seem to be in harmony with the custom followed by many Indians of offering their daughters and even wives as bedmates to guests. John Smith of Virginia was one of the first Europeans to explain that many American Indian men did not consider a sexual alliance between their daughter or wife and another man promiscuous if it was sanctioned by them. "Their women are carefull not to bee suspected of dishonesty without the leave of their husbands," he wrote in 1612.[199] In later years, other travelers also pointed out that a woman's sexual liaisons were not judged immoral when approved beforehand by a husband, father, or brother.[200]

Europeans also commented on what appeared to them to be similarly puzzling aspects of women's behavior and status. Bossu noted that Choctaw women were expected to leave their homes during their menstrual periods, supposedly to placate the men who believed that a menstruating woman could make them ill and cause them bad luck in battle. Bossu added that they had to go into the woods to bear their babies alone and that women could discipline their female children but never their male children.[201] Other Europeans recorded the existence of similar customs among other Indian groups, but noted that once a wife became a mother she was accorded a certain degree of respect.[202] "A crime considered frightful and unheard of among the Indians is that of a son rebellious to his mother," Chateaubriand wrote in 1827. "When she grows old, he feeds her."[203] According to Bremer, if a woman happened to be the mother of a distinguished warrior she was especially esteemed by the men of the tribe.[204] In return, native mothers appeared to be caring and affectionate toward their children, for many Europeans complimented them profusely in this area.[205]

What most struck European spectators about native American families was the women's total accountability for all domestic and agricultural labor, while the men were expected "only" to hunt, fish, care for their animals and weapons, and conduct warfare. The list of men's duties might appear to some to be demanding, dangerous, and exhausting; yet to most Europeans, who came from settled agrarian or industrial backgrounds, such tasks seemed incidental and even amusing. Montule depicted Indian males as "by nature very lazy in cultivating the land or in working as do civilized people." To him, they seemed to have energy only for the more interesting activities of hunting and fighting.[206]

Very rare indeed was the traveler such as Friedrich Gerstacker, who argued that "in a state of society where the lives of the family depend upon the success of the hunter, he must have his arms free and unencumbered for action at every minute, and dare not toil under a heavy load, for it would make his aim unsteady."[207] Rather, travelers endlessly lamented the plight of the poor woman who did all the domestic chores, labored in the fields, and took complete care of family and housing matters, while her mate did little or nothing (that is, he hunted, fished, fought, and attended to related duties).[208] Such statements were repeated so often that they became truisms. Some observers even claimed that American Indian men did no work at all and sometimes had to be carried on their wives' backs when they grew too lazy to walk home from hunting.[209]

These inaccurate portrayals of the roles and duties of men and women in most native cultures stemmed largely from the fact that commentators usually observed only the village life of traditional hunting and military societies. While they were afforded many opportunities to watch native women carry out the domestic chores that were their responsibilities, observers seldom had the same chance to witness native men engaged in their responsibilities: conducting a dangerous and demanding buffalo hunt, fighting in deadly warfare, or performing various rites such as a sweat lodge ceremony. Coming from an industrialized society where hunting and fishing were considered little more than leisure-time sports and where warfare was a matter for a trained few, most Europeans had little conception of the skill and peril involved in such pursuits. Thus, in their eyes, native women got the very worst of the bargain, while men seemed to get the very best.[210]

Complicating the matter still further was the absence of any direct contact between observers and Indian women, coupled with a lack of access to the words of Indian women, for words were seldom written down in societies that valued oral traditions and history. Even the few trappers and missionaries who did get to know American Indian women typically allowed their own self-interests or perceptions to bias their reports. Not only did most Europeans fail to reflect the average native women's feelings and attitudes about the societal system in which they functioned, but they almost totally neglected any recognition of exceptional women. Although American Indian women among many tribes became accomplished equestrians, daring warriors, revered medical practitioners, and venerated religious leaders, it has been left to modern anthropologists, historians, and native women who serve as tribal, family, and personal historians to reveal the stories of Indian women such as Elk Hollering, Running Eagle, and Old Lady Drives the Enemy.[211]

As a result of their blind spots, most nineteenth-century European commentators emphasized what appeared to them to be a cruelly unfair division of labor between American Indian men and women. "The man smokes peacefully while the woman grinds corn in a mortar." Louis Philippe wrote. "The men in domestic life are exceedingly slothful," traveler John Davis added, near the turn of the nineteenth century. "The women perform all the household drudgery. . . . The active employment of the men is war and hunting."[212] "The squaw has to toil," Pulzsky observed, "the man but to fight, to hunt, to play, and to speak in council."[213] And, according to Hodgson, "the women were hard at work, digging the ground, pounding Indian corn, and carrying heavy loads of water from the river, while the men were either setting out to the woods with their guns, or lying idle before doors."[214]

Many European onlookers concluded that the domestic toil performed by Indian women placed them in the category of an animal or a slave. "The wife of an Indian is his marketable animal; travelling, or in a compaign, she carries the burden of his baggage on her back," one observer explained in 1849.[215] "The women are forced to do the hardest work, and are treated like slaves," another author emphasized in 1845.[216] Indians "look upon women in a totally different light from what we do in Europe, and condemn them as slaves to do all the drudgery," yet another writer insisted in the 1790s.[217]

John Xantus was shocked to discover that women "do everything, even the most degrading tasks we would be embarrassed to ask our servants to do in Europe."[218] In 1817, English botanist John Bradbury thought that the plight of native women looked so dire that he was led to claim that "mothers frequently destroy their female children, alleging as a reason, that it is better they should die than lead a life so miserable as that to which they are doomed. . . . also it is said that suicide is not infrequent."[219]

European novelists reinforced these unhappy images of American Indian women by similarly representing them as drudges and their men as "haughty" husbands who "amuse themselves with hunting, shooting, fishing."[220] The men were frequently characterized as indolent, lazy tyrants who smoked and chatted while their women labored their lives away.[221] Only Karl May rejected this interpretation in favor of an enlightened Indian hero who vowed to make his wife "a lady of the hut and the tent, as the women of the palefaces!"[222] Perhaps May could not bear to present his friends, the American Indians, as complete tyrants. Or perhaps he suspected that such a depiction of the roles of Indian men and women was too extreme in its dimensions to be totally accurate.

There were, of course, reasons for these European perceptions of

Indian women. Because of their own traditional attitudes regarding the limited roles and inferior position of women in European society, it was difficult for them to grasp many native groups' concept of men and women as separate but equal.[223] Yet, to many Indians, it was a matter of pride that men and women had their appropriate duties, which they performed faithfully and well. An Indian woman could insult another most severely by saying, "You let your husband carry burthens [sic]." To European ears, however, this sounded like a complaint rather than an expression of pride in one's duties.[224] Europeans could not understand that an American Indian male walking in front of a female did not signify the woman's inferiority but indicated that since the male was expendable he was placing himself in the way of an attack and thereby protecting the more valuable female, who would propagate and care for the race.[225] Nor did they see that separate dances and amusements did not automatically indicate male disdain for women.[226]

In addition, European critics apparently did not realize the contradictions in their own descriptions of native women, who were portrayed as beribboned and bedecked with ornaments, beads, and finely worked clothing in a manner hardly signifying contemptible and degraded slaves. They also did not seem to see any problem in their accounts of love-struck Indian swains, who went to great lengths to court and capture their loved ones, and their descriptions of elaborate and elegant marriage ceremonies—with both suggesting great esteem for the wife's role. Another significant paradox in the Europeans' comments occurred when they praised the exquisite basketry, ingenious quill work, and fine weaving of the women. Maximilian, for example, admired the porcupine-quill work, leather dresses and shirts, and buffalo robes produced by the Crow women he encountered.[227] Europeans were apparently unaware that such skills could not be achieved nor such crafts produced by slavelike beasts of burden who had neither leisure time nor the necessary status to develop the marks of a cultured and productive society.[228]

Evidently, the view of native American women as unfortunate workhorses, who became brutalized and cruel as a result of their husbands' treatment, was more amenable to most Europeans than the depiction of Indian women as skillful, respected, and well treated. As a result, travelers frequently rendered accounts of "savage women" who were "as insolent as the men were cruel."[229] Novelists too—even May—often portrayed native women as outrageous figures who were capable of inflicting the worst kinds of tortures upon their victims.[230]

Occasionally a dissonant note challenged this account of American Indian women. In 1859, a Norwegian traveler described a huge, respectful assemblage gathered around the pyre of an Indian woman.[231] A German traveler claimed that an American Indian wife was "no longer degraded to be the slave of her husband" but received the "honour due to her as a wife and a mother."[232] A female British novelist stressed the existence among the Huron Indians of an elected governing council of matrons who ruled coequally with the council of elders.[233] And Fredrika Bremer pointed out that a native woman could achieve power "from her mystical, witch-like attributes, when she is possessed of a powerful character."[234]

In her 1850 travel letters, Bremer critiqued in more detail the usual European view of American Indian women as degraded savages. After watching native American women in St. Paul, visiting them in their homes, and commenting upon their heavy work loads, she was moved to write:

> With inward wonder I regarded these beings, women like myself, with the spirit and feelings of women, yet so unlike myself in their purpose of life. . . . I thought of hard, gray, domestic life in the civilized world . . . hedged in by conventional opinion, with social duties . . . with every prospect of independence, liberty, activity, and joy closed, more rigidly closed by invisible barriers than these wigwams by their buffalo hides . . . and I thought that the Indian hut and that Indian woman's life was better, happier as *earthly life*. . . . I thought that the wigwam of an Indian was better and a happier world than that of the drawing-room. There they sat at their ease, without stays or the anxiety to charm, without constraint or effort, those daughters of the forest.[235]

Bremer's remarks also suggest that the position of the white frontierswoman was not really very liberated, despite the tendency of many Europeans to paint it in rosy hues. Hemmed in by social convention, treated unequally in almost every area of life, and committed to a lifetime of low-status domestic labor, white frontierswomen did in fact face a great number of restrictions and problems. Yet most Europeans did not see the situation that way. Compared to the tradition-bound circumstances and restrictive status of European women, frontierswomen at least appeared to be free and equal. And as inhabitants of the wonderfully progressive New World of the American frontier, women were often assumed to be recipients of the many human rights and the pervasive spirit of equalitarianism that "enlightened" white people were supposedly cultivating throughout the West. To most European analysts, western women lived in a promised land indeed.

On the other hand, Indian women, who symblized the opposition and challenge to further white expansion across the West, had to be viewed as primitive and savage. While they could occasionally be credited with a spark of beauty, warmth, or creativity, in the last analysis they had to be grouped with their men as poor, degraded folks who were obviously meant for extinction. The willingness of Europeans to see white women as near saints and Indian women as total savages was the logical outcome of the belief that white people were destined to inherit the earth and, most immediately, the American West. This message was surely not lost on generations of European and American women who, when migrating westward, found themselves cast as "natural" opponents of American Indians.

These European views encouraged the idea that both the mettle and moral powers of women were to be severely tested as they entered the frontier. Confused by inaccurate beliefs about both themselves and American Indians, westering women were soon thrust into a climate of rumor and alarmism. Primed to believe the worst, many frontierswomen would need time before they could begin to replace the attitudes they had learned with more accurate perceptions derived from their own day-to-day experiences in the West.

❖⁍[3]⁌❖

Rumors and Alarms on the Trail and in Early Settlements

As a consequence of their long exposure to American and European thinking about the contradictory nature of American Indians, most westering women struck out for the trans-Mississippi West with their minds conjuring apparitions of inferior native peoples, who were hostile, vicious, and evil, interspersed with enigmatic visions of superior native beings, who were friendly, kind, and courageous. Because the likeness of the "bad" Indian was usually dominant, however, most female migrants' expectations tended to be negative rather than positive. When they finally reached the trail, their nerves were taut with fearful anticipation; they were ready for the worst of fates at the hands of American Indians.

Already anxious and overwrought, these women found themselves in a climate of thought rife with rumors and alarms. Numerous men as well as women were so thoroughly convinced that they were about to come face to face with the fiendish visages of creatures who were little more than consorts of the devil that they transformed almost every sight and sound into an avenging native. The specter of savage beings hung heavy around them as they stepped gingerly upon the trail or nervously slashed at the tree that was to become the foundation of their first cabin. Indian "sign" was everywhere they looked—lurking

83

beside the trail, hidden in every bush and tree, or outlined along the horizon by the rays of the rising or setting sun. If women's nerves were not already thoroughly frazzled by the time they turned westward, the gossip that enveloped them as they began their trek was enough to bring them to the edge of terror in a very short time. Aggravating the situation was the pettiness and meanness with which both whites and natives often treated each other; thus, in many cases, an element of truth was injected into the taletelling.

By translating their fears into ubiquitous rumors, frontier people created a climate marked by nervousness and tension. While a state of anxiety kept them alert to possible danger, it also tended to make them so nervous that they were incapable of dealing effectively with the native populations they encountered. That many violent outbreaks and tragic confrontations occurred between American Indians and the migrants intent upon settling the West is a widely known fact. But it is also true that many "uprisings" and "massacres" were often little more than the work of a fearful people's overactive imagination. Thus, problems with Indians were frequently derived far more from the migrants' anxieties about what could happen to them than from what actually happened.

From the start of their westward venture, a great number of women were particularly vulnerable to rumors and alarms because the media images of American Indians were reinforced on a more immediate level by family stories that enveloped them during the months, or sometimes years, before their departure for the West. This family lore often included a few episodes featuring "murderous savages" and leaving little to the imagination. As details were repeated and twisted into various shapes for the amusement or edification of listeners, they were often embellished to the point of the macabre. Because of a dearth of objective critics or of purveyors of factual knowledge about native Americans, these family mythmakers were free to embroider their legends with their own fantasies as well as those of their audience.

Thus, many women had already served childhood apprenticeships as potential victims before they even took their places in the wagons. Harriet Smith, migrating as a young girl in the 1840s, vividly recalled her grandfather's scary and thrilling tales of the Indians he had encountered while serving in the War of 1812. "Naturally we were somewhat afraid," she commented when the members of her party spied their first natives.[1] During the same decade Virginia Reed Murphy also carried with her the terror that her grandmother had instilled in her with frequent recitals about the "fearful deeds of the savages" and the trials of an aunt held captive for five years.[2] As late as 1900, Lucy Jennings admitted that she had heard so many horror stories about Indians that she was terrified to step out of the family wagon.[3]

Quite often the primary focus of these family yarns was the concern with the custom of scalping victims attributed to American Indians. Scalping was the very stuff of Indian tales. Dramatic, colorful, and capable of inducing little prickles of dread in an audience, stories of scalping could be depended upon for titillation. Often dominating the minds of many women, they eventually produced some extreme reactions. Going west as a child in 1861, Lucy Fosdick not only heard much about scalping, but as a protective measure she had her hair cropped short by her mother before departure.[4] In 1874, another young woman, Emily Andrews, was so certain that two Tonqua Indian guides had a peculiar "desire for light haired scalps" that she "kept a good distance from them" throughout the journey.[5]

Even by the end of the nineteenth century the situation had not noticeably improved. Although much more knowledge regarding Indian customs had become available—with "tame" Indians touring the country in circuses and Wild West shows, now that native Americans were in fact largely vanquished—the rumor mills continued to churn. Martha Lowrence remembered her neighbors in Missouri warning her family in 1899 that Indians "would kill us and scalp us and burn us up and that they were bad people."[6] Another woman of the decade said that she had heard so much about the Indians she was convinced that she would be scalped. One of her contemporaries related her own fears in more detail. As a girl of sixteen in 1895, Mary Ellen Williams joined her father's family, consisting of a Choctaw wife and offspring, and confessed that she "was absolutely scared to death." She continued, "I didn't expect anything else but to be scalped if Dad got out of my sight."[7]

It is little wonder then that many women were prepared to be scalped when they actually met American Indians for the first time. With so many traumatic stories fresh in their minds, it is not surprising that more than one woman's thoughts focused immediately upon her hair as natives approached. When shadows against the sky materialized into Indians, Annie Baker reacted in a typical fashion by "expecting momentarily to be scalped by the Redskins."[8] In 1870, some ten years after the Baker episode, Mabel Beavers displayed a similar response when she was met at the train by "a couple of full blood Indians." Despite the fact that she had come to teach school in the Oklahoma Indian Territory, Beavers was consumed by prejudice and fear. "I just knew," she said later, "that if one of those Indians had touched my hair, that my scalp would have come off without any pulling." Although they treated her with great respect and consideration, she remained a prisoner of her own anxiety. Her explanation was a simple and telling one: "They were Indians. Horrors!"[9]

The inflammatory family legends of American Indian atrocities that spurred such reactions pervaded the nineteenth century and continued into the twentieth century. Neither the actual degree of settlement of western regions nor the increasing white control and decimation of native populations seemed to affect the nature or proportions of these accounts. Rather, the legends were based apparently upon what whites living in Europe or in nonfrontier regions of America *believed* to be the situation in the West.

Those folks who decided to move westward, despite the American Indian horror stories, found little escape from the tales once they had embarked on their trek. One might think that the concern with more immediate issues, such as food and water supplies or exposure to jumping-off places or trails devoid of natives, would have deflected at least some of the migrants' fears. Instead, not only were the emigrants' guides filled with dire warnings about native Americans, but the jumping-off places were themselves hotbeds of rumor and gossip. One young traveler of 1852 wrote:

> As we drew near Council Bluffs on the Missouri River, the cry of "Indians, Indians," turned me into stone. . . . The air was thick at Council Bluffs with tales of Indian massacres, starvation and pestilence. . . . the one refrain was that the plains were alive with Indians on the war path.[10]

Once on the trail, travelers were thrust into an even more intense climate of dramatic reports regarding American Indian activities. They soon learned that there was little relief from terrible and often ill-founded portrayals of native peoples. One might reasonably expect that migrants' accounts of trails and eras that were especially plagued by poor relations with native Americans would yield greater evidence of such Indian rumors than would accounts from other routes and times. While one gets some sense of an increased prevalence of Indian alarms in documents from particular regions and years, it would be difficult to demonstrate clearly that they included noticeably more accounts of difficulties than documents from less turbulent areas and times. Here, as with the tales of American Indians circulating in the American East and in Europe, trail news seemed to depend more on the traveler's nervousness than upon his or her actual circumstance.

Consequently, narrations of trail experiences almost always included some mention of rumormongering regarding American Indians and what were termed their "depredations." Both male and female migrants recorded the alarms that they constantly encountered as they progressed along one of the many westward trails. On the Oregon Trail of the 1840s and 1850s scarcely a traveler could escape receiving secondhand intelligence of a horrifying nature.[11] Those heading toward California were also recipients of frequent rumors along their route.[12] As a case in point, in 1849 Dr. Jonathan Clark, journeying from Iowa to California, mentioned frequent notes relating Indian activities "stuck up in a conspicuous place near the road" by advance parties.[13]

Other migrants were exposed to other stark and more startling conveyors of news. On her way from Wisconsin to California in 1850, Lucene Parsons noted that bones were used as bulletin boards to report the exploits of native Americans. "We see writing on bones every day stating the deeds of the Indians," she wrote. A few days later she added, "Here we saw a bone stating that Indians had run off 17 mewls & horses."[14] Later in the decade, Helen Carpenter remarked that, in spite of the many rumors, her party had not really been concerned about Indians until they too "found little messages by the roadside, written in pencil, on the bleached bones of animals such as 'look out for the Indians; Indians ran off all the stock of train ahead;' etc. etc."[15]

Apparently, when it came to reporting "Indian troubles," whether real or fabricated, ingenuity and imagination were unlimited. In 1850, Margaret Frink was disturbed by a rather sophisticated alarm system that took the form of printed circulars distributed to emigrants. She was further distressed when the natives and "their doings" became so frequently the focus of camp conversation. Soon she began "to think that three men, one woman, and one eleven-year old boy, only armed with one gun and one Colt's revolver, are but a small force to defend themselves against many hostile Indian tribes, along a journey of two thousand miles."[16]

Other migrants were also intimidated as a result of the preoccupation of many travelers with conjecture and storytelling.[17] The after-dinner fireside especially seemed to encourage such activity. In Cyrus Hurd's view, "It will do in the States to tell those stories for fun, but when you come to the spot it ain't so pleasant."[18] More than a decade later, in 1864, Mallie Stafford also lamented the effectiveness of a fireside gathering that she attended in the middle of Colorado "Indian country." She declared that "the conversation naturally, under the circumstances, centered on Indian stories, Indian attacks, crossing the plains, etc., and as the night wore on they grew more and more eloquent—it seemed to me they were gifted with an *awful* eloquence on that particular subject."[19]

For most migrants, the word-of-mouth reports that constantly buffeted the wagon trains served as the main source of their recurrent consternation.[20] Helen Love said that she had listened to so many stories that by the time she reached Fort Kearney in 1853 she could no longer sleep because she thought she "heard wolves howling and Indians screaming and all sorts of noises."[21] While moving from Iowa to California in 1862, another woman remarked that "there is great tails about the Indians." During the following years, yet another woman had difficulty in sleeping because of constant reports of "depredations of the Indians."[22]

Such stories came from a bewildering variety of sources. The license to purvey Indian intelligence was to be had simply by asserting that one "knew" something, that one held a key piece of information that could avert a disaster or save a life. Thus, all kinds of people became reporters, and often their news was more alarming than informing to those who received it. In 1861, Lucy Fosdick pointed to the drivers of teams as the source of her unease. "The teamsters, to be sure, generally ended their advice by telling us that if we were well armed we should probably get through all right," she explained. "But we naturally felt very uneasy," she added, "and from that time dated my fear and hatred of 'Lo, the poor Indian.'"[23] Helen Carpenter mentioned trader's reports; Charles Robins cited the tales carried by a priest; and James Miller, on his way to Virginia City, identified a dragoon as the person who regaled him with stories of Indian attacks.[24]

In following decades other migrants were less specific. In 1862, heading toward California, one writer noted simply that "we hear many stories of Indian depredations." In 1868, in Texas another traveler mentioned that "we hear of Indians being seen at every foot." In 1875, in Wyoming Territory, still another wrote that "the air is full of Indian rumors."[25]

Because emigrants' nerves were honed to such a fine edge by reports like these, they mistook an incredible variety of occurrences for Indian raids.[26] Expecting to see a native at every turn, to lose one's scalp momentarily, or to receive the fatal blow at any time, a traveler's eyes and ears interpreted most things in one context only—Indian. They literally transformed the landscape, their stock, and their own companions into threatening menaces. In one instance, American Indians supposedly mounting a major offensive turned out to be only a ferry rope splashing in the water. On other occasions, images of Indians were evoked simply by a passing deer, a lost dog returning to camp, four little pigs that had escaped, and some jittery cattle.[27] Wolves were quite often the cause of terror in a camp. Maria Schrode related that one man's wife thought "some wolves was Indians and she screamed louder than the wolves howled and frightened some of us considerably."[28] Sometimes flocks of birds started the trouble, as in the case of Mary Powers, who wrote that "the Indians that had so frightened us were nothing but a flock of filthy bussards."[29]

Not infrequently it was the train members themselves who generated the scare. When two young women purposely rushed through the dark toward a young man on the fringe of camp, in revenge for some of his practical jokes, they were appalled to see him respond by dashing into camp and raising an Indian alarm.[30] Similarly, a man in another train jokingly fired a shot to awake a sleeping guard, thereby raising the entire camp, stampeding the stock, and causing the guard to be run over and seriously injured. In recounting the episode, Mary Saunders commented that "it taught Mr. Baker and all the guards that they could not break the rules with safety."[31] Harriet Ward also disparaged the tendency of some travelers to use such scares for their own purposes. When her son was hit by an arrow, the entire camp readied itself for a full scale assault, only to find that "the much dreaded arrow was but a harmless little stick" thrown into the midst of the children "to frighten them, by one of the boys whose slumbers were disturbed by their merriment."[32]

A variety of people along the trail were sometimes taken for native Americans. Mary Warner remarked that a member of her train was fired at by an Indian as he passed through a canyon, or rather, she explained, "he supposed it was them."[33] Lucy Cooke related a similar incident about one of her fellow travelers.

> He had not gone far when, looking back, he saw someone in pursuit, and fearing it to be an Indian, jumped off his horse and took to his heels and hid in the tall grass, leaving his horse for Mr. Indian. The pursuer proved to be one of his own men, so he got well laughed at for his fright, and would have lost his horse had not an Indian caught it and brought it to camp.

The captain of the train justly rewarded the Indian with a dollar for his honesty.[34]

The soldiers sent to protect the migrants also elicited their share of cases of mistaken identity. Ada Millington described the men of her party loading their guns and regrouping the train when they thought they had sighted wigwams in the distance and Indians firing guns. When the Indian camp turned out to be tents and United States soldiers, she said that "we had a good laugh over our scare."[35] Emily Andrews mentioned that her party grew very excited about a small body of riders on a distant hill, only to learn upon approaching them that they were in fact Texas Rangers.[36]

In this state of constant agitation, both male and female migrants readily blamed American Indians for any misfortune or irregularity that occurred. Indians automatically became the villain of virtually any mishap. Because prejudice and near hysteria achieved dimensions that defied rationality and reason, natives did not even need to be in the area, nor was it necessary for any shred of evidence to exist to suggest that they had perpetrated an incident; they were immediately and irrevocably indicted. When cattle stampeded, Mary Warner indicated that the guards assumed that Indians had been the cause.[37] Katherine Dunlap explained that when stock wandered it was "natural" to think that it had been stolen by Indians, who were assumed to be always "skulking around the camps."[38] Upon observing native Americans for her first time, Lucy Sexton noted that "they were mounted, and one of them on a fine American horse, undoubtedly stolen."[39] And Emily Horton offered a particularly harsh judgment when some of the men of her train brought a bleached skull into camp. According to her, it was "all there was to show that one of our race had perished far from home. No doubt death was caused by savages."[40]

When actual Indians *were* spotted the reports that resulted were the cause of great precautions. Despite either their actual demeanor or intentions, natives were blamed for all kinds of thoughts and deeds. One man rushed into his camp, claiming that he was being chased by Indians. He raised fifteen to twenty armed men, only to discover upon tracking the natives down that they wanted "to smoke peace," for they said that they had planned only to beg food. These same men remained convinced that a full-scale attack would be launched against them on that very night. Depite their fears, it failed to materialize.[41] In another instance, the presence of American Indians in the vicinity caused train members to dress and to prepare themselves for night combat. On the next day an ox, "full of arrows, but still alive," was found on the trail. After shooting the animal to put it out of its misery, these people concluded that some other train moving ahead of them must have been struck.[42]

Of course, there were in reality instances of disastrous armed confrontations between migrants and the American Indians whose lands they were invading as well as of Indians being deterred by the whites' aggressive behavior. The much more usual narrative was one that recounted numerous and seemingly unfounded scares but no actual Indian problems. In case after case, trail documents were punctuated by impending crises and predictions of doom, only to end on a rather anticlimactic and peaceful note. Oregon migrant Margaret Chambers's remark in 1851 that "we had no trouble with the Indians—only some scares" was typical of trail accounts.[43] In fact, in time many migrants became exceedingly suspicious of the Indian rumors flowing around them. When Charlotte Pengra heard a "frightful tale" about four hundred revengeful natives blocking her party's path she was understandably concerned. "Have seen no Indians and conclude the tale we heard was false," she soon noted. Some days later, the appearance of a "hostile" Indian village again caused distress; "we anticipated some trouble," she wrote, "but realised none." By the end of her 1853 chronicle of her move from Illinois to Oregon, she declared that "I have heard lots of bugbear stories about the Indians. . . . I conclude the stories are about as true as they ever will be."[44] On the way to California in 1859, Lavinia Porter exchanged what turned out to be her "groundless" fears for an almost favorable attitude toward Indians. "From their general demeanor they rather inspired us with a confidence which seemed to sanction our presence in their midst," she wrote at one point. On another occasion, when an Indian returned her train's wandering cattle to them, she remarked, "It truly seemed to us in our long journey traveling alone that the Indians watched over us."[45]

It is also instructive to pursue the writings of some of the individuals who were the most terrified when just beginning their westward journey. Their accounts repeatedly disclosed a reversal in their attitudes toward American Indians. Terror was routinely replaced by equanimity, aversion by acceptance, and hatred by affection. Elisha Brooks, for example, said that his family responded to the rumors that surrounded them by throwing themselves "on the tender mercies of the Red Men," only to discover that "though stern at times" they were "no worse on the whole than some of the degenerate sons of Japheth." According to Brooks, his party "concluded that Indians were not as bad as they had been painted."[46] Similarly, Lucy Jennings, the young woman who had been afraid to leave the family wagon, finally met some Oklahoma Indians who were "very nice" to her and her family.[47] Mabel Beavers, the young teacher who had been so terrified of her American Indian charges, discovered that "those people were lovely to me, and were and are yet, some of the warmest friends I have ever had."[48] And Mary Williams, the girl who had so dreaded living with her father's native wife and children, not only learned to love her new brothers and sisters but eventually married a Choctaw herself.[49]

Apparently, for many migrants rumor was far worse than reality. Their fears were seldom realized, and their trepidations proved to be largely unfounded. Although they tortured themselves and one another with apprehensions that kept everyone on tenterhooks, most travelers were actually more harassed and plagued by their own angst than by native Americans. A surprisingly small number of chronicles by emigrants and settlers recorded any actually violent interchanges with Indians.[50] Yet the majority of the documents did contain some mention of tension, agitation, and dread concerning the possibility of altercations with natives. The fact that such malaise often evaporated by the end of the westward trek, leaving a traveler feeling a bit sheepish, is perhaps best expressed in a succinct statement by a member of the Donner Party, Virginia Reed Murphy. Although terrorized by Indian tales before leaving home, Murphy later wrote, "let me say that we suffered vastly more from fear of the Indians before starting than we did on the plains."[51]

It should be recognized, however, that even though so many of the alarms lacked credence they did serve a purpose for the migrants in reminding them to be cautious.[52] As trail discipline gradually relaxed and people began to grow skeptical enough of the Indian threat to do things like taking what one woman called "fool-hardy" walks, scares encouraged them to exercise more precaution.[53] In response to the rumors, many trains regularly circled their wagons, posted guards, and kept night fires burning in an effort to protect their animals from theft. In 1840, for instance, Abigail Smith wrote to her brothers and sisters with the reassurance that her party was proceeding warily through Missouri by routinely circling their wagons and posting night guards.[54]

Interestingly enough, neither such prudence nor the rumors that had spawned it abated once the destination of any particular journey had been reached. The trail was far from being the only breeding ground for anxiety about Indians; rather, an omnipresent dread of native Americans accompanied the migrants into their new settlements. Although settlers had more time to get to know Indians, they also had longer exposure to the harsh fact that outbreaks of violence did occur between native and white groups. Consequently, the accounts left by western settlers were also replete with a continuing saga of apprehensiveness about Indians.

Here again, the number of American Indians living in a region, the degree of settlement that the area had achieved, the number of problems actually encountered, or the point in time did not seem to have any discernible correlation with the quantity of stories in circulation. Rather, people's own interpretation of the dangers inherent in their situations highly influenced both the number and scope of the tales. Thus, an Oregon woman of the 1840s remembered that "often the news would come that the Indians would murder us," rumors that resulted in her parents keeping all-night vigils.[55] Another Oregon woman, however, maintained that although her family received several native American scares they were never molested and were probably "never in actual danger."[56] A Texas woman of the 1860s recalled that an attack was believed to be so imminent that men "wore guns in the field and at all times." In explaining the situation, she exclaimed, "And Indians, Oh horrors, we expected to be massacreed at any time."[57] Significantly all these women not only survived to make these statements but retained both their wits and their scalps in the process.

The problem of rumor was exacerbated by local newspapers that were quick to print, and often enlarge upon, Indian stories circulating through their area. Hungry for news to fill their pages and anxious to enlarge their readership, editors often printed Indian atrocity tales that were unmarked by any degree of taste or discimination. As one woman noted in 1856, she was sure that a friend had received all the Indian news available from the Oregon Territory and "perhaps more" since news accounts "do not generally lose anything."[58] Local events often enhanced the credibility attributed to overstated or unfounded reports. Conducting a Civil War draft, for example, might suggest to a town's inhabitants that nearby natives would seize the opportunity to attack them during the state of general confusion caused by men preparing to leave home.[59]

The scare that resulted from such an interpretation often brought people flocking into a town center to prepare to dispel their enemies. Convinced that their strength as well as their ultimate survival lay in joining forces, settlers were willing to forsake their homes, fields, and businesses to devote excessive, and usually needless, amounts of time and energy to preparing their own defense. Men would drill, and women would sew all day to make tents for them, but often it came to nothing and the distraught populace soon dispersed.[60] One Oklahoma woman of the 1880s recollected many such gatherings, admitting that she could not "remember of there ever being a fight." On one occasion, her mother "cooked up a whole sack of flour into bread and baked several hens, boiled hams, etc." Rumor had it that the Indians were holding a war dance preparatory to killing all the "pale faces," yet, given a little time, it too blew over.[61]

This type of incident was repeated again and again with settlers "fortin up" at the slightest suggestion of troubles with their native American neighbors.[62] According to a Texas woman, Jonaphrene Faulkner, the worst times came during the full moon because it was believed that the Indians preferred nights of "Commanche moons" for attacks on settlers. The result for her community was that people "began to look forward with dread to those beautiful seasons that had

heretofore been our greatest joy; and many families accustomed themselves, upon such nights, to 'fort up,' in the largest and strongest
house in their settlement."[63] In another area of Texas, the women
and children would fort up and the men would lie out in the fence
corners under the full moon to protect their stock.[64]

As on the trail, however, settlers often mistook a dismaying array
of people and things for American Indians. With their consternation
at an untenably high level, they determined that an outbreak of hostilities was imminent from the flimsiest evidence. During the 1870s
in Texas, May Tansill concluded that a man approaching her was
indeed a native because of something red that he was wearing. "I had
always fancied that Indians wore some thing red about them," she
later explained, "so I jumped to the conclusion that an Indian was
approaching me."[65] Another young woman was embarrassed when,
armed with a shotgun and "thinking only of wild Indians come to
scalp us," she opened the door to encounter a startled young farmer
from Kansas standing on her doorstep.[66] Yet another woman precip-
itated a massive Indian scare when she "started running and screaming
to a neighbor's house" after mistaking her son—approaching home
and wearing a jaunty feather in a newly purchased hat—for an American Indian.[67]

Apparently, anything that moved was suspect by these anxiety-
ridden frontier people. Tumbleweeds driven by the passing wind were
imaginary native Americans for some Nebraska homesteaders. A colt
alarmed some Kansans, a screeching hoot owl frightened some Okla-
homans, and a lone mouse trying unsuccessfully to climb out of a tin
dish of water became an Indian intruder in an Iowa farmhouse.[68]
Shadowy Sioux dressed in their white blankets and stalking through
a dark and foggy barnyard were discovered by some other Iowa farmers to be no more than a flock of geese, while a hired man carrying
a featherbed through the fog alarmed still others.[69] Near Denver in
the early 1800s, some Mexican cattle drovers were discovered to be
the source of similar trouble.[70] In Oklahoma, in the 1890s, a noisy
charivari party following a wedding was enough to convince people
that native Americans were killing and scalping their neighbors. Although the citizens of the nearby town rallied to the call by organizing
an army of defense and emptying the hardware stores of arms and
ammunitions, no Indians appeared, and yet one more uprising failed
to occur.[71]

Understandably, frontier people living in the many forts stretching across the West were especially prone to such scares.[72] Because they were surrounded by native populations and because it was their primary function to control these peoples, conflict with American Indians was always an imminent possibility. Hence their nerves were frequently rubbed raw with foreboding. As a case in point, Frances Carrington warmly described the friendly Cheyenne living around Fort Laramie, the "feeling of perfect security" at the fort itself, and the large number of American Indian children who frequented the fort. Yet she noted that a serious alarm had been created by nothing more than a herd of buffalo.[73] Another army wife, Ada Vogdes, who considered herself a "nervous excitable person," stated that she was unsuited for life in places such as Fort Laramie and Fort Fetterman during the 1860s. As a result, she spent most of her time being "frightened to death." This state of mind caused her to mistake coyotes, dogs, two drunken cooks, and a soldier, who was returning stealthily from the quarters of a laundress, for Indians. She refused to leave the fort for outings with her husband because she was "frightened nearly to death for fear we might encounter some Indians." And when an unfounded alarm swept the fort she professed herself, once again, to be "frightened to death."[74]

Given the existence of such tension and worry on the part of so many settlers, it is little wonder that when actual native Americans appeared they were blamed for all manner of misdoing. Expecting Indians to be disreputable and troublesome, settlers eagerly laid a wide spectrum of offenses at the feet of available natives. An Iowa woman of the early 1830s described the alacrity with which some whites assigned a missing hat and ax to Indian theft. When they discovered the articles, they simply dismissed it with a "hearty laugh."[75] Some years later, during the Civil War, another Iowa woman quickly jumped to the conclusion that a begging Indian was undoubtedly a Sioux spy.[76]

Such reactions were usually irrational. Several Oklahoma women recollected that they had feared the American Indians they met because of their clothing, their dirtiness, their singing, and their "jabbering and grunting" speech, although Indians had never harmed them.[77] Another Oklahoma woman remembered that her distrust of Indians was instilled in her by her mother, who would spend Sunday mornings distractedly watching natives file by the house on their way to church at a nearby mission.[78] On one particular Sunday morning in 1884, in Cañon City, Colorado, ragged and begging Indians disrupted church service and caused a general chaos during which many people screamed and others fainted. Yet once they had been given bread and other foodstuffs, the Indians quietly departed.[79]

Many settlers responded to the approach of a native by immediately fleeing, either to hide for days or weeks in a barn or in the nearby woods or to desert the area entirely.[80] According to Ambrose A. Call, after the Spirit Lake disaster in Iowa in 1857,

> The air was filled with rumors, every stranger was viewed with suspicion, and if seen on the prairie was run down and captured as an Indian spy. Cranes were magnified into Indians, prairie fires were mistaken for Indian camp fires and the very howling of the April winds sent a chill of horror to the hearts of mothers as they clung closer to their babes. . . . A large number of settlers who had families fled, and some never returned.

Predictably, no Indians were ever found in the area so affected by their supposed presence.[81]

Despite the fact that native Americans rarely played out their parts in the dramas concocted by overwrought frontier people, some of the more timorous settlers never surrendered their inbred terror of Indians. As a child, Anne Ellis of Nebraska dreaded starvation, Indians, and ghosts. But long after she outgrew her qualms about food and spirits she still dreamed of fleeing from native pursuers, or, in her words, "of running from them till my feet rose from the ground and I ran in the air."[82]

Yet like many initially distraught trail folk who came to like or even to love Indians, many settlers *did* radically discard their negative attitudes with time. The young woman who had answered her door with shotgun in hand, and who on other occasions had run for the house and barred the doors and windows in the face of approaching Indians, recollected that the anticipated war whoop never reached her ears. "Finally we were not so afraid of them," she observed, "becoming well acquainted with dozens of bucks and squaws in later years and counting them as some of our best friends."[83] The little girl who timorously watched American Indians pass by her house on Sunday mornings grew up to marry "a full blood Comanche Indian," and upon his death she wed "a full blood Cherokee."[84]

Evidently, many migrants and settlers eventually came to realize that the copious Indian rumors that accosted them were usually nothing more than figments of someone's overactive imagination. As they became seasoned frontier people, many settlers recognized that they, other train members, or their neighbors seldom experienced serious altercations and confrontations with American Indians. The relaxation of defensive postures toward Indians that resulted allowed them to interact more freely with individual natives, which, in turn, often gave them even more confidence in the rationality of their supposed enemies.

This is not to argue that there were no violent and tragic interactions between frontier people and native Americans, for there were many such unfortunate instances. Rather, the suggestion here is that myth and media overemphasized such calamities to the point of distortion. Moreover, in light of the intense contemporary interest in Indian affairs, some migrants and settlers themselves were not above inventing incendiary tales. In turn, newspapers, always searching for ways to expand their subscription lists, published these fabrications with their own embellishments, and by the mid-nineteenth century mythical massacres were both sensational and commonplace.[85] However, as John D. Unruh's recent study of the overland trail has demonstrated, in reality frontier people killed more Indians than were killed by Indians between 1840 and 1860. In addition, some 90 percent of emigrant killings occurred west of the South Pass rather than on the Great Plains, as legend would have us believe. And even when such killings did take place they often resulted from individual incidents rather than from the large-scale murders so often described by the overworked term "massacre."[86]

This climate of fear created anxiety in both women and men. Yet women's accounts showed them to be frequently more hysterical in their reactions to alarms than were many men. Considering the nineteenth-century dictums concerning the woman's weak and nervous nature as opposed to the man's strong and calm disposition, it is not surprising that frontier people accepted the idea that the threat of Indian troubles was much more debilitating to women than to men. Thus, on a train en route from Illinois to the Willamette Valley in 1845, the cry of Indians caused the "frightened men," as one person described them, to arm themselves and to form a corral, while the women, all in a state of near panic, reacted by crying, wringing their hands, and praying.[87] During her 1853 trip from Texas to California, Maggie Hall was even more explicit about male and female behavior in the face of false alarms. The "groundless scares in the night," she said, were merely "very exasperating" to her father, but "they made the women nervous and sick."[88] Some years later, in 1873, on a train moving from Kansas to Texas, Olivia Holmes tersely noted that "we got up a little excitement about the Indians but it did not amount to anything" except to frighten "us women folks."[89]

Many trail documents do reveal that it was quite often these excitable females who initially raised the alarms, often to the scorn or amusement of their menfolk. In 1853, on her way from Iowa to Oregon, Catherine Washburn jotted in her diary that "some of the women were very much allarmed to night they thought they herd the Indians coming to attack us which turned out to be the ferry rope splashing in the water."[90] In 1900, when Lois Brown woke up her husband to inform him that natives were whispering and conniving against them among some nearby trees, her husband simply laughed and informed her that she heard only screech owls.[91] In another incident of "Indian excitement" at Fort Dawes in 1865, Samuel Newcomb rather disdainfully described the panicky women gathering their children and running "from place to place like they had lost all reason."[92]

When cautious men attempted to offset women's propensity to panic by holding drills, women's reactions were apparently as disruptive as they were during an alarm. In 1849, the captain of Catherine Haun's train called such a drill, only to watch the women go into a frenzy. "Some screamed, others fainted, a few crawled under the wagons," Haun wrote. "All of us were nearly paralized with fear." She later added that the fact that throughout the Platte River area they had seen "nothing living but Indians, lizards and snakes" was "trying, indeed, to feminine nerves." As the women watched the grotesque shadows cast by the campfires, Haun remarked that "the redmen needed only horns and cloven feet to complete the soul stirring picture!"[93]

Yet, in several cases when American Indians were actually thought to be attacking, some women maintained their composure. They neither cringed in terror nor fell into an incoherent state of hysteria. Instead, they not only conducted themselves admirably in the face of real danger but aided other women whose nerves were not quite so steady. At Fort Lapwai in Idaho Territory in 1876, for example, several officers' wives nearly exhausted themselves "trying to quiet the excited laundresses."[94] In an 1853 fray, Harriet Ward claimed that several of the women were not frightened in the least. She added tellingly that "I hardly think we ever suffer quite as much when anything of this kind really happens as we do in the anticipation."[95]

It was nothing short of remarkable that at least a few women were able to retain their sanity when confronted with an authentic siege. By being constantly reminded that they were by nature weak and nervous, women were at once being told that they were expected to behave in a panic-prone fashion when danger appeared and that it was acceptable for them to do so. That such cowardly behavior was both expected and allowed created a situation in which even the most self-possessed and spirited woman could easily succumb to the pandemonium created by her sisters. To maintain one's composure as native Americans were about to invade was difficult enough; to remain calm as one's companions were creating bedlam was nearly impossible.

In all fairness to frontierswomen, it should be noted that they had at least two gender-related reasons to especially fear native assaults. One of these was the sexual threat, the dread that almost every woman harbored of being raped, or, to use the nineteenth-century euphemism, of being "passed over the prairie" by Indian molesters. Terrifying accounts of such occurrences intimidated generations of frontierswomen, keeping them close to wagon, home, or fort. As Susan Newcomb phrased it in 1865, she was leery of going very far from Fort Davis, Texas, in this "Indian world."[96]

The other danger that women particularly feared was that their children would be seized and carried off by American Indian captors. Charged with child care and frequently lectured on their overwhelming maternal sensibilities, women reacted with horror to the stories of Indians who not only stole children but perpetrated all manner of atrocities upon them. In the 1876 Fort Lapwai attack that never materialized, Emily Fitzgerald stated that "for a few moments, I think, we women with our helpless little children suffered as much as if the Indians had really come."[97]

Naturally, men were cognizant of these two menaces to their women. Consequently, some men tried not to leave women and children alone for very long periods of time or alone at all if they could possibly avoid it.[98] To other men, however, this type of precaution was impractical or unattractive. Thus, many men left their homes and families to conduct business in a nearby town or county seat, to work the fields, to hunt, to fight Indians, and for a variety of other reasons. If necessity dictated their absence, many men left their women with a last resort should Indians appear. One woman, traveling with her small children, wore a locket on a thin gold chain; while beautiful, the locket contained a meticulously folded paper and inside were small pellets of cyanide for her and her children to consume rather than face capture by native Americans.[99] Another woman was told by her husband, who was preparing to defend her from approaching Indians, to take his gun and get in the back of the wagon. "Should they attack us and capture me and you see that you can not escape," he counseled her, "you will have the gun and can decide what you wish to do about your life."[100]

In both of these cases and one suspects in many others, the threat came to naught and neither the pills nor the gun were ever employed.[101] Yet the terror experienced by these and other frontierswomen was crushingly painful, even though it was more frequently inspired by imagination than by reality. Women's poignant anxieties cannot be dismissed or belittled. Rather, the intensity and the very existence of such terror, whether or not it was justified by circumstances, should elicit admiration for those women who *were* able to maintain a modicum of equanimity in the frontier environment or to reject alarmist thinking in favor of a more moderate outlook regarding natives.

Furthermore, despite nineteenth-century stereotypes of hysterical women and stoic men, overland trail accounts reveal that not all men were as imperturbable as they were reputed to have been. Despite the steady hands and stout hearts attributed to men by the social beliefs of the era, their supposed courageousness occasionally displayed some significant cracks. Many male migrants commonly tended to magnify a few American Indians into hordes. In one case, "hundreds" of Indians turned out to be closer to fifteen, and in another instance, "thousands were actually forty Indians."[102] This tendency toward exaggeration on the part of some men was viewed with scorn by others. Byron McKinstry, a member of a train headed toward the California gold fields in 1850, jeeringly wrote in his journal about one of his fellow travelers whose Indians had "vanished as well as all fear of them." He declared sarcastically that he wished "the Indians had Potts and half a dozen more of our co. that I could name, then our

Chapter 3

Indian trouble would be at an end, at least the imaginary part of them."[103] A few days later he added:

> We had a hard rain last night—and an alarm of Indians!!! Blood and murder what shall we do? We shall surely all be slain!! Why did we not make our wills and have our lives insured before we adventured among these horrible savages! As I was sleeping away in my tent . . . Bang! Bang! from the guns of the sentinels—then the cry of Indians! Indians! from voices in every direction . . . but finding the scalp still on my cranium . . . I commenced dressing quite cooly. . . . But soon the voice of our captain and the valiant Potts made us take to the rain to defend ourselves against those grim savages. . . . After walking round an hour or so, and listening to many valiant speeches . . . I was permitted to go to bed, and I got a fine nap before day.[104]

McKinstry thought that the women were as silly as Captain Potts. During another false alarm, the women of the camp screamed, swung their bonnets, and convinced the men that the natives were killing them. McKinstry wryly noted: "I don't expect that the poor souls will get over their fright in a month, and I am not sure that all the men will. If there had been Indians within hearing they certainly would have fled!"[105]

Apparently, at least from McKinstry's record, it was not just women who were inclined to allow their anxieties to overwhelm them. In fact, one male migrant on his way to Montana in the 1860s frankly admitted that he imagined that "every weed and bunch of grass" that stirred was an American Indian.[106] Like the women, many men imagined all types of people and things to be Indians.[107] In one case, three approaching native warriors who were the cause of an alarm turned out to be Indian women upon closer inspection, and in the last analysis, they were actually three emigrant women from that very train.[108] In another case, some distant objects determined to be warring Indians caused the men to prepare their weapons and to fall upon the ground to conceal themselves from their advancing opponents. "Every gun was charged & every eye gazed eagerly at the *Indians*," one of the participants wrote, "when, lo, & behold, the Indians proved to be six large elk crossing the river."[109]

It is significant that frontiersmen who behaved in such a fashion became the objects of derision by their companions or even at their own hands. Yet this study did not unearth one instance of frontierswomen chastising each other or themselves for such "cowardly" conduct. Clearly, women were expected and allowed to display a range of emotions that were not considered suitable for men. Charged with the protection of train members, wagons, and stock, and possessing a supposedly stronger inherent nature, men were expected to demonstrate bravery and equanimity. They were to stand implacable in the face of every danger, especially when threatened by an Indian offensive; they were not allowed to surrender to the luxury of panic that the women were permitted.

Accordingly, most men attempted to live up to macho dictates for their gender, which were so popular throughout the nineteenth century. Predictably, there were instances of outright cowardice, as in the case of the Englishman who took refuge under a wagon during a threatened siege and loudly proclaimed himself an alien while invoking the protection of King George.[110] But most men frequently maintained that indeed they did not fear native Americans and would route them through strength of arms.[111] This, in turn, resulted in the organization of numerous types of protective associations, in the appointment of military "captains" to lead trains, in arming and drilling by male overlanders, and in the posting of many guards.[112] Often such precautions were found to be what Fancher Stimson described as "cumbersome and undesirable," especially as the fear of Indians was quickly dispelled. Often, they were not only disbanded but became a "subject of merriment."[113] In other instances, such measures remained very much in force, based on the notion that the first priority was always to be prepared for attack.[114]

These military efforts by frontiersmen etched in sharp relief the differences between the men and women of an expedition. While Samuel Newcomb described the ineffective actions of women, his wife Susan noted in her 1867 diary that "the men over hauled the Indians yesterday." At another point she recorded that some men hunting Indians to locate their camps had returned with three native scalps. Stuck at home, unable to take any action herself, and fearful for her husband's safety, Susan retaliated with invective, the only way available to her to cope with the frustrating situation. She railed against both the United States government, which she felt did not supply them with adequate protection, and the American Indians themselves. In her view, President Ulysses S. Grant should be forced to battle Indians until he was willing to order out enough military power "to scalp every red skin in the universe." When soldiers were finally sent after the "red imps of the earth" she hoped that the army would "scalp the last one of them, for they are too bad to be endured."[115] Her husband Samuel, while also vitriolic in his complaints against the government and the natives, was much more capable of taking such action as negotiating treaties, redeeming captives, chasing Indians, and protecting the stock.[116]

Seemingly, such an aggressive stance on the part of frontiersmen should have allayed much of the women's distress. But women were not always impressed with either the good sense or the physical abilities of their men. Instead, they were often doubtful, even caustic, in their statements regarding the protection from American Indians afforded them by their menfolk. Should warlike natives actually appear, there seemed to be too much braggadocio in the air to indicate the possibility of reasoned and effective response by men. As Lydia Waters phrased it:

> I should say we had some mighty men of valor with us. The Indians would die of fright as soon as they saw them! These mighty men could fire forty shots out of their wagons without reloading![117]

And after a false alarm, Harriet Ward seemed puzzled about the crestfallen countenances of her would-be protectors. "After all the excitement," she commented, "I think the gentlemen were somewhat disappointed that they had not *even seen an Indian.*"[118] Other women joked about their men's military might. Surveying her well-armed husband with his bowie knife and pistols, Lucy Cooke remarked, "Hope he won't hurt himself."[119] And after watching the men of her family fire fifty shots to kill one cow, Maria Schrode wryly observed, "We think the Indians would be in great danger if they should attack us."[120]

Such remarks suggest a tension between men and women regarding their comparative abilities to handle themselves in the face of danger. The men clearly expected the women to be nervous and silly. Surprisingly, given nineteenth-century injunctions about male strength, many of the women seemed to anticipate ineptness and even irrationality on the part of their men. Their comments suggest that these women did not meekly accept the subordinate role of helpless protectee in relation to their men's dominant role of courageous protector. Barred by societal expectations from taking matters into their own hands, they could express their dissatisfaction with the lack of any effectual security only through jibes directed toward the men. One might even argue that if women had felt relatively safe and protected by their men they would not have acted in the panic-stricken manner that they so often displayed. This is pure speculation, of course, but it does seem that the inability of both male and female to grapple effectively with the threat of native violence was at least one of the contributing factors to the ubiquity of rumors and scares.

This propensity on the part of frontier people to magnify rumors as a result of their anxieties about their own ability to repulse attack was only one among many ways in which they helped to generate scares. Primed by eastern predictions that the frontier experience would be difficult and even violent, many settlers seemed to try to fulfill such expectations. They developed what one might call a "frontier psychology," that is, a near obsession with demonstrating the difficulties of the western environment as well as their own eventual victory over the challenges it presented. After the initial settlement period of frontier regions, this frontier psychology manifested itself in the proliferation of Old Settlers Associations. These groups of pioneers held regular meetings (often followed by the publication of their proceedings), during which they recalled and recounted the hardships and the triumphs of westering. During the early settlement years, however, this kind of thinking often resulted in the exaggeration of hardships, particularly those associated with native Americans since these experiences were of such widespread interest and were indeed fraught with potential dangers. The hyperbole that resulted included not only rumors and scares but hundreds, or perhaps thousands, of invented massacres, with the brave U.S. Cavalry often emerging victorious.[121] In 1876, Nebraskan Caroline Winne sarcastically denigrated this tendency to overstatement. "Oh what a farce it is," she wrote to her family back East. "Come to get down to the facts of Crook's expedition, the one hundred Indians killed amounted to just 4 killed," and, she continued, "as there were four soldiers killed and light wounded . . . we failed to see the success—'but twas a famous victory.'"[122]

On the other hand, some frontier people perpetrated hoaxes simply to scare their companions or to make an attempt at humor. More than one overlander reported that problems with American Indians were nothing more than the products of practical jokes.[123] Settlers also reported such perverse attempts at humor on the part of their neighbors. After a night of terror forted up with friends, one woman sarcastically remarked that had they been able to identify the prankster who raised the alarm "there would have been some hair lost, but not by scalping."[124] Another woman described her own participation in an attempt to reduce the bumptious male attitudes of a local judge and attorney by surrounding their wagon with whites masquerading as natives. When the "Indians" struck with appropriate shouting, yelling, and shooting, the driver of the wagon fell backward with the exclamation, "I am shot; everyone for themselves"; the judge fled the scene, and the attorney ran to a nearby fort to return with two groups of soldiers.[125]

Although it seems a rather extreme measure to expose male bumptiousness, this was not the only incident in which a female settler reacted negatively to protestations of male courage. After enduring several traumatic scares with other terrified women and children, Texan Julia Sinks came to the conclusion that they were largely the work of "ladies' men," who had created the threat of siege only to excite "a host of fears for the pleasure of allaying them." According to Sinks, there were several men in Austin "who fought windmills diligently, bringing in their somber visages as if laden with the news of terrible calamity." Once the women were sufficiently alarmed, these men would pass among them to offer their protection, solicitously attempting to quiet the very fears they had so assiduously cultivated. Sinks added that these episodes became "one of the entertainments of the times . . . a kind of stimulant against a stagnant timidity," always marked by "many visits from the ladies' men with pitying, doleful faces."[126]

As self-serving as Sinks's "ladies' men" may appear, there were other frontiersmen whose motives were more devious than the solicitation of attention and gratitude from the womenfolk. These were the various traders who used scares to further their own economic ventures and who were considered by some to be "as roguish and treacherous as the Indians themselves."[127] In some cases, they initiated alarms to draw cavalry to the area in order to sell them their corn and other goods. In other instances, they stirred up the natives themselves, intending to plunder their goods during the ensuing confusion.[128]

Government agents, renegade Frenchmen, Union and Confederate soldiers, Catholic priests, and Mormons were also often accused of inciting Indian scares to enhance their own economic and religious ends.[129]

In addition, frontier outlaws played upon settlers' terrors of American Indians. Frequently it was white thieves who ran off with stock and other items, sometimes even going to the trouble of disguising themselves as native Americans in case they were sighted.[130] Overlanders were often aware of the existence of these "white Indians," sometimes judging them to be more dangerous than the Indians themselves.[131] In 1859, a woman who was raped and shot by five "natives" was able to identify them as whites because they had neglected to paint their entire bodies. And army personnel sent to guard the overlanders during the 1850s were so accustomed to the existence of roving groups of "white Indians" that they viewed the phenomenon as a kind of tragic joke.[132]

But it was not just self-interested, fanatical, or aberrant individuals who fostered scares. Frontier people who considered themselves law abiding, righteous, and even well intentioned also established a rumor-prone climate through their mistreatment of native Americans. One of the saddest examples of such behavior was the efforts of whites to slaughter buffalo so that the Indians, robbed of their subsistence, would become dependent upon whites and thus more vulnerable to being "civilized."[133]

Other instances of mistreatment resulted from a pettiness of spirit that was often combined with an utter disregard for the American Indian as a human being. The conduct of frontier people toward natives ranged from distrustful attitudes to actual physical harm. Many overlanders, convinced of their inherent right to invade native lands, refused to pay tolls to cross bridges that natives had built. They also rejected entreaties for tribute to compensate Indians for destroyed grazing lands, exhausted game reserves, and depleted water supplies. Some even captured Indians who were forced to serve as guides for their parties.[134] A number of others seemed to derive satisfaction from needling native Americans and generally making them appear foolish. Lavinia Porter noted with disgust that some men of her train who swaggered and bragged that they could whip any band of natives also treated them contemptuously on a personal basis. "It was their usual

107

custom whenever the Indians approached our camp or sat by our camp fires," Porter complained, "to tease and play various tricks upon them."[135]

A common white prank on the frontier involved thoroughly fleecing an American Indian in a trade, an occurrence that seemed to elicit delight from many professed Christians. Disregard for the basic humanity of American Indians also motivated a variety of other schemes that would result in a white profit at native expense. In one of the more macabre tricks, a young doctor allegedly severed Black Hawk's head from his recently deceased corpse and boiled the flesh from it with the intention of publicly exhibiting the skull for a fee. Intimidated by the near uprising he provoked among Black Hawk's people, the doctor was reported to have deposited the skull with a friend, who sold it to a museum that subsequently burned down, destroying the skull.[136]

Frequently the prank involved potential physical danger to a native. One such incident was related by a Colorado settler:

> . . . the future divinity student—although at that time he was harboring no such holy intentions—loaded up some sticks of stove-wood with healthy charges of powder and left them on the woodpile in the hope that some of the roving Indians . . . would carry them off, put them on a camp fire and receive the benefits. The plan, though, resulted in a backfire. The young man himself forgot which were the doctored logs, carried some of them into the house, put one in the kitchen stove, and when the smoke of the explosion had cleared away he instantly realized that something was wrong.[137]

Although that prankster received his just reward, most of the others did not. Suffering was usually inflicted upon the Indians. One frontiersman, for example, traded the infested bedding of a dead companion to American Indians, who were soon widely infected with smallpox. Understandably, the Indians sought revenge and retaliated by stealing stock and keeping the settlers in a general state of upheaval.[138]

Unfortunately, some frontier people carried such misbehavior toward native peoples to an even more violent extreme. There were cases of white men physically abusing and assaulting American Indian women, and it was not uncommon for them to take potshots at the native men.[139] As such events tend to do, they often escalated to a pitch that caused not only bitterness and hostility but frequently the deaths of natives. More than one alarm was generated by the pointless murder of an Indian.[140]

This is not to argue that overlanders and settlers alone created rumors and scares, for American Indians themselves often contributed to the problem. They too seemed to possess a perverse sense of humor that frequently revealed itself in their teasing and torment of frontier people. An Oklahoma woman who was startled at the unexpected discovery of an aged Indian couple standing quietly in her kitchen claimed that they thoroughly enjoyed her discomfiture and laughed at her.[141] A male migrant was accosted by begging natives, who thrust their hands into his pockets, took a kerchief from around his neck, and mocked him with raised arrows; the migrant responded with predictable fright. As one of his companions described it, he gave them "leg bail for security"; the natives laughed uproariously as he scampered back to his camp.[142] Indian women also engaged in making migrants appear ridiculous before their companions. They particularly preyed upon inexperienced men who, responding to the women's blandishments, would hand over some money and head toward the bushes with one of them. The woman would lead the way and then suddenly run off to a group of her own people, leaving the greenhorn to face the giggling and applause of the native women, the guffaws of the Indian men, and the taunts of his own comrades.[143]

Aware of white fears regarding scalping, these native American tormentors were not above deriving amusement from threats of taking scalps. Mollie Sanford portrayed herself as almost scared to death when a "squad of Indian warriors" entertained themselves by seizing her two long braids and brandishing their hunting knives.[144] On another occasion, three Indians actually cut off two young boys' hair with their hunting knives. The terror that they inspired in local settlers was punished not only by a stern lecture from the Indian agent but by a drastic cut in their rations for that month.[145] Certainly, the fondness of many natives for the custom of wearing scalplocks dangling from their belts did nothing to allay white fears.[146]

An Oklahoma woman recalled that she had been teased by native Americans on another particular sore point of the settlers: the fear of having their children seized by Indians. When a "Chief" came to her and through gestures asked for her two-year-old boy, she drew back in alarm. When she shouted no, the man threw back his head, laughed heartily, and then departed. Hurrying to her neighbors for solace, she was dismayed to learn that, in their opinion, "the Indians meant no harm and were merely trying to be friendly."[147] Another Oklahoma woman learned to accept stoically the fact that, when intoxicated, several local natives enjoyed entering her house, carrying her daughter around, and shooting into the fireplace. She remembered that she had not fled, although she had been afraid. "They meant no harm," she explained, "but they enjoyed frightening white people."[148] But one Texas woman was not so calm. She was absolutely outraged by an intoxicated Indian who seized a young boy, telling him that the "sweetest morsel ever known was a white man's heart."[149]

Scares were not only caused by "Indians who became wild after a few drinks of the white man's 'fire water,'" as one woman phrased it, but also by those who had something to gain through raising an alarm.[150] Individual natives often warned overlanders of impending attack, but it is not clear whether they did so to ingratiate themselves with the migrants or to frighten a train away from their own territory.[151] More clear-cut were the instances in which one tribe would seek revenge against another tribe that had been friendly to settlers. By raising the cry of depredation, they hoped to turn the settlers against these amicable, or, in their eyes, traitorous Indians.[152] And occasionally, an individual American Indian attempted to aggrandize personal power through implementing the fear of an uprising. Nannie Alderson, for example, related the story of a Crow medicine man who, in 1889, used an alleged vision of white extermination to gain "a dangerous following of restless spirits among his own people."[153]

Perhaps the greatest single source of gossip and alarm was the frequent infighting among various groups of native Americans. Settlers who believed, as Agnes Cleaveland, that "from time immemorial, American Indians had lived by raiding, whether of the natural bounty of the land or the garnered resources of their neighbors," were understandably worried that the Indians' greed or ire would eventually be directed against them.[154] Hearing dramatic tales of internecine warfare and actually observing violent Indian outbreaks, many frontier people felt helpless.[155] Even if settlers had not yet been directly attacked by warring tribes, they would surely and inadvertently be caught up in the hostilities. As frontier people continued to think about and discuss the likelihood of such occurrences, their inclination toward panic increased. In their eyes, hunting parties were thus transformed into war parties, ceremonial makeup into war paint, religious dances into war dances, and a lone sentinel into an advance guard.

With such fears running rampant through their minds, it is not surprising that many frontier people did indeed panic when warriors actually approached them.[156] Making preparations to defend themselves became a visceral reaction for many settlers and was justified by the idea that in this type of situation it was better to jump first and to ask questions later. Understandably, such responses created misunderstandings between themselves and "warring" Indians, who wanted no more than to ask questions, to beg, or to simply visit. A common confrontation occurred when a large group of mounted and well-outfitted natives surrounded an Oregon-bound party in 1846. The men were preparing to defend themselves and their families immediately when they learned to their great surprise that, despite their warlike appearance, these native Americans "failed to molest them in any way, but told them that they were going to war with another tribe." Although outright disaster was averted, ruffled feelings were apparent, and a "generous supply of tobacco" was distributed before the Indians departed.[157]

Intertribal hostilities created another difficult problem for frontier people because they were occasionally placed in the curious position of being asked to extend protection to peaceful American Indians. As might be expected, reactions to such requests varied widely. One group of overlanders sheltered terrorized natives, treating them kindly by supplying them with food and other small gifts.[158] Another train simply allowed some Indians to follow them, as one migrant explained it, to take "advantage of our presence as security against the much dreaded Sioux."[159] But others had little sympathy for tribes such as the Pawnee who, due to their constant discord with Sioux and Cheyenne neighbors, were forlorn and starving. One overlander was dismayed when "the gallant men" of her train drove the Pawnee "forth without mercy," but another settler admitted that intertribal warfare was a great source of unrest for migrants.[160]

Of course, overlanders and settlers were not only upset by American Indian assaults upon other Indians but also by native forays upon both other frontier people and stock. Indians raided stock with some regularity and often caused outbreaks of violence in the process.[161] When physical harm or death resulted from a confrontation between Indians and whites, rumors flew with incredible speed for many miles

111

in every direction. Word-of-mouth reports, letters, and newspapers magnified the danger to unrecognizable dimensions. After the Spirit Lake disaster in Iowa in 1857, two Algona women were buffeted by one story after another for many miserable months. They wrote their family in Connecticut that the stories were "large" and so numerous that they did not know what to believe. One added, "If they all increase in proportion, I don't know what they would be when they get to you." The other woman assured her cousin that she hoped not to "see an Indian for ten years" because "it is not very pleasant to be in fear of them all the time." The upshot of the affair was that "for a week we had six persons beside our own family here nights, and six guns well loaded, but we did not use them."[162]

From these letters of Betsey and Abbie Rist it is apparent that one of the many repercussions of frontier alarmism was to reinforce in eastern minds the existing conceptions of marauding native Americans. One female visitor to Wyoming, whose travel account appeared in *Lippincott's Magazine* in 1875, refrained from even discussing the "Indian question," as she called it, because she was convinced that "everybody at the East has an opinion ready formed upon the subject."[163] But other writers were not so reticent. They not only offered accounts of "uprisings" to their readership; they embellished them mercilessly. As a result, Ellen Biddle had quite forgotten her own fright over a scare when she began to receive entreaties from her parents to return home. According to her, the reports of the alarm had reached her family through "newspapers in the East, and had lost nothing in transit."[164]

While rumors and scares occasioned the excessive use of literary license by journalists, periodicals, and newspapers, an actual outbreak of armed conflict received the grand treatment. With both westerners and easterners amplifying the event for their own reasons, a serious conflict such as the one near Fort Phil Kearney in 1866 had become even more tragic by the time it was reported. Margaret Carrington commented disgustedly that the newspapers acted immediately with all the "accuracy which wood engraving affords." She explained, "As there was no one to contradict, and no one who knew the truth, a large margin was left for the play of the fancy, and the imagination was drawn upon with great freedom and success."[165]

Thus, an interesting variation of the "vicious cycle" syndrome was activated. People in settled regions prepared migrants to encounter abusive natives and the migrants, taut with fear, reacted in such a way as to confirm the worst imaginings of those left behind. Small wonder then that with such repetition and reinforcement people in the "states" were consumed with a prejudice toward American Indians that has only just begun to abate during our own era. While the story of a film such as *Tell Them Willie Boy Was Here*, in which one lone Indian's defection from a reservation is enlarged into an uprising of thousands, may appear implausible to our generation, it would have been entirely believable during the nineteenth and the early twentieth centuries.

One of the many unfortunate consequences of this phenomenon was the tenacity with which people from the settled areas adhered to their negative images of native Americans, even though many of their frontier friends had long since renounced such beliefs. An Oklahoma woman of the 1890s tried many ways in which to persuade some eastern visitors that some of her best friends and favorite houseguests were Indians. She took her friends to a camp where her native acquaintances would "all gather around" and pat her on the back. Yet her friends "would draw back from the crowd," and they often told her that "they were ready to run." Sadly enough, she never did induce her visitors to think that American Indians were more than malicious and contemptible beings.[166]

As one might expect, all westerners did not surrender their biases against the native peoples they encountered. Many held tightly to their own preconceptions despite a barrage of challenging evidence. This tendency of many frontier people to cling to their views was encouraged by the prevalence of gossip about Indians. Not only did the constant talk confirm what they already believed to be true, but it impeded effectually any meaningful communication with native Americans that might have helped reshape white thinking.

This lack of communication between Indians and whites led to some pathetic situations. Because many overlanders believed that Indians would perceive them as cowardly or as easy marks for begging and thievery, they frequently refused to speak at all with the natives who approached them.[167] Following the advice of guidebooks, other migrants, and advisers they met along the trail, many travelers treated natives with disrespect, suspicion, and distrust. In 1857, Helen Carpenter recorded that the Pawnees came to her camp while they were "nooning," and immediately the order went out to not give them a thing. "It was thought," she explained, "that they would follow and be a nuisance if shown any kindness." But Carpenter discovered that she could not eat her lunch "with those poor wretches watching every mouthful like hungry dogs." Although her mother seized an opportunity to slip some food to the pitiable beggars, the Pawnees did not follow the train afterward or give the travelers any trouble. "We do not coincide with all of Uncle Sam's views," Carpenter added, "but he is the 'boss' of the train and as such his views must be respected."[168]

The hesitancy of frontier people to interact with American Indians also led to some humorous situations. Because whites were so nervous about what Indians might be plotting as they attempted to make their needs known through gestures and actions, settlers often totally misinterpreted the Indians' intentions. One result is that settlers often gave away a sizable part of their household goods in the process.[169] When seven native men pushed their way into her house, Ella Bird-Dumont was terrified, although she admitted that their leader appeared friendly and attempted to talk with her. The object of their visit seemed to be to trade their government-issue clothing for groceries, but her stock of food was short and she vehemently shook her head no. When the men discovered her rifle, however, their leader became determined to trade for it. As she continued to shake her head fearfully, hoping all the while that they would depart, he began showing her the items of clothing that he wore. "I did not understand him, and did not make any reply," she later wrote, "so he began laying off his clothes, one by one." She looked helplessly at her friend. This woman suddenly realized that he thought he had traded his clothing for the rifle, so he was removing it piece by piece. Just as things were on the verge of being "everlastingly too late," the women were able to sign to him that there was no trade and that he should re-dress himself immediately. Fortunately, *he* was not embarrassed and with laughter proceeded to put his clothes back on.[170]

Although neither of these episodes resulted in long-term physical damage to either side, they demonstrated a lack of sympathy, understanding, and compassion on the part of overlanders and settlers toward the native populations they were displacing. Had more positive feelings existed, they might have made the development of the frontier much easier and more pleasant for everyone involved. There are many pitiful stories that support the possible validity of this contention. During the Civil War, for example, several Arkansas women

114

sought to escape the ravages of battles around Fayetteville by removing to Washington, Arkansas. They inadvertently entered the Choctaw Nation of Indian Territory during their flight and became terrified of the fate that might befall them. When a lone Choctaw man approached them and offered them directions in broken English, they fled hastily, assuming that "he would bring a band of Indians and we hardly dared surmise the rest." When they encountered a soldier they told him their sad tale and pleaded for his help, only to be answered by his laughter. He reassured them that they had no cause for alarm because the Choctaws "to the last man were Southern," and far from intending to return with "a band of tomahawkers," as they had assumed, the man was actually trying to assist them.[171]

In the 1880s, another southern woman endured a different type of ordeal because of the communication barrier between settlers and natives. It began with one of her "guards" amusing himself by betting a companion that he could put a bullet hole through an old Indian's hat without touching his head. In fact, he grazed the old man's scalp. The upshot of the affair was that the Indians retaliated by burning the family home, destroying the silver and other personal items of value, and shooting their beloved dog. She later offered her own personal view of settler-native relations:

> It was all very kindly up to a point, but beyond the kindness there was a blank wall. In view of the cruelties that had been exchanged between white man and Indian, it was no wonder if real warmth was lacking between them or if the Indian attitude toward us was one of complete cynicism. I can understand this now, but at the time I was terribly disappointed. I came from the South, and despite the burning of our house I looked, unconsciously perhaps, for the same affectionate relationship with the Indians that had existed in my home between the colored people and the whites. One of the hard lessons I had to learn in Montana was that the affection I sentimentally wanted just simply was not there.[172]

The damage done by the inability or unwillingness of frontier people to communicate meaningfully with American Indians did not accrue to just one side. Indians too were often the victims of numerous, and often tragic, misunderstandings. The ingenuous, the curious, and even the most well-intended American Indians were blamed for an assorted variety of ills. Whether they had any part in the creation of

115

these problems was often not really germane to the consequences that they suffered. Indians experienced a range of effects from embarrassment to persecution for trouble they had not caused. In addition, they often experienced starvation, poverty, and the loss of their land due to misinformed government policies generated by prejudiced and harried bureaucrats. [173]

Even when an influential white leader like Samuel Houston of Texas attempted to take the part of American Indians and to divert harsh actions against them—such as the so-called Cherokee Bill of the 1840s, which annulled the Indians' right to all lands because of their "barbarity"—his entreaties fell upon closed ears. Julia Sinks emphasized that while Houston was a charismatic figure with a widespread following his eloquence had been wasted. According to her, most Texans "hardly classed" Indians "with the people in its usual sense," and Houston's "sympathies were outside the common pale of thought." [174]

Anti-Indian attitudes frequently resulted in the loss of Indian lives. Not only were they exterminated without quarter in many instances, but individual natives also fell at the hands of distrustful frontier people. Byron McKinstry told of one such case, in which an overlander swapped horses with an Indian who was overtaken the next day by a rear portion of the same party. When they recognized their companion's horse they quickly accused the Indian of stealing it. Fearing their ire, he fled. His flight was perceived as evidence of his guilt; thus, they fired immediately, killing the innocent man. [175]

In their haste to react to American Indian problems in a violent manner and with weapons that they were often ill prepared to use, overlanders and settlers regularly destroyed their own goods, stock, and companions. One fellow shot his own mule twice after mistaking it for an Indian intruder; another shot an oxen through the head; and an Arizona woman who fired at an "Indian" through her cabin door learned that she had wounded a neighbor's burro, for which her husband had to pay two dollars in damages. [176]

Settlers also frequently took aim at each other. Ella Bird-Dumont drew a bead on an approaching Indian, only to learn that she had almost shot her own husband while he was out searching for her. [177] In an Oklahoma scare of the 1890s, a local judge obligingly took command of the "troops" of local men. As he drilled them with supposedly empty rifles, he ordered them into formation and then gave the command to fire. One recruit discharged a cartridge that he had accidently left in the chamber, hitting the dust in front of the judge's feet. The judge, angry and disgusted with his recruit, threatened to resign and shouted at his men, "Let the confounded redskins butcher you all."[178] In another area of Oklahoma during the same decade, a native dance occasioned a scare that resulted in a young boy fatally shooting his own brother.[179]

The willingness of overlanders and settlers to permit rumors and gossip to rule their lives imposed great rigidity on their activities. On the trail they joined with so many other travelers that parties became unwieldy and often created difficulties in locating campsites, water, and grass. However, it was generally thought to be better to experience the problems of a train that was too large than to take the chance of being overpowered by unfriendly American Indians.[180] But as Lavinia Porter pointed out, the warmongering attitudes and actions of train members could actually create more danger than they deterred. After remonstrating in vain with hostile train members, she and her family, fearing retaliation from the Indians whom the migrants had abused, left the train to attempt the journey on their own. Their experience was instructive: not only were they never bothered by native Americans, but one traveled with them for three days as a guide. When she learned that he had actually been sent to protect them, she remarked, "If that were true, it went to prove that there was honor among these savage tribes of the wilderness."[181] Other overlanders who were not so trusting stuck close to their train, refraining from enjoying the countryside or even from killing game "for fear that the Indians might be near."[182]

Once settled, many frontier people continued to restrict their behavior and life-styles. Some men wore guns at all times, even while they worked in the fields.[183] Women refused to go out on rides or picnics, to attend war dances and other ceremonies, or to observe the splendid sight of a government-endorsed hunting party.[184] Others not only stayed close to home but engaged in subterfuge, such as lacing their own liquor supply with morphine in case troublesome Indians appeared or placing in their yards hollow logs in which they intended to hide.[185]

Both men and women spent overwhelming amounts of time, energy, and resources in "fortin up." Often this meant that they gathered in someone's well-built house, barn, or other outbuilding. Time after time they spent sleepless, terror-filled nights during which no siege

117

ever transpired.[186] Others resorted to utilizing mine shafts, specially dug caves, hotels, and town squares as their forts. One can only speculate how many people were bilked of their belongings; for example, a group of Texans entrusted their stock to an army captain while they forted up, never to see either the stock or the captain again.[187]

Many other frontier people engaged in even more substantial efforts to protect themselves. Band after band of informal "frontier guards," "rangers," and "brigades" drilled zealously, only to disband eventually without ever having seen action.[188] In many regions, actual forts, stockades, and blockhouses were built—or at least begun—to shelter settlers when the dreaded horde finally descended upon them.[189] Sometimes the local rangers staffed these garrisons; on other occasions, formal troops were ordered out, often by the thousands.[190] In some areas, such as Texas and Colorado, such precautions were frequently necessary. It would be interesting to know how many troops relocated in order to occupy a new and finally unnecessary fort, such as Fort Dodge in Iowa, where soldiers spent three quiet years without incident. When this fort was dismantled and sold at public auction in 1853, it was purchased by a local man who founded the city of Fort Dodge on its site in the following year. Sioux City's fort, in the absence of many threatened onslaughts, was never even finished, and its timbers were sold for firewood and building material.[191]

Despite the fact that many of these attempts at protection turned out to be unnecessary, the danger at the time seemed very real to the frontier people who initiated such actions. Perhaps the enormity of their fears can be better understood by noting the lengths they were willing to go to intimidate American Indians from attacking and to punish them when they did. Overlanders and settlers were not above taking scalps, captives, and hostages, or imposing torture and death upon natives, even though they disparaged Indians for engaging in such behavior.[192] Whites frequently proved to be just as vicious, savage, and barbarous as they claimed the American Indians were. Ignoring their own religious beliefs, frontier people argued that they were forced to react to Indians on their own murderous level if they were to survive. Consequently, frontier history is punctuated by episodes that many Americans would like to forget ever happened. For example, after the 1847 Whitman massacre in Oregon the settlers reacted with vitriolic rage against the Indians. As Polly Purcell described it:

> The soldiers killed the chief Pe Pe Mox-Mox, one of the boys put a rope around the chief's neck and tied it to the horn of his saddle, rode all around the camp and told the Indian prisoners if they killed any more of the white settlers they would be treated the same way. They also scalped the chief which was very humiliating to the Indians.[193]

It might be argued that these various reactions to such incidents were not extreme but were necessary measures against an unstable and threatened native population that did indeed assail and kill both overlanders and settlers. It might also be suggested that, in a sense, the actions involved in these incidents created as much trouble with native Americans as they averted. Such conduct and the harsh sentiments that accompanied it did nothing to encourage peaceful coexistence or harmonious relations between populations on the frontier.

Certainly the widespread existence of anti-Indian passions and the incidents that they spawned leave little doubt in one's mind concerning the reasons why so many frontierswomen were apprehensive, at best, and filled with terror, at worst, at the possibility of encountering real American Indians. Between the images they had been indoctrinated with *before* leaving home and the rumors, scares, and alarmism they had been subjected to *since* leaving home, they were clearly ready for a series of traumatic experiences. Interestingly enough, women's mental states often had little or nothing to do with real American Indians.

How then would women react when they were actually exposed to individual natives on a personal basis? Would they see only the Indians who they had been prepared to encounter, or would they prove to be flexible and open enough to revise their views once they had confronted real people? While living in a climate of fear and alarm, would women find it possible to think and act in a rational and independent fashion when judging particular people? These are all questions that have surprising and very significant answers.

4

Contact and Cultural Clash with Native Populations

Since the majority of both Americans and Europeans were usually more receptive to the idea of the "bad" Indian than to the image of the "good" Indian, most migrants headed west with a view of American Indians that was more negative than positive. Whether they turned westward during the early decades of the nineteenth century or started their trek later, frontier people were likely to anticipate encounters with barbarous savages. Such an expectation was intensified further by the climate of rumor and alarmism that prevailed on the trail and in the early settlements. At the same time, however, most of these people clung to the hope that American Indians might turn out to be the noble savages described by Jean Jacques Rousseau and James Fenimore Cooper.

These contradictory expectations, commonly held by both men and women, resulted from the long and complex conditioning process that all emigrants experienced in regard to native peoples. Female emigrants appear to have had additional reasons for searching out simultaneously both the despicable and the ennobling characteristics of American Indians. Many frontierswomen thus painted a picture of Indians that appeared to be paradoxical and fraught with ambivalence. In their writings, these women often presented portraits of Indians that seemed to exaggerate their favorable qualities while overstating their undesirable traits.

Further complicating the apparent inconsistency in women's views of western natives was the observable tendency of a number of them to begin to shift toward an increasingly generous interpretation of American Indians. For some women this change occurred rather quickly, often during the westward trek itself. For others, especially those who were abruptly deposited in a raw frontier settlement by a ship or a railroad, the metamorphosis came sometime after taking up residency on the frontier. Whatever the timing, the women's own words demonstrate that many of them did replace their conception of American Indians as a combination of saint and savage with a view of the natives as human beings to be empathized with, perhaps even liked.

Understanding the confused and changing images of Indians contained within the pages of numerous frontierswomen's diaries, letters, and reminiscences is a difficult and challenging task. Clear-cut contradictions and shifts were typical of these women. The men, however, almost never exhibited either the degree of contradiction or the process of change in their interpretations of Indians that the women did. Yet both women and men were exposed to similar influences, such as the ferocity or the gentleness of the natives they encountered, whether or not their party engaged in altercations with Indians, and the previous history of a trail or settlement that had created a calm or a volatile climate. Because women's perceptions often altered and men's seldom did, it may be possible that women's revised perceptions of American Indians were closely linked to their changing ideas about themselves as females. As women's views of themselves altered, they became more receptive to the attempt to see native peoples in a more humane way than they had been initially capable of doing. Consequently, a woman who headed westward with trepidation and dread regarding native Americans could, and often did, become a sympathetic supporter of those very Indians.

As a first step toward understanding the process of changing attitudes in these frontierswomen, it must be noted that the women, in addition to absorbing extensive information about American Indians, also were taught certain beliefs concerning themselves as females. Like Indians, women were considered by nineteenth-century society to have two sides to their natures, one superior and the other inferior. The superior side of women's characters derived primarily from their supposedly exceptional moral abilities, the quality that made them the moral guardians of home and family. In addition, women's superiority included a variety of other admirable traits; they were kind, gentle, passive, religious, domestic, pure, and refined. On the other hand, the inferior aspect of women's presumably inherent natures resulted from their obvious weakness. Although morally superior, women were believed to be physically and intellectually inferior. They had small brains and weak muscles. They were also helpless, childlike, nonassertive, indecisive, and unable to protect themselves.[1]

Having heard all their lives these assertions regarding female character, most women accepted them and carried them west. As they assessed the various American Indian groups that they met, their concepts of themselves helped to shape their interpretations of Indians. In considering women's "superior" side, it has been suggested that because they were taught to see themselves as moral guardians and as the protectors of civilization women were encouraged to perceive Indians as uncivilized, as morally deficient, and as brutalized by their primitive existence.[2] While seeing themselves as the harbingers of civilization, women were advised to view the Indians as potential subjects for women's reform efforts. Sara Smith, a recently wed minister's wife, remarked:

> I long to be at my journey's end. I long to be telling the dying heathen the story of the cross. O, how happy I shall be in my laboring for the good of those dear Indians. May God prepare me to do them good.[3]

Their assumed superiority often encouraged women to emphasize, and indeed even become obsessed with, the American Indian's supposed inferiority.

When women's convictions about their own moral powers and the Indians' hypothetical need for reform were combined with more generalized views of the savagery and rapacity of native peoples, large numbers of women suffered from ambivalent feelings. As a result, most women undertook the journey filled with both hopeful anticipation and a great deal of dread at the prospect of their first confrontation with a "real" Indian. In their anxiety, many of these women spent their early days on the trail scouring the countryside for any evidence of Indians.[4] When one California-bound traveler of the 1860s heard shots fired in a nearby camp, she immediately drew the conclusion that it indicated the presence of Indians. Another female emigrant recalled that the sight of an Indian dog following her party kept them "in a continual state of excitement."[5] In 1850, one woman even scanned the horizon with a telescope in order to detect the presence of native Americans. Although no one in her party was very alarmed when she spotted several Indians and everyone was able to sleep that night after posting adequate guards, she not only remained awake all night but did not bother to change her clothing, "neither shoe nor bonnet."[6]

Like trail women, female settlers also frequently demonstrated a willingness to see things in a very dramatic way. In the 1880s, for example, Agnes Morley Cleaveland viewed the long-deserted site of a massacre near her new home in New Mexico. Although it was marked by only two grave-shaped mounds of loose rock and the faintest suggestion of a covering of ash, she insisted that

> the mind's eye saw the sudden dash of yelling savages from the timber beside the dim wagon tracks that were the "road," . . . saw the swift, terrible slaughter of the surprised and helpless men; saw the oxen driven away to their own slaughter, leaving behind them the remnants of what had been human bodies and a fire that blazed fearsomely.[7]

What a surprise it must have been for these anxiety-ridden women to discover that the "first" Indians they met were often friendly; this was the case, at least, during the 1840s, 1850s, and 1860s.[8] This meeting usually occurred just beyond the Missouri River, since St. Joseph and Council Bluffs were the primary departure points for migrants. Because many of the American Indians in this region had become accustomed to a steady stream of travelers through their domain, they were generally not of the hostile disposition that women had been led to expect. Consequently, women's writings were filled with frequent notations that the first Indians they met were not nearly as troublesome to them as they had expected. In 1846, for example, while Polly Purcell's family was crossing the Missouri River on their way to Oregon they were surrounded by what she described as "500 warriors." Although Purcell's group prepared to defend themselves, they were both astonished and relieved to discover that no hostility developed.[9] Three years later, Martha Morgan noted that the Sioux her party met in the same area were "ostensibly very friendly."[10]

During the next several decades, women continued to report that the American Indians in the Missouri River region were peaceable, friendly, and annoying only in their habit of begging.[11] Women's fears frequently dissolved into curiosity or even amusement. When Pauline Wonderly crossed the Missouri River at Kanesville (Council Bluffs) in 1852, she felt that she was entering "the domain of the dreaded Indian." Instead of being attacked, however, she was treated to an "exhibition of Indian markmanship in which native men shot their bows and arrows at nickels which the gullible whites gladly threw into the air."[12] In 1853, while crossing the Kansas River, Elizabeth Goltra was amazed to learn that her first Indians accepted gifts of bread, meat, and a dime; then they thanked her and passed on their way.[13] In 1862, Ada Millington discovered that the first native Americans she met near Fort Kearney asked not for coins but simply wanted to shake hands with the migrants and say, "how, how."[14]

Ada Vogdes was another woman whose terror of American Indians was not borne out by her first meeting with them. On her way toward Fort Laramie in 1868, she commented in her journal that "it was a fearful feeling to me, in the midst of an Indian country, & far from home." By the time her party reached Chimney Rock, she added that though they had seen no Indians it was rumored that they were traveling in the midst of them. "This kind of life," she lamented, "does not suit the female portion of creation. A woman was never intended to cross these Plains." When she finally did meet some native Americans near the fort, the incident passed without a trace of drama, for they encountered only a small party of friendly Indians on a hunting expedition. Vogdes's relatively pleasant experience did little, however, to change her ideas. She insisted upon clinging to her terror of Indians, thus making herself miserable for some time. During this early period of her life on the frontier, she was unable to enjoy the social life of the fort, spent sleepless nights while her husband was away, and refused to leave the garrison's protective walls for outings.[15]

Clearly, years of being steeped in anti-Indian prejudice were not suddenly erased by a meeting with friendly tribes, and this was especially the case for women who viewed themselves as moral missionaries to "barbarians." Rather, those lessons concerning the moral nature of women and the "savage" natures of American Indians were likely to hold sway, for only a few weeks or for an entire lifetime, regardless of evidence to the contrary. Therefore, it is not surprising to discover that many women's first meetings with Indians, although cordial, were still marked by great tension. "I was very much scared," Rachel Rose wrote in 1852. Others reported that they stayed closer to camp or were caught up in "scares" as a result of the Indians' proximity.[16] In 1864, Mary Warner jotted this simple statement in her diary: "There were two Indians came to camp begging—they were the first we had seen and we were afraid of them."[17] A couple of years earlier, when another trail woman viewed her first native beggars, she remarked that although they may have looked very natural to some of the train members who had seen them before they looked "very savage" to her. She added that "they are monstrous looking creatures to inhabit such beautiful soil as we are now traveling through."[18]

Such revulsion was not uncommon. These women often reacted to the first native Americans they met in terms of their own expectations rather than considering the reality standing before them. As early as 1848, a young woman encountering her first Indians just outside of St. Joseph explained that to her "frightened vision, dressed in their long macinaw blankets, with eagle feathers in their hair, they looked ten feet high."[19] As late as 1886, Allie Busby, visiting the quiet Mesquakis at the Tama agency in Iowa, responded in a similar manner to her first Indians: "Wild visions of tomahawk or scalping knife arose, while the Indian of romance disappeared altogether from our imagination."[20]

Not all women were intimidated by the presence of native Americans along their routes. Some, like Lavinia Porter, were simply annoyed by the Indians, even though her party was not troubled by them to any extent.[21] Others were thoroughly disillusioned. "We had expected to see feathered head-gear and painted faces," one explained; while another, headed for Montana in 1864, complained that the first Indian she spotted was a ragged, ugly creature who "was very disappointing as the 'Noble Red Man' we read about."[22]

Such statements indicate that a characteristic of American Indians that first attracted women's attention was their style of dress or the lack of it. Coming from a culture that advocated covering the body with layers and complex types of apparel, these women were often shocked that many of these "barbaric" people—unlike the more "civilized" whites—wore little or no clothing.[23] Mary Sandford recalled that "the Indians were nude save for a throw over one shoulder, and a strap around the loins."[24] Mary Staples declared that their "clothing was very scant." Sallie Maddock added that they were "mostly naked." Margaret Hecox said that they frequently came "to our camp in a perfectly nude state." And Harriet Smith reported that, in encountering an Indian man, she was "a little streaked for he had nothing on but a blanket and great earrings and bracelet, all brass."[25]

Women were also appalled to discover that Indian children were seldom clothed.[26] Mary Fish wryly commented that the "papooses were perfectly naked and some of the seniors did not come very far from the same predicament."[27] This was not an uncommon interpretation. Helen Carpenter also was dismayed that some Pawnee Indians she met had "no clothing" but were wrapped only in "very unsanitary looking blankets." She was, however, pleased to note that they were so "adept in the management of them" that there was "no undue exposure of the person."[28]

It also seemed curious to many frontierswomen that while most Indians covered their bodies with little more than loin cloths, blankets, and moccasins they did wear a "profusion of ornaments" like a "Broadway belle."[29] A wide variety of brass, silver, feather, and shell jewelry and other personal decoration was often complemented by brightly colored hues applied to the face and torso.[30] The resulting combinations were usually judged by whites to be flashy or even outrageous. To Eveline Alexander, for instance, the Indian regalia was almost overwhelming because of its fullness and complexity. When she first encountered Utah Indians, she noted that their "costume exceeded anything" she had yet seen in terms of its elaborateness and profuseness.[31]

One might think that the intricate dress of some American Indians would meet with at least a modicum of approval from white women who favored a highly fashionable style and personal ornamentation in their own costumes. Yet when the Indians were dressed well, women's judgments still tended to be derogatory. Upon seeing her first Indians near Fort Kearney in 1856, Caroline Richardson wrote that they were "drest in their 'peculiar costome.'"[32] Another woman observed that though "some are nearly naked, some dressed most fantastically." Still another noted that they were "decorated in the extreme of Indian dandyism."[33] In 1853, Celinda Hines Shipley remarked that she couldn't really make up her mind about the first group of native Americans that she saw fully dressed. While they seemed rather well clad, she explained in a rather caustic way that she couldn't really judge them fairly since she hadn't seen very many clothed Indians.[34]

The only way in which American Indians seemed to elicit signs of approval from women was when their attire resembled white styles. If Indians approximated whites in their manner of dress, women viewed their appearance with a more positive tone.[35] Esther Hanna, for example, was pleased that some Sioux near Fort Laramie seemed "to prize any article of clothing from a white man very much."[36] Another group of Sioux, who were neatly attired like pseudo-whites, struck Margaret Hecox as "clean and wholesome in appearance."[37] And when Maria Norton came across some American Indians dressed "with pants and caps," she judged them to be "the most respectable that we have seen."[38]

This sample of comments by white women about the personal appearance of native Americans illustrates the propensity of women to impose the standards of their own society upon people representing an entirely different way of life.[39] Instead of being attracted by the color, spirit, and verve of native apparel, most women's early reactions tended toward discomfiture because American Indians dressed so differently from whites. Instead of admiring the craftwork involved in the jewelry, quill work, and beading, many women—at least initially—could only dismiss such decorations as pagan, ostentatious, or excessive. Given the style of white women's fashions, these judgments contained an element of paradox, even humor. Characterized throughout the nineteenth century by such devices of sartorial splendor as bustles, hoopskirts, and leg-o'-mutton sleeves, white women's styles seem now rather peculiar in themselves. Women who aspired to a fifteen-inch waist through severe corseting, beginning in childhood, or by the more extreme method of surgical removal of the lower ribs certainly might have been expected to have some tolerance for extremes of fashion. Yet these women, who saw themselves as the carriers of white civilization to aborigines, thought their own styles were not at all eccentric, while they condemned those of the Indians as absurd.

In a similar shortsighted manner, women were quick to pass harsh judgment upon what they perceived to be the low standards of cleanliness among Indian groups. Despite their own values in this area, which involved infrequent baths and the liberal application of toilet water, they commonly disparaged various native American groups for being dirty and even filthy.[40] Although many Indians bathed frequently and cleansed themselves in sweat baths, they were perceived as unclean. Garbed in their paint, jewelry, and colorful blankets, they were, according to Annie M. Zeigler, "picturesque" but "often dirty."[41] To Sallie Maddock, they were "disgusting and dirty looking." To Mary Staples, they formed "a filthy set," and to Mary Jane Guill, "a filthy and dirty set of Indians."[42] One woman was firmly convinced that "the romance of Indian life will not bear a closer inspection—they are neither more or less than filthy savages."[43]

Vitriolic as these opinions were, other women were even more vicious in their observations. One charged that "filth" and Indians were "inseparable." Another dismissed an entire village of natives with the statement that "the creatures looked too filthy to live."[44] Sarah Herndon maintained that native Americans were "the most wretched looking human creatures" that she had ever seen. To her there was "nothing majestic, dignified, or noble-looking about any of the Indians" she met. Obviously disappointed that she had not happened upon a Cooperesque Indian, Herndon caustically wrote, "I fail as yet to recognize 'The noble red man,'" adding that Indians were "lazy, dirty, obnoxious-looking creatures."[45]

A telling indication of their own conceit lay in the fact that these women frequently used the term "creature" when speaking of American Indians. The repeated usage of "creature," which implies something less than a human being, suggests that to many white women American Indians were not really people at all.[46] One of the Indian practices that helped to create this antipathy in women was the habit of some native groups of eating various types of insects, including crickets and locusts. Women who would sanction or even advocate drinking alcohol, devouring foods dripping with butter or pork grease, eating highly spiced or sugared dishes, as well as using tobacco and snuff, found the consumption of insects disconcerting, at best, and repulsive, at worst.

Women's appraisals of such practices were quick and acrimonious. When Algeline Ashley observed Utah Indians pulling wings off locusts and harvesting them in sacks, she declared that they were "very low Indians and very ugly looking."[47] The reaction was even more vituperative when the insects in question were lice. One California settler of the early 1850s watched an Indian woman eating lice from her husband's head, while, according to her, she was feeding him a few of the choice ones. The settler stated unequivocably that Indians were

contemptible objects because of the "extreme indolence of their nature, the squalid conditions in which they live . . . and the general
imbecility of their intellects."[48] Helen Stewart indicated that she preferred visiting Indians to avoid her camp altogether because they
were not only "the durtyist creatures I ever saw" but "they will pick
the lice out of there head and eat them."[49]

Unfortunately, these women were often slow to examine either the
economic demands or the customs of Indians, and so they were equally
slow to understand the eating of fare that they found so unacceptable.
Instead, while men encouraged native Americans to entertain them
by shooting at targets with bows and arrows, women amused themselves by watching Indians eat grasshoppers.[50]

In a comparable spirit of distortion, women associated "peculiar"
odors with American Indians. It was a very common notion that the
presence of Indians could be detected through their smell.[51] It was
not unusual for whites to mention that they could smell a nearby
Indian camp or that their own horses and dogs responded with fear
to the aroma of a native American.[52] This scent was supposedly odd,
unpleasant, and "strongly Indian."[53] Lydia Waters explained that the
smell derived, at least in part, from the Indians' habit of rubbing
themselves with "the entrails of some small fat animal, a skunk or
raccoon, which looked as if it were dried in smoke." Instead of bathing
with water, she said, they "took the greatest comfort lying in the sun
rubbing themselves with these greasy insides."[54] Mary Fish claimed
that the Sioux smeared their bodies with "oil which they procure from
polecats." She phrased her opinion of the practice delicately by saying
that the "effluvia arising from their persons is none of the sweetest."
Frances Roe was more direct in stating that the Indians she had met
struck her as "simply, and only, painted, dirty and nauseous-smelling
savages."[55]

In these women's eyes, American Indians were clearly deficient in
certain basic areas of life. Many frontierswomen, however, were in
for yet another shock. When they got close enough to an Indian to
hold a conversation, they discovered that many of them spoke little
or no English. With obvious dismay, Ellen Adams remarked, "Some
of the Indians could not understand a single word of English."[56] Helen
Carpenter thought them to be "stupid" because they didn't "understand French any better than they did English."[57] Other women also

noted that the native peoples they tried to converse with could not speak or understand English.[58] They were willing to denigrate the validity of native tongues and to assume that English should become the dominant means of communication for all western peoples. This ethnocentrism grew even more apparent when women found an American Indian who could manage a few words of the white's language, often a discovery to be recorded and sometimes derided.[59] "They do not understand any of our language," one woman declared with a sneer, "and when they can speak a word of it they seem to think that they have done something very smart."[60] Whether Indians spoke no English at all, some English, or "good" English, they were often the targets of disdain on the part of white women.

As frontierswomen came into contact with various Indian customs, they demonstrated a blend of puzzlement, derision, and outright racism in their judgments. Some were amused by the sight of native American villages moving from one campsite to another on pole carts pulled by dogs or with the sticks of wigwams strapped to ponies.[61] On her way to California in 1853, Harriet Ward wrote that when Indians moved their homes they constituted "a strange and altogether interesting sight." To her, they appeared to be "poor half naked creatures with their *all* packed upon their horses."[62] In 1854, when Mary Burrell counted 402 Sioux in a procession, she asserted blithely that this "astonishing" sight was "equal to 50 caravans or circuses."

Such disrespect turned into absolute irreverence when women encountered American Indian burial grounds with bodies exposed on open racks. To Marie Nash, migrating to California in 1861, the corpses seemed to be a "sad sight." Other women minimized the significance of Indian burial customs by seeing them as only a matter of practicality in raising the bodies far enough off the ground to prevent pillaging and mutilation by wolves.[63] In fact, some women had so little respect for Indian burial customs that they entered burial grounds to "visit" and to collect beads to wear as ornaments.[64]

American Indian mating practices also appeared peculiar to many white women. Some seemed obsessed with a need to chronicle every French trader they met who had an Indian wife and "half-breed" children.[65] Mary Fish seemed amused by it all. When she met one French trader with two native wives, she quipped that "the Frenchmen go for amalgamation," and when she saw another with a dozen

131

wives she joked that he was simply "fond of a plural number."[66] A more common reaction to intermarriage was surprise that all the parties involved got along quite well. In 1852, Frances Sawyer noted that the children of one such marriage seemed "playful and happy." Margaret Frink marveled that one trader's native wife was not only "quite good-looking" but "dressed in true American style."[67]

Even more representative of women's reactions toward intermarriage was their outright disparagement of it as a "shame and disgrace to our country."[68] One woman found it "perfectly astonishing" that "a man who has ever seen civilized people can intermarry with the natives and be contented to settle down and live as they do." She was also amazed that the Indian wife and little girls wore dresses, "looked decent," and were spoken to "pleasantly, even fondly" by their white husband and father.[69] Mollie Dorsey was astounded when she observed such a family living "like civilized people." She recorded in her diary her disbelief that a white man could "live such a way." Perhaps the most acrid remark of all came from Maria Norton, who viewed the idea of intermarriage as an abomination. To her, it was "the greatest absurdity . . . for a white man to live with black dirty squaws."[70]

Many women were distressed still further by their perceptions of marriage customs among native Americans. They concluded erroneously from their usually hasty, superficial, and misinformed survey of such customs that men could nonchalantly and crassly trade ponies and other goods for as many wives as they might happen to desire. Mary Bailey declared that she "was somewhat shocked to think of such a loose state of morals," but her husband pointed out that it was really "nothing more than Yankee men do."[71]

In spite of their outrage over what they perceived to be inhumane arrangements for procuring wives, most white women thought it was nothing more than a joke if an Indian male attempted to trade ponies for them.[72] Sometimes, in fact, they risked their own safety when they angered native men by agreeing to a trade as a prank. However, when the Indian male returned with the appointed number of ponies, it quickly became apparent that the incident had caused great discomfiture and embarrassment to everyone involved.[73] In other instances, reactions ranged from sarcasm to levity. When an Ottawa Indian proposed to Emily Horton on her way to California in 1852, she stated sarcastically, "I was too unsophisticated to appreciate the honor."[74] But in a similar situation in 1862, Harriet Smith jested, "I thought I would wait untill some one would give Unc a lot of ponies for me and I would go and stay awhile with them then run away, and then we would have some ponies."[75] Mary Warner jokingly noted in her diary that her "Uncle Chester traded Aunt Lizzie off for two ponies but she would not go."[76] And Catherine Bell wrote home that "there was an Indian chief offered Charlie two of his best ponys for me, dont you think he ought to have traded?"[77]

Many women were also often seriously outraged by what they perceived as degrading treatment of native women by their men. When they witnessed native men taking money from women who had earned it by selling their own handiwork, men riding while women walked, or men expecting women to carry the load while they went unburdened, white women labeled Indian men as detestable and contemptible.[78]

These observations of the treatment of native women by Indian males increased frontierswomen's forebodings regarding their own possible captivity.[79] "I have no desire to go among the Indians in that way," one emigrant asserted. A Kansas settler of the 1850s admitted that she asked her son to watch her while she fetched water so that Indians would not carry her off. She also guarded her children closely. When native Americans approached her cabin she gathered her children in her arms so that her babies would not be stolen from her.[80] When another woman sighted some Indians garbed in blankets and feathers, she too worried that "they would kill us all, and take my baby in captivity."[81]

In addition to their disapproval of these features of American Indian life, many frontierswomen concluded that Indian character was of the lowest order. As though they had not already heard enough about the "bad" Indian, what they now seemed to be seeing with their own eyes convinced them that the native population of the West was indeed debased, ruthless, and savage. Interpreting native cultures in terms of their own white values, most women were quick to judge Indians to be poor specimens of humanity (if they saw them as people at all). To frontierswomen, native cultures and customs were worthy of little more than eradication by progressive and enlightened white civilizers like themselves. As a result, epithets such as "hard-hearted & cruel people," "too devilish for any human beings," "most treacherous mortals on earth," "too indolent to exert themselves much," and "ever treacherous" were liberally scattered through women's writings.[82] According to many westering women, native Americans were "untrustworthy, thieving, and treacherous," of a "sly intriguing nature," "very cowardly," and "ignorant and simple."[83]

One of the most notable personality defects attributed to all American Indians was their reputed laziness. This tendency was noted in 1853 by Kate Furness, who did not question why Indians near Fort Laramie were behaving in an indolent fashion; she simply concluded that "doing absolutely nothing" but standing around and gazing "vacantly into space" made them contented.[84] In the mid-1870s, Ellen Biddle tried to train a Colorado Indian youth as a house servant, and she was not surprised when he ran away with some other "indolent" and "worthless" Indians. "Since then," she wrote, "I have never thought the plan of sending Indian boys to the schools in the East to educate them, and then allow them to go back to their reservations, a good one." To her way of thinking, "there are too many generations of Indians back of them, and the few years of civilization are soon forgotten."[85]

Another widely held assumption about all Indians was that they harbored a crazed desire for liquor. While neglecting to find out why some Indians might be seeking whiskey, many women dismissed with disdain any individual or group of natives who did so.[86] In the 1830s, settler Mary Rice wrote to her sister that some of the Creek Indians around Fort Gibson patronized a local white liquor peddler. The result, in her words, was that

> a great many of the indians almost live on whiskey they will a company of them git together and drink and git to quarilling and then they will stab one another. . . . they dance and hollow and scream all night and most always on a Satterday night they dont never truble us any by coming near the house onely by going by in the road and screaming.[87]

In 1852, a lone Indian man attempting to trade a buffalo robe for whiskey caused one female migrant on her way to Salt Lake to declare that "these poor creatures will part with anything for liquor."[88] An 1846 trail woman, Catherine Haun, fell prey to the same kind of thinking. When her party had to lighten their load, she explained that they buried "the barrels of alcohol lest the Indians should drink it and, frenzied thereby, might follow and attack us."[89] Yet another woman expressed surprise that Indians who came into her camp to trade said nothing at all about whiskey.[90]

As prejudicial as these various judgments about native Americans appear, they were taken very seriously by women who did not realize that they were judging a huge number of people on the basis of a relatively few and highly visible cases. Most women, at least in the early stages of their westering experience, still held eastern or European values. As transplanted westerners approaching their new neighbors, their fears impeded their ability to recognize the difficulties created by such negative beliefs. Thus, while these women's projected images of Indians do not provide useful or accurate information regarding American Indians, they do reveal a tremendous amount about the thinking of the women themselves.

Many women's reactions to the customs and problems of a once proud and self-sufficient people appear intolerant and heartless. To a great extent, these reactions were derived from cruel anti-Indian images as well as from a belief in themselves as the moral reformers of the Indians. Frontierswomen's intolerance was intensified by their need to survive the demanding frontier environment. They guarded their own safety and that of their children very closely, and as the primary providers of food and clothing for their families, they fiercely resented any possible incursions upon their limited supplies. While on the Oregon trail in 1853, Charlotte Pengra wrote plaintively, "I always have to improve every moment of time when not traveling to provide enough to eat."[91] Most western women had to work very hard to maintain even an adequate level of provisions for themselves and their dependents. Therefore, American Indians, as potential threats to both their safety and their resources, often seemed to many women to be their first and most obvious foes.[92]

Added to these anxieties was women's basic ignorance of American Indian customs. When they came to the frontier, women knew little about native standards of hospitality that demanded a token gift from strangers traveling through their territory.[93] Thus, many women were irked to find that Indians were, in Sarah Royce's words of 1849, "evidently desirous of getting something out of us if they could."[94] Early in the westward trek, complaints were numerous against Indian groups who supposedly begged and stole from the whites. Phrases such as "thieving people," "somewhat troublesome," and "troubled by beggin Indians" appeared many times in women's writings.[95]

135

Although Indians often asked for sugar, meat, flour, coffee, other foodstuffs, and tobacco, it apparently took a long time for frontiers-women to begin to question why once self-sufficient groups were in such economic straits or to attempt to understand Indian ideas of hospitality. Instead, they were often inclined to see Indians as sly, disgusting, or pesky.[96] One women caustically wrote, "They are the greatest beggars I ever saw. I do wonder if they are hungry."[97] Other women were even more stinging in their remarks. "The better Indians come to camp to pay us a visit," Mary Jane Guill wrote in 1860. "Always stay till after supper I suppose it is fashionable for them to stay."[98] In 1864, Mallie Stafford scoffed: "Two large powerfully built warriors, in all the glory of red paint, buckskin, beads, feathers, dignity and general magnificence, condescended to honor our humble camp with a call—a call long enough to eat up and devour everything we had cooked, that being an immense pot of beans and bacon."[99]

Women's accounts were not only punctuated with references to begging natives but were also filled with scathing indictments of such behavior.[100] In addition, many female observers were convinced that native Americans were not only "born beggars" but were "awful thieves" as well.[101] From the Pawnees to the Sioux to the "Diggers," Indians were reputed to "steal anything they can lay their hands on."[102] It particularly annoyed many women that Indians seemed so intent upon running off stock vital to the lives and livelihoods of frontier people. Notations regularly appeared in women's journals that referred to their concerns regarding the safety of their horses, mules, cattle, and sheep. Women frequently expressed the fear that a particular group of Indians was eyeing their animals.[103] It was an accepted part of trail lore that wagons must be circled to form a corral for protecting the animals and that guards must be posted because the Indians would steal the animals if given "half a chance."[104] Even at the trail's end, vigilance could not be relaxed. Both males and females were posted to guard barns, outbuildings, and fields, lying in fence corners at night in order to thwart the incursions of stock-hunting American Indians.[105]

Women evidently remained oblivious to rituals involving horses in many Indian cultures.[106] Although women could compliment them-selves on their own sharp deals or "good buys" in their trading with the Indians, they failed to see any validity in the Indians' attitudes toward white belongings. Instead, it was frequently assumed that

Indians were out to bedevil emigrants and settlers, that they were drunk, or that they were simply compulsive thieves.[107] On the occasions when Indians assisted white people in retrieving their stock or when they returned wandering stock to whites, the migrants were quite often skeptical of such benevolent actions. "That they were honest enough to be bringing the lost horses to us we could hardly believe," remarked one young trail woman.[108]

Clearly, women's anti-Indian prejudices were not rapidly diffused. Westering women, convinced of their own moral mission to these "depraved" Indians, were hesitant to part with their preconceptions about America's native population. Whether curious, amused, or decidedly negative in their views of American Indians, women were not to be easily dissuaded from the soundness of those views. Combined with women's convictions about white superiority, such stubbornness helped to create a situation in which it was very difficult for women to see native Americans as legitimate human beings. As one woman so tellingly remarked in 1853, she and her party never tired of watching the Indians, for "they were equal to a circus in interest to us."[109] This woman was not the first to condescendingly compare Indians to performers in a carnival or in some other form of entertaining show. It is interesting to note, however, that had the Indians been consulted about their feelings in the matter, they would probably have also compared the white invaders to show people. Many Indians spent hours in gazing through the doors and windows of white homes, churches, wagons, and other structures. To many westering women, however, this habit was just one more disconcerting and vexing characteristic of natives who already seemed to be pretty worthless people.[110]

But this picture of women's negative perceptions of American Indians is incomplete and thus inaccurate. While so many frontierswomen were recording disparaging and even vitriolic descriptions of the natives they encountered, they were also pointing out, often in lavish and extravagantly generous terms, some attractive qualities of Indian peoples. In a sense, it seems paradoxical that women who appeared to be so intent upon casting Indians as evil, criminal, and primitive could simultaneously recognize the presence of a number of positive qualities in natives. Of course, whites generally tended to detect both favorable and unfavorable qualities, or "good" and "bad" sides, in native Americans; women, however, had their own particular motives for viewing Indians in this way. It is conceivable that white women's view of themselves as inferior in certain respects to men apparently influenced them to search for some superior qualities in the Indians they met. Because they had been taught to think of themselves as weak, helpless, and incapable of protecting themselves, many women seemed to feel dependent on the nobility and strength of character of the "primitive savage" for their ultimate survival. Although their own men could defend them to some degree from the western environment and its inhabitants, it was the Indians, in the last analysis, who would decide whether or not to destroy women through thievery, sexual assault, or outright warfare. Therefore, many frontierswomen were inclined to seek out a glimmer of nobility, a hint of kindness, or an indication of intelligence in the native peoples they confronted. Thus, despite their negative judgments, many women could also cite certain positive aspects in the physical appearance, character, and customs of some Indian people; and this tendency created many contradictory portraits of American Indians in frontierswomen's writings.

Even those women who were the most malevolent in describing the ugliness, filth, and odor of some Indians would, at the same time, characterize other natives with such phrases as "an imposing sight in the wilderness," "good-looking," "fine-looking," and "noble-looking."[111] Others depicted some Indians as "grave" and "stately," and "fine looking," with "the appearance of wealth and independence," or as "tall, strongly made," with "firm features, light copper color, cleanly in appearance, quite well dressed in red blankets."[112] A few women punctuated their derogatory remarks with words such as "industrious" and "intelligent." One woman spoke of "mannerly conduct" and "a degree of refinement" that she had not expected to find among "just Indians."[113] Still other women pointed out that in spite of possessing some unattractive qualities the Indians to whom they had been exposed were also honest, proud, and responsible people, who would not lie, steal, or cheat as many whites they had known would do.[114]

Some women were quick to praise individual instances of ability on the part of native Americans. Since the home was their own particular bailiwick, women were naturally very interested in the Indians' household arrangements. Consequently, they often commented upon both the interiors and exteriors of wigwams, wickiups, and teepees. Many of their observations were surprisingly positive in tone. Lucene Parsons thought that a particular Indian town with its underground wigwams exhibited immense ingenuity. In 1867, Denver settler Emma Hill said that a nearby Ute wigwam village constituted a "pretty picture."[115] Other women emphasized the cleanliness of Indian dwellings. Esther Hanna, for example, admitted that she found a wigwam that she visited "more comfortable" than she had anticipated.[116] Hanna was also impressed with Indian handiwork, which she maintained was of a surprisingly high quality.[117] Lodisa Frizzell also regarded the needlework produced by the native women whom she visited as the finest and most beautiful that she had ever seen. "I must say that nicer work with a needle I never saw," she declared, "or any thing more beautiful, it looked like sattin, & was finely ornamented with various colored beeds."[118] Like Frizzell, many women were so taken with the fine Indian beaded bags, moccasins, and shawls that they became popular items of exchange between white and native women.[119]

Unfortunately, women seldom recorded their reactions to childbirth and child care practices among native Americans. Whether they did not have the opportunity to observe them or whether they felt such topics were improper to mention is unclear. Occasional mention *was* made of the love extended to Indian children, and women also remarked on the high standards of behavior that Indian parents expected from their children.[120] Susan Magoffin complimented American Indian women for bathing themselves and their infants immediately after giving birth. "No doubt many ladies in civilized life are ruined by too careful treatments during child-birth," she suggested.[121] For the most part, however, the topic of native children was not explored very fully.

Numerous women commented that when natives expressed personal warmth it was directed not only toward their children but toward everyone within their presence. A large number of frontierswomen who were highly critical of Indians also thought that they possessed the basic humanity to respond to fair treatment from the whites. Respect, courtesy, friendliness, and willingness to share food with the Indians were credited by many women as important factors that guaranteed the safe passage of their party.[122] Lavinia Porter particularly believed in the value of such an approach:

> Evidently our hospitality and courteous treatment won their hearts, for they showed no signs of hostility to us. In fact from their general

demeanor they rather inspired us with a confidence which seemed to sanction our presence in their midst.[123]

Moreover, some women began to blame whites, particularly men, instead of natives for "Indian troubles." In their view, whites too often treated kindly Indians in an unfair or exploitive manner. Showing her obvious sympathy for the Indians, Mary Hopping bitterly called two men, who had paid an irate Indian counterfeit money for moccasins, "smarties." She was also contemptuous of a young woman who had asked for a scalp as a trophy from an Indian-hunting expedition.[124] Similarly, Lavinia Porter claimed that she remonstrated in vain with the men of her party who teased and played tricks on visiting Indians.[125] In another instance, Pauline Wonderly empathized with displaced natives by criticizing male emigrants who refused to pay a "reasonable" toll to Indians who had constructed a bridge across the Elk Horn River. In the fight which ensued, eleven Indians were killed. Later parties, she prophesied, would have to pay for the "meanness of the men of that train."[126] Selling guns and ammunition to Indians was believed by some women to be another offense for which later parties of emigrants and settlers would eventually suffer.[127]

Evidently, women were willing and able to express some positive feelings toward American Indians. Prevailing beliefs about women's physical weakness seemed to encourage them to look for benign rather than savage qualities in the people who inhabited the western regions that they were invading. Thus, while their supposed moral powers encouraged them to see Indians as depraved beings in need of reform and rehabilitation, women's physical weakness led them to seek out qualities of goodness and nobility. The apparent ambivalence of many women toward Indians, which resulted from such dualistic thinking, was illustrated by Ada Vogdes, an army wife at Fort Laramie in the late 1860s. She filled her journal with the expression "frightened to death." She was awakened by imaginary Indian whoops during the night, mistook two drunken cooks for a native American uprising, and repeatedly declined her husband's invitations to explore the area surrounding the fort. Yet, when a dramatic Indian false alarm was followed by a council that brought Indian leaders into camp, she noticed that Red Cloud had a "pleasant smile," adding that Big Bear had "the most splendid chest, and shoulders, I ever laid my eyes upon." She thought that Red Leaf had "a fatherly looking countenance,

& one to whom you would go in trouble, were we in different circumstances." Although she remained in "constant fear" whenever she left the fort, she began to enjoy her position as "a *belle* amongst the red men of the Plains."

When Vogdes moved to Fort Fetterman she complained, "This frontier life is terrible for a nervous excitable person as I am, and it seems as if I could not endure it much longer. For nearly two years the Indians have been the bane of my existence." At Fetterman, she thought a soldier returning tardily from a laundress's quarters was an attacking Indian, and she shuddered with fear at the sight of Cheyenne Indians outside her windows. Yet when American Indian leaders came into the fort, she was again impressed by them. She said of Red Dog that he "had nothing on but the skin in which he was born . . . I never saw such shoulders, arms, & legs, & hands . . . his legs were equally fine looking." After sitting with him at a small table, she explained that it would seem strange to an easterner to see her with "this naked man," but it did not seem strange to her at all. "I am not shocked if I see them with no clothes on" she added. [128]

Such contradictory assessments and reactions by frontierswomen toward American Indians was not simply a result of what they had been taught about the two-sided natures of both women and Indians. Paradoxically, it was also a product of the gradual *erosion* of those attitudes. First of all, women were experiencing a change in their views of themselves. They were learning that their supposed ability to civilize was only one of a myriad of skills demanded of them by the relatively unsettled land that they now inhabited. Moreover, they discovered that nothing disastrous would happen either to them or to their immediate society if they could not fully exercise the role of cultural conservator. They washed clothes on the Sabbath, listened to oaths, came into contact with gambling, drinking, and polygamy; yet life went on. Under these circumstances, frontierswomen quickly realized that their value to society was not eroding but, instead, was taking a new direction. Thus, many women in the trans-Mississippi West quickly developed new functions and roles that involved them in driving teams, performing trail work, walking for miles over rough terrain, handling weapons, participating in decision making, and making significant economic contributions. [129]

Given the emergence of these new strengths and abilities in response to western life, many women began to suspect that the inferior portion of their nature was no more rockbound than the superior portion was proving to be. Women's inferiority was refuted by too many cases of western women who grew strong, assertive, and confident in their own talents and skills. Many women began to believe that they might play some role after all in shaping their own lives, in protecting themselves and their children, and in determining their ultimate survival in the West. If, then, women were not of value primarily as moral forces there was no longer such a pressing need for them to emphasize the inferior aspects of Indian character. And if women were not really weak or incompetent there was also little need for them to depend on the superior aspects of Indian character for protection. Women who had found that they could drive two-thousand-pound wagons, effectively wield rifles, and survive other rigors of westering no longer desperately needed to seek protection through an idealized vision of "noble" natives.

Secondly, these changes in women's views of themselves opened their eyes and minds to a more humane exchange with the American Indians they encountered, and the result was a growing awareness on the part of many frontierswomen that actual Indians were neither as "good" nor as "bad" as they had thought. As women began to see Indians as people like themselves, they gradually rejected their former interpretation of natives as a strange and unlikely combination of the terribly savage and the wonderfully noble. As a result, numerous women's narratives began to reflect a more balanced view of white and native peoples caught in a complex, tense, and potentially explosive situation.

Lavinia Porter, for example, recounted the usual tales of begging Indians who were infested with vermin, lazy native men who expected women to do all the work, and degraded American Indians who possessed low moral standards. Like Vogdes, she was frequently "speechless with fright," suffering extreme anxiety in her exposure to the "dangers of savage life." Yet increasingly interspersed with these statements were Porter's remarks about helpful and kindly natives. When an Indian returned the Porters' wandering cattle, Lavinia mused, "It truly seemed to us in our long journeys traveling alone that the Indians watched over us." At another point, she mentioned that an Indian had traveled with them for three days as a scout and guide, concluding that this "went to prove that there was honor among these savage tribes of the wilderness" after all. [130]

Pioneer family with covered wagon. White women were responsible for caring for their families both physically and emotionally although their "home" was now a small, crowded wagon. (Courtesy Museum of New Mexico, neg. no. 15069.)

Letter, newspaper account, clothing remnant, and portrait of Mrs. R. F. (Clara) Blinn, captured by Indians in Arkansas. Captivity narratives and newspaper accounts of Indian attacks played an important part in white women's attitudes toward American Indians. (Courtesy Museum of New Mexico, neg. no. 108329.)

Individually colored Fashion Plates from *Godey's Lady's Book* (1840). Although women on the frontier retained an interest in popular fashions, their changing roles led them to modify their costumes.

American Indian woman with travois, Calgary, Canada. White women often reacted with amusement and derision to Indian modes of transportation. (Keystone View Co., courtesy Museum of New Mexico, neg. no. 90571.)

Apache camp scene, circa 1885. Disappointed at not finding the "noble savage" of myth, many white women's initial impression of Indian living arrangements was one of poverty, filth, and degradation. (Ben Wittick, courtesy Museum of New Mexico, neg. no. 89917.)

Indians of the Miwok tribe. Under the appelation of "diggers," these American Indians were almost universally despised by whites because of their subsistence-level existence. (Keystone View Co., courtesy Museum of New Mexico, neg. no. 89917.)

Pawnee Indians and their wind lodges, circa, 1868–1870. (William H. Jackson, courtesy Museum of New Mexico, neg. no. 58632.)

Frontier dwelling, home of A. F. Miller, south of Bloomfield, N.M., near San Juan River, circa 1885. Despite such crude homes, women settlers had to carry on their duties as wives, mothers, and domestic artisans. (Courtesy Museum of New Mexico, neg. no. 14659.)

Similarly, Harriet Ward not only overcame her own dread of Indians, but she maintained that many other women had experienced a similar reaction. "I have conversed with many ladies," she declared, "and they all appear happy and in good health." At one point, Ward did admit that she felt uneasy knowing that "hostile" Indians "infested" the mountains, and at another time, she remarked that a few Indian groups she met seemed "wild," "miserable," and "not to be trusted." Yet she felt confident enough in American Indians generally to not lose any sleep over the matter. "We encamped beside the mountain, with not a living being near us except the Indians, who, they say, are watching all our movements," she declared. "We staked our horses near the tent," she went on, "and all laid ourselves down to sleep, which we enjoyed nicely."[131]

Army wives serve as a particularly good illustration of how white women grew to understand American Indians as their contacts with them increased and improved. Army women lived every moment under the threat of attack and the possibility of losing their husbands. They often survived bloody and mind-numbing Indian wars, and they were by affinity and marital relationship committed to subduing native populations. Therefore, their goodwill, affection, and sympathy toward native Americans are rather surprising. Despite the death of her first husband, killed in the Fetterman "massacre," Frances Carrington expressed sympathy for the Indians who had been forced to give away the hunting grounds upon which their lives depended. Margaret Carrington, whose husband commanded Fort Phil Kearney during the conflict, supported Frances in her interpretation of the events.[132] According to one recent study of the sentiments of army wives, even Elizabeth Custer became unsure of her position regarding Indians. She sympathetically related the story of the Battle of the Washita to a friend, who wrote that "it confused my sense of justice. Doubtless the white men were right, but were the Indians entirely wrong? After all these broad prairies had belonged to them."[133]

The wife of Orsemus Bronson Boyd also changed her mind about American Indians. Stationed at Camp Halleck, Nevada, in the mid-1860s, she was so regularly exposed to large numbers of Paiute and Shoshone Indians that she wrote, "I soon regarded red men as fearlessly as if I had been accustomed to them all my life." They too were interested in her and paid her long visits. They would often devote the entire day to watching her and her family. When she attended a native dance, she noticed that the dancers became so caught up in the performance that they returned to what she described as "their original savage natures." Yet, on reflection, she decided that these Indians were always so friendly to her that she could not really think of them as "savages." Thus, she added, her positive attitude helped her to avoid the overwhelming sense of terror "which has made life so hard for many army ladies."[134]

As frontierswomen began to recognize aspects of their own humanity and fallibility along with those of the Indians, their remarks about native Americans frequently became more gentle and kind in tone. Contradiction and ambivalence often gave way to warmth and even expressions of affection. As women became more balanced and realistic in their attitudes, they also came to the realization that there was no such concept as "Indian." Individually and gradually, women grew to discriminate between types of Indians, to realize that different groups possessed different qualities, and to reject the image of "Indian" as one amorphous collection of people. Women's journals almost always recorded the sighting of their very first Indians, but eventually they turned to more specific descriptions learning to specify, for example, that "we are now in the Pawnee nation" or that "we are now in the Sioux nation."[135]

As women learned to discriminate between Indians, they grew to dislike some groups while reacting favorably to others. The Pawnees of the Platte River country were frequently judged to be the most troublesome of all Indian tribes.[136] Reputed to be beggars and thieves, the Pawnees were considered by some women to be "one of the most dangerous of hostile tribes."[137] The Sioux, on the other hand, who were encountered farther along the northern trails to California and Oregon, were often viewed as the most handsome and the cleanest of all American Indians. They were described as "a fine intelligent looking race," a tall and athletic people who were "friendly to the whites."[138] While traveling toward California from Iowa in 1852, Lucy Cooke noted that the Sioux were "a noble-looking tribe . . . so well dressed; such gay trappings on them and their ponies, and beautiful beaded work they wear." During the same year, Lodisa Frizzell judged them to be the "best looking" Indians she had seen, explaining that they were "tall, strongly made, firm features, light copper color, cleanly in appearance."[139]

The Cheyennes also elicited some compliments concerning their intelligence, wealth, and stalwart appearance.[140] But when women encountered the so-called Digger Indians of the Plains region, the tone of their remarks usually became hostile. They almost universally agreed that the Diggers, given this name because of their custom of digging up roots for food, were the most loathsome of all native American tribes.[141] Elizabeth Ward described them as "repulsive creatures, squatty, dark and greasy."[142] When Lydia Waters spied her first Digger Indians she exclaimed that "greater brutes nature never made." She went on to say:

> They had never cut their hair which was full of sticks, dried grass and dirt, and their heads looked as large as bushel baskets for their hair stuck out straight. Their bellies were tremendous from eating so much when they could get it. They were very saucy and would have taken the guns out of the wagons in spite of all the women could do.[143]

Evaluations of other Indian groups along the many trails and their "cut-offs" were varied. The Bannock Indians were said to possess countenances that were "fine and some of them even intelligent." The "Piute" Indians "were fine looking" but not to be trusted, according to Harriet Ward.[144] The "Kioose," in Esther Hanna's view, were "intelligent, finely formed, well clad and very cleanly."[145] To Mary Pelham, the "Pima, Papgo, Maricopa," and Yuma Indians were the most interesting.[146] Helen Carpenter saw the "Puitahs" as friendly, but the Shoshone as aggressive and combative.[147] Harriet Bunyard found the "Lemore" Indians "detestable" and the "Maricopis" an "ignorant, silly looking people."[148] An early Texas settler, Mary Maverick, discovered the Tonkawa Indians to be treacherous and cruel. And a woman traveling along the Platte River felt honored to be able to give the chief of the Otoe tribe, "a very fine looking man," a loaf of bread.[149]

Considering the range of women's comments about various tribes and nations of native Americans, it is clear that they grew to recognize that all Indians were not alike. Frontierswomen also began to realize that natives not only varied from tribe to tribe but also from one region to another and from one era to the next. For instance, a group of once peaceful American Indians might have experienced the ravages of white migration so thoroughly by the 1860s that they became belligerent.[150] Lucy Sexton maintained that when her family moved to California in the mid-1850s "the Indians were peaceable all along the route, and we had no such contentions as later travelers over the same route did."[151] Mary Pelham claimed that there was a difference in both time periods and trails. She believed that the northern route was safer than the southern one that they followed on their way from Texas to California in the early 1850s. She also voiced a common complaint about changes among Indian groups: "How these Indians have changed. Not simple and childlike any more. Until that year (1853) very few had ever seen a white man and seldom a white woman or child. They never tired of watching us and our ways of living."[152]

In some cases, time improved Indian-white relations. During the late 1850s and the early 1860s, near San Francisco the natives were said to be peaceable, seldom causing settlers the trouble that was reported to be occurring in the interior portion of the country.[153] By 1867, Cynthia Capron, an army wife, said that most of these Indians were now settled on a reservation, where they were "very industrious for Indians," cultivating "a large farm of several thousand acres, and very well too."[154] In the Mount Hood region of Oregon, the Indians, particularly the Flatheads and Nez Perces, were also considered to be friendly, good looking, well clad, and clean.[155] In the late 1860s, Montana settler Mary Hopping maintained that when the Flathead and Nez Perce Indians came through on their way to hunt buffalo "everyone was glad to see them."[156]

But modifications in American Indian behavior did not always promote smooth Indian-white relations. When the Indians' changing behavior proved detrimental to peace with the whites, some women began to argue sympathetically that the problems were caused by the growing force of white population on the frontier. They believed that this pressure compelled native American groups to wage war with each other over dwindling resources as well as to make violent attempts to stem white incursions.[157] Kate Furness explained that when she encountered her first Indians just across the Missouri River they were engaged in a war with the Sioux, who had "encroached on their hunting-grounds and killed the buffalo."[158] Other women pointed to the pernicious effect of "renegade whites," who not only "incited" the Indians but also stole stock and then blamed the Indians for it.[159]

Clearly, there is much evidence in women's own accounts that many of them modified or radically altered the harsh conceptions of American Indians that they had brought with them on the trail west. Many women moved from hate and fear to warmth and sympathy. The writings women left behind also suggest that they did not fulfill the widely accepted image of inept and cowering creatures intimidated by vicious, marauding, and sexually abusive natives. Their words indicate that actual relations between themselves and natives was, for the most part, very unlike the dramatic, conflict-filled confrontations commonly portrayed by nineteenth- and even twentieth-century informants. How women really acted in their dealings with American Indians thus appears to be vastly different from the story that was usually told.

In order to explore this contention that many women's relations with American Indians were actually far less negative than they were usually assumed to be, a sample of 150 diaries, journals, memoirs, and letters was assembled. These documents represent most trans-Mississippi areas, the primary eras, and the thought and experiences of a variety of types of women. When the reactions to Indians that they document were studied and counted, it was discovered that 113 writers recorded no trouble whatsoever with native peoples, 22 noted minor problems, and only 15 reported major difficulties.[160] Although it is not very scientific or sophisticated, this rudimentary data provides just enough evidence to seriously question once more the image of the victimized white woman and her predatory native enemy. When woman after woman employs the phrase "no trouble with Indians" in their diaries, letters, or memoirs, one begins to suspect that there may well be another version of relations between white women and native Americans other than the one usually presented through myth and the media.[161] As a case in point, Ada Millington concluded her travel diary with the assertion: "Our journey has been as prosperous, with as little trouble as we expected. No Indian difficulties to speak of, and our stock was not stolen or lost."[162]

Yet both myth and the media have continued to promote the idea that white women and American Indians were at loggerheads more often than not. Violent confrontations that did harm frontierswomen have been emphasized, and Indians have too often been portrayed as barbarous natives who pillaged, burned, and raped whenever possible. A survey of nineteenth-century novels, poetry, drama, tracts, textbooks, newspapers, magazines, sermons, and lectures supports the traditional picture of the weak and victimized white woman and the fierce and rapacious American Indian. The widespread popularity of the captivity narrative was perhaps the best illustration of this point. Unfortunately, twentieth-century myth and media have also tended to perpetuate the customary view rather than to question and to reassess it. Television programs, for example, still deal to a large extent in circled wagons, flaming arrows, captured children, and violated women.

Was this view concocted to entertain an anti-Indian white audience while reconfirming the prejudices of that audience? This was clearly not the entire explanation, for there were indeed many actual instances of violence and disaster involving women and Indians in the trans-Mississippi West. For example, Texas in the mid-nineteenth century is the setting for a tragic drama filled with horror stories based upon the clashes of white and native peoples. Beginning with the memoirs of one of the earliest women to settle in Texas, Mary Maverick, the drama that unfolds is one of tragic misunderstanding and armed confrontation. Maverick relates early troubles between the Tonkawa Indians and the settlers. Then she proceeds to give a full description of the eruptions between the Comanches and the whites extending through the 1830s and into the 1840s. As she recounted many violent incidents, including the stories of white captives, Maverick was moved to exclaim that Texas Indians were "cruel and relentless savages" who "daily committed atrocities about us."[163] In a similar vein, Mary Rabb, an Indian Hill settler, maintained that in many years, and especially in 1835, the Texas Indians were so troublesome that whites had to go to nearby La Grange to "fort up."[164] The reminiscences of Elizabeth Owens also indicted the Comanches during the 1840s. Mary Locklin referred to the Texas natives as "red fiends" who interfered with the emigrants' "work of improvement" by "hatching their deviltry" and coming "down upon them without warning, burning their houses, killing stock, destroying property, and murdering defenseless women and children."[165]

Texan Martha Simmons wrote a narrative of a regrettable conflict with the Comanches in 1839, in which her father was killed and she, her brother, and her mother were taken captive. She recorded the way the "devils" tortured her and her mother until they were able to escape in 1840.[166] A similar chronicle by Rosalie Priour detailed a series of attacks and "atrocities" perpetrated by Texas Indians against settlers in the Corpus Christi area until well into the 1850s.[167] Julia Sinks added that not only were the various Texas tribes "demons" but that the Comanches, in particular, were cannibals—a charge that Maverick also included in her reminiscences.[168]

Throughout the 1850s, Texas women—Martha Gray, Eugenie Lavender, and Mary Baylor—reported that raids by the Tonkawa, Caddo, and Comanche Indians kept them in a constantly upset state.[169] Jonaphrene Faulkner explained that many such troubles occurred because the "Commanches had resisted all advances of the white man looking to their subjugation or control and roamed free and vindictive still, and blood thirsty, upon the far western plains."[170]

During the 1860s there was little abatement of difficulties between the native and the newly arrived populations in Texas. Susan Newcomb, an early Texas settler, recorded that the Indians were "thick and plenty and trying to brake our country." The tension in the situation drove her to lament her presence in "this country" and to express a desire to flee from it. "It was made for the wild Indians and buffalo," she noted in her diary. When some of the natives were captured after an Indian raid, she expressed the hope that all the native Americans in the area would soon be killed.[171] Ella Bird-Dumont was not quite so vicious as Newcomb, but she did endure so many Comanche problems in the panhandle region that at one point she almost shot her own husband as a result of her fear of attack.[172]

According to other women's narratives, such troubles continued in parts of Texas well into the 1870s. One woman maintained that "the Indians would often come down on raids during moonlight nights." Another said that in 1872 her family moved into town to escape altercations with Jack County natives.[173] During the same years, May Tansill reacted with great bitterness to the continuing conflicts between whites and American Indians. "I know the Indians have been unjustly treated and I have a great deal of sympathy for them," she wrote, "but I haven't quite so much sentiment concerning them as I had before I came here and learned so much about their cruelty and depredations."[174]

Relations between Texas settlers and native groups seemed to improve slightly during the 1880s. One woman, who migrated to Montague County in 1889, was able to live without incident near her Creek and Comanche neighbors. "We had no truck with them to speak of," she explained, "they let us alone and we let them alone."[175] But a woman who moved in 1890 to Indian Territory in Texas soon became disgusted with the unpredictable Choctaw Indians. According to her, Indian officers who had been appointed to keep the peace afforded the settlers little protection from Choctaws because "Choctaw Beer" made "them both drunk and crazy." By 1891, her family decided to relocate in the relatively saner and more stable Oklahoma area.[176] Furthermore, Mary Parker recalled that many Texas families caught Oklahoma fever about this time and moved there rather than live in fear of "mean and treacherous" Indians such as the Cheyennes and the Potawatomis.[177]

This overview of Texas women settlers demonstrates that disharmony and violence did occur between many women and Indians. The image of the frightened white woman, lying awake at night in her wagon and overcome by fear regarding her chances of surviving the trail because of antagonistic American Indians, was not a fabrication. Nor was the portrait of the disillusioned woman, less than happy with her new frontier home because of conflicts with the land's previous owners, imagined or invented.[178] Many accounts tell of both relatively minor violent interchanges and major confrontations throughout the frontier, from Minnesota and Iowa to Montana, Wyoming, Colorado, and New Mexico and extending into the Far West.[179] Numerous trail narratives also record the occurrence of both minor and major clashes between migrants and the natives whose lands they were invading.[180]

A closer examination of many of the chronicles, however, indicates that American Indians were usually interested primarily in livestock rather than in human lives.[181] Time after time, frontier people's records explain that Indians wanted horses and cattle, not captives or scalps.[182] In 1863, for example, while moving to California, Mattie Walker mentioned that the "men were kept on the alert on account of Indians who made several attempts to drive the stock off."[183] In referring to West Texas in the 1870s, Mary Jane Bell insisted that "the Indians didn't molest anybody, as all they seemed to want was to steal the horses."[184] Native forays on white people's livestock sometimes grew into calamitous events in the history of western settlement, but more frequently they simply presented one more type of difficulty to be surmounted.[185] As one historian of the West, John Unruh, pointed out, "almost everyone did complete the trip safely."[186] A significant number of settlers also survived unharmed what they commonly termed the Indian "threat" to their new western homes.

Although instances of coercion and mistreatment did occur, there is more to the story of women and Indians than conflict. One has only to turn to Oklahoma during the latter half of the nineteenth century to discover the other side of the story, which may be juxtaposed with the drama that occurred in Texas. Frontier Texas was characterized by warlike tribes, who stubbornly resisted white incursions into their hunting territories, and by a tradition of violent solutions to white-native problems. Texas women had little opportunity to alter their views of either themselves or of Indians. Kept in a nearly constant state of turmoil, they only occasionally developed a sense of understanding or a shred of sympathy for Indians.[187] In Oklahoma, however, women encountered the so-called Five Civilized Tribes, which included the Chickasaw, Cherokee, and Choctaw. A relatively peaceable manner of dealing with native-white problems prevailed in Oklahoma. Unlike Texas frontierswomen, Oklahoma women were able to adjust their perceptions of both themselves and their new neighbors.

Oklahoma women seemed to have arrived in the Indian Territory with the same kinds and degrees of anti-Indian prejudice that so many other women carried to the frontier. A great many women related their initial dread that, as one woman phrased it, the "Indians would kill us and scalp us and that they were bad people."[188] This woman, as well as many other Oklahoma women, eventually described her native American neighbors as lovely people. To her, they were honest and hard-working citizens, and she rated them among some of the "warmest friends" she had ever known.[189] Some Oklahoma women who were at first "scared to death" and anticipated losing their scalps eventually became "intermarried citizens" by marrying native men.[190]

Recollections by Oklahoma frontierswomen are thus significant illustrations of the process of change experienced by so many women in their perceptions of themselves and American Indians. Despite their initial terror, they came to feel confident enough to attend native dances, cries, and other ceremonies. In addition, they often became fast friends with American Indians. At least one woman felt that the Indians "were the dearest people in the world."[191] It was not uncommon for Oklahoma women to establish pleasant and friendly relationships with their Indian neighbors. Women of the 1880s, for example, recalled that some of their best friends were Indians; they exchanged medical care with them and taught them English and farming methods. As one Oklahoma settler said, the Indians "acted friendly and

159

we found that they were as good as we were and couldn't help liking them."[192] Only occasionally were such attitudes offset by a female settler who continued to fear American Indians and to think that they were "nasty" people.[193]

As a result of the big land rushes in Oklahoma during the early 1890s, scores of white settlers placed additional pressure on the land-holdings of the native population. Yet recollections of amicable relations still dominated women's accounts. These women remembered exchanging visits with Indians, feeling safe with them, admiring their honesty, and lacking any fear of them.[194] Others recalled sharing schools, towns, and reservation lands with them in a spirit of peace and friendship.[195] Only a few women thought that American Indians were wild, had peculiar habits, or were fearsome.[196] Rarer yet were the women who remembered "uprisings" and "massacres."[197] One such woman pointed out that although some native Americans may have even scalped people "at one time" they quickly became "civilized." In her words, "the Indians were sure mean those days but later became our friends."[198] Another Oklahoma woman who migrated to the area as late as 1901 noted that, as with white people, the quality of relations really depended upon the individual native in question. She recalled that her area had only one "bad" Indian, one who drank too much and terrorized the settlers. Most of them were very nice people, she continued, particularly a "fullblood" Chickasaw woman who was her "neighbor and the best friend" she ever had.[199]

The positive outlook of Oklahoma frontierswomen does not stand alone in the writings of western women. There were numerous other cases of women who could express positive feelings despite the continuing presence of the Indian "menace" and other related "hardships." Some spiritedly declared, as did Lucene Parsons, that "we have some fine times with all our troubles."[200] In 1853, a single woman traveling to Oregon with a train insisted that such a trip had a "refining and ennobling influence."[201] And Harriet Ward maintained:

> Indeed I think what is often termed suffering is merely a little inconvenience, for I had so often read and heard of the difficulties and dangers of the overland route to California, and I find from experience that the pleasure thus far quite overbalances it all.[202]

It is significant that many women actually slept very soundly despite their convictions about the ever-present threat of Indian attack.[203] In 1853, Oregon-bound emigrant Helen Love admitted that she feared the Indians, but, she said, "I was not so afraid as to keep me from sleeping."[204] In 1859, Catherine Bell stated that although the Indians were "very bad" she could sleep as well as she could in her own home.[205] And even after viewing the ghastly sight of a scalped Pawnee with four or five arrows implanted in his dead body, Frances Sawyer wrote, "Morpheus cozily wrapped us all in his arms last night, and the pleasant dreams of our faraway Kentucky home were not disturbed by the Indians, dead or alive."[206] Yet another woman added that she slept quite well but always with an ax by her side, a weapon that she never had occasion to use on an Indian.[207]

Numerous other frontierswomen's sources illustrate other changes in their thinking about American Indians. Some who began by admitting that they were "very much scared" progressed to infrequent and casual mention of Indians.[208] Allene Dunham, who crossed the plains to California in 1864, began the trip by curling up tightly in her short bed because she feared that the Indians would cut off her feet if they protruded from the wagon's confines. She concluded the journey by saying that she had greatly enjoyed her frequent visits to Indians camps.[209] Yet others not only rejected the negative ideas that had once been almost gospel to them, but they even grew to be amused by such thoughts. For instance, Carrie Strahorn, after traveling safely throughout the West with her journalist husband in the 1870s, derided the beliefs held by people east of the Mississippi River. She found it unthinkable that they saw life "on the other side" as composed only of hardship, danger, bandits, and "rubbing elbows with the slayers of Custer."[210] Still other women described their move from apprehensiveness to the development of a mutual confidence between themselves and native Americans. Some even became involved in friendships with Indians that meant more to them than white friendships.

Caroline Phelps, the wife of an Indian trader on the border of Illinois and Iowa between 1830 and 1860, provided an interesting illustration of the change that was possible. She began her life among the Indians by being greatly perturbed about their drinking, terrorized by the thought that they would rob her, and extremely distressed by their fighting among themselves. After a series of personal disasters and illnesses that she survived through a combination of her own fortitude and aid from various Indians, Phelps began to see herself and American Indians through different eyes. As a result, she gained enough confidence to attend native dances and other ceremonies. When her sister visited from Dubuque, Phelps persuaded her that there was no reason to be afraid or to feel in danger while attending an Indian dance. Phelps also called upon an Indian doctor for help and hired an Indian male nurse for her children. After an 1838 violent upheaval among the native Americans in the region, she simply stated that she was glad to "have peace & quietness again after so much howling in the wilderness, if we always had to live as I have for three weeks past I could not stay in the indian country, but I never was very much afraid of them." When John, her children's native nurse, died, she claimed that they mourned him as though he had been a member of the family.[211]

Many years later, another woman, Hilda Faunce, also the wife of an Indian trader, moved with no small amount of trepidation to a Navajo reservation in the Arizona desert. Feeling both superior and scared, she initially branded the residents as primitive, heathen, and immoral. She believed that they were liars, beggars, thieves, and drunkards.[212] After some time, however, she discovered that she had come to admire the Navajo people and to feel comfortable in her role on the reservation. "As the months passed," she wrote,

> I learned to respect the way the Navajos made the most of an arid, rocky land; I admired their architecture; the design of the blankets and the skill and sincerity in carrying it out were real art. As a rule they were industrious; the lazy and the indigent were less common than among whites. Their religion was wholesome and clean and their respect for their belief compared favorably with the white man's attitude toward his God.[213]

Faunce came to blame Navajo problems on the willingness of white men to supply the Indians with liquor. "Why do we try to thrust our civilization on a people like this?" she lamented.[214] As the time approached to leave the reservation for a ranch, she declared that she was glad to be free of the Indians, of whom she was heartily tired. Yet when the moment of actual parting arrived she was not happy.

"I had not realized that we had woven so many threads of friendship that it hurt to break them," she explained. "I stopped often to think that in all my life these four years were the most isolated and the most colorful."[215]

Like these traders' wives, military wives also often moved from misgivings to warmth in their relations with American Indians. According to historian Sandra L. Myres, these women arrived at their husbands' frontier posts filled with the usual misconceptions about American Indians. But, like so many other frontierswomen, they became more open and receptive toward native peoples. With time, Eveline Alexander discovered that the Navajo were not after all, as she had thought, a stolid, humorless people. Martha Summerhayes came to regard her Indian servants as quick learners as well as responsible and conscientious workers.[216] Alice Baldwin was another army wife who drastically changed her ideas regarding Indians. She aided several Indian captives, who she described as "pitiful creatures," and she firmly believed that even friendly Indians were not to be trusted. Eventually, however, she formed friendships with some Indian women, praised the sincerity of the native culture and value system, and described Chief Joseph as a "wonderful Indian."[217]

Another military wife, the timid and fearful Ada Vogdes, provides one of the outstanding examples of the process of changing attitudes experienced by so many frontierswomen. In "constant fear" whenever she ventured from Fort Laramie and "frightened to death" at any little irregularity while inside its sheltering walls, she was certainly not a likely candidate to become a friend and supporter of the people that she thought of as dreaded enemies. Yet she eventually became a firm friend of the hated and feared warrior, Red Cloud. When he brought his warriors into the fort for peace negotiations, she judged them to be "young bold & dashing." She jotted in her diary: "A more exciting day . . . I never experienced. . . . It was a grand sight." She came to feel comfortable trading with and entertaining American Indians. She even began to boldly leave the fort for outings and horseback rides that she "enjoyed very much."[218]

It would be a distortion of the data to argue that *all* women changed their minds about either themselves or American Indians during their time on the trail or in a frontier settlement. Some women's documents cannot even be assessed because they mention native Americans only sporadically or not at all. Other sources, such as an individual letter or a half-kept diary, are too truncated to indicate any conversion in attitudes.[219] Furthermore, some women's sources clearly exhibit a *lack* of shift in their perspectives. For example, Californian Mary Staples and Oregonian Caroline Budlong both had ample opportunity to revise their views of themselves and to learn to know the many native peoples who lived around them during the 1850s. Yet both women came to think that Indians were nothing more than cruel, lazy, and unreliable beggars.[220] During the 1840s, Iowan Susan Willeford had the same opportunities, and she was exposed to fewer and less intrusive Indian neighbors. She too, however, continued to feel that, as far as she was concerned, natives "were seldom if ever very welcome visitors."[221]

Unfortunately, existing source materials, fragmented and scattered as they are, cannot support the extensive investigation that would be necessary to determine the circumstances that caused some women to change their attitudes while others remained firmly attached to their prejudices. It would be both fascinating and significant, for example, to know whether women who objected to the westward migration held more firmly to their prejudices than those who were willing to go. Place of origin, previous contact with Indians, age, marital status, ethnicity, race, and religion are other factors that may have affected women's views, but such matters have gone unrecorded—at least they are impossible to determine in any systematic way—in frontierswomen's writings.

Sources do illustrate, however, that there were numerous cases of women who *did* radically alter their opinions and beliefs. As these women became more realistic and confident about their own roles, contributions, and strengths, they became more secure and sympathetic in their relations with American Indians. In fact, there are enough of these cases demonstrating the process of change to raise grave doubts regarding the validity of the more usual image of beleaguered frontierswomen living in constant terror of marauding and savage Indians. The writings of these women indicate that all westering women were not routinely at odds with natives, nor were they regularly attacked or debauched by them.

If then, this traditional image of white women–native relations is not useful or accurate, what was the reality of the situation? If "rape, pillage, and burn" is not a key phrase in understanding the experience of frontierswomen and American Indians, then what is it? If women did not always play the role of victim in relation to Indians, could they perhaps have become friends and empathetic with American Indians? Rejecting myth is a necessary first step toward gaining some insight into the relationships that developed between many women and Indians in the trans-Mississippi West.

❦❧ 5 ❦❧

The Development of
Relationships with
American Indians

Because relations between whites and American Indians have not been examined in terms of gender, the assumption stands unchallenged that both white men and women played similar, if not identical, roles in their dealings with Indians. Once the issue of gender is introduced into the study of migration and settlement, however, it becomes apparent that men and women actually fulfilled different capacities in this and in almost every other facet of the westering experience. Both on the trail and in frontier settlements, men were charged with the care of the equipment and livestock, while women supervised the home and were responsible for children. Men who farmed produced the raw materials in their fields that their wives and daughters then converted into finished products in their houses or work places. Men who labored or managed businesses produced cash income instead of raw materials, yet they still depended upon women to function as domestic artisans.

Although men and women occasionally shared work or overlapping functions, the division of labor along the lines described was generally accepted. Applied to their associations with Indians, these labor assignments cast men into something of an adversary position with American Indians, while women played more of a collegial role. It was the men who were responsible for cutting paths into the Indians' domain. They pushed wagons, people, and stock over the trails; seized native hunting grounds; and fended off Indians who might choose to resist such incursions through pilferage or outright assault.

As a result, male migrants and settlers were wary of their opponents. They were constantly alert for any indication that their enemies were in the vicinity, and regular guards were mounted. It was primarily the men's responsibility to corral the wagons or to lie in the corners of fences to thwart attack. Moreover, men were committed to the success of these efforts because of their great desire to establish themselves in livelihoods in the West. They were also motivated by their firm belief in their own aggressive character and their equally firm convictions regarding the inferiority of their foes. There was little in the contact between white males and native Americans that fostered sympathy, affinity, or friendship. Rather, males tended to approach the frontier and its native population as one piece; both were to be subdued, controlled, and made to serve the settler through militancy and, if necessary, actual violence. Frontier mythology, anti-Indian prejudice, and the male mystique all advocated this approach toward meeting and overcoming the challenges inherent in the settlement of the frontier.

Female migrants and settlers, on the other hand, did not share either the responsibilities or the bellicose way of thinking of their male counterparts. For one thing, in a large number of cases the decision to move westward was made by males. The enterprise itself was based on male desires and needs, with little thought for female wishes and concerns. A historian of western women, Lillian Schlissel, has argued that the westward move coincided perfectly with men's life cycles: it came at a time in their lives when they were "breaking away," that is, improving or bettering themselves. But for women the move was out of phase, for it usually disrupted their efforts to establish a home, produce children, and develop continuity for their families. Consequently, men's and women's accounts of the undertaking differed in predictable ways. Men focused on fighting, hunting, and conflict, while women concentrated upon family and domestic concerns, values, and other related matters.[1]

Whether as migrants or as settlers, women also differed from men in their primary responsibilities. In addition to child bearing and care, these duties centered around supplying food and clothing for their families. Therefore, women, like men, were dedicated to protecting themselves and their families from harm, but they were also constantly concerned with extracting vital resources for their families from the environment and its inhabitants.

Men too desired certain goods and services from American Indians. Grass, water, and route information were some of the commodities most commonly sought after, which men frequently attempted to wrest from the natives through cash payments, threats, or sheer pugnacity. In a typical action, the men of the Burrell party seized usage of an Indian-built bridge by brandishing their pistols at the American Indians who attempted to collect a modest toll.[2] But women, long taught to be soft and nurturing in their approach to problems and people, often derided their men for their aggressiveness. Women were usually dedicated to the success of their western venture because of their own involvement in it, the safety and survival of their families, or their own visions of frontier opportunity. Yet they did not necessarily support the means that men used to achieve that success. Steeped in the accepted female virtues of their era, these women frequently believed that "might" did not automatically make "right." To them, the thud of a heavy fist falling on a native's head did not guarantee survival. Furthermore, their own lack of physical strength did not encourage them to think in terms of belligerent action. Thus, women tended to pursue a more gentle course than men in their dealings with native Americans.

As a consequence, women's sources portray American Indians as guides, assistants, and purveyors of provisions far more often than they describe them as enemies. According to Schlissel's study of 103 overland diaries, women, "having no special stake in asserting their bravery, having no special need to affirm their prowess . . . correct the historical record as they write of the daily exchanges by which the Indians were part of life of the road."[3] Women routinely bartered, traded, and entered into acts of mutual assistance. In other words, in their attempts to provide food, clothing, and other commodities for those people who depended upon them for succor, women often formed relationships for mutual support with Indians.

This is not meant to imply that women regularly allowed themselves to be pushed around or intimidated by intrusive Indians. On the contrary, numerous incidents involved newly confident women who resisted Indian demands that they deemed unreasonable. Women short-circuited native commands by actions that ranged from slapping their faces to brandishing empty pistols under their noses.[4] They also resorted to using a variety of threats. On one occasion, Susanna Ede evicted an Indian interloper from her kitchen by threatening to pour hot grease on him; in another incident, she raised a pot of boiling water to be thrown on the trespasser.[5] Still other women relied upon direct action. One woman simply tore her belongings out of the hands of trespassing American Indians.[6] Some of the truly assertive women depended on raw bravado to repel unwelcome requests. Lavinia Porter, for example, refused a demand for bread only to have bleeding scalps thrust at her to count and admire. When she refused to give ground, her would-be oppressor muttered "white squaw no fear" and departed.[7]

Some frontierswomen were even willing to engage in unfeminine, violent action when it was necessary to thwart natives. To protect stock from nearby Indians, Mary Burrell and Barsina French's mother took turns standing guard with the men.[8] An Arizona woman defended her family's horses and mules by spending a long night shooting at a band of Pima Indians from one end of the stable roof and then the other.[9] An Iowa settler attempted to fend off an abusive Indian with a fireplace poker.[10] And when Susie Van De Wiele's officer husband asked her if she was afraid of the Indians surrounding Fort Leavenworth, she calmly replied, "No, give me a pistol."[11]

Apparently, some women were learning that their physical weakness was not as severe nor as debilitating as they had been led to believe. They also seemed quite willing to act in a martial fashion when they thought it was called for, even though they might decry such tactics as standard procedure.[12] These instances of aggressive action were, however, more often the exception than the rule. Women who recorded one or two such occurrences in their lives as migrants or settlers usually also noted many more occasions upon which they cooperated, traded, or had some other type of pleasant interaction with American Indians.[13]

Actually, the pattern that emerged in a great number of western women's accounts was one characterized by exchanges of goods and services between white women and native American men and women. Many frontierswomen overcame their anxiety to trade routinely items such as trinkets, clothing, and foodstuffs with Indians. Such trade occurred even during the years of intensified conflict during the 1860s and 1870s.[14] Both on the trail and in their new homes, women began to barter needles and thread, processed foods such as flour, articles of apparel, and trifles with natives, who usually offered fresh foods in return. Women's accounts frequently mentioned native American men and women bringing to them butter, eggs, potatoes, corn, pumpkins, melons, strawberries, blackberries, venison and other fresh meats, fish, and dried salmon.[15]

The various types of food items supplied by Indians were often savored as a welcome relief from a diet of bread, bacon or salt pork, and beans. "We have so little change in our diet," Miriam Colt, a Kansas settler of the 1850s, wrote, "that almost anything is relished."[16] Similarly, California-bound Martha Moore considered some mountain trout that she purchased from an Indian to be "quite a treat." On another occasion, she was very pleased to have "procured a fine mess of fish."[17]

Many women also became interested in obtaining specialized Indian products and crafts for themselves. They grew skillful at bargaining for buffalo hides and robes, antelope and elk clothing, moccasins, baskets, and beadwork.[18] Army wife Cynthia Capron was particularly delighted with a watertight basket that she purchased for one dollar near Camp Wright in the 1860s.[19] Moccasins were probably the single most popular trade item, and some women even ordered them from native women.[20] Buffalo robes were also coveted, so much so that at least one woman agreed to surrender her shawl to obtain one.[21] Some of the other beautifully tanned skins, including beaver and otter, were carelessly used for rugs, a practice that women sometimes came to regret when these items were no longer widely available.[22]

It is significant that some of the very women who headed west harboring great apprehension toward American Indians developed into very enthusiastic traders. Lucy Cooke, at first much in awe of Indians, became an expert bargainer, and by the end of her trail experience she had collected a fine cache of furs.[23] Army wife Eveline Alexander overcame her misgivings to barter not only for foodstuffs, such as berries, but also to purchase shields, bows, and arrows. She considered a war shield that she bought to be "quite a valuable trophy."[24] Even Ada Vogdes, who had spent so much of her time in fear of the Indians, acquired enough proficiency in local native dialects to bargain effectively with native Americans. "I rushed around all day to get a blanket worked with beads which I suceeded in doing," she wrote triumphantly.[25]

Women who engaged in trade with Indians soon learned, often to their amazement and occasionally to their dismay, that, in Catherine Haun's words, "the Indian is a financier of no mean ability." Bargains and good deals were not particularly easy to come by, for many natives had as strong a streak of Yankee cunning as the Yankees themselves. "Though you may, for the time congratulate yourself upon your own sagacity," Haun noted, "you'll be apt to realize a little later that you were not quite equal to the shrewd redman."[26] Katherine Dunlap, on her way to Montana in 1864, said that the Indians with whom she traded were so canny that they not only recognized the difference between "coin" and "greenbacks" but would only "take the latter at 50¢ on the dollar."[27]

Naturally, male migrants and settlers also traded with American Indians, but the types of goods involved were usually somewhat different from those purchased by women. Although men were also attracted by moccasins, buckskins, and buffalo hides, they generally spent more time on exchanges involving arms, ammunition, tobacco, horses, and other animals.[28] Men were generally judicious in distributing liquor or refused to do so at all.[29]

When they were part of an all-male expedition or settlement, many men found it necessary to purchase or swap food and clothing with the Indians. But when women were present they were not only primarily responsible for obtaining such items but commonly carried on the negotiations personally.[30] Apparently, as women's preconceptions concerning both themselves and American Indians began to dissipate they were able to enter into business dealings with their once-dreaded enemies. In so doing, they fulfilled their function as providers of domestic goods. They also demonstrated their ability to practice a relatively gentle style in their contact with American Indians.

In addition to trading with Indians, both male and female migrants and settlers began to hire native men, women and children to perform a myriad of services for them. Men frequently employed, or even kidnapped, Indians to serve as guides who would lead them to the best trails and to grass and water.[31] To help them ford swollen rivers safely, they paid Indians cash or, more often, items such as shirts and caps or ammunition.[32] Occasionally, men even entrusted their stock to an individual Indian hired to act as a herder.[33] It was also not uncommon for men to pay natives "rewards" for locating "lost" stock, but it is impossible to determine whether this was simply a variation of the age-old protection racket.[34]

There was a good deal of complaining about the amounts of money or quantities of goods charged by American Indians for these services.[35] So many men viewed the idea of employing Indian helpers as little more than extortion that they shunned native guides, pilots, herders, and other workers entirely. Due to their belligerent attitude, such men often left a sharp taste of bitterness in their wake. And because they shunned assistance they frequently met with disaster.[36]

Women also began to hire natives to perform chores for them. Californian Mary Ackley employed some Paiute men to shovel, cut wood, draw water, and even wash clothes.[37] Other women, evidently relieved of some of their former anxieties, began inviting Indians into their homes as domestic helpers. Native men, women, and children performed household chores, such as washing dishes and clothes. Their female employers frequently commented that they did a good job or that they were "a great help," and they were paid for their labors with such commodities as sugar, salt, and bread.[38]

The most significant capacity in which women employed both Indian men and women was as nursemaids to their children.[39] This practice seems almost unbelievable, given the widespread fear that American Indians were lying in wait to pounce upon white children and carry them away as adoptees or as captives. Yet many mothers grew to trust Indians so thoroughly that they brought them not only into their homes but into their nurseries. When army wife Eveline Alexander arranged for an Apache girl to care for her newborn baby in 1868, she wrote home to her father in New York:

> I wish the grandmothers of the young one, who are so afraid of her "falling" into the hands of the Apachees [sic] could have looked in upon us a while ago. They would have seen the infant prodigy awake in her cradle, cooing to herself, and being rocked to sleep by a bona fide wild Apachee, who a week ago was roaming the mountains, guiltless of any other covering but her "maiden modesty."[40]

Later, Alexander told her father that the Apache nurse seemed "to love to be with the baby" and "is quite useful already in drawing it around in its wagon and rocking the cradle."[41]

Interestingly enough, many of the women who engaged American Indian nurses did not appear to object to them teaching the children native customs, dialects, food preferences, and games. Nannie Alderson seemed delighted that her baby's "good and faithful" nurse carried the child on her back like a "papoose." She was pleased that the nurse crooned native songs to the baby, taught her a "squaw dance," made her pretty beaded moccasins, and followed the Indian custom of never spanking her.[42]

In addition, deep affection often developed between the children and their native caretakers as well as between the parents and the nurses. In one case, a young Puget Sound woman, who was raised by an Indian nurse during the 1850s, acquired a fondness for native food and gained some proficiency with her nurse's language. She also expressed a love for the woman that was overshadowed only by her feelings for her mother.[43] When her male Indian nurse died, Caroline Phelps said that her entire family felt his loss very much; her children cried for him "as much as though he had been a relative." She went on to explain:

> He was their friend truly they missed his singing, he used to fix a drum & then sing and drum & have them and the little papooses dance, any one could not tell which was which only by the color, many a time I have went in where they were dancing, all having blankets on, and I could hardly tell my own children . . . they would all sing, but just alike. My daughter could talk the indian language just as well as she could our own.[44]

Rachel Wright, a settler in the Upper Napa Valley, claimed that the key to such favorable working relations with American Indians rested with the migrants and settlers themselves. Indians could be "an advantage rather than otherwise," she argued, "as they were not only willing but glad to work if they were left free, well treated and properly paid for their labor."[45] It was in this same spirit of gentleness and fairness that many frontierswomen entered into various types of social affairs with American Indians. Women began to visit them in their homes and to attend their celebrations and ceremonies. They formed close friendships with Indians, particularly with native women. And they occasionally married native men.

These relations between women and Indians were often characterized by warmth and affection. They shared time together inside each other's homes, a stage seldom achieved by male migrants or settlers. Although men visited native camps and villages, they typically joined the "braves" and "chiefs" around the fire to smoke the pipe together, to talk about land and politics, and to negotiate trades. They were often treated to meals prepared by the women of the family, and sometimes they were expected to admire the children, but men were not welcomed into the bosom of the Indians' homes and families as women were. Moreover, men did not regularly form close friendships with Indian males, as women did with Indian females. Furthermore, when they married native women it was often done with an element of necessity or exploitation. Such marriages were almost never legalized or solemnized according to white terms, as with marriages between white females and native males. When a white man did marry a native woman according to white law, it was a matter for comment. In one such case, Alice Baldwin wrote that the man involved was "the soul of honor," who "had the decent courage to marry her legally."[46] In another instance, a woman claimed that Indian problems were caused in her area of Washington state by men not only refusing to legalize their unions with native women but by already having wives back East.[47]

Thus, although both men and women conducted trade with Indians and employed them along the trail and in their new homes, they did not achieve the same degree of closeness with native Americans. Men's accounts generally lacked the fond references to American Indian friends and neighbors that filled many women's writings as the time they spent on the frontier lengthened. Rather, men tended to remain in their adversary position to the Indians, while women tended to develop and expand their collegial role.

Relationships between women and American Indians often began with group visits to Indian camps. Even the women who had been at first very apprehensive about native Americans described pleasant social time spent with them. "We often visited Indian camps," Allene Dunham maintained. "They always treated us to a piece of dried buffalo, or venison, or some other kind of meat."[48] Another woman on the way to Salem, Oregon in 1851 claimed that "if there were Indians we would go visiting their lodges and go around among them."[49]

While such occasions nourished cordiality on both sides, it was usually the more personal visits between white women and native women that fostered warm feelings. One trail woman of the 1850s who visited some Sioux women came away favorably impressed by both their hospitality and their skill with a needle.[50] Another female migrant of the 1860s recorded frequent and very genial social calls between her friends and "the Cherokee Ladies."[51] A Mormon woman added that the Indian women whom she visited were "really friendly." She remarked that they had enjoyed "quite a dish of conversation" together.[52] An Iowa settler of the 1870s explained that she grew up with friendly feelings toward the Indians who roamed the woods and camped in the fields around her home. She attributed this to the fact that her Aunt Liza had regularly taken her and her sister to a nearby native village, where the women had given them beads that they "treasured greatly."[53] An Oklahoma woman recalled a similar experience from her childhood of the 1890s. She often visited a Choctaw woman, whom she called Aunt Sophia. She was especially impressed by Aunt Sophia's "wonderfully clean house," extensive collection of handiwork, and the many little kindnesses that she extended to her young caller.[54]

Pleasant contacts between white and native women often blossomed into deeper associations. Once army wife Alice Baldwin had invested some time in crimping and waving native women's hair she discovered that "thereafter the Indian women were my firm friends, and rendered me various favors and kindnesses." She commented perceptively that they were brought together by "feminine vanity and tastes," which she felt were "much the same the world over, no matter what the race or color." On one occasion, Baldwin consented to undress partially to allow Indian women to see the paraphernalia that she wore. "Crinoline and corsets they marveled at, but did not admire," she remarked. As they examined her various articles of clothing and fussed over her beautifully dressed hair, she was struck by their voices, which seemed "naturally soft and melodious." She wrote that as she sat among them, "listening to their chatter and laughter, and no doubt passing uncomplimentary comments about me, I felt that it all meant sincerity, which does not always prevail in a cultured and fashionable society."[55]

Many other white and native women also exchanged bits of female knowledge, lore, and folk medicine with each other. For instance,

Mormon migrant Eliza Roxey Snow learned about the sego root from native women, and she claimed that it "proved to be a nutritious, substantial article of food, and not unpalatable."[56] An Oklahoma woman recalled that she had acquired an extensive knowledge of "palatable and very healthful" greens and roots by accompanying Indian women on their gathering and digging expeditions into nearby woods.[57] Others learned how to use herb remedies or how to treat a rattlesnake bite with raw turkey meat.[58] White women were assisted in childbirth by Indian midwives, and often they received thoughtful and sometimes ornate gifts for their new babies. One California woman raved about the "beautiful baskets and elaborate moccasins worked with beads and feathers" that Indian women brought to her mother upon the occasion of the birth of her baby, the first white child to be born in that part of the country. Another remembered the native American woman who had brought her persimmon bread and a papoose board that was intricately worked with beading and fringe.[59]

A representative case of this congenial and helpful exchange between white and native women was Leola Lehman, an Oklahoma settler who befriended Indian women. In turn, they visited her, bringing small presents to her, and gathered around in admiration when she displayed her new baby. As Baldwin and other women mentioned, elements of female culture drew these women of different races into a close and easy bond. Lehman particularly liked one native woman who had come to see her because she thought that the transplanted white woman "might be lonesome." Lehman eventually came to "like and respect" this native woman and to regard her "as one of the best women she had ever known." She suggested that many such friendships between whites and natives were possible. However, whites must realize, she said, that American Indians were afraid of white people because they had heard terrifying stories about them. When she left the Indian region, Lehman wrote, "I was glad to be back among my own people but had learned to like the Indians. I was no longer afraid and understood that many of their ways that seemed strange to me were caused by fear of white people."[60]

Once other Oklahoma settlers, both male and female, were given the oppotunity to interact on an amicable and rational basis with their Indian neighbors, they also became fast friends with both native men and women.[61] These settlers occasionally entertained native Americans in their homes. In one rather unusual case, a white and native male became so close that the Indian cried when his white comrade died. "Not much stoicism there," the deceased man's sister commented.[62]

Women's friendships were more common, however, due to the crucial role played by female values in drawing together white and native women. They shared their interest in home, family, children, and domestic matters, and they were both committed to certain values, such as the ability to be open, nurturing, and supportive, which created a connection that was largely unavailable to the males of both cultures. It is unlikely, for example, that a native man would call upon a settler and tell him that he had come because he had thought the other might be lonely. An even more ridiculous picture emerges when one thinks of a settler partially disrobing to allow his new Indian friends to admire and assess his intimate apparel. Instead, males helped each other with weapons, stock, hunting, fighting, and similar activities that only infrequently resulted in the kind of mutuality and confidentiality that women so easily developed and shared.

It should be noted that frontierswomen almost never entered into close friendships with Indian males. They did, however, often find that their business and social relations with Indians generally, and with women particularly, fostered a sense of acceptance and admiration toward their male native acquaintances. As women overcame their anxieties and allowed themselves to know Indians, they soon realized that the natives were not as threatening as they had once appeared. Harriet Ward, for example, clearly contradicted her earlier negative attitudes when she wrote in her diary that her friends back home would "be surprised to see me writing so quietly in the wagon alone . . . with a great, wild looking Indian leaning his elbow on the wagon beside me, but I have not a single fear except that he may frighten the horses."[63] Women were often glad to see Indians arrive and sorry to see them leave. "We have parted with white folks that we did not regret so much," insisted one woman.[64]

Women's statements regarding their kindly feelings toward American Indians generally lacked the patronizing note so often found among Southerners when speaking of some of their slaves as good friends. It has become an occasion for humor when minority peoples hear Gentiles avowing that some of their best friends are Jews, whites declaring that some of theirs are blacks, or men acknowledging that some of theirs are women. But when a frontierswoman offered an observation such as "She-wickey was my best friend," the statement carried a ring of veracity.[65] As far as it is possible to judge from mute documents—incapable of revealing the tone of voice, the telltale inflection, or the writer's facial expressions—these women seemed to be sincere. Granted, women like Ward or Vogdes may well have been aware of potential shock value as they wrote to their old friends about their willingness to share space with an authentic "savage" companion. Most of these women, however, were not reluctant to act upon their sentiments by actually visiting Indians and by attending native functions.

Women did, for example, turn to Indian medical men for treatment for themselves or for other family members, and particularly for their children.[66] When her daughter's face was badly burned, Caroline Phelps called in a native doctor, who treated the child effectively.[67] In another case of Indian doctors treating settlers' ailments, a woman remarked that the Indians cared for her people "like a brother should treat a brother."[68] Women also aided native Americans upon occasion. Nannie Alderson restored two "almost frozen" Indian men with a warm fire and a hearty meal.[69]

Gradually, frontierswomen demonstrated their readiness to attend Indian activities, including cries, weddings, funerals, beef issues (distribution of government rations), stomp dances, war dances, and mock battles. They regarded weddings, cries (mourning ceremonies), and funerals as times for respect and empathy.[70] They viewed beef issues as a colorful and entertaining gathering of native peoples, although they were sometimes repulsed by the ferocity with which the Indians slaughtered and disemboweled the animals.[71] Ball games and stomp dances were usually entertaining and interesting to them, even though they sometimes suspected that some Indians ingested drugs and hallucinogens during the course of a dance.[72]

Indian war dances and mock battles received very mixed reviews from frontierswomen. Some women regarded them simply as pleasant and interesting social affairs.[73] One woman seemed pleased when Nez Perce Indians prepared a mock battle for her mother's first visit to Oregon, even when they pretended to take each other's "sham scalps."[74] Other women, however, revealed their own anxieties in their reactions to such performances. In 1875, Wyoming visitor Laura Johnson watched nervously as Sioux filed toward Fort Fetterman to stage a dance. Although she was impressed with their beautiful attire, she felt that the dancers represented "a piece of *real* savage life." To her,

179

these Sioux were "of the wildest kind, about as savage as any there are." When she saw them dance she was convinced that it was "the real thing" rather than an imitation.[75] Similarly, during the 1890s, Ellen Biddle observed Indians moving toward Fort Robinson in "full regalia," writing that, "few people, I imagine, can see a tribe of Indians marching toward them, even when not in their war paint, without feeling a thumping of the heart and a trembling of the limbs; at least that was my experience." She added that the dance, attended by people from miles around the fort, was a tremendous success.[76]

Other women responded fearfully to the dances that they witnessed. Stunned by the ferocity of the dancers, one woman was convinced that the Indians had actually lured them within range for an ambush.[77] Another enjoyed the Paiute dance, but due to a recent "unpleasant experience with their neighbors, the Shoshones," she "felt more comfortable when they were gone."[78] Yet it was not always the women who were afraid of the possible outcome of these native dances. A Colorado settler of the 1860s, Emma Hill, described the Indian dances held around fires and late into the night. Many of her neighbors attended, and the "whole affair," according to Hill, was "dignified and impressive." When some American Indians requested the town's permission to present an exhibition of a war dance, it was the men of the town who refused; they decided that the Indians would get too excited during the course of the dance and would do harm to the settlers.[79]

While some women may have been intimidated temporarily by native Americans attired in battle dress and acting in an aggressive and warlike manner, they usually maintained their equilibrium. Laura Johnson, for example, later attended a Sun Dance involving thousands of Sioux, and she enjoyed it especially because of the skilled dancing of one particularly handsome and graceful young native man.[80] Ellen Biddle regularly traded with Indians and took a young native man into her home as a house servant.[81] It seemed that frontierswomen were able to adjust to individual Indian men more easily than they could to a large number of them, especially when they were dressed in warlike costumes and imitating military actions. The experiences of both Harriet Ward and Ada Vogdes demonstrated that women could indeed learn to deal with even the most ferocious-looking native Americans on a one-to-one basis. In fact, some women not only learned how to cope with individual Indian men, but they discovered in the process that they liked, admired, and even loved them.

When romantic love blossomed between a white woman and a native man, it often resulted in marriage. Since it is difficult for long-term affection to develop from occasional or superficial contact, it is not surprising that when intermarriage occurred it was usually the result of frequent contact based on mutual interests. In 1886, for example, a young New England woman of genteel family and demonstrated literary ability went to teach at the Great Sioux Reservation in the Dakota Territory. Here, Elaine Goodale came to see Indians as human beings, to respect their complex culture, and to like them as individuals. During her first five years among them, she wrote many articles and tracts about them and their problems. In 1891, she married a Sioux physician named Charles A. Eastman, with whom she shared a deep commitment toward helping the Sioux people adjust to a rapidly changing world. Together, the Eastmans wrote nine books, with Elaine continuing to write extensively about native American concerns.[82] That Elaine Goodale Eastman's decision to marry an American Indian was not unique among missionary women is supported by occasional and often passing references to other such instances in frontier accounts.[83]

Another situation that fostered marriages between white females and native males existed in Oklahoma during the 1880s, the 1890s, and the early 1900s. As large numbers of settlers took up land leases on Indian agencies, pushing into the region as "Sooners" in well-publicized land rushes, congenial associations often developed between whites and American Indians. These contacts, in turn, produced a large number of intermarriages. While reading through the hundreds of interviews with female settlers in Oklahoma during this era, one is struck by the recurrent references to intermarriages. A former Texas woman recalled, "I have two nieces who married Comanche Indians, one Clinton Red Elk, and one Buster Work-a-wam."[84] Other women mentioned that relatives, acquaintances, or they themselves had married native men.[85]

Oklahoma women chose a variety of Indian men as their mates. One woman explained that her husband was "a quarter-blood Choctaw Indian" who farmed near the Little Washita River.[86] Another woman said that she married a Cherokee who was a teacher trained at Tahlequah's male seminary.[87] Another chose as her husband "a full blood Chickasaw," an interpreter for the governor of the Chickasaw nation; she married him first under state law in 1892, and again under Indian law in 1897.[88]

Although the government fully recognized intermarriage by allowing the wives of native men to draw an allotment and payments made to blood Indians, there was some opposition to the idea from individual settlers.[89] Interviews with these Oklahoma women do not mention any objections being raised by other women, but they do call attention to male disapproval. One woman remembered that her father, a "one-half Cherokee," refused to prove a land claim because he thought it "a disgrace to be part Indian," and he would not publicly admit his background even to obtain a homestead.[90] Another woman spoke of her father's vehement objections to the possibility that any of his daughters would ever marry a native American. Yet, in a curious twist of fate, after his sudden and tragic death, neighboring Indians were so kind to these women that, in the words of the interviewee, "my sister married a full blood and we have always been glad that she did."[91]

Unfortunately, current scholarship does not supply enough data or evidence to allow one to judge whether women and men were more, less, or equally accepting of the idea of marriages between white women and American Indian men. It might be hypothesized, however, that the female value system permitted relatively easy adjustment to the concept of intermarriage. Female values made it possible for women to enter into warm and comfortable situations with Indians in which intimate relationships could develop. In addition, because female ideals focused on home and family, women were not usually as dedicated as men to the eradication of native Americans and the seizure of their property. Thus, it can be argued that it was at least possible that white women were more accepting of the idea of marriage between themselves and native men than were their white menfolk.

While white male and native female alliances have received much coverage through both myth and the media, little has been said about the existence of white female and native male relationships. At best, this is a very complex and thorny issue. Since the time of Pocahontas, white men believed that they had a mission to rescue native women from primitivism, degraded status, and low levels of sexuality in Indian men. By entering an association with an Indian woman, a man often stood to gain land, stock, and the friendship of the woman's people, to say nothing of the help and affection of the woman herself. Because white men knew that their own position would usually determine that of the family they created when adding a woman and children to their household, they were not afraid that they would lose status by marrying a woman from a group believed to be inferior.

There was, therefore, usually much to be gained and little to be lost when a white man entered a relationship with a native woman. Since it was not very threatening, the alliance could be widely publicized and accepted. Popular literature, the press, and more recently, movies and television, could all make much out of male migrants and settlers forming personal relationships with native women. From dime novels to the Hollywood movie *Jeremiah Johnson,* illegal and unsolemnized alliances (at least according to white prescriptions) could not only be openly presented to general audiences, but they could be glorified. Even objections to such alliances, which resulted in the use of the epithet "squaw man" for males involved with native females, generally receive trifling or sympathetic treatment by the media.

But what of the missionary woman married, both in legal and religious terms, to an Indian man? Why haven't the stories of women such as Elaine Goodale Eastman received attention from novelists and screenwriters? Where is the media saga of the female settler who went west to become the happy wife of an Indian and the fulfilled mother of "half-breed" children? When nineteenth-century media did broach this theme, it usually described female captives who wanted to return to their Indian husbands and children. The standard explanation for such "odd" behavior was that these women had been permanently dehumanized through their association with American Indians or that they were ashamed to face white society because of their debasement. When twentieth-century media considers the topic in movies, such as *Soldier Blue* and *Tell Them Willie Boy Was Here,* it is treated with a tone of shame and censure for all involved. After all, didn't Willie Boy have to flee the reservation because the agent interfered in the relationship that had developed between Willie Boy and the agent's daughter?

These issues are not easily resolved, if at all. Perhaps the topic of white male sexuality is relevant. If a white woman chose of her own free will to marry a native man, as did Elaine Goodale Eastman or the Oklahoma women, what was the attraction that influenced their decision? In almost every instance, women did not stand to gain status, wealth, power, or the approval of society. Could it be then that the supposedly inferior native male, with his assumed minimal ability in the sexual realm, was really not so impotent after all? Was it perhaps possible that women chose Indian men as mates or pined to return to their native husbands because these men were actually very sexually competent and virile? If white men admitted or even recognized this possiblity, their views of their own superiority could be damaged. It might force them to admit that Indians were not so inferior after all, and thus one of the primary rationales for their destructive anti-Indian policies might be undermined. According to at least one researcher, white women were not immune to the sensual appeal of American Indian culture and personality.[92] If, indeed, women were attracted to elements of native life and to individual Indians, this could create an additional pressure on men to recognize the potentiality of relations between their women and natives or to deny such a possibility. Just how men handled these threats is, at this point, unclear, but it appears that they tended to deny the existence or the validity of such white female and native male liaisons.

What is clear is the fact that white women and white men developed quite dissimilar types of relationships between themselves and with American Indians. These differences in white female–American Indian and white male–native American contacts derived in large part from the roles and functions that women and men played in their dealings with Indians on the frontier. Because men were cast as aggressors and as land grabbers, they were pushed into an adversary role. Women, on the other hand, frequently had the opportunity—as procurers of food, clothing, and other domestic goods—to develop a collegial relationship with Indians in their mutual quest for survival.

It should be pointed out that the contrasting roles played by women and men were also reflected in many of their interests, values, perceptions, and observations. Women and men on the frontier often asked different questions of the landscape and the people they encountered. They applied diverse sets of standards to both their adventures on the frontier and their contacts with its indigenous populations. And they frequently noticed and remarked upon divergent aspects of the same scene.

In order to substantiate the differences between women and men, it is useful to compare at some length the observations and emotions that they recorded in their diaries, letters, and memoirs. To facilitate such a comparison, a sample of 150 frontiersmen's documents as well as an equal number from women were assembled. This latter sample included the women's documents discussed in the previous chapter and followed as closely as possible in its representation of major trails, regions of settlement, and eras the accounts of frontiersmen. It differed markedly, however, in that it included a large number of migrants and settlers who were members of all-male expeditions, parties, and communities. These male groups were formed because many men went west while they were still single or made the initial move without their families. While they sometimes migrated with groups of men, women, and children, they often banded together, especially in their attempts to reach and then to exploit the mineral frontiers. Also unique to all-male groups were the scientific or military expeditions that pushed into virtually every frontier area at one time or another. Women lacked a parallel experience in their westering. Although some single women did migrate and settle on their own, the predominant number of frontierswomen were married and were often mothers as well.[93] And although there were a few female parties of Sooners in Oklahoma, a few predominantly female settlements, and several female communes such as the one in Belton, Texas, they were relatively unusual phenomena.

While this difference between the male and female samples somewhat skewed the data, it also provided for some interesting comparisons. It might be expected, for example, that the men's sample with its all-male groups would demonstrate a higher proportion of reports of trouble with Indians. This expectation is based on the assumption that men tended to take fewer precautions when women and children were not present. The male sample actually showed a slightly lower rate of such reports than did the female sample. Out of 150 male documents, 124 reported no trouble with American Indians, 17 recorded minor problems, and 9 noted serious confrontations. One hundred and thirteen women reported no discord, 22 documented minor difficulties, and 15 recorded major conflicts. Although the differences between the two groups are not statistically significant, they do suggest that men exhibited roughly the same degree of caution when in male groups or in mixed parties.

The two samples were further contrasted in twelve categories to determine the similarities and dissimilarities in interests and in attitudes toward native Americans. Sources were rated for relative frequency of mention and for changes in attitude toward Indians over a period of time. In the area of men's and women's interests, the sources were compared in the following categories: domestic affairs; childbirth and child care; general observations, such as scenery and weather; and social affairs. With regard to the topic of Indians, they were contrasted in the ways that they described native people, villages, and artifacts; military preparedness; customs and morality; contacts with native Americans; tribal differences; and personal views of American Indians.

The basic divergences between female and male perspectives generally became very clear in their comments on matters of daily concern. As might be expected, most frontiersmen were by role and function much more concerned than frontierswomen with details of wagons, terrain, directions and maps, finances, land purchase and clearing, crops, equipment, and innumerable other technical and mechanical matters. Men typically recorded meticulous descriptions of a watering place or campground, a ford or ferry, a land investment, a crop failure, a harvest, or a house-raising. One male migrant of 1841 began his account with a thorough statement regarding the number of people in the party as well as the number of oxen, mules, and horses. In addition, he detailed the amount of flour that he had "laid in," and he explained in very precise terms why he had chosen to take an old but good flintlock rifle as his weapon.[94]

Men were also very aware of distances covered. Crossing the western plains in 1850, Iowan William Edmundson included mileage figures in each day's notations.[95] Similarly, Ohioan Hiram Shutes was very concerned with distances traversed. He concocted a device that, when attached to a wagon wheel, counted the number of revolutions of the wheel, and, in turn, these could be translated into approximate mileage figures.[96] Men also displayed great interest in the details of fording flooded streams and rivers, which was a frequent challenge to their strength and ingenuity. "Went 6 miles to Dry Creek," wrote A. W. Harlan, while on his way across the plains in 1850. He added that

it lacked only nine feet of answering to its name, with a swift current. We set stakes & stretched ropes & chains across & built a bridge of willow brush, rolled our waggons over by hand, swam our teams across. By this time there was 60 other waggons waiting. We loaned them our chains, ropes & bridge & left.[97]

Since the care and safety of stock was of such primary importance to western ventures, men also concentrated upon activities such as herding and resting animals, searching for grass and water for stock, and hunting for lost, strayed, or stolen animals.[98]

Although women were often interested in these matters in a general way, they usually did not record them in such detail. They might remark on the crossing of a ford or on problems with stock, but they reserved writing space for matters more crucial to themselves. For instance, as men were counting the miles as carefully as possible, women were meticulously counting the number of graves that they passed.[99] Women also noted distances covered and men remarked on the number of graves, but the level of intensity in the comments of each varied. Furthermore, while women offered observations on such topics as wagons and provisions they did so from their own point of view. Kitturah Belknap spent several paragraphs explaining how she sewed inner and outer wagon covers by hand, what dishes she packed for the journey across the Oregon Trail, what medical supplies were included, what her workbasket contained, and even the nature of the tablecloths that she tucked into the wagon.[100]

Men, on the other hand, had little to say about domestic arrangements. They mentioned cooking and washing only in passing, if at all.[101] On occasion, they did help out with these tasks to a small degree. Helen Carpenter remarked on a father and his sons who regularly joined "mother" around the fire and cooked their own provisions.[102] One young man noted that he did all the cooking for "seven adults and a boy about 3 years old," after the regular cook suffered an accident along the trail.[103]

A great number of men involved in all-male undertakings seldom, or never, commented on domestic matters. It would seem likely that they recorded some of their adventures, since they were entirely responsible for such tasks as cooking and other household chores. Yet they commonly showed a definite lack of interest in commenting on their involvement in domestic affairs.[104] Those men who did record their domestic efforts accomplished the task with great brevity. Fortyniner Edwin Hillyer, for example, was bemused by the sight of men cooking. "Who'd a thunk it, three months ago," he wrote, "that they would see John and Ed away out on the plains . . . cooking over a bush fire?" Later, he noted cryptically: "I baked bread. Yes I made and baked bread."[105] Another male migrant on the road to Virginia City in 1865 stated, "Baked my first loaf of bread, very good."[106] A migrant on the Oregon Trail supplied his wife with slightly more information when he wrote that he did "not mislike" camp life, and

> on the contrary am much pleased with it thus far—Hank & self have done most of the cooking, and have succeeded thus far, admirably— The great difficulty we find, is to cook enough—All of us have most voracious appetites. . . . But truly we get along finely.[107]

A captain in the Army Corps of Topographical Engineers, surveying the Salt Lake Valley in 1849, sounded as if he too got along "finely," for on at least one occasion he noted that he was quite pleased with his dinner of buffalo meat, two bottles of claret, coffee, and a "segar."[108]

Other than cooking for themselves, the other major domestic hurdle that confronted these men was the problem of cleaning their soiled clothing. One man devised the simple solution of tying his dirty clothes in a blanket and then submerging the bundle in a swift stream.[109] Another complained that when he had first attempted "the art of washing dirty clothes" he "suceeded admirabley," although his fingers "suffered some from the effects of very good soap."[110] A man who had hurt his back and knuckles in his first brush with washday wrote that he and his companions often thought of their wives and "wondered that we were ever dissatisfied with their impatience on washing day." He said that "had they been present, we should have asked their pardon."[111]

Men alone did miss women, but not just for their domestic services. One forty-niner wrote that he and his comrades were "quite cheered by the sound of a female voice" when they visited a nearby emigrant camp.[112] Another would-be miner was depressed because there were no women for miles around his trail camp. As he contemplated the home and family that he had left behind, he wrote, "I am not doing this for fun or from selfishness, but for the hope that I can secure more gold with which to give them more than the comforts of life." He declared, "There is no selfishness mixed in it."[113] Once they had reached the California diggings, men expressed a loneliness for women and sometimes the regret that they had left home at all.[114] They confided their feelings to their diaries, wrote long letters home, and turned to the few women who lived in the region. As one miner wrote plaintively, "Came across a camp of Indians. We had a bottle of Brandy along & treated them. Tried to honey up to some of the squaws, but couldn't come it."[115] An unmarried emigrant of 1850 recorded a similar lament, writing that "what goes hardest with me is the loss of the company of young ladies." He followed this with a complimentary description of a Sioux woman, "a chief's daughter, that was really good looking."[116]

Since women did not migrate in all-female groups, their accounts are not filled with similar complaints. Domestic tasks were at the center of a woman's world, whether she lived at home, on the trail, or in a crude frontier dwelling. There was never any squabbling about who would perform the cooking and other household tasks. Everyone concerned understood that these were female duties.[117] Thus, female writers concentrated upon their primary function in life, their domestic responsibilities. Unlike men, frontierswomen frequently listed an awesome catalog of domestic tasks, including recipes, directions for producing goods such as soap or butter, comments about basic as well as fashionable clothing, and numerous remarks on related subjects.[118] Unlike those men who succinctly recorded their attempts to bake bread, Kitturah Belknap offered a complete sketch of her "salt-rising" bread.[119] And while Catherine Haun's trail account depicted women walking along in the dust and heat of the trail to share bits of gossip and exchange recipes, men's writings illustrated an eagerness to swap with other men tidbits of information about the care of stock or the selection of the best trail.[120] A comparison of men's and women's documents from the same family collection clearly demonstrates these differences. Although both male and female family members experienced the same western region during the same time period, their chronicles are often noticeably dissimilar.[121]

Differences between male and female accounts became even more apparent when the topics of childbirth and child care were considered. Although they traveled with mixed groups that included their own wives and children, men infrequently recorded pregnancies, births, or activities and problems concerning children. The male's pragmatic attitude toward such matters was evidenced by Dr. Thomas White, while moving from Indiana to Oregon in 1852. "I was called on to perform the duties of obstetrician," he observed, "for the rule of multiplication, will go on, on the plains, as well as in other relations of life."[122] In the same vein, other men apparently accepted pregnancy, childbirth, and even infant mortality as natural functions to which they accorded little notice. The terseness of the following diary entry was not uncommon:

> Feb. 25, 1868—Tacy, my wife, had a new daughter this A.M. at 6–1/2 o'clock.
> Sat. March 7th—I went to Salem and paid Dr. Siveter $10.00. I had expected him to charge only $5.00.
> Sun. May 3—Baby died![123]

A dramatic contrast emerges when this diary notation is set beside the statement that Kitturah Belknap made after her baby died from lung fever. It was, she wrote, the "first real trial" of her life. When another of her children died, she noted in her diary:

> I have to pass thru another season of sorrow. Death has again entered our home. This time it claimed our dear little John for its victim. It was hard for me to give him up but dropsy on the brain ended its work in four short days. . . . We are left again with one baby and I feel that my health is giving away.[124]

This is not meant to suggest that men cared nothing about the birth, care, and death of their children. Men, after all, were expected to play the roles of the strong male and the family provider. The first role prevented them from expressing many deep emotions, and the second role riveted their attention to matters more immediate to their own functions in life. Furthermore, according to nineteenth-century standards of modesty and their own reticence to discuss such things, women did not have much to say about pregnancy or childbirth, either. But they did write a great deal about the problems of protecting and caring for children in a frontier setting. They continually worried about children's health and safety, attempting to prevent disasters such as rattlesnake bites or the jolting of a child off a wagon seat.[125] Men also took precautions to protect their children, and they went to great lengths to retrieve them when lost. But they were more likely to make an offhand remark such as one jotted down by a prospector in 1865: "The Indians are still camped near us. There are a good many pappooses with them, and their squalling reminds me of my own parental home and village."[126]

Although men's and women's writings differ in these areas, they converge in the categories of general observations and social life. Both genders made many comments on scenery, weather, meetings with old neighbors, the beginnings of new friendships, loneliness and homesickness, illness, death, disaster, entertainments, schools and churches, and similar matters of joint concern. Both men and women were taken with the grandeur of the rolling plains and the rugged mountains, the color and profuseness of the prairie flowers, the clarity of the water, and the vastness of the sky. Neither gender was reticent to relieve the boredom of the trail by describing at great length sights such as Scotts Bluff, Independence Rock, and Salt Lake City. Both men and women recorded the minute details of magnificent yet frightening prairie fires, hordes of locusts, blizzards, and spring floods.

In addition, frontiersmen occasionally expressed their deeper emotions, although perhaps not in the detail with which frontierswomen wrote of their own feelings. Men revealed themselves to be just as delighted as women to encounter old friends along the trail. Men, however, were sometimes more private with their sentiments. Hiram Shutes, for example, slipped off to quietly bid his mother good-bye, while Catherine Haun was more public with her farewells.[127] In the Kenyon family, one of the women sadly wrote home that the family's letters were like "bread and 'lasses' to a hungry child." When John Kenyon read the letters, his wife suggested that he may have wept over them.[128]

If men were a little more scientific and women slightly more literary in the style of their observations in these areas, it was perhaps another reflection of societal prescriptions for women and men. Women tended to emphasize color and light intensity, openness and vastness, and nature's flair for the dramatic, while men were more likely to focus upon soil types, dimensions, and nature's ability to enrich or deplete the earth's resources. Women often envisioned Chimney Rock as a castle or as some other fanciful form, while forty-niner Byron McKinstry typically portrayed the area as follows:

I can see several very high rocks . . . one of them looks like a large building, also more Bluff Ruins on this side 2 or 3 m. farther up. I should suppose the highest of the "Bluff Ruins" were from 300 to 400 ft. high, and are composed of somewhat differently colored strata. The top of one was of a hard brown rock for 10 feet, then chocolate or clay color for 10 or 15, then white for 3 or 4, then 15 or 20 of the chocolate or clay again . . . the strata nearly horizontal, and any of it except the hard cap rock could be cut easily, and the water had worn some frightful chasms among these hills.[129]

Another depiction of the same area clearly displaying a male perspective was written in 1851 by gold-seeker J. Goldsborough Bruff:

This basin, among the singular and romantic bluffs, is a beautiful spot. It appears to extend E. & W. about 5 ms. and about 3 ms. wide. In a deep gulch lies a cool clear spring and brook.—Close by is a group of Indian lodges & tents, surrounding a log cabin, where you can buy whisky for $5 per gallon; and look at the *beautiful* squaws, of the traders.[130]

Yet these gruff men, apparently so aware of whiskey and women, also occasionally responded to the beauty of the plains by gathering a bouquet of wild flowers for themselves.[131] And a Utah emigrant who meticulously recorded the dimensions of Court House Rock and its environs even took a moment to compare it to a European castle.[132]

Turning to the topic areas concerning American Indians, the men's and women's documents analyzed here also demonstrated differences and similarities in their approaches, their opinions, and their willingness to alter their views of the native peoples of the West. Both their gender and their responsibilities dictated to a great degree what elements they would single out for comment as well as the ways in which they would perceive them. The resulting observations offer an interesting and significant contrast between male and female perspectives.

In the first category—aspects of native people, villages, and artifacts—men regularly remarked on the physical appearance and dress of American Indians, although their comments were usually not as detailed or couched in as judgmental a tone as those by women. If anything, men seemed to be impressed by native dress when intricacy and display were involved, and unlike many women, they did not think it was ostentatious. One man described several Potawatomis as "splendidly dressed in white deerskins ornamented with black cloth, small sleigh bells, ribbons, feathers, and so forth." In the early 1850s, another man portrayed some Indians near Fort Hall as "fine looking fellows with there caps and feathers on and there Beed shoes and Bo and arrows."[133] Men also remarked in an awed way about the ornaments, beadwork, feathers, and paint worn by many American Indians.[134] However, men concurred with women in their dismayed response to states of native undress. In 1859, Joseph Camp judged some Pawnee Indians to be "very degraded" because "some of them are almost naked and most of the men wear nothing but a tattered blanket and a breechclout. . . . women wear short petticoats and leggins."[135]

When American Indians attempted to emulate white clothing styles, men tended to find it amusing. Women, however, applauded Indian efforts toward emulating the whites. A male emigrant of the 1860s, upon meeting some Dacotah Indians, wrote that "our indians are evidently somewhat civilized as they have trowsers" and "soldiers blouses," while "one gay chap had on a caloco shirt."[136] Another man, on his way to California, observed that the emigrant trains had so influenced the Pima Indians that they were hardly to be seen without "a shirt, coat or a pair of Pants—though never an entire suit." He was "much diverted" at the sight of a tall, good-looking Indian with a stovepipe hat on his head, a heavy blue blanket coat covering the upper portion of his torso, and absolutely nothing on his "lower extremities."[137] A Utah-bound traveler of 1859 was similarly entertained by the sight of Cheyenne and Sioux Indians dressed in white-style clothing. "I was quite amused," he remarked, "to see some of the Indian women dressed so neatly in calico and crinoline, and some of the boys had on pants, suspenders, calico shirts, and straw hats, but these were rare cases. There were more of them with only such clothing as is peculiar to the Indian."[138] A military officer of the 1840s encountered an "old savage" who had tried to make himself look "as respectable as possible" by dressing in a green frock coat "not of the latest cut," an old pair of epaulets, leggings, and a cap of grizzly bear skin topped by a red feather. The officer wrote that "it did afford us a little amusement."[139]

When men turned their attention to Indian homes and villages, they only occasionally saw them as picturesque, concentrating instead upon the manner of construction involved.[140] Men's writings were filled with detailed accounts of building techniques, materials, styles, and dimensions of native dwellings. A typical journal entry read: "This morning I examined the lodge referred to yesterday. It was of a conical form made of dressed buffalo hides nicely stretched over sixteen cottonwood poles."[141] Another male migrant commented on wigwams that, according to him, were made of "dressed bufaloe skins sewed together" and "are round in shape with a pole passing through the top."[142] A Texas settler of the 1830s offered more details:

> Their tents are made of Buffaloe skins tanned or dressed perfectly white. They sew together a number of hides, making a long roll of it. When they wish to pitch a tent, they form a circular frame work of forks & hickory with[e]s around which they wrap this roll of skins beginning at the ground and winding round until they reach the top leaving a small hole for the escape of the smoke; the entrance into the tent is a small hole just large enough for a man to creep through; thus forming a habitation very much in its outward configuration resembling a hornet's nest, and having inwardly very much also of the hornet-temperament & severity.[143]

Other frontiersmen took similar pains in their reports of huts, tee-pees, houses, and even ruined native villages.[144] Men only occasionally included descriptions of the interiors of these Indian homes, presumably because their interest in such matters was not very intense.[145] Even when they were curious, it was often difficult for them to gain access to the interior of these dwellings. When Isaac Wistar insisted upon visiting an Indian town that intimidated his friends, he did so because he, unlike many white men, was interested in observing the "domestic arrangements at home" of the Sioux. He approached a lodge, and the chief invited him to talk, but so many young men jostled him and attempted to examine his weapon that he decided not to dismount. "The train was passing out of sight, evening was coming on, and I did not care to tempt them too much," he explained. Although he did get a glimpse of several native women sitting on buffalo robes inside the teepee, he proceeded no farther because he did not wish to be "too presuming on a first acquaintance." He shook hands all around, working his way through the male population, who, according to him, "were loudly discussing me or some other inter-esting object." The conclusions that he drew from this abortive visit were superficial: the Sioux were excessively curious and friendly, and their lodges were well laid out in patterns and characterized by lances and shields in front of each one.[146]

Wistar's emphasis on weapons as outstanding features of native American lodges was a common focus among frontiersmen. Charged with the defense of themselves, their families, and their stock, they were sometimes almost obsessed with the weaponry and martial skills of American Indians. Men therefore emphasized the numbers and strength of Indian groups, the number and types of weapons in evidence, and the quantity and quality of horses. At the same time, they showed an overriding interest in their own weapons, military organization, and ability to resist native American incursions.[147] Although men did on occasion offer descriptions of native baskets, beadwork, or other crafts, they spent a great amount of time in recording and discussing artifacts such as bows and arrows, lances, and other weapons.[148] When men drew vignettes of the various Indians they met, they often included statements such as the following: "The braves were armed with small tomahawks or iron hatchets which they carried with the powder horn, in the belt . . . over their shoulders were leather targets, bows and arrows, and some few had rifles."[149] Other notations included these two examples: "their bows & arrows are formidable weapons . . . the arrows about 3 feet long with a steel point sharp as a knife"; "chief—had his bow & arrows—one had a spear—no fire arms."[150]

Details of native military techniques also filled the writings of frontiersmen.[151] Arriving settlers were inundated with less than reassuring bits of lore about the various tribes. "The Comanchas," explained an early Texan, "are warlike and fight on horseback; they drill themselves & horses on the prairie, their mode of fight is to form a circle round their enemy, & keep riding round & round like circus riders . . . they then draw their arrows and commence attack; still keeping their circular gallop."[152]

Some of these male commentators felt that American Indians were "marauding and erratic savages" who especially threatened women: "all females that have the misfortune to fall into their merciless clutches" faced "an ordeal worse than death."[153] But the majority of them expressed more concern for protecting or retrieving their stock than for protecting their lives or those of their families.[154] According to their writings, one of men's chief worries was the protection of their animals from Indians, while women were more preoccupied with the protection of their children.[155]

Many men, like many women, quickly came to the realization that most American Indians were more anxious to steal the emigrants' and settlers' animals than to annihilate their owners. Given the crucial role that stock played in their own ventures, frontiersmen could not afford to be either generous or understanding where their animals were concerned. As Isaac Wistar explained after the Digger Indians had run off his party's mules, "most of the men have gone after the mules in a desperate hope of recovering them, for life itself here depends on the all-important help of that indispensable but hated animal." He added that the terror induced in the men by the loss of their mules had made them "savage by sympathy."[156]

Although women recognized the need for adequate defense measures, they mentioned it less often than men and sometimes even joked about it at the men's expense. Women tended to be much more inquisitive than men about the domestic organization, marital customs, child raising practices, and crafts of American Indians.[157] Women remarked upon Indian customs and standards of morality, which seemed to elicit their shock, disapproval, and indignation in writings that were often of great length.[158] Men often observed that native Americans had unusual "burial" practices, were polygamous, intermarried with French settlers, ate insects, were fond of liquor, were lazy, and were inveterate beggars. They were, however, generally terse in their moral judgments of such practices.[159]

Many frontiersmen seemed to be especially curious about the manner in which American Indians treated their dead. Male documents offered many more particulars than female accounts about burials above the ground.[160] One emigrant of the 1860s noted that these burying grounds were "quite interesting" to him, but he, like most other men, extended them the greatest respect.[161] Only one man from the group surveyed here violated the sanctity of these cemeteries by invading one to get a bead as a souvenir.[162] Most agreed with the army officer who observed that "in no instance will one nation disturb the dead of another or anything that may be about them, not even when at war." He went on to maintain that "the Indians deserve great credit for the respect they show their dead." He added that an order was given that a nearby burial lodge not be disturbed, "as there has been some thoughtless person who would not have considered it a very heinous offense to have taken for a curiosity a beautiful pipe, which was lying on a scaffold inside the lodge."[163]

Most men also seemed to be respectful of native marriage customs, including intermarriage and polygamy. They seldom disparaged these customs in the way that women did. Often, they simply made notations such as the following: "there is quite a village with 7 stores owned by white men, the most of whom are married to Indian women." Another man said that "there are some ten or a dozen Frenchmen liveing here in lodges or wigwams, withe Squaws for their wives." Still another man noted, "I saw a white man with a squaw and several children."[164] When they considered the offspring of intermarriages, most men noted only in passing that, judging from the "variation of complexion" to be found, miscegenation was apparently practiced successfully. When Byron McKinstry noticed that "the little ones at the trading posts are much whiter than their mothers," he dismissed it by remarking that "the cause of this extraordinary phenomenon I shall have to leave to be solved by the learned in such matters."[165] Only a few argued that interbreeding caused "degeneracy, physical as well as moral," and thus produced a villainous horde who disgraced "the beautiful plains."[166]

Men also spent a good deal less time than women in attacking some Indians' custom of marrying several wives. Frontiersmen recognized that while some American Indians believed in a form of marriage that was unacceptable to most migrants and settlers they did not engage in what one emigrant termed "indiscrimnate cohabitation."[167] They tended to agree with their womenfolk, however, on the topic of Indian treatment of women. They were often under the impression that native males, when not satisfied with one wife, simply purchased another for the price of a good horse.[168] Another common view was expressed by an explorer of the 1830s, who claimed that American Indians were cruel to their women, compelling them to do all the work while the men had only to hunt and fight.[169]

Men were less condemnatory than women of Indian drinking habits. The usual comment was simply that some natives had requested whiskey. This observation was often accompanied by the statement that they had no liquor to give to the Indians.[170] Other men, as well as some women, remarked that they "heard none of them asking for whisky."[171] Of course, some men did offer accounts of incidents involving drunken Indians, but again little censure was included.[172]

Instead, frontiersmen tended to lament the Indians' "insatiable thirst for ardent spirits." They also condemned the "unprincipled men" who, "for the sake of gain, will supply them with the means of drunkenness and destruction."[173] Given all the emotional overtones and the economic threat inherent in the image of a drunken male, women were understandably much less willing than men to overlook the issue or to offer sympathy.

Men's tolerance for native customs began to decline somewhat when it came to the eating of vermin. Men not only recorded the existence of this habit among some Indians but referred to it as a "disgusting practice." They reacted with great surprise to the "apparent relish" and "evident gusto" which some natives seemed to display when engaged in the practice.[174] One forty-niner claimed that he refrained from eating Indian cooking after he "saw a woman catching vermin from the head of a little boy, with which she pieced out her supper, which fully satisfied my curiosity as to their epicurism."[175]

When it came to the Indian habit of requesting gifts or of actually appropriating goods for their own use, men were almost as vitriolic as women in their reactions. Epithets such as "indolent," "thieving," "lieing," and "begging" punctuated frontiersmen's writings.[176] Derogatory references to panhandling and pilfering Indians were only occasionally relieved by an observation concerning the industriousness or ingenuity of American Indians.[177] Unlike women, men did not often praise the inventiveness or skillfulness of native Americans. Although they may have been slower than women to condemn certain native cultural practices and rituals, they were also much more hesitant to discern a spark of imagination, originality, or enterprise in American Indians.

Men did, however, join women in quickly learning to discriminate among tribal groups of American Indians. From emigrants to settlers to gazetteers, they regularly logged journal entries regarding the various types of American Indians that they encountered.[178] Their opinions of these groups usually demonstrated great consensus. The Pawnees were commonly judged as very "hostile." The Snake Indians were considered the "greatest beggers in the world." The California Mission Indians were thought to be exceedingly friendly to settlers.[179] As in women's writings, the Sioux were reported to be powerful, wealthy, and beautiful in form, figure, and dress.[180] The "Diggers," however, were the target of universal opprobrium. Seen as a "thievish and rascally race," they were considered by many to exist in "the lowest state of human existence."[181]

Men frequently recorded observations of intertribal warfare.[182] Like women, they also theorized that it was white men rather than Indians who stole stock and created other problems for emigrants and settlers.[183] White traders were sometimes deemed to be "as roguish and treacherous as the Indians themselves." So-called white Indians were regarded as even more dangerous than warlike tribes such as the Pawnees.[184]

Apparently, there were some men who, like many women, could see beyond superficial appearances. They could also reject their own prejudices about the cruel nature of American Indians to discover that it was not always Indians who caused the settlers' problems. Many men came to realize that Indians were also subject to various pressures and unfair practices. Some men tried to reach out to Indians, hoping to alleviate some of the bitterness that often resulted from native contact with white people. They visited Indian camps and met with the leaders in an attempt to prevent loss of goods or lives. Unfortunately, because these meetings were usually rather formal affairs, they were not designed to foster sympathy or understanding. Following the accepted practices, the men exchanged gifts, smoked the pipe together, and then discussed questions of trade, passage, landownership, and other related issues. These talks often involved a large number of onlookers, whose presence added to the tension and impersonality of the situation.[185] Lacking in personal interaction between white and native males, such meetings contrasted sharply with women's accounts of visiting with Indian women, conversing and exchanging tidbits of female lore, and sharing cooking methods, modes of dress, and child raising techniques.[186]

In spite of the common practice of concluding male conferences with a feast, the stiffness was not alleviated. One army officer parleying with an Oglala Sioux leader smoked the pipe and feasted in the Indian's lodge, yet he felt that although much superficial "good will" was involved very little had really been accomplished. For his company's belongings disappeared despite the leader's promises to the contrary.[187] Forty-niner Reuben Shaw also came away with a negative impression from a similar ceremony. In his call on a village of Blackfeet, Shaw was appalled by the "filthy, repulsive interiors" of the dwellings, the "filthy cooking methods" of the women, and the preponderance of dogs. "What struck us as being most abundant about the Indian camp was, first, dirt," he asserted, "second, dogs; third, more dirt." His disgust was compounded when he discovered that he had to offer gifts of jewelry and buttons to the women in order to view their babies and to give a variety of articles to the leader in order to obtain hunting rights in the area. In the last analysis, Shaw was convinced that the "crafty" chief—whom he dubbed "Saint Brag" based on the chief's propensity to boast of his own exploits—got the best of the bargain and that his people had spirited off many of his party's goods in the process. "We were," he said, "glad to be done with the Blackfeet, though we looked upon them as a very interesting people and as noble types of the American Indians."[188]

These two men's adventures were common. Their contact with Indians accomplished little in fostering real communication between Indians and whites. They also failed to bring white and native men any closer together than they had been at the beginning of their meetings. Unfortunately, this was a frequent occurrence for most frontiersmen. Consequently, their writings seldom demonstrated positive changes in their responses to American Indians. Usually committed from the inception of their ventures to an adversary position toward Indians, most men had little motivation or opportunity to learn to know Indians or to develop sympathetic feelings for them.[189]

There were, of course, exceptions to this behavior. One was Alonzo Delano, who came to believe that nine-tenths of the trouble between frontier people and native Americans was created by the whites themselves. Yet even he concluded that peaceful coexistence was impossible and that American Indians would have to yield to white pressures because of their obvious inferiority.[190] Another exception to the pattern was Howard Egan, who found at least one "good" Indian whom he took back to Salt Lake City as a combination friend and servant.[191]

Other men—such as missionaries, teachers, fund-raisers for missions, explorers, and religiously oriented individuals—expressed some compassionate feelings toward American Indians. They did not, however, adopt these feelings after contact with Indians. Rather, they carried these attitudes to the frontier and continued to cling to them.[192] There were also a great number of male emigrants who came to the frontier with negative attitudes and continued to adhere to them. Captain Randolph Marcy, for example, argued in several of his books about the West that native Americans were "marauding and erratic savages," who were controllable only by punishment and harsh chastisement.[193] Another man remembered that his father maintained his intense bitterness toward the Sioux right down to "the latest moment of his life."[194] Yet another man harbored so much animosity toward Indians that he held his pistols in readiness from the moment he left Council Bluffs. Willing to kill any Indians who might appear, he wrote home to a friend, "I do not think there was any wrong about it. I fought for my rights, and tried to kill them lest they might attack our camp we knew not when."[195]

Other men, however, went west claiming to have an open mind toward American Indians. One of these, Dr. Thomas White of Indiana, soon found himself disenchanted. After only a few days of contact with the "hateful wretches," he explained that he had lost any pity that he might have had for Indians. "I used to think the Emigrants at fault, but I know it is not the case," he insisted.[196] Another medical doctor, traveling on the plains in the 1860s, indicated that the more he thought about Indians the more he was inclined to dislike them. Having observed the Omahas, Pawnees, and Sioux, he decided that all Indians were "filthy," "sneaking," and "treacherous." Having read an acquaintance's description of an Indian council, he was convinced that natives erroneously considered themselves superior to frontier people. His evidence was fragmentary, and he admitted that he knew little from "personal observaton of their customs." Yet he did not hesitate to advocate that the "tribes of the plains must be given a tremendous thrashing. . . . and forced into subjection."[197] A Mormon settler in Salt Lake City urged a similar approach to the natives in his area of the frontier. He explained that he had "lost all of the good feeling I ever had for them and that was not much." He wrote to his uncles that "last winter we killed one tribe off and will have to kill a few more before we can make them behave that is the way to convert them to the Mormon faith."[198]

The dominant tone of the men's writings represented in this sample was one of acrimony and hostility. If men joined the westward movement with deep commitment to aiding American Indians, they usually maintained it. But if they started out with vague sentiments or with deep-seated prejudices, they usually managed to discover that their pessimistic expectations were confirmed. Only a few of these men were able to convert their cynicism into a more empathetic view of American Indians. This pattern deviates sharply from that demonstrated by the women's writings studied here, the majority of which did show positive changes in women's prejudicial reactions toward Indians. Women and men differed in their roles and functions in relation to Indians and in their dissimilar perceptions of the frontier and its indigenous inhabitants. Perhaps the greatest difference between them lay in their willingness or unwillingness to modify their attitudes toward Indians. While men tended to remain rigid and inflexible in their views, many women exhibited a capacity to alter their ideas considerably, particularly with regard to American Indians.[199]

Why was this so? It is true that women's roles allowed many of them to enter into relatively close and warm relationships with individual Indians. Yet sociologists have long argued that stereotypes and prejudices against a group of people do not alter solely through pleasant experiences with representatives of that group.[200] Rather, they believe that such experiences must be supplemented by an educational process that promotes changes in attitudes as well.

It seems that frontierswomen did undergo a type of educational process in making their adjustment to the frontier. The increased demands on their physical capabilities helped them to see that they were not as weak as they had thought. At the same time, the realities of the moral climate showed them that their supposed talent for reform was not as significant as they had believed. As women began to accept these alterations in their views of themselves, they became open to the possibility of similar alterations in their attitudes toward others.

Women's views, once they had been deemed illusory, were then susceptible to the types of influences provided by their amicable contact with Indians. Men did not participate in this same educational exercise. Convinced of their own strength, their inalienable right to wrest a livelihood from land inhabited by other peoples, and the immutable inferiority of the previous tenants of the land, men had no reason to modify their original convictions. In fact, the stresses and strains placed by the demands of the frontier on these male attitudes may well have caused them to reaffirm such convictions in order to justify their endeavors. Men, therefore, tended to treat the American Indians they encountered in a way that would produce the very results that they had anticipated. Men expected the Indians to be a problem, so they often boasted, threw their weight around, and acted arrogantly; and the Indians involved had little alternative but to respond in a militant fashion. When conflict inevitably erupted,

men's worst suspicions were confirmed and their anti-Indian prejudices reinforced. Added to the tension was the virtual absence of the
warm, personal contacts with American Indians that frontierswomen
experienced.

Unlike their female counterparts, men had either little motivation
or opportunity to revise their ideas about American Indians. Women,
on the other hand, frequently discovered that their preconceptions
about themselves and Indians, rather than being confirmed, were
being eroded. As a consequence, many frontierswomen were eventually able to develop a sympathetic and humane stance toward their
formerly mortal enemies. This would not prove to be the case, however, with all minority groups that westering women were to encounter on the American frontier.

✥❦ 6 ❧✥

The Selective Nature of Frontierswomen's Sympathies

Diaries, letters, memoirs, and other writings of frontierswomen offer evidence that many of them transformed their anti-Indian attitudes into more positive sentiments during the course of their westering experiences. A large number of women were able to modify or even reverse their negative ideas and emotions. As their views of themselves became more fluid and open, their contact with Indians increased. As a result, numerous women revised their prejudices toward American Indians.

Women's willingness to change their views was not, however, applied indiscriminately to all racial, ethnic, and religious groups that they encountered on the frontier. While some women did express as well as display empathy toward American Indians under even the most trying circumstances, they did not extend the same measure of humaneness to groups such as Mexicans, Orientals, Blacks, Mormons, or natives along the Panama Route to California. Women lacked or avoided the opportunity for close or extended contact with representatives of these groups. Also, women's self-images did not undergo any changes that might directly affect their feelings about these groups of people. Moreover, unlike American Indians, these groups were not as numerous, as visible, or as pressing in their demands for some type of contact with emigrants and settlers. Women, therefore, were able to offer their sympathies in a selective manner. They gave compassion or affection to American Indians while continuing to deprecate most other minority group members.

Before considering women's relations with some of these other groups, it is important to thoroughly understand the full extent of their growing compassion toward natives. Women developed and expressed their sympathies for Indians on many different issues and in a wide variety of situations. Some simply called for an understanding of the human condition to be applied to American Indians. One settler of the 1880s, for example, agreed that Indians had many faults, but she pointed out that whites demonstrated many character flaws as well. The Indian "has also his trials," she added, advising her contemporaries to "judge him not harshly."[1] A Kansas settler of the same decade also felt that it was unfair for whites to denounce what she referred to as the Indians' state of degradation. "Are our souls refined and free from all impurity?" she asked.[2]

Even those women who did not reject the idea of the innate inferiority of American Indians were able to develop at least a shred of pity for them. An Iowa settler of the 1880s remembered that Indians roamed the prairies around her homestead with "native dignity." Unfortunately, according to her, "the footprints of the white man soon became the aggressor," and the Indians were "compelled to give place to a higher order of civilization." There was a note of melancholy in her observation that "where the wigwam stood now stands the prosperous city with its church steeples lifting their lofty heads to the heaven."[3] Interestingly enough, this pensive remark came from a woman whose views concerning Indians did not change significantly. Until they finally disappeared from her area entirely, she continued to regard them as unwelcome visitors. Although she did not alter her views of Indians, she was, however, able to develop at least some sympathy for their misfortunes. Another woman of the same era also held on to her basic conviction that Indians were "murderous savages" capable of "diabolical deeds." Yet she softened just enough to express sadness that the American Indian would "soon be numbered among the extinct races."[4]

Apparently, even those women who never came to express any affection for American Indians could still commiserate with Indians about their plight. This was certainly true of army wife Frances Roe,

who had called the Indians "dirty, and nauseous-smelling savages."
Yet she came to believe that there was blatant injustice involved in
the mass killing of the buffalo that, in turn, deprived the Plains Indians
of their primary source of subsistence. She wrote bitingly:

> If the Indians should attempt to protect their rights it would be called
> an uprising at once, so they have to lie around on sand hills and watch
> their beloved buffalo gradually disappear, and all the time they know
> only too well that with them will go the skins that give them tepees
> and clothing, and the meat that furnishes almost all of their sustenance.[5]

Another army wife who, unlike Roe, developed amicable feelings
toward Indians was even more adamant about the unfairness of taking
precious resources from indigenous populations. While at Fort Laramie during the 1860s, Frances Carrington observed that

> at the time of my arrival it had become apparent to any sensible
> observer that the Indians of that country would fight to the death for
> home and native land, with spirit akin to that of the American soldier
> of our early history, and who could say that their spirit was not com-
> mendable and to be respected?[6]

Many other women who exhibited varying degrees of warmth toward Indians took the position that it was highly unjust for whites to
seize Indian lands. Loss of these lands condemned native inhabitants
to a life of poverty and virtual homelessness.[7] But women couldn't
seem to agree upon the wisdom of restoring certain patches of land
to Indians through the reservation system. Although some women
thought that it provided a partial atonement for past injury, others
believed that the reservation concept was the result of little more
than white patronization and arrogance, especially on the part of the
federal government in Washington. "Now the government allows them
a portion to themselves as a great favour and taken as such," Oregon-
bound emigrant Agnes Stewart Warner contended in 1853, "but this
does not make it right."[8] When she saw eight thousand Navajos confined to a reservation in the 1860s, army wife Eveline Alexander was
moved to write that "as most of them were prisoners of war, I expected
to find them of a sullen and unhappy appearance, but on the contrary
those I saw looked very contented and cheerful." The rations that she

saw being distributed were sparse. "Not much to support life on, one would think," she concluded.[9] Two decades later, Carrie Strahorn observed Navajo reservations in Arizona and Utah. One of their worst features, she was convinced, was that "the Government divided families by taking them to different localities making them justly angry and revengeful."[10]

Land policies and the reservation system were not the only sources of women's distress. In addition to lamenting the harshness of land decisions affecting native Americans, many women also decried the Indians' basic lack of adequate food and clothing. They pitied the needy Indians, gave what they could, and recorded their frustrations in their diaries and journals.[11] "Oh, dear, but they do look so uncomfortable," sighed one emigrant woman of the 1860s, after passing a native village.[12] Army wife Ada Vogdes, overcoming her own intense fears of native peoples, also felt pity when she noted the Indians' destitute condition. When some twenty Indians came into Fort Laramie for food, she logged her compassionate response in her journal. "I did pity these poor things paddling around in the cold & snow," she noted.[13] Other women regretted their own inability to help the unfortunate natives. Rather than disparaging Indians as beggars or resenting their demands on their own families' resources, these women felt helpless and inadequate. For instance, when Lois Murray turned away a hungry Indian for lack of food he coughed so hard that she later insisted, "If I could have called him back, I would have given him bread." Murray claimed that she never again refused to aid a needy Indian.[14]

These women all developed some degree of compassion, respect, or even affection for Indians. Perhaps they were altruistic and even solicitous in their commentaries because they were not facing the immediate threat of disfigurement, dismemberment, or death at the hands of rancorous Indians. They could afford to be gracious, kind-hearted, and benevolent. But what of the women who *were* facing such dangers? Did the women directly involved in conflicts between whites and natives and those held as captives by Indians differ radically in their reactions to American Indians?

Despite the captivity legend, women who were drawn into violent conflicts between the two groups were not always negative in their reactions toward either their own situations or toward all of the Indians involved. Close examination of their writings reveals that women involved in armed conflicts and those held as captives were able to empathize with, and even to develop affection for, their enemies. Although one might reasonably expect such women to be bitter and malevolent, they were, in truth, frequently understanding and forgiving.

Of course, attacks, massacres, and captivity were not all that they were frequently reputed to be. There were outrages routinely committed by both sides, and not just by American Indians. Captives were taken by both natives and whites and were sometimes treated in a regrettable manner. In other cases, they were accorded fair treatment as prisoners of war, as adoptees, or as potential cultural converts. Nor was captivity by Indians aimed primarily at women and children. A study of the gender of captives in the New England area between 1675 and 1763 indicated that 349 were male, as opposed to 186 female and 35 of undetermined gender. It also showed that 22 were infants between birth and two years of age, 128 were children between two and six, 117 were youths between seven and fifteen, 288 were adults over sixteen, and 15 were of unknown ages.[15] It is possible, if such data were collected for the trans-Mississippi West, that a similar pattern would emerge. Certainly the anecdotal evidence available on the gender and age of captives in the trans-Mississippi region does not uphold the widespread belief that natives were single-mindedly intent upon seizing women and children as their prisoners.

There is also little support for the idea that American Indians routinely sexually abused their female captives. Captivity narratives involving women, and particularly those that included inferences of sexual mistreatment, appealed to a wide market, and their high sales gave them a visibility and a dominant position in the captivity genre. Captivity narratives therefore suggested that women accounted for a large number of Indian captives and that they were always raped, forced into unwanted marriages, or otherwise assaulted. Yet numerous women's accounts do not mention or even hint at sexuality, nor do they include fears about impending rape by Indian males.[16]

It might be argued that nineteenth-century women, schooled as they were in modesty and in aversion to speaking of sexual matters, would refuse to comment upon even an immediate sexual threat. Women did, however, discuss such issues in published captivity narratives in appropriately veiled terms. They also mentioned sexual matters in memorials entreating the Congress of the United States to compensate them for indignities that they had suffered.[17] Furthermore, captivity accounts divulge a tremendous amount of detail about every type of "atrocity" imaginable. It is therefore difficult to believe that the writers of captivity narratives could or would restrain themselves from providing some coverage to sexual misuse if it had been as widespread as believed.[18]

Another important question regarding captives was their desire to remain with their American Indian captors. The New England study discussed above revealed that, among those sampled, 569 Indian captives were exchanged or ransomed, 68 returned on their own, 16 probably returned, 38 returned after staying awhile, 12 returned against their will, 67 escaped, 149 died in captivity, 45 were killed by Indians, 30 more probably died, 228 remained with their captors, 58 perhaps remained, and 361 met undetermined fates. Of those who chose to remain among the Indians, a greater number of females than males stayed. Although nearly a third of the female captives chose to remain, less than one in ten males stayed.[19]

In spite of the lack of comparative data for the trans-Mississippi West, there are occasional indications that a similar situation existed. There was, for exammple, the widely told story of Olive Oatman. Once she had been ransomed, she spent most of her time longing for and attempting to return to her native husband and children. "For four years she lived with us," a friend explained, "but she was a grieving, unsatisfied woman, who shook one's belief in civilization." Although the Indian tattoo marks were removed from her face, Oatman's white family and friends could not erase "the wild life from her heart."[20]

Oatman's case and similar stories of other female captives were explained away by assertions that these women had been too brutalized by the Indians to function in white society or that they were perhaps too ashamed to face their families and friends again. These arguments, however, are not upheld by the writings of female captives.[21] In fact, some female captives actually expressed favorable feelings toward their captors. Sometimes these cases were recorded secondhand. Texan Harriet Bunyard, leaving her home in 1868 for California, encountered a young woman captive who had been recently ransomed from the Indians and who claimed that they "were very kind to her."[22] Another Texas woman of the 1860s, Ruth Thompson, recounted the story of an eleven-year-old female captive who insisted that she had been well cared for by an Indian woman. According to Thompson, the girl said of her native "mother" that "as long as I stayed with the Indians she was my adopted mother, and always treated me as her own child."[23] A similar tale revolved around the Fletcher sisters, captured in 1865 in Wyoming by Arapaho Indians. After Amanda Mary was ransomed, she located her baby sister Lizzie. When she wrote to General George Custer about the possibility of obtaining Lizzie's release, she was told that her sister was "in good health and was kindly cared for by the Indians being considered a great favorite by them." Upon pursuing the matter, Amanda Mary learned through an interpreter that Lizzie, now fifteen years old, denied being white, maintaining that she was an Arapaho and refused to be ransomed away from "her" people.[24]

In addition to these tales of female captives who were treated well by American Indians, there are also a number of firsthand captivity accounts that reiterate the same theme in more detail. Many of these narratives are from the 1860s and 1870s, the era in which native American resistance to the white invasion of their lands and hunting grounds peaked. Since conflict increased during these decades the number of captivities also proliferated. Women's reactions to Indians did not, however, automatically become more disparaging in tone as the climate of violence intensified. If anything, the troubles and tragedies generated from increased white and native contact during these years seemed to convince many women that they must intensify their own efforts to understand and to aid the situation. Women's documents from this time period indicate that growing numbers of women became missionaries and teachers to the Indians. Many women also grew increasingly sympathetic with natives on the issue of taking prisoners of war.

The case of Minnie Carrigan illustrates the willingness of some women to empathize with their captors. Taken prisoner in the 1862 New Ulm conflict, she later spoke with fondness of the two Indian women who cared for her early in her captivity. "It seems wrong for me to call those two Indian women squaws," she stated. "They were as lady-like as any white women, and I shall never forget them." When the prisoners were dispersed to other camps, she was protected first by a young native woman and was then taken in by an Indian family, who made quite a "pet" of her. "Their conduct toward me was so considerate," she later declared, "that I really liked them."[25]

Perhaps Carrigan's empathy can be better understood through a survey of the events leading up to the hostilities. The conflict began with an altercation between some begging Indians and resistant whites that involved the death of several settlers. It soon escalated into the settlers' severe and dehumanizing retaliation against the natives. Carrigan recalled that people were given the right to shoot an Indian if he or she were discovered off the reservation. When soldiers shot one errant Indian the people brought his body into town and "celebrated" with it in the streets. "The boys put firecrackers in his nose and lit them," Carrigan remembered. "After they were through celebrating, they scalped him and threw him into a ditch." Later, someone removed his head and decided "to have it fixed up in a showcase." This "celebration" was followed by a bad winter, during which the government neglected to pay the Indians their allotments. All of this, Carrigan said, resulted in the Indians becoming "disagreeable and ill-natured." Carrigan did not seem surprised that violence flared up, nor did she condemn the native Americans for their behavior.[26]

Another very different chronicle of the New Ulm tragedy, which gained wide circulation in published form, was Mary Renville's *Thrilling Narrative of Indian Captivity*. Renville's account seemed designed to titillate and shock. The incidents it recounted included the rape of white women captives by several drunken Indian men. But a close reading reveals that Renville attempted to justify Indian actions by castigating whites for their corrupt influence. Who supplied the liquor for the Indians in the first place? Renville asked. And how many crimes committed by Indian have actually been caused by corrupt or thoughtless whites? she continued. She blamed greedy traders and government agents for introducing some of the white's "most flagrant vices" to native Americans. She concluded her narrative of captivity and cruelty with the thought that Minnesota settlers must restrain themselves from punishing all Indians for this "massacre," a move that would only drive the peaceful ones into the ranks of those more warlike. Furthermore, Renville suggested, those settlers who would go among American Indians in the future must learn from the past and establish the basis of "Justice, Morality, and Truth" rather than continue to encourage dishonesty and dissipation.[27]

Other narratives of conflict between whites and Indians focused upon very young women. Some years before the New Ulm episode, a teenage brother and sister lost their family in a cholera epidemic on the plains. When they continued their trek toward California, they were seized by some Indians along the north fork of the Platte River. During their time with these Indians, the young woman, Ruth, "cured" the chief's daughter of cholera. Ruth calmed the girl and helped her gain faith in her recovery. In the meantime, Ruth's brother Curtis joined the native men in buffalo hunts and other activities. The natives finally put the two young emigrants back on the road near Fort Laramie, supplying them with blankets and other items. The narrator of the story claimed that a true bond of affection had developed between the young people and their captors, especially between Ruth and the young woman whom she had aided.[28]

Bianca Babb Bell of Texas related a similar incident. It involved her own experience as a young woman when she was taken prisoner by the Comanche Indians in the late 1860s. The Comanches killed her mother, carried her and her brother off in a grueling three-day trek, and neglected at first to feed her regularly. Later, however, she grew very fond of her adoptive mother who, in her words, "was always good to me." Her Indian mother held a "great feast" in Bianca's honor on the night of her arrival, and she continued to show Bianca many little kindnesses. "On cold winter nights my Squaw Mother would have me stand before the fire, turning round occasionally, so I could get good and warm," Bell recalled. "Then she would wrap me up in a buffalo robe and tuck me in good and warm." Bell maintained that her native mother was "always very thoughtful" of her and seemed to care for her as much as if she were "her very own child."[29]

Bell was not only fond of her Indian mother, but respected the other Indians in the group as well. Later, she declared:

> The majority of the Indians that I knew were of a jovial, happy disposition, always friendly and playing some kind of joke on the other fellow. I think they must have had exceptionally good children for in all the time I was with them I do not remember seeing them correct or punish one. One might imagine that the Indians were ignorant, but they were well educated in legends handed down from generation to generation. . . . All their history was handed down from one generation to the next.

She also emphasized that most of the Indians regularly worshipped their "heavenly Father," or "as they would say our sure enough Father." Other Indians "worshipped the moon," while still others prayed by "singing and dancing." She remembered that Indians "always gave a big dance, before going out on the war path, everybody joining in the dance. . . . it was always fun to go to a war dance." When her father finally ransomed her from the Indians, and to her native mothers' great despair, she was pleased to return to her own people. Yet Bell always retained happy memories of her time among the Comanches.[30]

Also instructive are the writings of some of the women who were involved in the violent clashes between settlers and American Indians around Dr. Marcus Whitman's mission in Oregon in the late 1840s. Writing of those tragic events, these women told of the "outrages" and "depredations" committed by the Indians. But they also emphasized the aid and support given to them by "friendly" natives.[31] They particularly commended the Nez Perces for saving settlers' lives, for treating them with "decency and respect" throughout the siege, and for bringing the guilty Indians back for trial and execution.[32]

During the years following the Oregon conflicts, these women's responses ranged from denying any fear of Indians to becoming their generous benefactors.[33] Typical reactions included retaining Indian friends for life or feeling moved "to weep & pray for those dark dying nations."[34] Rather than becoming bitter, many women were able to take a large and generous view of the unfortunate events that had transpired around the Whitman mission. By the fiftieth anniversary of these events, some women were willing to commemorate them. A ceremony was held at the original site, to which the local railroad company gave all survivors free transportation, and a monument built to Dr. Whitman dislodged a great many bones and skulls that had offered mute testimony to the disastrous nature of the "massacre."[35]

This discussion is not intended to imply that clashes between whites and natives were anything less than calamitous or that prisoners of war spent enjoyable interludes while away from their own families and friends. It is meant to suggest, however, that the captivity scenario presented by myth and by the media was not totally accurate. Mired in anti-Indian prejudice and seeking rationalizations for their inhumane treatment of natives, many white folks were willing to have their biases confirmed by horror stories of attacks and captivity. Yet the women's sources surveyed here indicate that a wide discrepancy may have existed between the scenario and the reality.

Clearly, even during the height of actual violence, women were not universally terror stricken by American Indians. Neither were they always physically or sexually abused by natives. Nor did women routinely blame Indians for the ills and strife that plagued so many areas of the frontier. Actually, a large number of frontierswomen pointed the finger of blame at white men. Mary Bailey, for one, claimed that her heart ached for the "extreme ignorance" of native Americans but that she pitied even more the "many white men" who passed them by "without thinking of doing them any good."[36] Other women recorded their complaints against men who set up incendiary situations with their swaggering and braggadocio, acting petty, mean, and heartless in their dealings with American Indians. One Iowa settler of the 1840s maintained that she had always pitied the Indians and would fully expect her own people to be just as "mean" as the Indians if they were driven out by native reprisals.[37] Two decades later, another Iowa woman criticized white ruthlessness, arguing that

> the heaped up graves, filled with the victims of starvation, disease, or cruelty in all its various forms, prove conclusively that the Indian— no matter how vindictive, or diabolical his acts may have been—has had his counterpart in the age of all most favored, whose watchword has ever been enlightenment and progression.[38]

Other women censured men for particular brutalities toward American Indians. Kate Furness, for example, singled out for blame the trail men who created catastrophes along their way. When a young man carelessly shot at some native American women to startle them, accidentally killing one woman, the Indians seized him and skinned him. "From a peaceful tribe," Furness argued, "these Indians had been turned into demons, a wild, revengeful nation," and simply because one young man had indulged in "a foolish, thoughtless act." Another occurrence in the Sierra Nevada mountain area made it even more clear to Furness that the typical male approach to Indians was harmful. When a group of American Indians approached on horseback, the men of the party immediately surrounded their stock and raised their weapons. The Indians insisted that they were peaceful and did not intend to fight. Furness's mother offered the leader bread and sugar, a kindly gesture that convinced the Indians to allow the train to pass. When dealing with Indians, Furness added, it was her mother's custom to initiate friendly acts, in contrast to the men's belligerent reactions.[39]

Still other women chided white males for taking advantage of Indians at every turn. An Oregon settler felt that many of the problems on the local reservation were caused by "lecherous white men" who preyed upon young Indian women. A Kansas settler believed that men who cheated Indians in trading also created many difficulties. "Is it right," she queried, that white men paid Indians "three dollars for a buffalo robe, worth twelve at home?"[40]

According to Margaret Carrington of Fort Kearney, military men were particularly reprehensible in their bargaining with Indians. She was enthusiastic about an 1866 fort policy that barred soldiers from bartering with Indians. This policy, she argued, deterred "the possibility of collisions growing out of trades in furs, beads, and other articles, in which the Indian is generally the unlucky one, and often exhibits his disappointment by becoming revengeful and wicked."[41] The military was also admonished by some women for their brutality in fights with natives. Rachel Wright mentioned a detachment of soldiers sent to "exterminate" some peaceful Indians in the Upper Napa Valley. According to her, these "harmless natives" stood and stared unsuspectingly at the "strangely clothed men," and the soldiers shot into their midst, wounding and killing many of them. The Indians, frightened and grief stricken, fled into the canyons. The settlers protested to the government, but relations between the two peoples were never restored to their formerly happy state.[42]

Civil War troops were also accused of making trouble across the frontier. In Oklahoma, soldiers terrorized Choctaw women by tearing their earrings from their ears and locking them all in a stuffy room for days.[43] And in California, Eleanor Taylor condemned soldiers who perpetuated "horrible butchery" in their battles with natives, displaying "quite as much of the savage nature as did the redskins." When two young soldiers deserted their troop, Taylor applauded their action.[44] The cause of suffering during the Indian wars of the 1870s was also laid at the feet of the military by some women. Caroline Winne, for example, rebuked Sheridan for being "drunk all the time in Chicago in his fine house," and she blamed Sherman—"on his general's pay in Washington, never having fought an Indian & knowing nothing at all about them"—for regularly making uninformed and ruinous decisions.[45]

Mother and child, circa 1900. White women were often moved to change their views of American Indians after observing their homemaking and child-rearing practices. (Keystone View Co., courtesy Museum of New Mexico, neg. no. 91528.)

Chippewa woman making a birch canoe, circa 1900. White women frequently came to admire and respect the skillfulness and ingenuity of native women. (Courtesy Museum of New Mexico, neg. no. 90554.)

Water carriers, circa 1880. Both white and Indian women of all ages worked under difficult conditions to provide food, water, and clothing for their families. (John K. Hillers, courtesy Museum of New Mexico, neg. no. 102081.)

Navajo Indian women weaving blanket, circa 1885. Many white women became enthusiastic traders for quality Indian-made goods. (Christian Barthelmess, courtesy Museum of New Mexico, neg. no. 70418.)

Mormon settlers. Women on the frontier rarely overcame their antipathy to Mormonism, fueled by lurid newspaper and fictional accounts. (Ben Wittick, courtesy School of American Research Collections in the Museum of New Mexico, neg. no. 15615.)

"Wild Fandango at Santa Fe." Myths surrounded the Roman Catholic Hispanic culture of the Southwest as well as the American Indian culture.

"Mexican Women." Indolence and uncleanliness were two stereotypical qualities attributed to Mexican women.

White Mountain Apache woman named "Na-tu-ende" or "Forty Horse Cayet-ro," daughter of "Brigham," circa 1883. Many white women overcame their early prejudices and developed relationships with Indians based on mutual respect and trust. (Ben Wittick, courtesy Museum of New Mexico, neg. no. 15910.)

The United States government came in for its share of the blame
as well. Greedy land policies, a misguided and inadequate reservation
system, and gross mismanagement of allotments and supplies were
all cited by women as sources of American Indian troubles.[46] After an
Indian war of the mid-1850s, Oregonian Elizabeth Lord maintained
that "there was never any doubt that the Indians were treated unjustly" by local government and men who had allowed and supported
wholesale seizures of native lands.[47] Mary Ann Tatum, writing in 1870
at Fort Sill, the Kiowa-Comanche Agency, also grumbled about whites:
"The heart grows sick with the repeated tale of wrongs and broken
promises by the whites & government why must it be so, why must
the poor untutored redman suffer so from the whites who feel that
they are so much further along."[48]

Women reprimanded a variety of specific types of white men for
their brutishness. Government agents, renegade Frenchmen, Catholic priests, and other representatives of religious groups were often
accused of corrupting or agitating native Americans.[49] White thieves
were particularly excoriated for stealing from both the settlers and
the Indians.[50] One Texas woman of the 1870s considered white fu-
gitives from other states to be the real problem on the Texas frontier.
According to her, fear of these "desperadoes" played on her mother's
mind "far more than fear of Indians."[51] Renegade and other "unprincipled" white men were also condemned for "inciting" Indians and
leading them "on to desperate deeds."[52] Still other women believed
that Indian problems in their areas were created by Mormons, who
either perpetrated heinous deeds themselves or encouraged Indians
to do so.[53] One such woman, emigrant Allene Dunham, insisted that
the "Mormons were to be dreaded more than the Indians themselves."[54] This charge often evoked countercharges, with Mormons
claiming that it was the "foul tricks" of the emigrants that caused the
difficulties for which they had been unfairly accused.[55]

Many women realized the need to consider solutions to the problems that were plaguing both settlers and American Indians in many
areas of the frontier. It seemed apparent to them that violence and
acrimony could not be allowed to continue if the people involved
expected to attain a degree of stability and productivity. Conflict was
eroding both the peace of mind and the physical energy of both
groups, to say nothing of the wanton destruction of resources that
was involved. Many women thus came to grips with the question of

what could be done about the flare-ups that so frequently characterized relations between whites and natives.

When they considered solutions to the so-called Indian problem in the West, many women were prone to talk in rather vague terms about "civilizing" American Indians.[56] In 1885, Alice Fletcher cited the example of Omaha farmers in Nebraska as proof that Indians could indeed be "civilized." In her view, the Omaha people were successful farmers independent of all government support; they offered living proof of what could be "actually accomplished in bringing a people from barbarism to civilized life." To her, the Omahas demonstrated that "civilization is no fanciful theory, but, under proper care and influences, is within the grasp of all the Indians." She argued that "while many persons are still questioning whether the Indian will work, whether he can be educated, whether it is possible for him to become self-sustaining" the Omaha people had already demonstrated that all of these things were possible.[57]

To Fletcher, civilizing American Indians apparently meant turning Indians into economically productive beings engaged in livelihoods acceptable to whites, and it also meant educating them, presumably in white ways. But to others the idea of civilizing American Indians assumed larger dimensions. It implied the need to "elevate" Indians by introducing "white standards" into their lives. This was generally believed to be an appropriate job for women, who were regarded as the moral and civilizing forces of American society.[58] More than one woman arrived on the frontier charged with the duty to elevate native Americans while supervising their metamorphosis into pseudo-whites. Interestingly enough, these women were often indoctrinated with the need to bring to men of the frontier a civilized "way of living." Civilizing both the Indian and the frontiersman presented huge challenges. An Oklahoma woman maintained that only by dint of "courage and long hours of labor" were she and her co-workers able to fulfill both charges.[59]

In order to achieve this uplifting of American Indians, some women advocated a combined emphasis on work habits, education, and religious instruction.[60] Reformer Annie K. Bidwell of California took the position that reservations had to be replaced by individual farms. Her rancher husband partially underwrote her scheme by donating land to Indian families. Bidwell herself then added to the structure a mission school and a temperance brigade. In a 1904 letter soliciting aid for her experiment, Bidwell declared that "these Indians have proven themselves worthy of the position of any white citizen."[61]

Other women concerned about Indian problems emphasized the need for teachers among the Indians. Some of these women insisted that teachers must civilize as well as educate their pupils. In 1840, Abigail Smith wrote to her family from Kansas lamenting the lack of white teachers among natives: "Oh that there might be teachers sent to show them the way to be saved and the arts of civilization."[62] Other women shouldered the task of teaching Indians what whites felt they needed to know to survive peacefully in the increasingly white world of the West.[63] A large number of women who taught in the mission schools throughout the frontier soon learned that their duties included more than teaching. One teacher in Oklahoma recalled that "I was matron and teacher to say nothing of being nurse and seamstress and besides I usually helped at the Saturday morning bath."[64]

A number of other women believed that American Indians could only achieve their leap from primitivism to civilization through religion. They tended to believe that Indians were "buried in ignorance" because they knew "nothing of Christ or the way of salvation."[65] To "Christianize" American Indians thus became their particular focus.[66] Perhaps the best known of these female missionaries was Narcissa Whitman, a young woman who was so intent upon the idea of carrying religious teachings to the Indians in Oregon that she hastily wed a missionary in order to meet the church board's requirement that all female missionaries be married.[67]

Clearly, a large number of women discussed, advocated, or implemented various kinds of solutions to the difficulties that erupted as emigrants and settlers increasingly displaced native populations throughout the West. They not only allowed their sympathies to be engaged by the sad state of affairs between whites and natives, but they also felt that they could have a positive effect on them. They were apparently quite willing to devote their time and energy to a thoughtful consideration of the issues involved, and sometimes they also invested their lives in their attempt to improve the situation. These women were probably encouraged in their efforts by concepts of female morality that still persist in our own day. And they were also motivated by their increasing understanding of and empathy for natives.

As women came to realize that American Indians were not stock characters—inherently bestial, wanton, and licentious—in captivity narratives, dime novels, or stage plays, they began to hope for the salvation of at least some Indians. These women's objectives were misguided and based on cultural arrogance inasmuch as they wanted to replace Indian culture, language, art, crafts with white value systems. Yet they did illustrate a firm belief in the Indian's ability to adapt, change, and learn. They did not argue, as did so many male reformers, that natives were hopeless because not only were they dying out naturally, but they were basically incapable of learning, growing, and contributing to white society.[68]

Oddly enough, the kindheartedness and spirit of optimism that many frontierswomen expressed concerning American Indians was not generally extended to other minority groups on the frontier or along any of the routes leading to the American West. Since Orientals, Mexicans, and Blacks were visibly different from emigrants and settlers in appearance, language, and cultural characteristics, they were easily identified targets of prejudice. Thus, it is easy to understand why women may have felt constrained and reserved in their relations with these groups. However, Gentile frontierswomen also maintained an enmity toward Mormons, a group of people very much like themselves in appearance, culture, and ethnic origin. Because of these obvious similarities, it might be assumed that Gentile women would have had more incentive to associate with members of the Church of the Latter-Day Saints than with native Americans. Yet Gentile women adamantly refused to relinquish even a fraction of their bigotry toward Mormons. At the same time, these women were softening and modifying their views of Indians, who were clearly a group of people very unlike them.

Women took their negative views of Latter-Day Saints with them to the West and held to them throughout their time there. Before leaving their eastern homes, they had been thoroughly indoctrinated with anti-Mormon prejudice by a spate of critical sermons, speeches, tracts, novels, newspaper articles, satirical cartoons, and caricatures. Consequently, many women expected the Mormons to be more difficult to deal with than American Indians.[69] They had heard many horror stories about the practice of polygamy, and they had also become convinced that, as one *New York Times* reporter phrased it, most Latter-Day Saints were fanatically "intense and zealous religionists."[70] They considered the Mormons as high-handed, corrupt, and unfeeling people who would take advantage of emigrants and settlers whenever the opportunity presented itself. One woman recalled that she had heard "so many vile things of these Mormons that I expected to see them with cloven feet," while another insisted that she was "suspicious of anything connected with Mormons."[71] Yet another woman stated that she dreaded Mormons and fully anticipated unfair treatment from them because "the tales told of the Mormons in those days were worse than those of the Indians." Even after learning that the Mormons at Council Bluffs charged reasonable prices and were fair in their dealings with the emigrants, she was delighted when her party bypassed Salt Lake City; she had "no desire to see the Mormon settlement."[72] One California-bound emigrant who wintered in Council Bluffs in 1853 came away with a different set of impressions about the Mormons living there. "We found before spring," she wrote later, "that with all their zeal and devotion they were a treacherous set and sect." She claimed that these Mormons "made it a business" to steal from the Gentiles. Her party also decided to skip Salt Lake City, a decision that pleased her since she too nurtured a very definite aversion to Mormons.[73]

Because the Latter-Day Saints lived in tightly knit religious communities, there was seldom little more than superficial contact between Mormon and Gentile women. Consequently, female emigrants and settlers had few actual experiences with Mormons to offset the many dramatic and incendiary tales they had heard. A common rumor, for instance, was that Brigham Young, to conserve resources for the Mormons themselves, had ordered that no grass or other provisions be given to Gentiles.[74] Another widely circulated story concerned the Mormons' supposed practice of stealing stock from emigrants and settlers and often blaming it upon the Indians. Accounts flourished of Mormons swooping down on Gentiles to ruthlessly kill them and carry off their possessions.[75] After hearing a number of such reports, one female migrant insisted that "any means to rob the 'Gentile' was considered commendable."[76] Latter-Day Saints were often reputed to be very willing to join American Indians in their attacks on emigrants and settlers.[77] In addition, they were regularly blamed for "inciting" the Indians to attack whites in an effort to reduce the number of Gentiles settling in the Southwest as well as to impair their progress and power in the area.[78]

Feared and hated to an extreme, Mormons were frequently the

target of judgmental comments by female migrants. Diary and journal entries not only noted Mormons moving westward in all kinds of wagons and handcarts, but assessments of them were offered as well.[79] Given women's preconceived notions about these people, it is not surprising that their remarks about Mormons were generally disparaging. To one woman, Mormon men were "a very hard looking set," while to another, the women were "very plain looking, many of them absolutely ugly."[80] Other women recorded their impressions that Mormons were "not always inclined to be friendly," that they were "poor, ignorant and dirty," and that their ranks often seemed to include "the dregs of some foreign country."[81] One of the most rancorous observations came from Mary Fish. While crossing the plains in 1860, she saw groups of Mormon women valiantly dragging handcarts behind them. She asserted harshly: "They must be sadly in want of husbands to level themselves to brutes & after all their trouble to obtain one 4th or perhaps one 20th part of a man."[82]

Only a few frontierswomen were willing to extend any understanding or sympathy to the Latter-Day Saints whom they met. One young female migrant who deprecated Mormons grudgingly admitted that some of them were "good people, but very common: border people."[83] Another woman who did not hold a very high opinion of them pointed out that Mormons suffered as much as Gentiles from fear of the Indians.[84] And Margaret Hecox, an emigrant on her way to California in 1846, expressed some pity for them. She explained that as her party traveled slowly to avoid overtaking a train of Mormons they grew increasingly distressed by the badly rutted roads that the Mormons left in their wake. They were also upset by the discriminatory treatment they received at the hands of people along the way who took them to be Mormons. Apparently, the Latter-Day Saints had no money, offering their labor in return for their purchases, and this practice so infuriated settlers that they subsequently refused to sell food, fodder, or clothing to Hecox's train. Although these settlers mentioned that the Mormons appeared to be half-starved, Hecox observed that they "had not a particle of sympathy to waste on their pitiable condition." In her view, however, the Latter-Day Saints were not quite "as black as they were painted." When her group finally overtook the Mormons, she found their "abject poverty" to be "an extremely pitiful sight." She was appalled that "some trundled wheel-

230

barrows before them, containing all of their worldly possessions." Yet when the Mormons were finally behind them, she felt "greatly relieved" to be clear of them, and anxious that her train move faster "lest they overtake us."[85]

These women's expressions of sympathy were certainly hesitant in nature and reserved in tone. Moreover, their remarks were far outweighed by the many exclamations about the Mormons who were heading back from Salt Lake to the "States." Women seemed to revel in delight at this apparent sign of Mormon failure.[86] Quite often, women simply assumed that these Latter-Day Saints had had their fill of Mormonism and were fleeing Zion. Other women claimed that the Mormons themselves had described to them their secret escape from Salt Lake City.[87] In 1857, Helen Carpenter said that a contingent of these returning Mormons were "in rags and tatters and, must I say it, scabs." To her, they were "the very worst lot" she had seen. These "poor creatures" existed in poverty and squalor, and they were, she was convinced, only a few of the many who "would be glad to leave Salt Lake if they could only get away."[88] Some years later, in 1884, Mallie Stafford recorded her party's occasional encampments with a party of returning Mormons. "They had escaped the terrors of the law and the 'Avenging Angels,'" Stafford explained, "and after a residence of years in Zion, at last were *going home*." She claimed that "they conversed but little on the subject of Mormonism," and she added that "the slightest reference made to the subject from time to time, convinced us that it stirred up a flood of painful and unpleasant recollections."[89]

Mary Fish added another dimension to women's images of these returning Latter-Day Saints. In her 1860 overland journal, she chronicled a meeting with two Mormon women headed for the "States." According to Fish, these women had fled Salt Lake because of their antipathy toward the plural marriages in which they were involved. In Fish's words, one woman was now returning to her parents with "four little responsibilities," while her companion, also "a fourth or fifth wife of a Saint," had "consoled herself for the loss of a small portion of a man by taking a whole one as she has married a trader."[90]

Given these unkind views of Latter-Day Saints, it is little wonder that many female emigrants were pleased when their trains circumvented Salt Lake City altogether. But other women were intently curious, were driven on by dwindling supplies, or were propelled into Salt Lake City by a combination of these two factors. Others were simply glad, as Rachel Rose said, "to see where folks lived once more."[91] Whatever their basic motivation, they were lured on by rumors about Brigham Young, his elaborate home, and his many wives, who were sometimes reported to be only seventeen in number and at other times to be as many as sixty-one.[92] Their curiosity was further aroused by the Latter-Day Saints who swarmed into their camps to bargain for old clothes, dishes, and other items in exchange for stock.[93] Their wonder was stirred by their first glimpses of the spiraled city, and one group was amazed by the Mormon woman who said that she had been in that splendid spot for eighteen months and had not yet seen as much as fifty cents in actual money.[94]

Thus, the emigrants flocked into the fabled city of Salt Lake. They pushed into the shops as anxious customers for the goods that the Mormons were only too willing to sell them. The Latter-Day Saints were pleased to become a supply station for those on their way to California, and the harassed migrants were equally happy to restore their depleted supplies before they moved onward for the last lap of their trek. The emigrants thronged into the streets, gazing in awe at the Mormon Temple, the Mormon Tabernacle, Young's house, the house of his many wives, and the homes of elders. As migrant women described it, the city was beautiful, marked by lovely adobe houses surrounded by well-tended gardens, and crowned by the impressive temple and tabernacle buildings.[95] To one woman, the city looked like "a herd of white castles," while another characterized it as being "as singular as its inhabitants." She added that

it is built entirely of sunburnt bricks, without blinds. Not one house can boast them. Still, some of them have neat, pleasant appearances, and could you divest yourself of the idea that they were inhabited by Mormons, would in some instances be truly beautiful.[96]

When these Gentile women entered the Mormon Tabernacle to witness the religious services of the Latter-Day Saints, they were much less complimentary. In 1851, one woman claimed that "it was not anything dignified on the Sabbath, but they were very rough and coarse with their remarks." She was upset that the congregation responded with cheers when slurs were hurled against the United States, with the leaders actually threatening to roll rocks down upon the heads of U.S. soldiers should they try to enter the city. She concluded that "their remarks were all coarse; there was nothing refined or elevating in it."[97] A year later, Mary Bailey reported that the Mormon service consisted primarily of people relating "dreamy visions." She was not shocked by the exhortations but by the fact that so many of the Latter-Day Saints were Europeans. It seemed strange to her "that such delusion should spread so far."[98] Another female observer offered yet another perspective on the Mormon services by describing one that included "a ranting Mormon oration," superb music, and an overly long benediction.[99]

In spite of their often positive impressions of Salt Lake City and its inhabitants, most women did not radically alter their anti-Mormon views. The basic ideas that they carried into the city were frequently the same ideas with which they left. One young woman of the 1870s who was duly impressed with the beauty of the city declared, "Still I should not want to live there, even in the Gentile part and among Gentiles."[100] There were, however, some exceptions. After a winter among the Mormons in the 1850s, Sarah Cooke became a member of the church. Yet she staunchly withstood all suggestions that she and her husband engage in plural marriage.[101] Much more typical, though, was the vehement statement of a woman who spent a reasonably pleasant period of time in Salt Lake City during the mid-1850s:

> To-morrow we turn our back upon the Mormon capital, with its wretchedness, abominations, and crimes. . . . how we rejoice to escape from a region of human depravity, the terrible features of which have opened more and more distinctly to view the longer our sojourn has continued.[102]

These women's words sound bitter and pitiless, but they seem to contradict both the image of Salt Lake City as a pleasing oasis in the desert and the impression of Mormons as industrious folks whose energy made that forsaken spot bloom. Against all odds and in the face of all predictions to the contrary, these religiously committed people were able to turn persecution to their own advantage and to wrest a living from a region marred by salt flats and a desert climate. Through gruelling effort, they crowned their city with an intricately engineered tabernacle, whose acoustics are still considered remarkable in our technological age. Yet most women both entered and left Salt Lake City with the firm conviction that the Mormon oasis was not Zion at all but the center of degeneracy and depravity marring an otherwise progressive continent. While they would enter American Indian villages haltingly and with disapproval and leave them with good words for their inhabitants on their lips, most women evidently could not transform their views of Mormons in a similar manner.

It is not difficult to discern the primary reason for women's tremendous hostility toward the Mormon capital and the sect that it represented. The reason lies in one word: polygamy. Women saw plural marriage as a demoralizing institution that presented a potential threat to their own monogamous marriages and limited kinship family structures.[103] Most women thought this practice abhorent and despicable, and they spoke of it as "wicked" and "demoralizing" in the extreme.[104] Whereas they found forgiveness in their hearts for the "primitive" and "ignorant" American Indians who engaged in polygamy, they could not extend the same understanding to Mormons, who were white, well educated, and claimed to be Christians. Women thus displayed no forbearance toward the polygamists of the Church of Latter-Day Saints but denounced them in blistering terms for their depravity.

Lucene Parsons spent the winter of 1851 among the Latter-Day Saints in Salt Lake City before she continued on to California. For her, coming to know Mormons was not to be equated with learning to like them. She thought that "a meaner set lives not on this earth," and she was convinced that any "honest person" would come to the same conclusion after a few months among them. She was distressed at the Mormons' discriminatory hiring practices that barred a Gentile from working on a job that a Mormon wanted. Her real barrage, however, was leveled at polygamous marriages. Because of this custom, she felt that Latter-Day Saints were an "unprincipled sect" who "live like the brute creation more than like white folks." According to her, not only did these "demons" marry women as young as ten years old, but they married mothers, daughters, and sisters even at the cost of persuading them to abandon their own husbands. She added that the Mormon men did not treat their wives well, and quarreling, desertion, and divorce were all too common in the Salt Lake City family scene.[105] Another female migrant supported Parsons's views. She scathingly referred to Brigham Young's wives as a "harem," and she was disgusted that they were housed in a "poor, miserable log and adobe affair, directly in front of his elegant, Gothic-windowed barn!" She saw no reason for polygamy except male whim. "They marry and unmarry at pleasure several times a year if they choose," she insisted. Employing a frequently cited comparison, she added that "the state of society corresponds well with the Age of Barbarism in the east."[106]

Harriet Ward had a slightly different understanding of the rationale behind the concept of plural marriage. "They boast that all owned a plurality of wives for the purpose of raising up a perfect race to inhabit this new Jerusalem forever," she noted in her 1853 journal. "But," she added, "not any of them believes a word they preach, and they are a miserable lot of extortioners upon whom the wrath of God will yet be poured out." Ward's severe reaction is particularly interesting because she was one of the clear-cut cases of a woman initially terrified and distrustful of Indians who grew to like and admire them. In the case of the Mormons, Ward not only retained her disgust, but she felt that it was intensified by the time she had spent among them. As she left the Salt Lake area, she disputed the Mormons' right to occupy such a lovely land: "The country through which we have passed today is beautiful and should be inhabited by a different set of beings than the Mormons."[107]

In 1865, Sarah Herndon supported Ward's feelings with even more acerbity:

> This is a beautiful valley. Too good to be possessed by a community of bigamists. What a stigma upon the Government of these United States that whole communities are allowed to live criminal lives with impunity. I wonder how many are paying the penalty for bigamy in the penitentiaries of the United States? What is crime in one place, under the same Government, I would think, would be crime in all other places.

To Herndon, the effect of plural marriage on Mormon women was disastrous, for they were sad and sorrowful with never a smile on their lips.[108] Parsons too had emphasized the unhappiness of the "spiritual wives" she had known. According to Parsons, Mormon wives constituted "a poor heart broken & deluded lot" who were "made slaves to the will of these hellish beings who call themselves men."

She railed against male Mormon leaders who trampled on women's rights by denying Mormon women even as much liberty as was extended to "common slaves" in the South.[109]

Other women who also censured Mormon males expressed great perplexity concerning the females. One who hoped that "swift and terrible" punishment would befall profligate Mormon men wondered about the "superstitous credulity of their dupes," the women confined to Mormon "harems." To this woman, the personal histories of these polygamous unions presented "one unvarying picture of rascality, folly, imposition, credulity and crime." She could only conclude that female Latter-Day Saints were "good-natured, stupid fools" for consenting to the idea.[110]

Some female observers believed that Mormon women accepted polygamy because they were intimidated and fearful of the power structure. Gentile women frequently claimed that Mormon women confided to them tales of the destructive and demeaning nature of polygamy, and then pledged them to absolute secrecy. "An old woman told me they would drown her in the lake if they knew she talked against them," one young woman recalled. She emphasized that during her time in the Mormon capital she did not meet one woman who was "satisfied with her lot," and indeed, she had received many "applications from women that wanted to get away."[111] Sarah Cooke also remembered female friends who had prayed in agony over their plural marriages, with some believing that they would die from the distress of it.[112] Mary Powers's 1856 journal revealed similar instances of Mormon women confiding their feelings about polygamy after extracting a promise from her never to reveal them. Explaining that they feared reprisals, these women expressed bitterness against plural marriage and cautioned Powers to beware lest her husband be "sucked into the system" before she could prevent it.[113]

Gentile women not only perceived polygamy as a practice that should be shunned by white and supposedly civilized people; they also feared that it might affect their own men and marriages. Even if polygamy did not have a direct appeal to Gentile males, there was always the threatening possibility—as the Mormon women who talked with Powers had pointed out—that it would enmesh an unwary man before he knew it. Thus, frontierswomen could dredge up some tolerance for American Indians engaged in polygamy because that situation did not seem to pose a peril to the status of their own marriages.

However, when white traders "married" several native women or when Mormon men took plural wives, it hit too close to home to elicit any sympathy or understanding.

Because Gentile frontierswomen were so thoroughly convinced that polygamy was morally corrupt and personally menacing, they often projected their feelings to Mormon women, assuming that they must also hate and despise not only polygamy but the male leaders of the Latter-Day Saints who had imposed it upon them. It is useful, then, to examine this point in some Mormon women's documents. Mormon women were, after all, also frontierswomen. Just as the Gentile women, they crossed the plains to Salt Lake City and settled in a frontier region. Their responses to anti-Mormon prejudice and their frequent defense of polygamy must therefore be included in a consideration of frontierswomen's attitudes.[114]

One of the most prolific writers and speakers among Mormon women was Eliza Roxey Snow, a wife of Joseph Smith. She migrated to Salt Lake shortly after Smith's murder in 1844. Maintaining that she had learned to "love" the "principle and design of Plural Marriage," she was very upset by the negative reactions that she encountered as she moved toward Salt Lake. According to her, the inhabitants of Des Moines "manifested as much curiosity as though viewing a menagerie of wild beasts." She concluded that "their levity and apparent heartlessness was proof of profound ignorance."[115] Many other Mormon wives who made the trek to Salt Lake City described their initial introduction to the idea of plural marriage as a "bitter pill," a concept repugnant to their feelings, and as a crushing trial.[116] But, like Snow, they came to an acceptance of polygamy as a religious duty and sacred proclamation. In 1857, one of these women's husbands decided to take another wife after twenty-eight years of monogamous marriage with her, and said that she was willing to accede to his decision because "it was a duty her religion demanded." The advantage, according to her, was that she was now "freer and can do herself individually things she never could have attempted before; and work out her individual character as separate from her husband."[117]

Shortly after their relocating in Salt Lake in the 1840s, another Mormon wife accepted the presence of a second wife because it was a "sacred revelation." Her religion required her to support polygamy, and she maintained that her family lived happily with no jealousy. She expressed great hostility against those who invaded Mormon homes with "impudent questioning" and held Mormon women "up to scorn!" While arguing that polygamy was a religious duty rather than a practice derived from wicked or base motives, she was violently opposed to a proposed law to make plural marriage illegal because it would deprive women of their lawful husbands while marking their offspring as illegitimate. This Mormon woman's acrimony in blaming the outside world for a plethora of Mormon troubles seemed almost unbounded.[118]

Other Mormon female migrants to Salt Lake also railed against laws passed by Gentiles that, in their view, would force Mormons to flee the United States in order to follow the sacred precepts of their religion.[119] Others could not understand why Latter-Day Saints were so widely maligned for polygamy. They felt that Mormons had committed none of the crimes and misdemeanors charged to them.[120] They argued that when a man took an additional wife it was done only in the presence, and with the full approval, of his other wives; hence, there was nothing secretive, corrupt, or underhanded about it.[121] Moreover, some of these Mormon women contended that the children of plural marriages were happier, healthier, and "brighter intellectually and physically than those born under the restricted law of Monogamy."[122]

Mormon wife Margaret S. Smoot could not fathom why plural marriage, if all its advantages were conceded, was so "unjustly condemned by the world." As a migrant to Salt Lake after Smith's death and the destruction of Nauvoo in 1844, Smoot was already one of two wives. After her arrival in Salt Lake in 1847, she lived a "poor but happy" life in a community characterized, according to her, by virtue and chastity. "Vice and prostitution were things unknown to our society," she recalled. The only "houses of ill fame" in the area were those established by "Monagamists, Interlopers and defamers of women."[123] According to another Mormon woman, abortion and infanticide were also unknown among them because of the ability of extended families to absorb all pregnancies and births; they were not like Gentiles, who sought "to destroy the life of an infant before it is born and after because their deeds have been evil."[124]

From this sampling of the writings of Mormon frontierswomen it appears that many of them supported the system of polygamy.[125] Was it only from the outside that plural marriages of the Latter-Day Saints seemed so reprehensible? Were Gentile women laboring under gross misconceptions about polygamy? Did Gentile women imagine or invent the unhappy confessions of Mormon wives that they recorded in their diaries and journals? Did they perhaps refuse to listen to the true feelings of women who favored plural marriage simply because the idea was so frightening to them?

While these are all interesting and potentially significant questions, they are impossible to answer considering the current state of available data on plural marriage among the Latter-Day Saints. One scholar, Marilyn Warenski, herself raised as a Mormon, has recently argued that Mormon women were thoroughly indoctrinated in the principles advocated by the church and that their public support of controversial issues had been superbly orchestrated by the Mormon male power structure. According to her, when Latter-Day Saints came under attack for polygamy while seeking statehood in the 1870s, church leaders encouraged women to undertake a voluble defense of polygamy. In what she termed "an institutional political maneuver," Mormon women demanded their rights as women, that is, the right to chose their own marriage style. Warenski charged that

> here, in this uprising of Mormon women in defense of polygamy, is perhaps the ultimate example of how women have been coerced, in the name of God, to participate in their own oppression; and in this case there was the ironic twist of the argument being presented under the guise of women's rights.[126]

Yet, even after Utah attained statehood and polygamy was formally outlawed, some women chose to remain in or to enter plural marriages. Although this often created a situation in which Mormon women had to repudiate publicly their marital status, skip around the country to elude the authorities, or enter voluntary exile in other countries such as England, there is evidence that some unsanctioned polygamy still existed in the twentieth century.[127] Was it, as one woman suggested, that Mormon women were simply accustomed to plural marriages from childhoods spent in polygamous homes? Had they been led to believe that such an experience prepared them for the afterlife?[128] Or were they really convinced of the religious validity of plural marriage, believing that it could not be altered by any legal code foisted upon them by the Gentile world?

Of course, there are no clearly defensible answers to any of these questions. Regardless of whether Mormon women truly accepted and supported polygamy, the significant factor for this study is that a very large number of frontierswomen disdained Mormons for engaging in plural marriage and refused to modify their stance despite any evidence to the contrary. They often refused to pity Mormon women for their "delusions," castigating them instead for their weak-mindedness. While these same frontierswomen were beginning to extend understanding, kindness, and even affection to American Indians, they denied such feelings to Latter-Day Saints. Women's sympathies, distinctly selective in nature, were directed toward American Indians and away from those people known as Mormons.[129]

But not *all* aboriginal populations automatically elicited women's sympathies. The mere fact that a group of people were "primitive savages" or untutored natives did not guarantee that frontierswomen would extend their aid, understanding, and friendship to them. The collegial relationships that so often developed between white women and native Americans was in the trans-Mississippi West a complex process, the result of which is illustrated by a survey of women's responses to another native group very similar in appearance and culture to American Indians but one that failed to inspire female benevolence. In spite of their close contact with women during an intensified period of time, these native people remained the objects of women's venom and disgust. They were the natives along the Panama Trail, a route chosen by many emigrants who were anxious to get to the California gold fields as quickly as possible. Like the Mormons, Panamanians remained as despicable in women's eyes when they reached the end of the trail as when they had set out. Women who carried anti-native prejudices into the eastern portion of Panama also carried them, often in an intensified form, out of the western region of the country.

Because of the arduous nature of the crossing, female emigrants along the isthmus route were probably not very numerous. The entire trip took anywhere from twenty-one days to a month and a half. It involved boarding a steamer in New York; crossing the isthmus on the back of a mule led by a Panama native or, after 1855, crossing by railroad; and boarding another steamer to make the passage to San Francisco. The journey was not only marked by seasickness, overcrowding, bad food, and boredom while on shipboard, but during the Panama crossing it was characterized by disease, terrible accommodations, a hot and steamy jungle climate, and resentful natives. Although the Panama route was the quickest and most traveled path to California during the Gold Rush years, it also presented some of the worst hardships to the argonauts and to others who chose it.[130]

Although it is virtually impossible to determine what proportion of those people already flocking into Panama by the end of 1848 were women, historians of the isthmus crossing usually insist that their numbers were insignificant.[131] One historian has argued that because the trip was much too severe to attract women passengers the few women who did attempt it were prostitutes anxious to reap lucrative rewards from their timely appearance among male travelers.[132] The number of women on the Panama Trail was probably limited by the fact that most of them traveled with family units who sought not only routes cheaper than the Panama crossing but trails that would allow them to carry larger amounts of baggage and supplies. Yet women's diaries and journals exist which prove that women, both single and married, were among the passengers of virtually every Panama-bound steamship from the beginning. On the initial voyage of the *California* to San Francisco, 14 of the 364 passengers were women.[133] After a portion of the railroad opened in 1851 and accommodations had improved, the number of women making the crossing increased. By 1867, they accounted for a significant but undetermined proportion of the four hundred thousand passengers transported across Panama by the railroad within thirteen years.[134]

Like the women who made the overland crossing along the various land routes, these female migrants across Panama were fully, if not always accurately, informed about what treatment they might expect from the natives. Guidebooks published specifically for Panama travelers emphasized the necessity to be "liberal to the men who work the canoe." Migrants were advised to negotiate written contracts with porters and other native workers to hold them to their agreements.[135] These less than encouraging bits of advice were supplemented by newspaper stories that warned of the rampant vice and corruption, especially an addiction to gambling, among Panamanians.[136] Newspapers also carried lurid accounts of riots and other violent confrontations between natives and emigrants, which were introduced by dramatic headlines, such as the following: "Fearful Riot at Panama! Twenty-Five Americans Massacred by the Natives."[137] The texts of such stories referred to "excited savages," "a general melee," or "a general massacre." Their authors reported that when Panamanian troops were dispatched to quell the rioters they joined their "fellows" in the attack on the migrants and engaged in altercations that resulted in "natives killing, wounding and robbing" ship passengers.[138]

After hearing a number of such tales, many women quickly developed an intense fear of the land portion of the trip. Sarah Brooks, migrating with her three-and-a-half-year-old child in 1852, related that "the interest of all centered in that much-dreaded part of the journey," the crossing of the isthmus. "The papers had given accounts of the dangers to be met with there," she explained, accounts that mentioned "robbers, loss of baggage, of people being left behind and having to wait for another steamer; and, worst of all, getting the much dreaded Panama fever."[139] In addition, these women were imbued with the concept of Manifest Destiny, which argued that their "little brown brothers" were an inferior race of people awaiting the infusion of enlightenment and civilization which the travelers would introduce to them. Therefore, they fully expected the Panamanians to be, as one woman said, "intellectually little above the animals."[140]

Many women who departed from New York, after they had been exposed to these demeaning images of the native peoples they would encounter in Panama, seldom mentioned the natives in their diaries, journals, letters, and memoirs of the trip. Other features of the journey engaged their attention. They wrote of rough seas and seasickness, magnificent scenery, inadequate meals, friendly companions, and the mule ride across the isthmus.[141]

Other women, however, were quite taken with the native population of Panama and devoted a good deal of space in their writings to them. Like women on the overland trails, Panama migrants were at first interested in the physical appearance and style of dress of the natives they met. They routinely described the nearly naked state of both the men and children, observing that the men seldom wore anything more than a breechcloth, or as one woman said, a "bit of cloth about their loins."[142] One woman, making the passage in reverse from California to New York in 1854, portrayed the men as "swarthy-visaged, half-naked Carthaginians. . . . a mongrel race of natives, whose appearance and features were equally as repulsive."[143] Another woman added unkindly that most of them were "intolerably ugly."[144]

The women of Panama received some compliments from female travelers about their dress. Some white women thought that they dressed "fantastically," although their many ruffles and beads made them seem to be dressed perhaps a bit "comically."[145] One woman declared that "the females were dressed quite fancifully" in their frocks of thin white gauze, while another felt that their outfits bordered on the gaudy.[146] Some female observers were so delighted with these colorfully attired women that they liked to watch them as they set out their wares in the meat market, moved through the streets with baskets on their heads, or spread their sparkling white wash on the grass to dry.[147] One woman asserted that she was so "perfectly fascinated with them and their wares" that she purchased "bananas, oranges and limes and a basket" despite warings not to consume local produce due to the dangers of disease.[148]

When it came to native homes, hotels, and other buildings, women were much less likely to be so admiring. Instead, they wrote disparagingly of filthy native huts, miserable thatched dwellings, and such overwhelming dirt and stench that they were, according to one, "obliged to hold our noses and have cologne to go to sleep by."[149] In 1861, Julia Twist was horrified by the shanties she saw and scornfully wrote that they were "occupied by a race of beings hardly fit to be classed as human. They are the nearest to the brute creation of any I have yet seen."[150]

Apparently, many women travelers across Panama possessed a great deal of interest in the native population. Panama's natives, like their American Indian counterparts along the overland route, were also exceedingly curious about the female migrants. Women mentioned that they were disconcerted by the natives' habit of invading hotels and other buildings in order to stare at them "in perfect astonishment," as if they were "one of the greatest curiosities in the world."[151] One woman was very annoyed that Panamanians not only stared at her but yelled at her as she passed by; she said that they looked to her "frightful in the extreme."[152]

There is little documentary evidence regarding the thoughts that filled Panamanians' minds while observing these female emigrants. However, there are many examples of women's writings indicating that migrants' views of the natives were largely negative. Women were generally harsh, cruel, and spiteful as they described the native inhabitants of Panama's towns and villages, who carried their luggage, led their mules, piloted their canoes, carried them on their backs from the steamers to shore, and performed a wide variety of other services. Sarah Brooks demonstrated a common attitude toward Panamanians when she stated that "desperately ugly in looks, they proved equally so in character."[153]

Other women were more specific than Brooks in their assessments of the "ugly" nature of the natives, particularly in their accusations that they were greedy and probably dishonest as well.[154] One woman was convinced that the natives resorted to subterfuges such as hiding mules and bribing boatmen "in order to secure as many pieces of money as possible" from the helpless and vulnerable emigrants. To her, Panamanians were crafty as well as indolent and stupid, and she concluded that they were "perfectly happy and contented in their ignorance."[155] An 1849 traveler also took the stand that the natives were "simple, inoffensive people" who nevertheless "understand perfectly the getting of dimes from the Americans."[156] Her position was supported, in turn, by another forty-niner who insisted that the natives "extort all they can from the travelers."[157]

Still other women were very upset by what they considered to be the temperamental nature of the Panamanians. Jessie Benton Fremont portrayed them as "naked, screaming, barberous" people, while May Ann Harris Meredith jotted in her diary that "the natives were so impetuous and excitable that it was almost impossible to do anything with them." At another point, Meredith complained that the natives "speak the Spanish language and create the greatest confusion and noise I ever heard." She declared that "they almost make me crazy."[158] Other female travelers reported that the natives' tempestuousness was further aggravated by their tendency to drink, gamble, and fight.[159]

This unfavorable picture of Panamanians in women emigrants' writings was almost totally unrelieved by approving remarks. Unlike their sister migrants on the overland routes, the women who crossed the isthmus seemed oblivious to any signs of personality, creativity, or energy in the natives they encountered. During the approximately ten days that it took to traverse Panama, women had neither the opportunity nor the motivation to revise either their images of themselves or their conceptions of the natives along their route. Consequently, nearly all of them maintained their anti-native prejudices throughout their time on the Panama trail.

In fact, many women travelers found their prejudices intensified by the outbreaks of violence that frequently erupted between migrants and natives. Since most emigrants entered Panama with expectations of brutish treatment from the natives, they may have tended to act in a belligerent or arrogant manner that, in turn, produced the results that they had anticipated. Considering the boredom, heat, and tension of the situation, travelers' attitudes and actions could have easily created trouble between themselves and the Panamanians, and the results would only have confirmed their view that such conflict was inevitable.[160]

Women's documents frequently chronicle native uprisings, massacres, and attacks. In 1852, for example, Sarah Brooks was involved in an altercation with "an ugly set" of boatmen, one of whom shed his breechcloth due to the heat and ignored all orders to put it back on. The women sheltered themselves with umbrellas, and the other boatmen retired to nearby trees for a nap. The "stormy scene" resulted in the male migrants drawing knives and pistols on the natives, who "sullenly" returned to their work.[161]

As a result of such petty squabbles, the Panamanians were accused of causing trouble and gained a reputation as bold, insolent, and dangerous people. Crossing Panama in 1854, Mallie Stafford was surprised that despite the dangers of attack from these "hordes of merciless savages" great numbers of gold-seekers pushed onward toward California. She quickly learned that many travelers were well armed due to reports of atrocities and massacres, whose "bare recital" was enough in her view to make "the stoutest female heart quail with apprehension." She was frightened when a male migrant impetuously drew a pistol on a native mule driver who had told him to "go to hell." And she was terrified when another native man pulled her mule off the main trail. She flailed at him ineffectually with her riding whip, but she was fortunately saved by a runner sent out from their destination hotel to meet them. After this episode, she began to believe the many rumors that were circulating about the Panamanians:

Men had been murdered for their money and clothing, and women had been stolen away and murdered for their jewelry. The natives appeared to be the lowest type of humanity, treacherous, malicious, deceptive, and avaricious, many of them being capable of committing the foulest murder for a small sum of money. Only a few months before the natives, armed, had waylaid a train of passengers, and robbed and massacred them in open daylight.

When she met two other women who had been saved from would-be assailants, she concluded that "this incident, added to my own personal experience convinced me that we had heard no idle rumors, that dark and mysterious deeds had been committed, and that 'the half had not been told.'"[162]

A few years later, several women were caught in the disastrous 1856 riot that finally occurred in Panama City as a result of rumor, prejudice, and conflict.[163] One of these recollected that during the course of the eighteen-hour seige "families were separated. . . . many were knocked down, beaten, left for dead in the streets, and some of the women had their earrings torn from their ears, and brooches from their dresses." She suggested that "the natives seemed angry at the constant streams of 'Yankees' who were using their town as a convenient stepping stone to the treasure land of California."[164] A year after the outbreak, Lucy Sexton discovered that the safety of her party across the isthmus was now ensured by a sizable contingent of United States Marines. Like the U.S. Cavalry stationed throughout the American West, these marines guarded the intrusive immigrants from the resistance of the native people.[165]

Within only a few years, the flood of migrants moving thoughtlessly and aggressively through Panama had created an incendiary situation between themselves and the natives. When added to the rigors of the trip itself, this tension and discord were not conducive to a very pleasant passage. Consequently, women had neither the time nor the inclination to adjust their interpretations of Panama's natives during the course of their journey. Their memories of the trek were well summarized by Mallie Stafford, who depicted her trip as "a ride over a wild, inhuman country on the back of a wild, irresponsible mule driven by a wild, demoralized, irrepressible son of the tropics."[166]

Of course, there were many women who harbored very similar sentiments about their overland passage to the Far West. Their negative comments were, however, balanced by many other women who found much to enjoy and savor not only in the trip itself but in the native peoples they encountered along the trail and in their new homes. The understanding, affection, and empathy that these women developed toward American Indians was not extended to other minority groups.

This selective nature of frontierswomen's sympathies is crucial to an understanding of the significance of relations between white women and native Americans. The relationship that developed between these frontierswomen and American Indians was unique, for it was not replicated in women's contacts with any other group of frontier people or aboriginal population. Friendly and collegial interchanges between women and Indians demonstrates that the traditional interpretation, perpetuated by myth and media, of women and Indians as adversaries is neither accurate nor useful.

✤[7]✤

The Legacy of Image and Myth

Widely touted legends and myths regarding the nature of women, American Indians, and the interaction of the two have exerted tremendous influence from the beginning of settlement of the American colonies to the present day. Advocating the view that women were weak and vulnerable while Indians were savage and rapacious, myth and media promoted the idea that contact between the two groups was almost always calamitous. According to the typical scenario, women often ended up broken in spirit and body as a result of their encounters with American Indians. Such occurrences contributed weighty evidence to the argument that the unmanageable native must be exterminated or at least physically constrained under the watchful eye of a reservation agent.

As women turned westward their minds were filled with both American and European attitudes about themselves, American Indians, and the many dangers of the venture for females. Westering women carried with them white ideas about the native groups they would meet. They also labored under a set of beliefs about females in nineteenth-century America that helped to shape their own views of Indians. Accordingly, frontierswomen tended to emphasize and react to particular aspects of native culture, society, and value systems.

More specifically, women were taught that they were, on the one hand, superior beings because they possessed exceptional moral abilities and, on the other, that they were inferior beings because they were physically weak. Because women were enjoined to see themselves as the guardians of morality, the protectors of ethics and civilization, they tended to conceive of American Indians, as uncivilized, deficient in morality, and brutalized. In effect, they sought out the "bad" Indian. However, because women were taught that they were weak, they also paradoxically pursued the "good" Indian, that being whose natural purity and virtue would protect women from the ravages of the environment and of the natives themselves.

Consequently, frontierswomen viewed their westering experiences, and particularly those involving American Indians, with a jaundiced eye. Influenced by anti-Indian prejudices, overwrought from listening to horror stories about Indians, and prepared to discover a largely unattractive set of characteristics in the natives they encountered, these women's initial contacts with American Indians were largely predetermined before they even set foot upon the westward trail. Clearly, one legacy of image and myth was its detrimental effect upon contact and relations between females and natives. Such tension prevailed that disasters often did result. The anxiety-ridden woman who grabbed an ax when an Indian approached, only to be confronted with a startled native also grasping for a weapon, was the unfortunate victim of her own fears.

Under these strained circumstances, it was remarkable that numerous women were able to move beyond the customary beliefs about themselves and American Indians. A crucial change in frontierswomen's responses frequently occurred as they met various types of Indians. At the same time, they observed their own resilience in the face of the harsh demands imposed on them by the frontier. As women associated with actual American Indians, they came to realize that natives were neither as "good" nor as "bad" as tradition had presented them. Most women were also simultaneously undergoing changes in their attitudes toward themselves. They discovered that their supposed moral superiority was only one of the many attributes required of them and that it could not be exercised with any regularity in the frontier setting. They also learned that they were not physically inept but could participate in heavy work, handle weapons, and protect themselves. If, then, women were not of value first and foremost as civilizers there was no need for them to emphasize the inferior aspects of native character. If they were not weak there was little necessity for them to depend on the superior aspects of native character for protection. As a result, many frontierswomen began to trade with, hire, socialize with, and become friends with American Indians.

Again, image and myth exerted a powerful influence. The reality of these often pleasant, and frequently empathetic, relationships between women and American Indians did not filter back to eastern and southern Americans or to Europeans. Casual observers and scholars alike were too steeped in customary lore to comprehend what was actually happening between women and Indians on the frontier. Since there was much more interest in the adventures of frontiersmen than in those of women, western women's diaries and letters were not widely published, nor were women asked by newspapers to become correspondents or by publishing houses to become authors. As women, they were not usually welcome on the lecture platform or lyceum circuit. Moreover, they were largely ignored as subjects of the interviews, sketches, and essays about the American West turned out in huge numbers by primarily male writers.

Needless to say, even fewer people were paying attention to what American Indians might have had to say about their true feelings and adventures. Indians toured with Buffalo Bill Cody and with other wild West shows, appeared in sideshows, circuses, and expositions, and made incongruous appearances as "savages" in delegations visiting Washington, D.C. and other major cities. When they were serious they were usually ignored, but when they engaged in antics they became the focus of attention. Most Americans seemed happy to believe that these odd creatures were indeed representatives of a rapidly vanishing breed.

It is not surprising that an era that considered these two groups of people as inferior beings would overlook women's and Indians' own personal interpretations of their experiences in favor of more customary and comfortable beliefs about them. It might be hypothesized that the reason that most Americans clung so tenaciously to the usual picture of women and Indians was more complex than simply their dismissal as insignificant people. It might be argued that most nineteenth-century Americans and Europeans could not surrender their prejudicial images of women and American Indians to pursue a more accurate portrayal of them as rational, capable beings. Such revisionist thinking would have upset prevailing concepts of inferiority and would have interfered with related discriminatory actions toward these groups. It was necessary to perpetuate accepted interpretations of women and Indians in order to support and rationalize social treatment of these two groups. Thus, most people could not allow themselves to see or hear what was actually taking place between women and American Indians in the trans-Mississippi West.

Therefore, image and myth regarding women and Indians impaired their interaction on the frontier and prevented generations of observers from perceiving its real nature. But image and myth also served to support and perpetuate prejudice and discriminatory treatment toward frontierswomen and natives. It is both curious and significant that these phenomena did not dissipate sometime during the twentieth century. Rather, the nineteenth century bequeathed to the twentieth century its own selective interpretation of the experiences of frontierswomen and American Indians. That many twentieth-century people must have shared the needs and prejudices of nineteenth-century people is indicated by their willing acceptance and continued perpetuation of these inaccurate interpretations. Many people would now agree, particularly those who are women and American Indians, that it is time to move beyond the view of relationships between females and natives embodied in both myth and media. It is time to reassess and revise the attitudes that supported the erroneous presentation of this particular chapter in the history of the American West.

Notes

Introduction

1. See for example, Robert F. Berkhofer, Jr., *The White Man's Indian: Images of the American Indian from Columbus to the Present* (New York: Alfred A. Knopf, Inc., 1978; Vintage Books, 1979).

2. Roy Harvey Pearce, "The Significances of the Captivity Narrative," *American Literature* 19 (1947), 1–20; Richard Van Der Beets, "The Indian Captivity Narrative as Ritual," *American Literature* 43 (1972): 548–62. One investigator has argued that these captivity narratives sold so well because they "focused on Indian brutality," which "served to justify the extermination of the Indian" who "still inhabited and defended the lands which whites coveted." James A. Levernier, "Indian Captivity Narratives: Their Functions and Forms" (Ph.D. diss., University of Pennsylvania, 1975), 27.

3. John Frost, *Pioneer Mothers of the West; or, Daring and Heroic Deeds of American Women* (Boston: Lee and Shepard, 1875), 22.

4. David T. Haberly, "Women and Indians: *The Last of the Mohicans* and the Captivity Tradition," *American Quarterly* 28 (Fall 1976): 431–43; Donald L. Kaufman, "The Indian as Media Hand-Me-Down," in Gretchen M. Bataille and Charles L. P. Silet, eds., *The Pretend Indians: Images of Native Americans in the Movies* (Ames, Iowa: Iowa State University Press, 1980), 24–25; Abbie Gardner-Sharp, *The Spirit Lake Massacre and the Captivity of Miss Abbie Gardner* (Des Moines: Iowa Printing Co., 1885).

5. Calvin Martin, "The Metaphysics of Writing Indian-White History," *Ethnohistory* 26, no. 2 (Spring 1979): 153; James Axtell, "A Moral History of Indian-White Relations Revisited" (unpublished paper presented at the annual meeting of the Organization of American Historians, Philadelphia, 1 April 1982), 1, 4, 8–9.

6. Reginald Horsman, "Recent Trends and New Directions in Native American History," in Jerome O. Steffen, ed., *The American West: New Perspectives, New Dimensions* (Norman: University of Oklahoma Press, 1979), 124–28.

Chapter 1

1. *Ladies Repository,* 3 (February 1843), 54.

2. Cotton Mather, *Ornaments for the Daughters of Zion* (Cambridge, Mass.: Printed by Samuel & Bartholomew Green for Samuel Phillips at Boston, 1692).

3. Julie Roy Jeffrey, *Frontier Women: The Trans-Mississippi West, 1840–1880* (New York: Hill and Wang, 1979), 10–13, 22–24; John Mack Faragher, *Women and Men on the Overland Trail* (New Haven: Yale University Press, 1979), 179–87.

4. Helen S. Papshively, *All the Happy Endings* (New York: Harper & Brothers, 1956), xiv–xv, 35–41. Regarding novels and other books, see Herbert R. Brown, *The Sentimental Novel in America, 1789–1860* (Durham, N.C.: Duke University Press, 1940), 282–87, 290–95, 300–322, 360–69; Leslie A. Fiedler, *Love and Death in the American Novel* (New York: Criterion Books, 1960), xvii–xxxiii, 49–55, 62–67; James D. Hart, *The Popular Book: A History of America's Literary Taste* (New York: Oxford University Press, 1950), 51, 67–68, 85–93; Ernest E. Leisy, *The American Historical Novel* (Norman: University of Oklahoma Press, 1950), 13–14; Ralph Thompson, *American Literary Annuals and Gift Books, 1825–1865* (New York: H. W. Wilson Company, 1936), 5, 30.· Regarding periodical literature, see Frederick Lewis Allen, William L. Chenery, and Fulton Oursler, "American Magazines, 1741–1941," *Bulletin of the New York Public Library* 45, no. 6 (June 1941), 439, 442–49; Eleanore P. Hartman, "Magazines—Molders of Opinion," *Wilson Library Bulletin,* 21 (April 1947), 600–601; Frank Luther Mott, *A History of American Magazines* (New York: D. Appleton & Company, 1930), 341–42, 351, 581–89, 594. Regarding children's books and periodicals, see Florence V. Barry, *A Century of Children's Books* (New York: George H. Doran, 1923); Rosalie V. Halsey, *Forgotten Books of the American Nursery* (Boston: C. E. Goodspeed & Company, 1911), 121, 127, 141, 150, 171, 188, 192–97, 201; Monica Kiefer, *American Children through Their Books, 1700–1835* (Philadelphia: University of Pennsylvania Press, 1948), 1–2, 18–20;

Abraham S. Rosenbach, *Early American Children's Books* (New York: Kraus Reprint Corporation, 1966), xxviii–xxxix, liii; Catherine M. Sedgwick, *A Love Token for Children* (New York: Harper & Brothers, 1838), and *Stories for Young Persons* (New York: Harper & Brothers, 1841); Lydia H. Sigourney, *The Boy's Reading-Book* (New York: J. Orville Taylor, 1839), and *Letters to My Pupils: With Narrative and Biographical Sketches* (New York: Robert Carter & Brothers, 1851); Elva S. Smith, *The History of Children's Literature* (Chicago: American Library Association, 1937).

5. Clifton J. Furness, ed., *The Genteel Female* (New York: Alfred A. Knopf, 1931), xvi–xxi, xliv.

6. Ann Douglas, *The Feminization of American Culture* (New York: Alfred A. Knopf, 1979), 12–13.

7. Susan P. Conrad, *Perish the Thought: Intellectual Women in Romantic America, 1830–1860* (New York: Oxford University Press, 1976), 95–98.

8. Abigail Adams, *Letters* (Boston: Wilkins, Carter & Co., 1848), 416.

9. Margaret Fuller Ossoli, *Memoirs of Margaret Fuller Ossoli* (Boston: Phillips, Sampson, and Company, 1852), 195.

10. *Ladies Companion* 20 (May 1844), 24–25; *Ladies Repository* 4 (October 1844), 312.

11. T. S. Arthur, *Advice to Young Ladies on Their Duties and Conduct in Life* (Boston: Phillips and Sampson, 1848), 124–31.

12. *Ladies Repository* 1 (April 1841), 121.

13. Hester Chapone, *Letters on the Improvement of the Mind* (New York: Evert Duyckinck, 1826), 151, 160.

14. Harriet Beecher Stowe, *The Minister's Wooing* (New York: Derby and Jackson, 1859), 37.

15. Barbara Welter, *Dimity Convictions: The American Woman in the Nineteenth Century* (Athens: Ohio University Press, 1976), 21.

16. Caroline Lee Hentz, *Ernest Linwood* (Boston: J. P. Jewett and Company, 1856), 459.

17. Maria Cummins, *The Lamplighter* (Boston: J. P. Jewett and Company, 1854).

18. Marion Harland, *Alone* (Richmond: A. Morris, 1855), 282.

19. *American Monthly Magazine* 9 (March 1837), 290–92.

20. Elizabeth Sandford, *Woman in Her Social and Domestic Character* (London: Longman, Brown, Green, and Longmans, 1842), 5.

21. *The Ladies Companion* 12 (December 1839), 62.

22. Mrs. A. J. Graves, *Women in American* (New York: Harper, 1844), 67.

23. Lydia H. Sigourney, *Letters to Young Ladies* (New York: Harpers, 1841), 13.

24. *Ladies Repository* 8 (September 1848), 277–78.

25. Catharine Beecher, *The American Woman's Home; or Principles of Domestic Science* (New York: J. B. Ford, 1870), 13, 466.

26. Kathryn Kish Sklar, *Catharine Beecher: A Study in American Domesticity* (New York: W. W. Norton & Company, 1973), 156–58.

27. Catharine Beecher, *Essay on Slavery* (1837; reprint, Freeport, N.Y.: Books for Libraries Press, 1970), 99–100.

28. Lydia Maria Child, *History of the Condition of Women*, vol. 1 (New York and Boston: C. S. Francis & Co., 1854), 9.

29. *Ladies Repository* 4 (October 1844), 313.

30. *Ladies Repository* 6 (October 1846), 305.

31. Nancy Cott, *The Bonds of Womanhood: "Woman's Sphere" in New England, 1780–1835* (New Haven: Yale University Press, 1977), 200–201.

32. Sarah Josepha Hale, *Northwood*, vol. 2 (New York: H. Long, 1852), 407.

33. Glenda Riley, "Origins of the Arguments for Improved Female Education," *History of Education Quarterly* 9 (Winter 1969), 455–70; Sarah Josepha Hale, Letters, Vassar College, Poughkeepsie, Mass.

34. Glenda Riley, "The Subtle Subversion: Changes in the Traditionalist Image of the American Woman," *The Historian* 32 (February 1970), 210–27.

35. *Godey's Lady's Book* 41 (July 1850), 355.

36. *Ladies Repository* 5 (June 1845), 163.

37. *Burlington Hawk-Eye*, 9 January 1851.

38. T. S. Arthur, *Ten Nights in a Barroom* (Boston: L. P. Crown, 1854).

39. Ida Husted Harper, *The Life and Work of Susan B. Anthony* (Indianapolis and Kansas City: Bowen Merrill Company, 1898), 66–68.

40. *Ladies Repository* 3 (May 1843), 139.

41. *Godey's Lady's Book* 21 (August 1840), 89.

42. Margaret Coxe, *Claims of the Country on American Females*, vol. 1 (Columbus: Isaac N. Whiting, 1842), 42.

43. Elizabeth Sandford, *Female Improvement* (London: Longmans, 1836), 114–15, 118.

44. *Godey's Lady's Book* 18 (June 1839), 283; ibid. 25 (December 1847), 330–32; ibid. 43 (August 1851), 122; ibid. 45 (August 1852), 193.

45. *Godey's Lady's Book* 61 (December 1860), 556.

46. Lydia H. Sigourney, *Poems* (Philadelphia: Key & Biddle, 1834), 29, 77–78, 171; and idem, *Sayings of Little Ones* (Buffalo: Phinney and Company, 1855), 244–45.

47. *Ladies Repository* 8 (January 1848), 17; ibid. 1 (April 1841), 113; *Godey's Lady's Book*, 37 (August 1848), 61–68.

48. *Ladies Repository* 8 (January 1848), 17.

49. *Ladies Repository* 1 (April 1843), 113.

50. Harland, *Alone*, 282.

51. *Godey's Lady's Book* 32 (January 1846), 1.

52. Angelina Grimke, *Appeal to Christian Women* (New York: American Anti-Slavery Society, 1836), 16–18.

53. Elizabeth Chandler, *Political Works and Essays* (Philadelphia: L. Howell, 1836), 17–20, 175, 47–48.

54. Lydia Maria Child, *The Right Way, the Safe Way* (New York: Published at 5 Beekman Street, 1860), 96.

55. Calvin Stowe, *Harriet Beecher Stowe* (Boston: Houghton Mifflin and Company, 1889), 259–60.

56. Elizabeth Cady Stanton, et al., *The History of Woman Suffrage*, vol. 1 (Rochester, N.Y.: Charles Mann, 1889), 67, 71.

57. Ibid., 73.

58. *New York Times*, 13 May 1859.

59. *The Knickerbocker* 23 (January 1844), 79–80.

60. *Godey's Lady's Book* 22 (April 1841), 155.

61. Ibid., 150–56.

62. *Burlington Hawk-Eye*, 26 December 1850.

63. Sklar, *Catharine Beecher*, 266–67.

64. Maria J. McIntoch, *Woman in America: Her Work and Her Reward* (New York: D. Appleton & Co., 1850), 102.

65. Lydia H. Sigourney, *The Western Home and Other Poems* (Philadelphia: Parry & McMillan, 1854), 27.

66. Charles F. Hoffman, *A Winter in the West by a New-Yorker*, vol. 2 (New York: Harper, 1835), 235; Hector E. Lee, "Tales and Legends in American Western Literature," *Western American Literature* 9 (Winter 1975), 239.

67. *Iowa News*, 24 June 1837; ibid., 26 August 1837.

68. Reprinted in *New York Tribune*, 27 July 1846.

69. Richard Drinnon, *Facing West: The Metaphysics of Indian-Hating and Empire Building* (Minneapolis: University of Minnesota Press, 1980), 131.

70. *Waterloo Courier*, 10 July 1860.

71. William W. Fowler, *Woman on the American Frontier* (Hartford: S. S. Scranton & Co., 1880), 3, 33, 359, 365, 502, 505.

72. Sklar, *Catharine Beecher*, 113–15, 168–83; *Burlington Weekly Hawk-Eye*, 6 April 1849.

73. Catharine Beecher, *Suggestions Respecting Improvements in Education* (Hartford: Packard & Butler, 1829), 52.

74. Catharine Beecher, *The Evils Suffered by American Women and Children* (New York: Harper & Brothers, 1846), 12.

75. Arthur J. Larsen, ed., *Crusader and Feminist: Letters of Jane Grey Swisshelm, 1858–1865* (St. Paul: Minnesota Historical Society, 1934), 191.

76. Herbert R. Brown, *The Sentimental Novel in America, 1789–1860* (Durham, N.C.: Duke University Press, 1940), 349.

77. F. A. Briggs, *Buffalo Bill's Witchcraft; or, Pawnee Bill and the Snake Aztecs* (New York: Street & Smith, 1911), 24, 28.

78. Leslie A. Fiedler, *The Return of the Vanishing American* (New York: Stein & Day, 1968), 177.

79. Ronald J. Quinn, "The Modest Seduction: The Experience of Pioneer Women on the Trans-Mississippi Frontier" (Ph.D. diss., University of California—Riverside, 1977), ii, 9, 11, 45–50.

80. Jeffrey, *Frontier Women*, 33–34; Sara Smith, "Diary," in Clifford Merrill Drury, *First White Woman Over the Rockies*, vol. 3 (Glendale, Calif.: Arthur H. Clark, 1966), 61–125; Patricia V. Horner, "Mary Richardson Walker: The Shattered Dreams of a Missionary Woman," *Montana, The Magazine of Western History* 32, no. 3 (Summer 1982), 22.

81. Drinnon, *Facing West*, 176.

82. Roy Harvey Pearce, *The Savages of America* (Baltimore: Johns Hopkins Press, 1965), 3–5; Frederick Turner, "The Terror of the Wilderness," *American Heritage* 28, no. 2 (1977), 59–62; Alden T. Vaughn, "From White Man to Redskin: Changing Anglo-American Perceptions of the American Indian," *American Historical Review* 87 (November 1982), 917–53.

83. Robert F. Berkhofer, Jr., *The White Man's Indian: Images of the American Indian from Columbus to the Present* (New York: Vintage Books, 1979), 2, 23–28.

84. Ronald T. Takaki, *Iron Cages: Race and Culture in Nineteenth-Century America* (New York: Knopf, 1979), 55–65, 92–107. See also Bernard W. Sheehan, *Seeds of Extinction: Jeffersonian Philanthropy and the American Indian* (New York: W. W. Norton & Company, 1973), and Michael Paul Rogin, *Fathers and Children: Andrew Jackson and the Subjugation of the American Indian* (New York: Vintage Books, 1975).

85. Quoted in Nancy B. Black and Bette S. Weidman, *White on Red: Images of the American Indian* (Port Washington, N.Y.: Kennikat Press, 1976), 41–48.

86. Robert J. Denn, "Captivity Narratives of the American Revolution," *Journal of American Culture* 2 (Winter 1980), 575–82.

87. James E. Seaver, ed., *The Story of Mary Jemison* (Canadaigua, N.Y.: J. D. Bemis & Company, 1824).

88. David T. Haverly, "Women and Indians: *The Last of the Mohicans* and the Captivity Tradition," *American Quarterly* 28 (Fall 1976), 431–33.

89. Abbie Gardner-Sharp, *The Spirit Lake Massacre and the Captivity of Miss Abbie Gardner* (Des Moines: Iowa Printing Company, 1885).

90. Mary Butler Renville, *A Thrilling Narrative of Indian Captivity* (Minneapolis: Atlas Company's Book and Job Printing Office, 1863).

91. Emeline L. Fuller, *Left by the Indians. Story of My Life* (Mt. Vernon, Iowa: Hawk-Eye Steam Print, 1892), 29.

92. Lonnie J. White, "White Women Captives of Southern Plains Indians, 1866–1875," *Journal of the West* 8, no. 3 (July 1969), 332, 336.

93. *New York Times*, 4 January 1868.

94. *New York Times*, 22 September 1851; ibid., 4 October 1851; ibid., 17 January 1853; ibid., 24 January 1853; ibid., 2 June 1859; ibid., 4 October 1870; ibid., 9 October 1870; ibid., 28 April 1871; ibid., 22 May 1878; ibid., 4 June 1878; ibid., 6 June 1878; ibid., 11 July 1887.

95. Robert V. Hine, *The American West* (Boston: Little, Brown, and Company, 1973), 191, 68.

96. See Gardner-Sharp, *Spirit Lake Massacre.*

97. Roy Harvey Pearce, "The Significances of the Captivity Narrative," *American Literature* 19 (1947), 2–6.

98. James A. Levernier, "Indian Captivity Narratives: Their Functions and Forms" (Ph.D. diss., University of Pennsylvania, 1975), 27, 31–36, 323.

99. Richard Van Der Beets, "The Indian Captivity Narrative as Ritual," *American Literature* 43 (1972), 553–62.

100. Fanny Kelly, *To the Senators and Members of the House of Representatives of Congress*, Broadside, undated, Newberry Library, Chicago, Illinois.

101. Black and Weidman, *White on Red*, 1–2.

102. Berkhofer, *White Man's Indian*, 95.

103. Ibid., 101.

104. *Burlington Daily Hawk-Eye and Telegraph*, 20 July 1855.

105. "Glimpses of Indian Life at the Omaha Exposition," *Review of Reviews* 18 (October 1898), 436–43.

106. "A Tenderfoot in the Indian Territory," *The Literary Digest* 91 (13 November 1926), 54–56.

107. An Old Scout, *The White Boy Chief or, The Terror of the North Platte* (New York: Frank Tousey, 1908), 3, 7, 20; Captain Latham C. Carleton, *Dave Bunker; or, The Outlaws of the Frontier* (Cleveland: Arthur Westbrook Company, 1908), 26, 51, 55, 76, 78, 80.

108. Chickering Carter, *Kid Curry's Last Stand* (New York: Street & Smith, 1907), 8.

109. Karen Ordahl Kupperman, *Settling with the Indians* (Totowa, N.J.: Rowman & Littlefield, 1980), 60–61; Valerie Sherer Mathes, "Native American Women in Medicine and the Military," *Journal of the West* 21, no. 2 (April 1982), 41–48; March C. Wright, "Economic Development and Native American Women in the Early Nineteenth Century," *American Quarterly* 33, no. 5 (Winter 1981), 525–28, 535–36; and Mary E. Fleming Mathur,

"Who Cares that a Women's [sic] Work Is Never Done . . . ?" *The Indian Historian* 4, no. 2 (1971), 11–16.

110. William J. Snelling, *Tales of the Northwest* (Minneapolis: University of Minnesota Press, 1936), 151.

111. James Fenimore Cooper, *The Pathfinder; or, The Inland Sea* (1840; New York: G. P. Putnam's Sons, n.d.), 234–35, 367, 389.

112. James Fenimore Cooper, *The Prairie: A Tale* (1827; New York: Dodd, Mead, & Company, 1954), 315.

113. *New York Times,* 1 August 1868.

114. Kupperman, *Settling with the Indians,* 58–59.

115. Jack D. Forbes, *The Indian in America's Past* (Englewood Cliffs, N.J.: Prentice-Hall, 1964), 79, 156–59; Snelling, *Tales of the Northwest,* 11–12.

116. Ron Tyler, "Artist on the Oregon Trail: Alfred Jacob Miller," *American West* 18, no. 6 (November–December 1981), 52, 55.

117. Hine, *American West,* 55.

118. Caroline Kirkland, *A New Home—Who'll Follow?* (New York: Charles S. Francis, 1841), 45.

119. James Hall, *Legends of the West* (New York: T. L. Magagnos & Co., 1854), 317–19.

120. James Fenimore Cooper, *The Last of the Mohicans: A Narrative of 1757* (1826; New York: Heritage Press, 1932), 255.

121. Drinnon, *Facing West,* 177.

122. Paul A. W. Wallace, "Cooper's Indians," in *James Fenimore Cooper: A Reappraisal,* ed. Mary E. Cunningham (Cooperstown, N.Y.: New York State Historical Association, 1954), 423–46.

123. Cooper, *Prairie,* 367.

124. Cooper, *Last of the Mohicans,* 254–55.

125. Snelling, *Tales of the Northwest,* 101.

126. William Gilmore Simms, *The Yemassee* (New York: W. J. Widdleton, Publisher, 1878), 299–300.

127. Old Scout, *White Boy Chief,* 2.

128. Gretchen M. Bataille and Charles L. P. Silet, eds., *The Pretend Indians: Images of Native Americans in the Movies* (Ames, Iowa: Iowa State University Press, 1980).

129. Barbara Welter, "The Cult of True Womanhood: 1820–1860," *American Quarterly* 18 (Summer 1966), 158–59.

130. Almira H. Phelps, *The Female Student, or Letters to Young Ladies on Female Education* (New York: Leavitt, Lord, & Co., 1836), 16.

131. Sandford, *Female Improvement,* 14–15.

132. George W. Burnap, *The Sphere and Duties of Woman* (Baltimore: J. Murphy, 1848), 45, 158.

133. *Godey's Lady's Book* 42 (January 1851), 65.

134. E. D. E. N. Southworth, *Retribution; A Tale of Passion* (Philadelphia: T. B. Peterson, 1856), 173, 188.

135. For example, Frances Wharton in James Fenimore Cooper, *The Spy: A Tale of the Neutral Ground* (1821; New York: G. P. Putnam's Sons, n.d.).

136. James Fenimore Cooper, *The Sea Lions, or, The Lost Sealers* (1849; New York: D. Appleton & Company, 1901), 223.

137. James Fenimore Cooper, *Jack Tier; or, The Florida Reef* (1848; New York: G. P. Putnam's Sons, n.d.).

138. John Frost, *Pioneer Mothers of the West; or, Daring and Heroic Deeds of American Women* (Boston: Lee and Shepard, 1875), iii–iv, 22.

139. Catherine Maria Sedgwick, *A Poor Rich Man and a Rich Poor Man* (New York: Harper and Brothers, 1836).

140. Hannah F. S. Lee, *Elinor Fulton* (Boston: Whipple and Damrell, 1837).

141. Hannah F. S. Lee, *Three Experiments of Living* (Boston: W. S. Damrell, 1837); Papshively, *All the Happy Endings*, 45.

142. E. D. E. N. Southworth, *Capitola* (Stockholm: P. A. Huldberg, 1865), 394.

143. James Fenimore Cooper, *The Pioneers; or, The Sources of the Susquehanna: A Descriptive Tale* (1823; New York: G. P. Putnam's Sons, n.d.).

144. *Godey's Lady's Book* 30 (March 1845), 99–100.

145. *Godey's Lady's Book* 31 (July 1845), 267–69; ibid. 31 (February 1845), 84–88.

146. *Godey's Lady's Book* 34 (April 1847), 215–17.

147. *Godey's Lady's Book* 37 (November 1848), 317.

148. *Godey's Lady's Book* 36 (January 1848), 67.

149. *Godey's Lady's Book* 22 (June 1841), 281.

150. *Godey's Lady's Book* 23 (July 1841), 41–42.

151. *Godey's Lady's Book* 27 (January 1843), 56. See also Jane A. Farrell, "Clothing for Adults in Iowa," *The Annals of Iowa* 46, no. 2 (Fall 1981), 118.

152. *Godey's Lady's Book* 26 (March 1843), 134; ibid. 26 (February 1843), 105–8.

153. Edward L. Wheeler, *Deadwood Dick's Eagles; or, The Pards of Flood Bar* (Cleveland: Arthur Westbrook Company, 1899), 8, 10.

154. Carleton, *Dave Bunker*, 77–78, 82.

155. Wheeler, *Deadwood Dick's Eagles*, 28.

156. Old Scout, *White Boy Chief*, 10–13, 19–20.

157. An Old Scout, *Young Wild West Surrounded by Sioux; or, Arietta and the Aeronaut* (New York: Frank Tousey, 1917), 10–11, 18.

158. Edward S. Ellis, *Hurricane Gulch* (New York: P. F. Collier, 1892), 109.

159. See, for example, Arthur Stringer, *The Prairie Wife* (New York: A. L. Burt Company, 1915).

160. Berkhofer, *White Man's Indian*, 28.

161. Cornelius J. Jaenen, *Friend and Foe: Aspects of French-Amer-Indian Cultural Contact in the Sixteenth and Seventeenth Centuries* (New York: Columbia University Press, 1976), 24.

162. Black and Weidman, *White on Red*, 132.

163. Cooper, *Last of the Mohicans*.

164. Quoted in Donald L. Kaufman, "The Indian as Media Hand-Me-Down," in Bataille and Silet, eds., *Pretend Indians*, 24.

165. Ibid., 23.

166. Berkhofer, *White Man's Indians*, 89.

167. *Frank Leslie's Illustrated Newspaper* 33, no. 857 (2 March 1872), 385, 391.

168. *New York Times*, 9 July 1865.

169. *New York Times*, 29 September 1851; ibid., 21 July 1865; ibid., 11 October 1870; ibid., 16 April 1871; ibid., 4 June 1878; ibid., 3 July 1887.

170. *New York Times*, 16 July 1887.

171. Helen Hunt Jackson, *A Century of Dishonor* (1881; Minneapolis: Ross & Haines, 1969); Carter, *Kid Curry's Last Stand*, 5, 11.

172. Wheeler, *Deadwood Dick's Eagles*, 17.

173. *The Winona Saturday Morning Post*, 5 July 1980; ibid., 17 January 1981.

174. Sherry Ann Sullivan, "The Indian in American Fiction, 1820–1850" (Ph.D. diss., University of Toronto, 1979), 195–97.

175. Bernard W. Sheehan, *Savagism and Civility* (Cambridge: Cambridge University Press, 1980), 127–31. See also Jay B. Hubbell, "The Smith-Pocahontas Story in Literature," *Virginia Magazine of History and Biography* (July 1957), 275–300.

176. Wilcomb W. Washburn, *The Indian and the White Man* (New York: Anchor Books, 1964), plates 3–5 between 134–35.

177. Marilyn J. Anderson, "The Best of Two Worlds: The Pocahontas Legend as Treated in Early American Drama," *The Indian Historian* 12, no. 2 (Summer 1979), 54–59, 64; Rayna Green, "The Pocahontas Perplex: The Image of Indian Women in American Culture," *The Massachusetts Review* 16, no. 4 (1975), 698–714; Philip Young, "The Mother of Us All: Pocahontas Reconsidered," *Kenyon Review* 24 (Summer 1962), 391–415.

178. Lydia H. Sigourney, *Pocahontas and Other Poems* (New York: Harper & Brothers, 1841), 32.

179. Berkhofer, *White Man's Indian*, 99.

180. Old Scout, *White Boy Chief*, 24–26.
181. Cooper, *Prairie*, 256–57.
182. Ibid., 346.
183. Ibid., 338.
184. Snelling, *Tales of the Northwest*, 50–61.
185. Simms, *Yemassee*, 311–13.
186. Cooper, *Pathfinder*, 336–55, 367–408, 494–501.

Chapter 2

1. Helen S. Papshively, *All the Happy Endings* (New York: Harper & Brothers, 1956), 2.
2. Kathleen M. Tillotson, *Novels of the 1840's* (Oxford: Clarendon Press, 1954), 13–14, 24.
3. Richard D. Altick, *The English Common Reader: A Social History of the Mass Reading Public, 1800–1900* (Chicago: University of Chicago Press, 1957), 83–86, 97, 100–110, 128–29, 131–35, 141–42, 152, 173, 188, 191–93, 200, 212–17, 239–40, 260–69, 277, 286, 293, 318, 330–39, 364–68.
4. Allan Nevins, ed., *America through British Eyes* (New York: Oxford University Press, 1948), v–vi, 3, 9; Oscar Handlin, ed., *This Was America* (Cambridge: Harvard University Press, 1949), 1–4, 7–8.
5. Mattie Austin Hatcher, ed., *Letters of an Early American Traveller: Mary Austin Holley, Her Life and Works, 1784–1846* (Dallas: Southwest Press, 1933), 99.
6. Frederick von Raumer, *America and the American People* vol. 1 (New York: Johnson Reprint Corporation, 1970), 500.
7. Isabella Bird, *The Englishwoman in America* (Madison: University of Wisconsin Press, 1966), 137.
8. Ray Billington, *Land of Savagery, Land of Promise: The European Image of the American Frontier in the Nineteenth Century* (New York: W. W. Norton & Company, 1980), 30.
9. An Old Scout, *The White Boy Chief or, the Terror of North Platte* (New York: Frank Tousey, 1908), 3–4, 11, 20; F. A. Briggs, *Buffalo Bill's Witchcraft; or, Pawnee Bill and the Snake Aztecs* (New York: Street & Smith, 1911), 8.
10. Edward L. Wheeler, *Deadwood Dick's Eagles; or, The Pards of Flood Bar* (Cleveland: Arthur Westbrook Company, 1899), 8, 10, 28; An Old Scout, *Young Wild West Surrounded by Sioux; or, Arietta and the Aeronaut* (New York: Frank Tousey, 1917), 18.
11. Bird, *Englishwoman in America*, 143.
12. Fredrika Bremer, *The Homes of the New World; Impressions of America* (New York: Harper & Brothers, 1868), 555.
13. This is a phenomenon that continues to exist in contemporary Amer-

ica. See Bryant M. Wedge, *Visitors to the United States and How They See Us* (Princeton, N.J.: D. Van Nostrand, 1965), 73.

14. See for example François René de Chateaubriand, *Atala and Rene* (London: Oxford University Press, 1963), and *Travels in America* (Lexington: University of Kentucky Press, 1969).

15. Ray A. Billington, "Cowboys, Indians and the Land of Promise: The World Image of the American Frontier" (Opening Address, Fourteenth International Congress of Historical Sciences, San Francisco, 22–29 August 1975), manuscript, Bancroft Library, Berkeley, Calif.

16. Chateaubriand, *Travels in America*.

17. William Cobbett, *A Years Residence in the United States of America* (Carbondale: Southern Illinois University Press, 1964); Alexis de Tocqueville, *Journey to America* (New Haven, Conn.: Yale University Press, 1960); Dr. Albert C. Koch, *Journey through a Part of the United States of North America in the Years 1844 to 1846* (Carbondale: Southern Illinois University Press, 1972); and Moritz Busch, *Travels between the Hudson and the Mississippi, 1851–1852* (Lexington: University Press of Kentucky, 1971).

18. Bird, *Englishwoman in America*, 144.

19. Jerzy Jedlicki, "Images of America," *Polish Perspectives* 18, no. 11 (November 1975), 26–28.

20. Preston A. Barba, *Balduin Möllhausen, the German Cooper*, vol. 17, *Americana Germanica* (Philadelphia: University of Pennsylvania Press, 1914), 19–20.

21. D. L. A. Ashliman, "The American West in Nineteenth Century German Literature" (Ph.D. diss., Rutgers University, 1969), ii–iii, 47, 54.

22. Richard H. Cracroft, "The American West of Karl May" (Master's thesis, University of Utah, 1963), 1, 153.

23. Hugh Honour, *The European Vision of America* (Cleveland: Cleveland Museum of Art, n.d.), 1, 4; Phillip D. Thomas, "Artists among the Indians, 1493–1850," *Kansas Quarterly* 3, no. 4 (Fall 1971), 3–6.

24. Thomas, "Artists among the Indians," 7.

25. Honour, *European Vision of America*, 12.

26. Thomas, "Artists among the Indians, 10–11, 8.

27. D. L. Ashliman, "The American West in Twentieth-Century Germany," *Journal of Popular Culture* 2, no. 1 (Summer 1968), 84–90; Billington, "Cowboys, Indians and the Land of Promise," 1.

28. Francis J. Grund, *The Americans in Their Moral, Social, and Political Relations* (New York: Johnson Reprint Corporation, 1968), 255.

29. Charles Dickens, *American Notes for General Circulation* (New York: Charles Scribner's Sons, 1911), 295; J. P. Brissot de Warville, *New Travels in the United States of America, 1788* (Cambridge: Harvard University Press,

Belknap Press, 1964), 418; W. Faux, *Memorable Days in America: Being a Journal of a Tour to the United States* (New York: A.M.S. Press, 1969), 180.

30. Robert G. Athearn, *Westward the Briton* (New York: Charles Scribner's Sons, 1953), 65.

31. Andrew J. Torrielli, *Italian Opinion on America as Revealed by Italian Travelers, 1850–1900* (Cambridge: Harvard University Press, 1941), 186–87; Arthur Schlesinger, "What Then Is the American, This New Man?" *American Historical Review* 48 (January 1943), 235–36.

32. Athearn, *Westward the Briton*, 67; *American Settler*, 16 July 1881.

33. Charles Hooton, *St. Louis' Isle or Texiana* (London: Simmonds & Ward, 1847), 51, 53, 149–50.

34. *American Settler*, 9 April 1887 and 5 July 1884.

35c. Edouard de Montule, *Travels in America, 1816–1817* (Bloomington: Indiana University Press, 1951), 142, 112, 174.

36. Charles Sealsfield, *The Americans as They Are* (New York: Johnson Reprint Corporation, 1970), 9; Fredrika Bremer, *America of the Fifties: Letters of Fredrika Bremer* (New York: American-Scandanavian Foundation, 1924), 259.

37. Jane L. Mesick, *The English Traveller in America, 1785–1835* (New York: Columbia University Press, 1922), 89–92; John G. Brooks, *As Others See Us: A Study of Progress in the United States* (New York: Macmillan, 1908), 309.

38. Athearn, *Westward the Briton*, 36.

39. Alexis de Tocqueville, *Democracy in America* (London: Oxford University Press, 1953), 465–66.

40. Friedrich Gerstacker, *Wild Sports in the Far West: The Narrative of a German Wanderer beyond the Mississippi, 1837–1843* (Durham, N.C.: Duke University Press, 1968), 200, 233.

41. Frances Trollope, *Domestic Manners of the Americans* (New York: Dodd, Mead, & Company, 1927), 60; Montule, *Travels in America*, 142.

42. Tocqueville, *Journey to America*, 129; Busch, *Travels*, 162; Francis and Theresa Pulszky, *White, Red, Black: Sketches of Society in the United States during the Visit of Their Guest*, vol. 1 (New York: Negro Universities Press, 1968), 80.

43. Charles Sealsfield, *The United States of North America as They Are* (New York: Johnson Reprint Corporation, 1970), 109; Augustus J. Prahl, "America in the Works of Gerstacker," *Modern Language Quarterly* 4 (June 1943), 220.

44. Mesick, *English Traveller in America*, 95; William J. Baker, ed., *America Perceived: A View from Abroad in the Nineteenth Century* (West Haven, Conn.: Pendulum Press, 1974), 31.

45. Sealsfield, *United States of North America*, 119; Gerstacker, *Wild Sports*, 239–40.

46. Kalikst Wolski, *American Impression* (Cheshire, Conn.: Cherry Hill Books, 1968), 85.

47. William A. Baillie-Grohman, *Camps in the Rockies* (New York: Charles Scribner's Sons, 1910), 22–23.

48. Harriet Martineau, *Society in America*, vol. 1 (London: Saunders and Otley, 1837), 117, 105.

49. Trollope, *Domestic Manners of the Americans*, 67.

50. Clarence Evans, "Friedrich Gerstacker, Social Chronicler of the Arkansas Frontier," *Arkansas Historical Quarterly* 6 (1947), 444; Henryk Sienkiewicz, *Portrait of America: Letters of Henryk Sienkiewicz* (New York: Columbia University Press, 1959), 35.

51. Alice H. Finckh, "Gottfried Duden Views Missouri, 1824–1827," pt. 2, *Missouri Historical Review* (October 1949), 22; Charles Dickens, *American Notes*, vol. 2 (London: Chapman and Hall, 1842), 47; Charles Lyell, *Travels in North America*, vol. 1 (London: J. Murray, 1845), 57.

52. Richard L. Rapson, *Britons View America* (Seattle: University of Washington Press, 1971), 107.

53. Eilert Storm, *Alene i Urskogen: Fortælling fra Amerika* (Kristiania: J. M. Stenersen & Company, 1899), 372.

54. Lyell, *Travels in North America*, 43; John Xantus, *Letters from North America* (Detroit: Wayne State University Press, 1975), 154; Baker, *America Perceived*, 31–32; Athearn, *Westward the Briton*, 66.

55. Von Raumer, *America and the American People*, 499; Prahl, "America in the Works of Gerstacker," 220.

56. Ole M. Raeder, *America in the Forties: The Letters of Ole Munch Raeder* (Minneapolis: University of Minnesota Press, 1929), 122–23.

57. Ernest Duvergier de Hauranne, *A Frenchman in Lincoln's America*, vol. 1 (Chicago: Lakeside Press, 1974), 230.

58. Mary S. Owen, "The American Frontiersman: A French Portrait" (unpublished manuscript, n.d., privately held, Mary Owens, England), pt. 7, 18–19.

59. Xantus, *Letters from North America*, 154–55.

60. Marilyn M. Sibley, *Travelers in Texas, 1761–1860* (Austin: University of Texas Press, 1967), 105–7.

61. Athearn, *Westward the Briton*, 66–67.

62. Pulszky, *White, Red, Black*, 119.

63. Busch, *Travels*, 136; Trollope, *Domestic Manners of the Americans*, 68.

64. Bremer, *Homes of the New World*, 615.

65. Charles V. Crosnier de Varigny, *The Women of the United States* (New York: Dodd, Mead & Company, 1895), 18–19.

66. William A. Bell, *New Tracks in North America*, vol. 1 (London: Chapman and Hall, 1869), 16.

67. Sealsfield, *Americans as They Are*, 9.

68. Baker, *America Perceived*, 39–40.

69. Ibid., 45–46.

70. Frances Wright, *Views of Society and Manners in America* (Cambridge: Harvard University Press, Belknap Press, 1963), 23, 221.

71. Martineau, *Society in America*, 1:108.

72. Harriet Martineau, *Retrospect of Western Travel*, vol. 1 (London: Saunders and Otley, 1838), 24.

73. Bremer, *America of the Fifties*, 245.

74. Martineau, *Society in America*, 1:108.

75. O. Drevdahl, *Fra Emigrationens Amerika* (Oslo, 1891), unpaged; Franklin D. Scott, "Soren Jaabaek, Americanizer in Norway," *Norwegian-American Studies and Records* 17 (1952), 92.

76. Axel Bruun, *Breve fra Amerika* (Christiana: A. Cammermeyer, 1870), 47.

77. Alan Conway, ed., *The Welsh in America: Letters from the Immigrants* (Minneapolis: University of Minnesota Press, 1961), 257; William and Robert Chambers, *Journey from New Orleans to California, 1849, and Other Interesting Excerpts from Chamber's Journal* (London: W. & R. Chambers, 1856), 13.

78. *American Settler*, 6 September 1884.

79. James Axtell, ed., *America Perceived: A View from Abroad in the Seventeenth Century* (West Haven, Conn.: Pendulum Press, 1974), 193.

80. Ibid., 122–23.

81. E. Stanley, *Journal of a Tour in America, 1824–1825* (London: Privately printed, 1930), 152; Percy G. Ebbutt, *Emigrant Life in Kansas* (London: S. Sonnenschien & Company, 1886), 45. See, for example, Blain T. Williams, "The Frontier Family: Demographic Fact and Historical Myth," in Harold M. Hollingsworth, ed., *Essays on the American West* (Austin: University of Texas Press, 1969), 40–65.

82. Athearn, *Westward the Briton*, 65.

83. Tocqueville, *Democracy in America*, 468; William P. Dallmann, *The Spirit of America as Interpreted in the Works of Charles Sealsfield* (St. Louis: Washington University Studies, 1935), 44–45; Merle Curti and Kendall Birr, "The Immigrant and the American Image in Europe, 1860–1914," *Mississippi Valley Historical Review* 37 (September 1950), 221.

84. Owen, "American Frontiersman," pt. 5, 20–22.

85. Pulszky, *White, Red, Black,* 234–35.

86. Handlin, *This Was America,* 252.

87. Clyde Thogmartin, "Prosper Jacotot: A French Worker Looks at Kansas in 1876–1877," *Kansas Historical Quarterly* 41 (September 1975), 19.

88. *American Settler,* 8 October 1892.

89. Schlesinger, "What Then Is the American," 235–36.

90. Dorothy B. Skardal, *The Divided Heart: Scandanavian Immigrant Experiences through Literary Sources* (Lincoln: University of Nebraska Press, 1974), 57; William Savage, *Observations on Emigration to the United States of America* (London: Sherwood, Neely, and Jones, 1819), 57.

91. Simon A. O'Ferrall, *A Ramble of Six Thousand Miles through the United States of America* (London: E. Wilson, 1832), 55–56.

92. Tivador Acs, ed., *Hungarian Pioneers in the New World* (Budapest: Lathatar Kiadasa, 1942), 190; Skardal, *Divided Heart,* 242–43.

93. James Axtell, ed., *America Perceived: A View from Abroad in the Eighteenth Century* (West Haven, Conn.: Pendulum Press, 1974), 225; von Raumer, *America and the American People,* 500.

94. Sealsfield, *United States of North America,* 131.

95. William N. Blane, *An Excursion through the United States and Canada, during the Years 1822–23* (London: Baldwin, Cradock, & Joy, 1824), 258–59.

96. Charlotte Erickson, *Invisible Immigrants, the Adaptation of English and Scottish Immigrants in Nineteenth-Century America* (Coral Gables, Fla.: University of Miami Press, 1972), 121; William and Robert Chambers, *Counsel for Emigrants and Interesting Information from Numerous Sources, with Original Letters* (Aberdeen: W. & R. Chambers, 1834), 127–28; Drevdahl, *Fra Emigrationens Amerika,* unpaged; Conway, *Welsh in America,* 257.

97. Axtell, *America Perceived: Seventeenth Century,* 202.

98. Mesick, *English Traveller in America,* 99.

99. Robert Barclay-Allardice, *Agricultural Tour in the United States and Upper Canada* (Edinburgh: W. Blackwood & Sons, 1842), 155–56.

100. Finckh, "Gottfried Duden Views Missouri," pt. 2, 21–22; George M. Stephenson, "Typical America Letters," *Yearbook of the Swedish Historical Society of America,* no. 7 (1921–1922), 60.

101. Theodore C. Blegen, *The Land of Their Choice: The Immigrants Write Home* (Minneapolis: University of Minnesota Press, 1955), 76; Michael Chevalier, *Society, Manners and Politics in the United States* (Boston: Weeks, Jordan, & Company, 1839), 430; Henry B. Fearon, *Sketches of America* (New York: Benjamin Bloom, 1969), 221.

102. Marcus L. Hansen, *The Atlantic Migration, 1607–1860* (Cambridge: Harvard University Press, 1940), 166; James Flint, *Letters from America* (Edinburgh: W. & C. Tait, 1822), 192.

103. H. Arnold Barton, *Letters from the Promised Land: Swedes in America, 1840–1914* (Minneapolis: University of Minnesota Press, for the Swedish Pioneer Historical Society, 1975), 42.

104. Thogmartin, "Prosper Jacotot," 19.

105. David T. Nelson, ed., *The Diary of Elisabeth Koren, 1853–1855* (Northfield, Minn.: Norwegian-American Historical Association, 1955), 346.

106. Pauline Farseth and Theodore C. Blegen, eds., *Frontier Mother: The Letters of Gro Svendsen* (Northfield, Minn.: Norwegian-American Historical Association, 1950), 28.

107. Milo M. Quaife, ed., *A True Picture of Emigration* (New York: Citadel Press, 1968), 91.

108. Busch, *Travels*, 174; Gustave Aimard, *The Border Rifles, A Tale of the Texan War* (Philadelphia: T. B. Peterson & Brothers, 1840), 67, 106.

109. *American Settler*, 5 July 1884; Torrielli, *Italian Opinion on America*, 186–87; Henri Herz, *My Travels in America* (Madison, Wis.: State Historical Society, 1963), 66.

110. Gustaf Unonias, *A Pioneer on Northwest America, 1841–1858: The Memoirs of Gustaf Unonias*, vol. 1 (Minneapolis: University of Minnesota Press, 1950), 227–29; Terry Coleman, *Passage to America, A History of Emigrants from Great Britain and Ireland to America in the Mid-Nineteenth Century* (London: Hutchinson and Company, 1972), 53, 257.

111. Athearn, *Westward the Briton*, 66.

112. Bird, *Englishwoman in America*, 151.

113. Athearn, *Westward the Briton*, 66.

114. Felix P. Wierzbicki, *California as It Is and as It May Be* (San Francisco: Bartlett Company, 1849), 50–51; Charles Sealsfield, *The Courtship of Ralph Doughby, Esquire* (Stuttgart: J. B. Metzler, 1843), 103–4.

115. Henryk Sienkiewicz, *Western Septet: Stories of the American West* (Cheshire, Conn.: Cherry Hill Books, 1973), 108.

116. See, for example, Auguste Carlier, *Marriage in the United States* (Boston: DeVries, Ifarra, & Company, 1837); Michael Chevalier, *Society, Manners, and Politics*.

114. Sibley, *Travelers in Texas*, 105–7; Patrick Shirreff, *A Tour through North America* (Edinburgh: Simpkin, 1835), 76; Fredrika Bremer, *The Homes of the New World; Impressions of America*, vol. 1 (New York: Harper & Brothers, 1853), 190–91.

118. J. W. Schulte Nordholt, "This Is the Place: Dutchmen Look at America," *Delta: A Review of Arts, Life and Thought in the Netherlands* 16 (Winter 1973–1974), 46.

119. *American Settler*, 12 December 1885.

120. Nordholt, "This Is the Place," 46–47; Varigny, *Women of the United States*, 13–14.

121. Ibid., 58–59.

122. Baker, *America Perceived*, 31.

123. Ibid., 43–44.

124. Herz, *My Travels in America*, 65.

125. Charles P. Trevelyan, *The Great New People: Letters from North America and the Pacific, 1898* (Garden City, N.J.: Doubleday, 1971), 113.

126. Alfred J. Morrison, ed., *Travels in the Confederation, 1783–1784 by Johann David Schopf* (New York: Bergman Publishers, 1968), 281, 283–84, 289.

127. Chateaubriand, *Travels in America*, 81.

128. Jens Tvedt, *Sihasapa-Indianerne: Norske Udvandreres Hendelser i Amerika* (Stavanger, 1887), 104–5.

129. George R. Brooks, "The American Frontier in German Fiction," in John F. McDermott, ed., *The Frontier Reexamined* (Urbana: University of Illinois Press, 1967), 165.

130. Karl May, *Winnetou* (New York: Seabury Press, 1977), xii–xiv.

131. Louis Philippe, King of France, *Diary of My Travels in America* (New York: Delacorte Press, 1977), 67.

132. Isaac J. Weld, *Travels through North America and the Provinces of Canada 1795–1797* (New York: Augustus M. Kelley, 1970), 217; Fearon, *Sketches of America*, 261; Paul Wilhelm, Duke of Württemberg, *Travels in North America, 1822–1824* (Norman: University of Oklahoma Press, 1973), 385.

133. Axtell, *America Perceived: Seventeenth Century*, 69.

134. Herz, *My Travels in America*, 97; Xantus, *Letters from North America*, 85; von Raumer, *America and the American People*, 1:137.

135. Rupert Brooke, *Letters from America* (London: Sidgwick & Jackson, 1931), 143.

136. Tocqueville, *Journey to America*, 199.

137. Ibid., 133; Wilhelm, *Travels through North America*, 2:196; Dickens, *American Notes*, 234.

138. John H. Vessey, *Mr. Vessey of England* (New York: G. P. Putnam's Sons, 1956), 140; David J. Jeremy, ed., *Henry Wansey and His American Journal, 1794* (Philadelphia: American Philosophical Society, 1970), 51.

139. Thomas Campbell, "Gertrude of Wyoming," in J. Logie Robertson, ed, *The Complete Poetical Works of Thomas Campbell* (London: Henry Fronde, 1907), 50; E. L. Jordan, ed., *America, Glorious and Chaotic Land: Charles Sealsfield Discovers the Young United States* (Englewood Cliffs, N.J.: Prentice-Hall, 1969), 192; Ulrich S. Carrington, *The Making of an American: An Adaptation of the Memorable Tales by Charles Sealsfield* (Dallas: Southern Methodist University Press, 1974), 47.

140. Tocqueville, *Journey to America*, 133–37, 199–200.

141. Xantus, *Letters*, 88; Frederick Marryat, *Diary in America* (Bloomington: Indiana University Press, 1960), 229; Adam Hodgson, *Remarks during a Journey through North America in the Years 1819, 1820, 1821* (Westport, Conn.: Negro Universities Press, 1970), 75; Vilhelm Dinesen, "Fra et ophold i de Forenede Stater," *Tilskueren* (October–December 1887), unpaged.

142. Billington, *Land of Savagery*, 125; Athearn, *Westward the Briton*, 126.

143. Wilhelm, *Travels through North America*, 184; Tocqueville, *Journey to America*, 328.

144. Chateaubriand, *Travels in America*, 178, 27.

145. Pulszky, *White, Red, Black*, 2.

146. J. P. Brissot De Warville, *New Travels in the United States of America 1788* (Cambridge: Harvard University Press, Belknap Press, 1964); Balduin Möllhausen, *Diary of a Journey from the Mississippi to the Coasts of the Pacific* (New York: Johnson Reprint Corporation, 1969), 24.

147. Athearn, *Westward the Briton*, 129; Billington, *Land of Savagery*, 134.

148. Von Raumer, *America and the American People*, 1:138–39.

149. Grund, *Americans*, 225–27.

150. Lyell, *Travels in North America*, 149; Bremer, *America of the Fifties*, 233; Wright, *Views of Society and Manners*, 135.

151. The term "squaw was probably a European corruption of an Indian word. Its connotation of a demeaned slave seems to have existed originally only in the minds of non-Indians. Susan Gouge, "Let's Ban the Word 'Squaw,'" *Ohoyo: Bulletin of American Indian–Alaska Native Women* 9 (July 1981), 10. See also Jean C. Goodwill, "Squaw Is a Dirty Word," in Norman Sheffe, ed., *Issues for the Seventies: Canada's Indians* (Toronto: McGraw-Hill, 1970), 50–52; Lillian Schlissel, *Women's Diaries of the Westward Journey* (New York: Schocken Books, 1982), 85.

152. Finckh, "Gottfried Duden Views Missouri," pt. 2, 22; Wilhelm, *Travels in North America*, 318.

153. Louis Philippe, *Diary of My Travels*, 85; Franz Löher, *Land und Leute in der Alten und Neuen Welt*, vol. 1 (Gottingen: G. H. Wigand, 1855), 173; John V. Cheney, ed., *Travels of John Davis in the United States of America, 1798 to 1802*, vol. 1 (Boston: Privately printed, 1610), 62.

154. Jean Bernard Bossu, *Travels in the Interior of North America, 1751–1762* (Norman: University of Oklahoma Press, 1962), 131; Gerstacker, *Wild Sports*, 108; Montule, *Travels in America*, 155–56.

155. Frederick Marryat, *Narrative of the Travels and Adventures of Monsieur Violet, in California, Sonora, and Western Texas*, vol. 1 (London: Longman, Brown, Green, & Longmans, 1843), 111–12, 131–32.

156. Tocqueville, *Journey to America*, 133.

157. Louis L. Simonin, *The Rocky Mountain West in 1867* (Lincoln: University of Nebraska Press, 1966), 92; Marian Schouten, "The Image of the American West Evoked in the Netherlands" (unpublished manuscript prepared for Ray A. Billington), Huntington Library, San Marino, Calif., 36–37; J. C. Beltrami, *Pilgrimmage in Europe and America*, vol. 2 (London: Hunt & Clarke, 1828), 145–46.

158. Paul Wilhelm, Herzog von Württenberg, *Erste Reise nach dem Nördlichen Amerika in den Jahren 1822 bis 1824* (Stuttgart: J. G. Cotta, 1835), 179; Jacob H. Schiel, *Journey through the Rocky Mountains and the Humboldt Mountains to the Pacific Ocean* (Norman: University of Oklahoma Press, 1959), 96–97; John T. Irving, *Indian Sketches Taken during an Expedition to the Pawnee and Other Tribes of American Indians*, vol. 1 (London: J. Murray, 1835), 170.

159. Weld, *Travels through North America*, 228.

160. Reuben Gold Thwaite, ed., *Early Western Travels, 1748–1846*, vol. 23 (Cleveland: Arthur H. Clark Co., 1906), 223, 271, 325; Byron Y. Fleck, "The West as Viewed by Foreign Travellers, 1783–1840" (Ph.D. diss., University of Iowa, 1950), 233–34.

161. Weld, *Travels through North America*, 235–36.

162. Cheney, *Travels of John Davis*, 62; Alexander Farkas, *Journey in North America* (Philadelphia: American Philosophical Society, 1977), 122, 136.

163. Wilhelm, *Travels in North America*, 318; Farkas, *Journey in North America*, 122.

164. Xantus, *Letters from North America*, 34.

165. Trevelyan, *Great New People*, 97.

166. Martineau, *Retrospect of Western Travel*, 85.

167. Bremer, *America of the Fifties*, 229.

168. Marryat, *Narrative*, 1:131–32.

169. Percy B. St. John, *The Trapper's Bride* (London: J. Mortimer, 1845), 81–82.

170. Mayne Reid, *The Scalp Hunters; or, Romantic Adventures in Northern Mexico*, vol. 1 (London: C. J. Skeet, 1851), 277–79; Sygurd Wisniowski, *Ameryka, 100 Years Old: A Globetrotter's View* (Cheshire, Conn.: Cherry Hill Books, 1972), 64.

171. Gustave Aimard, *Stronghand: A Tale of the Disinherited* (London: J. & R. Maxwell, 1878), 98.

172. J. Martin Evans, *America: The View from Europe* (San Francisco: San Francisco Book Company, 1976), 108–10.

173. Marryat, *Diary in America*, 126.

174. Ibid.

175. Finckh, "Gottfried Duden Views Missouri," pt. 2, 22.

176. Von Raumer, *America and the American People*, 144.

177. Scott, "Soren Jaabaek," 92; Wilhelm, *Travels in North America*, 198.

178. Weld, *Travels through North America*, 221; Hodgson, *Remarks during a Journey*, 271.

179. Tivador Acs, ed., *A Számüzöttek, Fiala Janós, 1848* (Budapest: Hungary, 1943), 245–46.

180. Mor Jókai, *Vándoroljatok ki!* (Berlin: Von L. Wechsler, 1893), 29, 50.

181. Wisniowski, *Ameryka*, 67–68.

182. Count Francesco Arese, *A Trip to the Prairies and in the Interior of North America, 1837–1838* (New York: Cooper Square Publishers, 1975), 66, 72.

183. Loher, *Land und Leute*, 174.

184. Magnus Bech-Olsen, *Min Amerikafaerd* (Copenhagen: S. L. Wulff, 1900), unpaged; Fleck, "West as Viewed by Foreign Travellers," 242–44.

185. Cracroft, "American West of Karl May," 57.

186. St. John, *Trapper's Bride*, 8–9.

187. Chateaubriand, *Travels in America*, 88; Louis Philippe, *Diary of My Travels*, 71; Gustave Aimard, *The Bee-Hunter: A Tale of Adventure* (London: J. A. Berger, 1868), 79; Gustave Aimard, *The Pirates of the Prairies: Adventures in the American Desert* (London: Ward & Lock, 1861), 62; Arese, *Trip to the Prairies*, 164–65.

188. Louis Philippe, *Diary of My Travels*, 72; von Raumer, *America and the American People*, 281–82.

189. Heinrich Luden, ed., *Reise seiner Hoheit des Herzogs Bernhard zu Sachsen-Weimar-Eisenach durch Nord-Amerika*, vol. 2 (Weimar: W. Hoffman, 1828), 33; Bremer, *Homes of the New World* (Harper & Brothers, 1853), 30.

190. Bossu, *Travels, in the Interior*, 131.

191. Wilhelm, *Travels in North America*, 198.

192. Bremer, *America of the Fifties*, 232.

193. See, for example, Marryat, *Narrative*, 2:12–13; and James A. Jones, *Traditions of the North America Indians*, vol. 2 (London: H. Colburn and R. Bentley, 1830), 131–40.

194. Wisniowski, *Ameryka*, 64–65.

195. Marryat, *Diary in America*, 234; Marryat, *Narrative*, 2:111–12; Wilhelm, *Travels in North America*, 316.

196. Frances Brooke, *The History of Emily Montague*, vol. 1 (London: Printed for J. Dodsley, 1769), 18–19.

197. Bossu, *Travels in the Interior*, 132, 171; Louis Philippe, *Diary*, 72.

198. Bossu, *Travels in the Interior*, 132.

199. Axtell, *America Perceived: Seventeenth Century*, 54–55.

200. John Bradbury, *Travels in the Interior of America* (Ann Arbor, Mich.: University Microfilms, 1966), 168.

201. Bossu, *Travels in the Interior*, 171.

202. Chateaubriand, *Travels in America*, 88.

203. Ibid., 32.

204. Bremer, *Homes of the New World* (Harper & Brothers, 1868), 593.

205. Axtell, *America Perceived: Seventeenth Century*, 56, 71; Montule, *Travels in America*, 160; Handlin, *This Was America*, 13–14.

206. Montule, *Travels in America*, 161.

207. Friedrich Gerstacker, *Narrative of a Journey Round the World*, vol. 1 (London: Hurst and Blackett, 1853), 356–57.

208. Wilhelm, *Travels in North America*, 338; Fleck, "West as Viewed by Foreign Travellers," 236–44; Baillie-Grohman, *Camps in the Rockies*, 273–75.

209. Acs, *A Számüzöttek*, 245–46.

210. John U. Terrell and Donna M. Terrell, *Indian Women of the Western Morning* (New York: Doubleday, 1976), 38–40; Karen O. Kupperman, *Settling with the Indians* (Totowa, N.J.: Rowman & Littlefield, 1980), 60–63; Margot Liberty, "Hell Came with Horses: Plains Indian Women in the Equestrian Era," *Montana, The Magazine of Western History* 32, no. 3 (Summer 1982), 10–19. See also Patricia Albers and Beatrice Medicine, *The Hidden Half: Studies of Plains Indian Women* (Washington, D.C.: University Press of America, Inc., 1983).

211. Rayna Green, "Native American Women," *Signs* 6, no. 2 (Winter 1980), 248, 250, 255, 260, 262; Valerie S. Mathes, "Native American Women in Medicine and the Military," *Journal of the West* 21, no. 2 (April 1982), 41, 47; Sue Armitage, "Western Women: Beginning to Come into Focus," *Montana, The Magazine of Western History* 32, no. 3 (Summer 1982), 4–5; Liberty, "Hell Came with Horses," 18–19.

212. Cheney, *Travels of John Davis*, 68.

213. Pulzsky, *White, Red, Black*, 6.

214. Hodgson, *Remarks during a Journey*, 265.

215. Napoleon A. Murat, *America and the Americans* (New York: W. H. Graham, 1849), 212.

216. Von Raumer, *America and the American People*, 138.

217. Weld, *Travels through North America*, 290.

218. Xantus, *Letters from North America*, 37.

219. Bradbury, *Travels in the Interior*, 89.

220. Brooke, *History of Emily Montague*, 1:18–19.

221. Charlotte Lenox, *Euphemia*, vol. 3 (London: T. Cadell & J. Evans, 1790), 190–91; Gustave Aimard, *The Indian Scout: A Story of the Aztec City*

(London: Ward & Lock, 1865), 229; Gustave Aimard, *The Trappers of Arkansas, or, The Loyal Heart* (New York: T. R. Dawley, 1858), 186; Ashliman, "American West," 154.

222. Cracroft, "American West of Karl May," 153–54.

223. Karen Sacks, "State Bias and Women's Status," *American Anthropologist* 78, no. 3 (September 1976), 565–69; Liberty, "Hell Came with Horses," 12; Mathes, "Native American Women," 41.

224. Marryat, *Diary in America*, 248.

225. Terrell and Terrell, *Indian Women*, 37; Mathes, "Native American Women," 41.

226. Gerstacker, *Wild Sports*, 110; Bradbury, *Travels in the Interior*, 146.

227. Bossu, *Travels in the Interior*, 132; Weld, *Travels through North America*, 259; Jeremy, *Henry Wansey*, 51; Möllhausen, *Diary*, 98; Thwaites, ed., *Early Western Travels, 1748–1846* (Cleveland: Arthur H. Clark Co., 1906), 22:352.

228. Terrell and Terrell, *Indian Women*, 71–90; Liberty, "Hell Came with Horses," 13–15.

229. Martineau, *Retrospect of Western Travel*, 94; Simonin, *Rocky Mountain West*, 134; *American Settler*, 19 July 1884.

230. Gustave Aimard, *The White Scalper: A Story of the Texan War* (London: Ward & Lock, 1861), 234–35; Aimard, *Pirates of the Prairies*, 107–8; Aimard, *Trappers of Arkansas*, 191–97; Bénédict Henry Révoil, *Le Bivouac des Trappeurs* (Paris: Brunet, 1864), 201–2; Karl May, *Der Schatz im Silbersee* (Bamberg, West Germany: Karl-May-Verlag, 1973), 340.

231. C. Ax Egerström, *Borta är bram, men hemma är bäst* (Stockholm: A. Bonier, 1859), 128.

232. Möllhausen, *Diary*, 26.

233. Brooke, *History of Emily Montague*, 1:69.

234. Bremer, *Homes of the New World* (Harper & Brothers, 1868), 593.

235. Bremer, *America of the Fifties*, 229–31.

Chapter 3

1. Harriett A. L. Smith, "My Trip across the Plains in 1849," California State Library, Sacramento.

2. Virginia Reed Murphy, "Across the Plains in the Donner Party (1846): A Personal Narrative of the Overland Trip to California," *Century Magazine* 42, no. 3 (July 1891), 409.

3. Lucy Jennings, interview 10025, vol. 48, Indian-Pioneer Papers, University of Oklahoma, Norman.

4. Lucy H. Fosdick, "Across the Plains in '61," Beinecke Collection, Yale University Library, New Haven, Conn.

5. Emily K. Andrews, "Diary of Emily K. Andrews of a Trip from Austin

to Fort Davis, 1874," Barker Texas History Center, University of Texas, Austin.

6. Martha Lowrence, interview 7884, vol. 56, Indian-Pioneer Papers, University of Oklahoma, Norman.

7. Lola Clark, interview 4547, vol. 18; Mary Ellen Williams, interview 6877, vol. 98; both in Indian-Pioneer Papers, University of Oklahoma, Norman.

8. Annie Muthart Baker, interview 10601, vol. 4, Indian-Pioneer Papers, University of Oklahoma, Norman.

9. Mabel Sharpe Beavers, interview 6850, vol. 6, Indian-Pioneer Papers, University of Oklahoma, Norman.

10. Elisha Brooks, *A Pioneer Mother of California* (San Francisco: Harr Wagner Publishing Company, 1922), 13–15.

11. Robert L. Munkres, "The Plains Indian Threat on the Oregon Trail before 1860," *Annals of Wyoming* 40 (1968), 203.

12. Thomas D. Clark, ed., *Off at Sunrise: The Overland Journal of Charles Glass Gray* (San Marino, Calif.: Huntington Library, 1976), 78; James A. Pritchard, *The Overland Diary of James A. Pritchard* (Denver: Old West Publishing Company, 1959), 58.

13. Dr. Jonathan Clark, "The Diary of Dr. Jonathan Clark," *The Argonaut*, 1 August 1925, 3.

14. Lucene Pfeiffer Parsons, "The Women in the Sunbonnets" (1850), Stanford University Library, Stanford, Calif. See also Lydia Waters, "Account of a Trip across the Plains in 1855," *Quarterly of the Society of California Pioneers* 6 (March 1929), 65, 72.

15. Helen Carpenter, "Diary" (1856), Huntington Library, San Marino, Calif.

16. Margaret A. Frink, *Journal of the Adventures of a Party of California Gold-Seekers* (Oakland, Calif.: n.p., 1897), 28–29.

17. Isaac Jones Wistar, *Autobiography of Isaac Jones Wistar, 1827–1905: Half a Century in War and Peace* (New York: Harper & Brothers, 1937), 74.

18. Margaret S. Dart, ed., "Letters of a Yankee Forty-Niner," *The Yale Review* 36, no. 4 (June 1947), 658.

19. Mallie Stafford, *The March of Empire through Three Decades* (San Francisco: George Spaulding & Co., 1884), 126–27.

20. Clark, *Off at Sunrise*, 78; Jane Augusta Gould, "Diary" (1862), Iowa State Historical Society, Iowa City; Pritchard, *Overland Diary*, 58; Harriet Bunyard, "Diary of Miss Harriet Bunyard from Texas to California in 1868," *Annual Publications, Historical Society of Southern California* no. 13 (1924), 94, 97; David M. Kiefer, ed., "Over Barren Plains and Rock-Bound Mountains," *Montana, The Magazine of Western History* 22, no. 4 (1972), 22, 26.

21. Helen Marnie Stewart Love, "Diary" (1853), Huntington Library, San Marino, Calif.

22. Louisa Miller Rahm, "Diary" (1862), Bancroft Library, Berkeley, Calif.; Ellen Tompkins Adams, "Diary of Ellen Tompkins Adams, Wife of John Smalley Adams, M.D." (1863), Bancroft Library, Berkeley, Calif.

23. Fosdick, "Across the Plains."

24. Carpenter, "Diary"; Louise Barry, comp., "Charles Robinson—Yankee '49er: His Journey to California," *Kansas Historical Quarterly* 34, no. 2 (1968), 186; Andrew F. Rolle, ed., *The Road to Virginia City: The Diary of James Knox Polk Miller* (Norman: University of Oklahoma Press, 1960), 8.

25. Gould, "Diary"; Bunyard, "Diary," 97; Laura W. Johnson, *Eight Hundred Miles in an Ambulance* (Philadelphia: J. B. Lippincott Company, 1889), 43.

26. Munkres, "Plains Indian Threat," 212–15.

27. Catherine Amanda Stansbury Washburn, "Journal (1853) from Iowa to Oregon Territory," Huntington Library, San Marino, Calif.; Ward G. DeWitt and Florence S. DeWitt, *Prairie Schooner Lady: The Journal of Harriet Sherrill Ward, 1853* (Los Angeles: Westernlore Press, 1959), 46; Ada Millington, "Journal Kept while Crossing the Plains" (1862), Bancroft Library, Berkeley, Calif.; Fosdick, "Across the Plains"; Bunyard, "Diary," 100.

28. Maria Schrode, "Journal" (1870), Huntington Library, San Marino, Calif.

29. Mary Rockwood Powers, "A Woman's Overland Journal to California" (1856), California State Library, Sacramento.

30. Susan Thompson Parrish, "Westward in 1850," Huntington Library, San Marino, Calif.

31. Mary Saunders, "The Whitman Massacre; A True Story by a Survivor of This Terrible Tragedy which Took Place in Oregon in 1847," Bancroft Library, Berkeley, Calif.

32. DeWitt and DeWitt, *Prairie Schooner Lady*, 132.

33. Mary Eliza Warner, "Diary" (1864), Bancroft Library, Berkeley, Calif.

34. Lucy Rutledge Cooke, *Covered Wagon Days: Crossing the Plains in 1852* (Modesto, Calif.: Privately published, 1923), 22.

35. Millington, "Journal."

36. Andrews, "Diary."

37. Warner, "Diary."

38. Katherine Dunlap, "Journal" (1864), Bancroft Library, Berkeley, Calif.

39. Lucy Sexton, *The Foster Family, California Pioneers* (Santa Barbara, Calif.: Press of the Schouer Printing Studio, 1925), 123.

40. Emily McCowen Horton, *My Scrap-book* (Seattle, Wash.: n.p., 1927), 17.

41. Mary Burrell, "Diary of a Journey Overland from Council Bluffs to Green Valley, Cal., April 27 to Sept. 1, 1854," Beinecke Collection, Yale University Library, New Haven, Conn.

42. Pauline Wonderly, *Reminiscences of a Pioneer* (Placerville, Calif.: El Dorado County Historical Society, 1965), 9.

43. Margaret W. Chambers, *Reminiscences* (n.p., 1903), 13.

44. Charlotte Stearns Pengra, "Diary" (1853), Huntington Library, San Marino, Calif.

45. Lavinia H. Porter, *By Ox Team to California: A Narrative of Crossing the Plains in 1860* (Oakland, Calif.: Oakland Enquirer Publishing Company, 1910), 65, 67, 69–70.

46. Brooks, *Pioneer Mother*, 16, 23.

47. Jennings, interview 10025.

48. Beavers, interview 6850.

49. Williams, interview 6877.

50. In a study of 103 women's overland diaries Lillian Schlissel discovered that only 7 percent recorded attacks by American Indians. Lillian Schlissel, *Women's Diaries of the Westward Journey* (New York: Schocken Books, 1982), 154. Other scholars who have also argued that the Indian threat was vastly exaggerated are Munkres, "Plains Indian Threat," 193–221; John D. Unruh, *The Plains Across: The Overland Emigrants and the Trans-Mississippi West, 1840–1860* (Urbana: University of Illinois Press, 1979), 9, 135–36, 156–200, 386, 395–96, 408–9.

51. Murphy, "Across the Plains," 409.

52. Unruh, *Plains Across*, 135.

53. May Callan Tansill, "Narrative" (n.d.), Barker Texas History Center, University of Texas, Austin.

54. Abigail Raymond Smith to her brothers and sisters, 5 May 1840, Beinecke Collection, Yale University Library, New Haven, Conn.

55. Polly Jane Purcell, "Autobiography and Reminiscence of a Pioneer," Graff Collection, Newberry Library, Chicago, Ill.

56. Quoted in Sandra L. Myres, "The Westering Woman," *Huntington Spectator* (Winter 1980), 1–2.

57. Ella Bird-Dumont, "True Life Story of Ella Bird-Dumont, Earliest Settler in the East Part of Panhandle, Texas" (n.d.), Barker Texas History Center, University of Texas, Austin.

58. Susan Cranston to Huldah P. Fairchild, 6 April 1856, in Susan and Warren Cranston, "Letters, 1852–1859, from Oregon Territory," Bancroft Library, Berkeley, Calif.

59. Sarah Kenyon to her mother-in-law and sister-in-law, 9 October 1862, in John Kenyon, "Letters" (1856–1865), Iowa State Historical Society, Iowa City.

60. Harriet M. Hill Townsend, "Reminiscence" (n.d.), privately held by Frank Kerulis, Waverly, Iowa.

61. Minnie Lee Parks, interview 8039, vol. 69, Indian-Pioneer Papers, University of Oklahoma, Norman.

62. Abigail Malick to her children, 8 December 1855, in Abigail Malick, "Letter" (1855), Beinecke Collection, Yale University Library, New Haven, Conn.; Lily Klasner, *My Girlhood among Outlaws* (Tucson: University of Arizona Press, 1972), 78; M. A. Rogers, "An Iowa Woman in Wartime," pt. 3, *Annals of Iowa* 36 (Summer 1961), 26–28; Mrs. Warren R. Fowler, "A Woman's Experience in Cañon City" (1884), Bancroft Library, Berkeley, Calif.; Chambers, *Reminiscences*, 45–47; Mollie Dorsey Sanford, *Mollie* (Lincoln: University of Nebraska Press, 1976), 186–89; Bessie L. Lyon, "Hungry Indians," *The Palimpsest* 9 (October 1928), 369.

63. Jonaphrene S. Faulkner, typescript of novel "Prairie Home" (n.d.), Barker Texas History Center, University of Texas, Austin.

64. Elizabeth Montgomery Neelley, "History of the Montgomery Family, from 1825 to the Present Time, 1937," Barker Texas History Center, University of Texas, Austin.

65. Tansill, "Narrative."

66. Maud Parshall Norris, interview 9837, vol. 67, Indian-Pioneer Papers, University of Oklahoma, Norman.

67. Neelley, "History of the Montgomery Family."

68. Anne Ellis, *The Life of an Ordinary Woman* (Lincoln: University of Nebraska Press, 1980), 12; Sondra Van Meter, "Pioneer Women," *Wichita State University Magazine* 2, no. 1 (Winter 1976), 18; Sarah Jane Alice Proctor, interview 9050, vol. 73, Indian-Pioneer Papers, University of Oklahoma, Norman; Harriet M. Hill Townsend, "Reminiscences" (n.d.), privately held by Frank Kerulis, Waverly, Iowa.

69. M. A. Rogers, "An Iowa Woman in Wartime," pt. 1, *Annals of Iowa* 35 (Winter 1961), 528; Louise Sophia Gellhorn Boylan, "My Life Story: Reminiscences of German Settlers in Hardin County, 1867–1883," Iowa State Historical Society, Iowa City.

70. Sanford, *Mollie*, 188.

71. Mrs. C. W. Callerman, interview 1080, vol. 15, Indian-Pioneer Papers, University of Oklahoma, Norman.

72. Robert C. Carriker and Eleanor R. Carriker, eds., *An Army Wife on the Frontier: The Memoirs of Alice Blackwood Baldwin, 1867–1877* (Salt Lake City: Tanner Trust Fund, University of Utah Library, 1975), 105.

73. Frances C. Carrington, *My Army Life and the Fort Phil Kearney Massacre* (Freeport, N.Y.: Books for Libraries Press, 1971).

74. Ada Adelaide Vogdes, "Journal" (1866–1872), Huntington Library, San Marino, Calif.

75. Caroline Phelps, "Diary" (1830–1860), Iowa State Historical Society, Iowa City.

76. Rogers, "Iowa Woman in Wartime," pt. 1, 526.

77. Mrs. A. L. Patrick, interview 7773, vol. 69; Annie M. Zeigler, interview 10088, vol. 101; Iona Goar Paxton, interview 9108, vol. 70; all in Indian-Pioneer Papers, University of Oklahoma, Norman.

78. Julia C. Bolen, interview 9113, vol. 9, Indian-Pioneer Papers, University of Oklahoma, Norman.

79. Fowler, "Woman's Experience in Cañon City."

80. Lois L. Murray, *Incidents of Frontier Life* (Goshen, Ind.: Evangelical United Mennonite Publishing House, 1880), 147, 155–56, 181–84; Bessie L. Lyon, "Grandmother's Story," *The Palimpsest* 5 (January 1924), 8.

81. Florence Call Cowles, *Early Algona: The Story of Our Pioneers, 1854–1874* (Des Moines, Iowa: The Register and Tribune Company, 1929), 111–12, 115.

82. Ellis, *Life of an Ordinary Woman*, 11.

83. Norris, interview 9837.

84. Bolen, interview 9113.

85. Unruh, *Plains Across*, 156, 175–76.

86. Ibid., 184–85, 189.

87. Sarah J. Cummins, *Autobiography and Reminiscences* (La Grande, Oreg.: La Grande Printing Company, 1914), 28.

88. Margaret Hall Walker, *The Hall Family Crossing the Plains* (San Francisco: Privately printed by Wallace Kibbee & Son, 1952), 13.

89. Olivia Holmes, "Diary" (1873), Bancroft Library, Berkeley, Calif.

90. Washburn, "Journal."

91. Lois Brown, interview 4496, vol. 12, Indian-Pioneer Papers, University of Oklahoma, Norman.

92. Samuel P. Newcomb, "Diary" (1 January 1865 to 21 December 1865), Barker Texas History Center, University of Texas, Austin.

93. Catherine M. Haun, "A Woman's Trip across the Plains, from Clinton, Iowa, to Sacramento, California, by Way of Salt Lake City (1849)," Huntington Library, San Marino, Calif.

94. Erwin N. Thompson, "The Summer of '77 at Fort Lapwai," *Idaho Yesterdays* 21, no. 2 (1977), 14.

95. DeWitt and DeWitt, *Prairie Schooner Lady*, 46.

96. Susan E. Newcomb, "Diary" (1869, 1873), Barker Texas History Center, University of Texas, Austin.

97. Thompson, "Summer of '77," 14.

98. Carriker and Carriker, *Army Wife*, 78; Nannie T. Alderson, *A Bride Goes West* (Lincoln: University of Nebraska Press, 1969), 48.

99. Owen P. White, *A Frontier Mother* (New York: Minton, Balch & Company, 1929), 68.

100. Baker, interview 10601.

101. See, for example, Agnes Morley Cleaveland, *No Life for a Lady* (Lincoln: University of Nebraska Press, 1977), 41; and Bird-Dumont, "True Life Story."

102. Milo M. Quaife, ed., *Across the Plains in Forty-Nine* (Chicago: Lakeside Press, 1948), 48–49; James Hewitt, ed., *Eye-Witnesses to Wagon Trains West* (New York: Charles Scribner's Sons, 1973), 12.

103. Byron N. McKinstry, *The California Gold Rush Overland Diary of Byron N. McKinstry* (Glendale, Calif.: Arthur H. Clark Company, 1975), 94.

104. Ibid., 95–96.

105. Ibid., 101.

106. Charles W. Martin, ed., "Joseph Warren Arnold's Journal of His Trip from Montana, 1864–1866," *Nebraska History* 55, no. 4 (1974), 532.

107. John O. Holzhueter, ed., "From Waupun to Sacramento in 1849: The Gold Rush Journal of Edwin Hillyer," *Wisconsin Magazine of History* 49, no. 3 (1966), 222.

108. Alonzo Delano, *Life on the Plains and among the Diggings* (Ann Arbor, Mich.: University Microfilms, 1966), 218–19.

109. David M. Potter, ed., *Trail to California: The Overland Journal of Vincent Geiger and Wakeman Bryarly* (New Haven, Conn.: Yale University Press, 1945), 93.

110. Gilbert Drake Harlan, ed., "The Diary of Wilson Barber Harlan," *Journal of the West* 3, no. 2 (1964), 153.

111. Wistar, *Autobiography*, 74.

112. Barry, "Charles Robinson," 179–88; Harlan, "Diary of Wilson Barber Harlan," 148.

113. Fancher Stimson, "Overland Journey to California by Platte River Route and South Pass in 1850," *Annals of Iowa* 13, no. 6 (October 1922), 406.

114. Holzhueter, "From Waupun to Sacramento," 221.

115. Susan Newcomb, "Diary."

116. Samuel Newcomb, "Diary."

117. Waters, "Account of a Trip," 61.

118. DeWitt and DeWitt, *Prairie Schooner Lady*, 46.

119. Cooke, *Covered Wagon Days*, 58.

120. Quoted in Sandra L. Myres, ed., *Ho for California! Women's Overland Diaries from the Huntington Library* (San Marino, Calif.: Huntington Library, 1980), 271.

121. Unruh, *Plains Across,* 175–76.

122. Thomas R. Buecker, ed., "Letters of Caroline Frey Winne from Sidney Barracks and Fort McPherson, Nebraska, 1874–1878," *Nebraska History* 62 (Spring 1981), 20.

123. Parrish, "Westward in 1850."

124. Sanford, *Mollie,* 152.

125. J. H. Lowry, interview 10332, vol. 56, Indian-Pioneer Papers, University of Oklahoma, Norman.

126. Julia Lee Sinks, "Reminiscences of Early Days in Texas Taken from Articles Published in the *Dallas* and *Galveston News,* February, 1896," Barker Texas History Center, University of Texas, Austin.

127. Burton J. Williams, ed., "Overland to the Gold Fields of California in 1850: The Journal of Calvin Taylor," *Nebraska History* 50, no. 2 (1969), 142.

128. Buecker, "Letters of Caroline Frey Winne," 6; Howard Egan, *Pioneering the West, 1846 to 1878* (Richmond, Utah: Howard R. Egan Estate, 1917), 23.

129. Mary Butler Renville, *A Thrilling Narrative of Indian Captivity* (Minneapolis: Atlas Company's Book and Job Printing Office, 1863), 43; Mary Jane Caples, "Overland Journey to California;" (1911), California State Library, Sacramento; Eleanor Taylor, "Ross Kin: Early Settlers of the West" (1978), Bancroft Library, Berkeley, Calif.; Rogers, "Iowa Woman in Wartime," pt. 1, 525, 534; Eliza Spalding Warren, *Memoirs of the West* (Portland, Oreg.: March Printing Company, 1916), 177; E. Allene Dunham, "Across the Plains in a Covered Wagon" (n.d.), Graff Collection, Newberry Library, Chicago, Ill.; Nancy N. Tracy, "Narrative" (1880), Bancroft Library, Berkeley, Calif.; Ruth Peterson, comp., "Across the Plains in '57" (1931), California State Library, Sacramento.

130. Munkres, "Plains Indian Threat," 214–15; Faulkner, "Prairie Home," 209; Unruh, *Plains Across,* 193–96; May Callan Tansill, "The Trek to Texas" (n.d.), Barker Texas History Center, University of Texas, Austin.

131. Walker D. Wyman, ed., *California Emigrant Letters* (New York: Bookman Associates, 1952), 101.

132. Unruh, *Plains Across,* 192–93.

133. Bird-Dumont, "True Life Story."

134. Unruh, *Plains Across,* 157, 169–70, 177.

135. Porter, *By Ox Team to California,* 79.

136. Sarah Welch Nossaman, "Pioneering at Bonaparte and near Pella," *Annals of Iowa* 13 (October 1922), 444–45.

137. White, *Frontier Mother,* 23.

138. Klasner, *My Girlhood among Outlaws,* 52.

139. Myres, *Ho for California!,* 167; Alderson, *Bride Goes West,* 101.

140. Elsie Pierson, interview 8538, vol. 71, Indian-Pioneer Papers, University of Oklahoma, Norman; Harold F. Taggart, ed., "The Journal of David Jackson Staples," *California Historical Society Quarterly* 22 (June 1943), 146.

141. Baker, interview 10601.

142. McKinstry, *California Gold Rush Overland Diary,* 92.

143. Ibid., 90.

144. Sanford, *Mollie,* 123.

145. Lorene Millhollen, interview 8957, vol. 63, Indian-Pioneer Papers, University of Oklahoma, Norman.

146. Fosdick, "Across the Plains."

147. Mrs. N. J. Brown, interview 4597, vol. 12, Indian-Pioneer Papers, University of Oklahoma, Norman.

148. Sarah Luster, interview 8530, vol. 56, Indian-Pioneer Papers, University of Oklahoma, Norman.

149. Elizabeth McAnulty Owens, "The Story of Her Life" (1895), Barker Texas History Center, University of Texas, Austin.

150. Dora Miller, interview 9373, vol. 64, Indian-Pioneer Papers, University of Oklahoma, Norman.

151. Johnson, *Eight Hundred Miles,* 93–94.

152. Murray, *Incidents of Frontier Life,* 127.

153. Alderson, *Bride Goes West,* 215–16.

154. Cleaveland, *No Life for a Lady,* 38.

155. Rogers, "Iowa Woman in Wartime," pt. 1, 526; Myres, *Ho for California!,* 149.

156. Porter, *By Ox Team to California,* 36–37.

157. Purcell, "Autobiography and Reminiscence," 2.

158. Jacob H. Schiel, *Journey through the Rocky Mountains and the Humboldt Mountains to the Pacific Ocean* (Norman: University of Oklahoma Press, 1959), 97.

159. Harlan, "Diary of Wilson Barber Harlan," 153.

160. Wyman, *California Emigrant Letters,* 53, 103.

161. Klasner, *My Girlhood among Outlaws,* 34–35, 73–77; White, *Frontier Mother,* 34–35; Miller, interview 9373.

162. Doris Faulkner, ed., "Letters from Algona, 1856–1865," *The Palimpsest* 61, no. 6 (November–December 1980), 187–89.

163. Johnson, *Eight Hundred Miles,* 116.

164. Ellen McGowen Biddle, *Reminiscences of a Soldier's Wife* (Philadelphia: J. B. Lippincott Company, 1907), 134.

165. Margaret I. Carrington, *Ab-sa-ra-ka, Home of the Crows: Being the Experience of an Officer's Wife on the Plains* (Philadelphia: J. B. Lippincott and Company, 1868), 219.

166. Margaret Cring Adams, interview 8499, vol. 1, Indian-Pioneer Papers, University of Oklahoma, Norman.

167. Unruh, *Plains Across,* 177.

168. Carpenter, "Diary."

169. Baker, interview 10601.

170. Bird-Dumont, "True Life Story."

171. Francena Martin Sutton, "Civil War Experiences of Some Arkansas Women"(n.d.), Barker Texas History Center, University of Texas, Austin. See also LeRoy H. Fischer, ed., "A Civil War Experience of Some Arkansas Women in Indian Territory," *Chronicles of Oklahoma* 57 (Summer 1979), 137–63.

172. Alderson, *Bride Goes West,* 99–103, 132–33.

173. Buecker, "Letters of Caroline Frey Winne," 9–10; Fosdick, "Across the Plains."

174. Sinks, "Reminiscences of Early Days," 11–12.

175. McKinstry, *California Gold Rush Overland Diary,* 223.

176. Kiefer, "Over Barren Plains," 23; Waters, "Account of a Trip," 76; White, *Frontier Mother,* 81.

177. Bird-Dumont, "True Life Story."

178. Pierson, interview 8538.

179. Meta Cresse Breuer, interview 10090, vol. 12, Indian-Pioneer Papers, University of Oklahoma, Norman.

180. Munkres, "Plains Indian Threat," 198–200.

181. Porter, *By Ox Team to California,* 79–83, 95–96.

182. Fosdick, "Across the Plains."

183. Bird-Dumont, "True Life Story."

184. Vogdes, "Journal"; Lizzie Bomhoff, interview 10350, vol. 9, Indian-Pioneer Papers, University of Oklahoma, Norman; Frances M. A. Roe, *Army Letters from an Officer's Wife, 1871–1888* (New York: D. Appleton and Company, 1909), 263.

185. Rogers, "Iowa Woman in Wartime," pt. 1, 526; Bessie L. Lyon, "Prospecting for a New Home," *The Palimpsest* 16 (July 1925), 226.

186. Cleaveland, *No Life for a Lady,* 40–41; Alderson, *Bride Goes West,* 216–17.

187. Owens, "Story of Her Life."

188. "Frontier Fear of the Indians," *Annals of Iowa* 3, no. 29 (April 1948), 315–22.

189. Mary Fokes Locklin, "Experience of Abigail McLennan Fokes and Family as Told by Her Daughter" (n.d.), Barker Texas History Center, University of Texas, Austin; Faulkner, "Letters from Algona," 186–88.

190. Faulkner, "Letters from Algona," 187.

191. Ruth Beitz, "They Guarded Iowa's Last Frontier," *The Iowan* 9, no. 3 (February–March 1961), 11–12, 46.

284

192. Klasner, *My Girlhood among Outlaws*, 86; Myres, *Ho for California!*, 166–68.

193. Purcell, "Autobiography and Reminiscence," 4–5.

Chapter 4

1. Carl N. Degler, *At Odds: Women and the Family in America from the Revolution to the Present* (New York: Oxford University Press, 1980), 26–27, 30–31, 150–51, 283, 351–53; Ann Douglas, *The Feminization of American Culture* (New York: Alfred A. Knopf, 1979), 8–10, 45–48, 56–60, 68–76; John Mack Faragher, *Women and Men on the Overland Trail* (New Haven, Conn.: Yale University Press, 1979), 94–97; Gerda Lerner, *The Majority Finds Its Past: Placing Women in History* (New York: Oxford University Press, 1979), 25–28, 162–65, 185–86; Glenda Riley, "The Subtle Subversion: Changes in the Traditionalist Image of the American Woman," *The Historian* 32, no. 2 (February 1970), 210–27; Glenda Riley, *The Origins of the Feminist Movement in America* (St. Charles, Mo.: Forum Press, 1973), 1–13.

2. Leslie A. Fiedler, *The Return of the Vanishing American* (New York: Stein and Day, 1968), 24, 177; Julie Roy Jeffrey, *Frontier Women: The Trans-Mississippi West, 1840–1880* (New York: Hill and Wang, 1979), 33–34; Ronald J. Quinn, "The Modest Seduction: The Experience of Pioneer Women on the Trans-Mississippi Frontier" (Ph.D. diss., University of California, Riverside, 1977), i–iii, 8–9, 11, 15, 18, 23, 30, 39, 45–50.

3. Sarah White Smith, "Diary," in Clifford Drury, ed., *First White Woman over the Rockies*, vol. 3 (Glendale, Calif.: Arthur H. Clark Company, 1966), 87.

4. Annie D. Tallent, *The First White Woman in the Black Hills* (Mitchell, S.D.: Educator Supply Company, 1923), 47.

5. Louisa M. Rahm, "Diary" (1862), Bancroft Library, Berkeley, Calif.

6. Margaret A. Frink, *Journals of the Adventures of a Party of California Gold-Seekers* (Oakland, Calif.: n.p., 1897), 29–30.

7. Agnes M. Cleaveland, *No Life for a Lady* (Lincoln: University of Nebraska Press, 1977), 39.

8. Ruth B. Moynihan, "Children and Young People on the Overland Trail," *The Western Historical Quarterly* 6, no. 3 (July 1975), 286.

9. Polly Jane Purcell, "Autobiography and Reminiscence of a Pioneer," Graff Collection, Newberry Library, Chicago, Ill.

10. Martha M. Morgan, *A Trip across the Plains in the Year 1849* (San Francisco: Pioneer Press, 1864), 7.

11. Catherine M. Haun, "A Woman's Trip across the Plains" (1849), Huntington Library, San Marino, Calif.; Susan M. Cranston, "Daily Journal" (1851), Bancroft Library, Berkeley, Calif.; Frances H. Sawyer, "Overland to California" (1852), Bancroft Library, Berkeley, Calif.

12. Pauline Wonderly, *Reminiscences of a Pioneer* (Placerville, Calif.: El Dorado County Historical Society, 1965), 3–4.

13. Elizabeth J. Goltra, "Journal" (1853), Bancroft Library, Berkeley, Calif.

14. Ada Millington, "Journal Kept while Crossing the Plains" (1862), Bancroft Library, Berkeley, Calif.

15. Ada A. Vogdes, "Journal" (1866–1872), Huntington Library, San Marino, Calif.

16. Mary F. H. Sandford, "A Trip across the Plains" (1853), California State Library, Sacramento; Ward G. DeWitt and Florence S. DeWitt, *Prairie Schooner Lady: The Journal of Harriet Sherrill Ward, 1853* (Los Angeles: Westernlore Press, 1959), 39–46.

17. Mary E. Warner, "Diary" (1864), Bancroft Library, Berkeley, Calif.

18. Mrs. Nicholas H. Karchner, "Diary" (1862), California State Library, Sacramento.

19. Mary Jane Caples, "Overland Journey to California" (1911), California State Library, Sacramento.

20. Allie B. Busby, *Two Summers among the Musquakies* (Vinton, Iowa: Herald Book and Job Rooms, 1886), 75.

21. Lavinia H. Porter, *By Ox Team to California: A Narrative of Crossing the Plains in 1860* (Oakland, Calif.: Oakland Enquirer Publishing Company, 1910), 26.

22. Sarah R. Herndon, *Days on the Road: Crossing the Plains in 1865* (New York: Burr Printing House, 1902), 73.

23. Smith, "Diary," 78.

24. Sandford, "Trip across the Plains."

25. Mary P. Staples, "Reminiscences" (ca. 1886), Bancroft Library, Berkeley, Calif.; Sallie H. Maddock, "The Diary of a Pioneer Girl" (1849), California State Library, Sacramento; Margaret M. Hecox, *California Caravan: The 1846 Overland Trail Memoir of Margaret M. Hecox* (San Jose, Calif.: Harlan-Young Press, 1966), 40; Fleming Fraker, Jr., ed., "To Pike's Peak by Ox-Wagon: The Harriet A. Smith Day-Book," *Annals of Iowa* 35, no. 2 (Fall 1959), 132.

26. Louisa Cook to her mother and sisters (Kearney, 1862), in Cook, "Letters" (1860–1865), Beinecke Collection, Yale University Library, New Haven, Conn.

27. Mary C. Fish, "Across the Plaines in 1860," Bancroft Library, Berkeley, Calif.

28. Helen Carpenter, "Diary" (1856), Huntington Library, San Marino, Calif.

29. Esther B. Hanna, "Journal" (1852), Bancroft Library, Berkeley, Calif.;

Rex C. Myers, "To the Dear Ones at Home: Elizabeth Fisk's Missouri River Trip, 1867," *Montana, The Magazine of Western History* 32, no. 3 (Summer 1982), 44; Smith, "Diary," 80, 84–85.

30. Cook to her mother and sisters (Kearney, 1862); Thomas R. Buecker, ed., "Letters of Caroline Frey Winne from Sidney Barracks and Fort McPherson, Nebraska, 1874–1878," *Nebraska History* 62 (Spring 1981), 6–7; Frances M. A. Roe, *Army Letters from an Officer's Wife, 1871–1888* (New York: D. Appleton & Company, 1909), 13.

31. Sandra L. Myres, ed., *Cavalry Wife: The Diary of Eveline M. Alexander, 1866–1867* (College Station: Texas A. & M. University Press, 1977), 79, 100.

32. Caroline L. Richardson, "Journal" (1856), Bancroft Library, Berkeley, Calif.

33. Leo M. Kaiser and Priscilla Knuth, eds., "From Ithaca to Clatsop Plains: Miss Ketcham's Journal of Travel," pt. 2, *Oregon Historical Quarterly* 62, no. 4 (1961), 368; Mrs. B. G. Ferris, *The Mormons at Home* (New York: Dix & Edwards, 1856), 13.

34. Celinda E. Hines Shipley, "Diary" (1853), Beinecke Collection, Yale University, New Haven, Conn.

35. Myers, "To the Dear Ones," 47.

36. Hanna, "Journal."

37. Hecox, *California Caravan*, 32.

38. Maria J. Norton, "Diary of a Trip across the Plains in '59," Bancroft Library, Berkeley, Calif.

39. A. D. Fisher, "Cultural Conflicts on the Prairies: Indian and White," *Alberta Historical Review* 16, no. 3 (1968), 22.

40. Ellen Tompkins Adams, "Diary" (1863), Bancroft Library, Berkeley, Calif.; Buecker, "Letters of Caroline Frey Winne," 11.

41. Annie M. Zeigler, interview 10088, vol. 101, Indian-Pioneer Papers, University of Oklahoma, Norman.

42. Maddock, "Diary of a Pioneer Girl"; Staples, "Reminiscences"; Mary Jane Guill, "The Overland Diary of a Journey from Livingston County, Missouri, to Butte County, California, May 5 to September 5, 1860," California State Library, Sacramento.

43. Ferris, *Mormons at Home*, 68.

44. Carrie A. Strahorn, *Fifteen Thousand Miles by Stage* (New York: G. P. Putnam's Sons, 1911), 15; Mollie Dorsey Sanford, *Mollie: The Journal of Mollie Dorsey Sanford in Nebraska and Colorado Territories, 1857–1866* (Lincoln: University of Nebraska Press, 1976), 122.

45. Herndon, *Days on the Road*, 106, 159.

46. Nellie Slater, "Travels on the Plains in Eighteen Sixty-Two," (journal), Denver Public Library, Denver, Colo.

47. Algeline J. Ashley, "Diary, Crossing the Plains in 1852," Huntington Library, San Marino, Calif.

48. Mrs. D. B. Bates, *Incidents on Land and Water* (Boston: James French and Company, 1857), 151–52.

49. Helen M. Stewart Love, "Diary" (1853), Huntington Library, San Marino, Calif.

50. Millington, "Journal."

51. Maria Schrode, "Journal" (1870), Huntington Library, San Marino, Calif.

52. Hecox, *California Caravan*, 29; Erwin N. Thompson, "The Summer of '77 at Fort Lapwai," *Idaho Yesterdays* 21, no. 2 (1977), 11.

53. Hecox, *California Caravan*, 29; Thompson, "Summer of '77," 11.

54. Lydia M. Waters, "Account of a Trip across the Plains in 1855," *Quarterly of the Society of California Pioneers* 6 (March 1929), 61–62.

55. Fish, "Across the Plaines"; Roe, *Army Letters*, 10.

56. Adams, "Diary."

57. Quoted in Sandra L. Myres, ed., *Ho for California! Women's Overland Diaries from the Huntington Library* (San Marino, Calif.: Huntington Library, 1980), 117.

58. Hanna, "Journal."

59. Guill, "Overland Diary"; Buecker, "Letters of Caroline Frey Winne," 10; Hanna, "Journal"; Hecox, *California Caravan*, 28; Lucy Sexton, *The Foster Family, California Pioneers* (Santa Barbara, Calif.: Press of the Schouer Printing Studio, 1925), 134.

60. Kaiser and Knuth, "From Ithaca to Clatsop Plains," pt. 2, 368.

61. Guill, "Overland Diary"; Norton, "Diary"; Katherine Dunlap, "Journal" (1864), Bancroft Library, Berkeley, Calif.; Marie Nash, "Diary" (1861), California State Library, Sacramento.

62. DeWitt and DeWitt, *Prairie Schooner Lady*, 78.

63. Nash, "Diary"; Carpenter, "Diary"; Millington, "Journal."

64. Julia L. Hare, "Reminiscences" (n.d.), California State Library, Sacramento.

65. Cranston, "Daily Journal"; Mary Stuart Bailey, "A Journal of the Overland Trip from Ohio to California" (1852), Huntington Library, San Marino, Calif.; Waters, "Account of a Trip," 64; Charlotte Stearns Pengra, "Diary" (1853), Huntington Library, San Marino, Calif.; Jane Augusta Gould, "Diary" (1862), Iowa State Historical Society, Iowa City; Sexton, *Foster Family*, 124, 131.

66. Fish, "Across the Plaines."

67. Sawyer, "Overland to California"; Frink, *Journals*.

68. Sara Hiveley, "Journal" (1863–1864), Denver Public Library, Denver, Colo.

69. Kaiser and Knuth, "From Ithaca to Clatsop Plains," pt. 2, 371.

70. Norton, "Diary."

71. Bailey, "Journal."

72. Sandford, "Trip across the Plains"; Mary Horne, "Migration and Settlement of the Latter Day Saints, Salt Lake City" (1884), Bancroft Library, Berkeley, Calif.; Nannie T. Alderson, *A Bride Goes West* (Lincoln: University of Nebraska Press, 1969), 48; Harger Family Papers, privately held by Delores Gros-Louis, Bloomington, Indiana; Sanford, *Mollie*, 128; Helen E. Clark, "Diary" (1860), Denver Public Library, Denver, Colo.

73. Mrs. H. T. Clarke, "A Young Woman's Sights on the Emigrant's Trail" (Salem, Oreg., 1878), Bancroft Library, Berkeley, Calif.

74. Emily McCowen Horton, *My Scrap-book* (Seattle, Wash.: n.p., 1927), 17.

75. Fraker, "To Pike's Peak," 134.

76. Warner, "Diary."

77. Catherine Jane Bell to Julia, 31 October 1859, Oroville, Calif., Bancroft Library, Berkeley, Calif.

78. Millington, "Journal"; Harriet Bunyard, "Diary of a Young Girl" (1868), Huntington Library, San Marino, Calif.; Porter, *By Ox Team to California*, 39; Sanford, *Mollie*, 164.

79. Frink, *Journals;* Ruth Peterson, comp., "Across the Plains in '57," California State Library, Sacramento.

80. Leo M. Kaiser and Priscilla Knuth, eds., "From Ithaca to Clatsop Plains: Miss Ketcham's Journal of Travel," pt. 1, *Oregon Historical Quarterly* 62, no. 3 (1961), 262; Miriam D. Colt, *Went to Kansas; Being a Thrilling Account of an Ill-Fated Expedition* (Watertown, N.Y.: L. Ingalls & Company, 1862), 136–61.

81. Caples, "Overland Journey."

82. Martha Ann Minto, "Female Pioneering in Oregon" (1849), Bancroft Library, Berkeley, Calif.; Emeline L. Fuller, *Left by the Indians: The Story of My Life* (Mt. Vernon, Iowa: Hawk-Eye Steam Print, 1892), 29; Margaret W. Chambers, "Reminiscences" (1894), Graff Collection, Newberry Library, Chicago, Ill.; Bates, *Incidents*, 156; Mary A. Hodgson, "The Life of a Pioneer Family" (1922), California State Library, Sacramento.

83. Caroline D. Budlong, *Memories: Pioneer Days in Oregon and Washington Territory* (Eugene, Oreg.: Picture Press Printers, 1949), 38; Colt, *Went to Kansas*, 132; David Edward Blaine, "Letters, 1824–1900," from his wife Kate (no salutation given, Seattle, 1854), Beincke Collection, Yale University Library, New Haven, Conn.; Annie D. Tallent, *The Black Hills: or, The Last Hunting Ground of the Dakotahs* (Sioux Falls, S.D.: Brevet Press, 1974), 82.

84. Kate McDaniel Furness, "From Prairie to Pacific" (1853), California State Library, Sacramento.

85. Ellen McGowen Biddle, *Reminiscences of a Soldier's Wife* (Philadelphia: J. B. Lippincott Company, 1907), 183.

86. Mrs. E. Van Court, "Reminiscences of Her Life in California" (26 March 1914), Beinecke Collection, Yale University Library, New Haven, Conn.; Mary Rice to her sister (Fort Gibson, Okla., 1835), Beinecke Collection, Yale University Library, New Haven, Conn.; Lodisa Frizzell, *Across the Plains to California in 1852* (New York: New York Public Library, 1915), 10; Sarah May Baldwin, no interview number, vol. 4, Indian-Pioneer Papers, University of Oklahoma, Norman.

87. Rice to her sister (1835).

88. Ferris, *Mormons at Home*, 63.

89. Haun, "Woman's Trip."

90. Lucene Pfeiffer Parsons, "The Women in the Sunbonnets" (1850), Stanford University Library, Stanford, Calif.

91. Pengra, "Diary."

92. Susan Armitage, "Women's Literature and the American Frontier: A New Perspective on the Frontier Myth," in L. L. Lee and Merrill Lewis, eds., *Women, Women Writers, and the West* (Troy, N.Y.: Whitson Publishing Company, 1979), 7–9.

93. Lillian Schlissel, *Women's Diaries of the Westward Journey* (New York: Schocken Books, 1982), 118.

94. Sarah Royce, *A Frontier Lady* (New Haven, Conn.: Yale University Press, 1932), 50.

95. Augusta Pierce Tabor, "Cabin Life in Colorado" (1884), Bancroft Library, Berkeley, Calif.; Rebecca Hildreth Nutting Woodson, "A Sketch of the Life of Rebecca Hildreth Nutting Woodson and Her Family" (1909), Bancroft Library, Berkeley, Calif.; Guill, "Overland Diary"; Kenneth L. Holmes, ed., "Letters from a Quaker Woman," *The American West* 20, no. 6 (1983), 42.

96. Mary Hall Jatta, "Journal" (1869), Bancroft Library, Berkeley, Calif.; Haun, "Woman's Trip"; Love, "Diary."

97. Herndon, *Days on the Road*, 235.

98. Guill, "Overland Diary."

99. Mallie Stafford, *The March of Empire through Three Decades* (San Francisco: George Spaulding & Co., 1884), 117.

100. E. Allene Dunham, *Across the Plains in a Covered Wagon* (possibly Milton, Iowa: n.p., ca. 1920s), 6–7; Martha M. Moore, "Journal of a Trip to California in 1860," Beinecke Collection, Yale University Library, New Haven, Conn.; Mary Burrell, "Diary of a Journey Overland from Council Bluffs to Green Valley, California, April 27 to September 1, 1854," Beinecke Col-

lection, Yale University Library, New Haven, Conn.; Buecker, "Letters of Caroline Frey Winne," 7; Gould, "Diary"; Haun, "Woman's Trip"; Porter, *By Ox Team to California*, 27, 32–33.

101. Tallent, *Black Hills*, 106; Hecox, *California Caravan*, 29; Eliza Ann Egbert, "Diary" (1852), Bancroft Library, Berkeley, Calif.

102. Hecox, *California Caravan*, 29; Nash, "Diary"; DeWitt and DeWitt, *Prairie Schooner Lady*, 139; Margaret Hall Walker, *The Hall Family Crossing the Plains* (San Francisco: Privately printed by Wallace Kibbee & Son, 1952), 29.

103. Bunyard, "Diary"; Catherine A. Washburn, "Journal, 1853, from Iowa to Oregon Territory," Huntington Library, San Marino, Calif.; Sawyer, "Overland"; Mattie Walker, "A Brief History of the William B. Walker Family" (n.d.), California State Library, Sacramento; Kaiser and Knuth, "From Ithaca to Clatsop Plains," pt. 1, 257–58, 284; Dunlap, "Journal"; Harriett A. L. Smith, "My Trip across the Plains in 1849," California State Library, Sacramento; Susan Thompson Parrish, "Westward in 1850," Huntington Library, San Marino, Calif.; Gould, "Diary"; Parsons, "Women in Sunbonnets"; Slater, "Travels."

104. Parrish, "Westward"; Emma S. Hill, *A Dangerous Crossing and What Happened on the Other Side: Seven Lean Years* (Denver: Bradford-Robinson Printing Company, 1924), 19; Mary Saunders, "The Whitman Maccacre; A True Story by a Survivor of This Terrible Tragedy which Took Place in Oregon in 1847," Bancroft Library, Berkeley, Calif.; Sawyer, "Overland"; Hanna, "Journal."

105. Mary Rabb, "Reminiscences" (1875), in Rabb Family Papers (1823–1922), Barker Texas History Center, University of Texas, Austin; Lizzie C. Stillwell Saunders, "Life Experiences of Pickey, Reminiscences of Mrs. L. C. Saunders" (1930), Barker Texas History Center, University of Texas, Austin.

106. Robert L. Munkres, "The Plains Indian Threat on the Oregon Trail before 1860," *Annals of Wyoming* 40 (1968), 221.

107. Sanford, *Mollie*, 129; Moore, "Journal"; Haun, "Woman's Trip"; Minto, "Female Pioneering"; Hecox, *California Caravan*, 40.

108. Kaiser and Knuth, "From Ithaca to Clatsop Plains," pt. 2, 392.

109. Maggie Hall, "The Story of Maggie Hall," Bancroft Library, Berkeley, Calif.

110. Blaine, "Letters"; Tallent, *First White Woman*, 138; Buecker, "Letters of Caroline Frey Winne," 8–9; Sanford, *Mollie*, 166; Vogdes, "Journal"; Carpenter, "Diary"; Lydia S. Lane, *I Married a Soldier; or, Old Days in the Old Army* (Philadelphia: J. B. Lippincott, 1893), 65–66.

111. Hecox, *California Caravan*, 28; Haun, "Woman's Trip"; Georgia Willis Read, "Diary" (1850), California State Library, Sacramento; Pengra, "Di-

ary"; Lucy R. Cooke, *Covered Wagon Days: Crossing the Plains in 1852* (Modesto, Calif.: Privately published, 1923), 30.

112. Eliza S. Warren, *Memoirs of the West: The Spaldings* (Portland, Oreg.: March Printing Co., 1916), 13; Elizabeth L. Lord, *Reminiscences of Eastern Oregon* (Portland, Oreg.: Irwin-Hodgson Company, 1903), 42; Frizzell, *Across the Plains*, 18.

113. Barsina French, "Journal of a Wagon Trip" (1867), Huntington Library, San Marino, Calif.; Cynthia J. Capron, "Life in the Army," *Journal of the Illinois State Historical Society* 13, no. 3 (October 1920), 367; Pengra, "Diary"; Dunlap, "Journal"; Hecox, *California Caravan*, 33.

114. Lula Nixon, interview 8011, vol. 67; Emma Clayton, interview 9672, vol. 18; Mary Clavin, interview 13643, vol. 18; Mrs. Eddie Brown, interview 7680, vol. 12; Sarah Luster, interview 8530, vol. 56; and Mrs. L. Johnson, interview 10227, vol. 48; all in Indian-Pioneer Papers, University of Oklahoma, Norman.

115. Parsons, "Women in Sunbonnets"; Hill, *Dangerous Crossing*, 82.

116. Mrs. John Barnes, interview 9735, vol. 5, Indian-Pioneer Papers, University of Oklahoma, Norman; Hanna, "Journal."

117. Hanna, "Journal."

118. Frizzell, *Across the Plains*, 25.

119. Katherine Provost, interview 1419, vol. 73, Indian-Pioneer Papers, University of Oklahoma, Norman; Barbara Baker, interview 10089, vol. 4, Indian-Pioneer Papers, University of Oklahoma, Norman; Lois L. Murray, *Incidents of Frontier Life* (Goshen, Ind.: Evangelical United Mennonite Publishing House, 1880), 134; Hodgson, "Life of a Pioneer Family"; Lois Smith Brown, interview 4496, vol. 12, Indian-Pioneer Papers, University of Oklahoma, Norman; Juliette Fish Walker, "Crossing the Plains," *Noticas* 16, no. 2 (1970), 4.

120. Haun, "Woman's Trip"; Barnes, interview 9735; vol. 5, Nixon, interview 8011.

121. Susan S. Magoffin, *Down the Santa Fe Trail and into Mexico: The Diary of Susan Shelby Magoffin, 1846–1847* (New Haven, Conn.: Yale University Press, 1926), 68.

122. Rachel C. Rose, "Diary" (1852), California State Library, Sacramento; Nancy A. Hunt, "By Ox Team to California," Bancroft Library, Berkeley, Calif.; Furness, "From Prairie to Pacific"; Sandford, "Trip across the Plains"; Walker, *Hall Family*, 28; Hanna, "Journal."

123. Porter, *By Ox Team to California*, 67.

124. Mary E. Hopping, "Incidents of Pioneer Life as I Remember and as I Have Been Told" (1962), California State Library, Sacramento.

125. Porter, *By Ox Team to California*, 79.

126. Wonderly, *Reminiscences of a Pioneer*, 4.

127. Hecox, *California Caravan,* 38.

128. Vogdes, "Journal."

129. Glenda Riley, *Women on the American Frontier* (St. Louis, Mo.: Forum Press, 1977), 3–4; Glenda Riley, "Women in the West," *Journal of American Culture* 3, no. 2 (Summer 1980), 314–18.

130. Porter, *By Ox Team to California,* 26–27.

131. DeWitt and DeWitt, *Prairie Schooner Lady,* 87, 123, 144, 158, 166.

132. Sandra L. Myres, "Romance and Reality of the American Frontier: Views of Army Wives," *Western Historical Quarterly* 13, no. 4 (October 1982), 414.

133. Sherry L. Smith, "Officers' Wives, Indians and the Indian Wars," *Order of the Indian Wars Journal* 1, no. 1 (Winter 1980), 38, 42–43.

134. Quoted in Christiane Fischer, ed., *Let Them Speak for Themselves: Women in the American West, 1849–1900* (Hamden, Conn.: Archon Press, 1977), 120–21.

135. Goltra, "Journal."

136. Saunders, "Whitman Massacre"; Goltra, "Journal"; Kitturah Penton Belknap, "Reminiscences" (1839), Iowa State Historical Society, Iowa City; Dunlap, "Journal."

137. Hecox, *California Caravan,* 29.

138. Mary A. Jones, "Recollections" (1915), Bancroft Library, Berkeley, Calif.; Porter, *By Ox Team to California* 34; Carpenter, "Diary"; DeWitt and DeWitt, *Prairie Schooner Lady,* 77; Sexton, *Foster Family,* 127; Virginia Reed Murphy, "Across the Plains in the Donner Party (1846): A Personal Narrative of the Overland Trip to California," *Century Magazine* 42, no. 3 (July 1891), 414.

139. Cooke, *Covered Wagon Days,* 30; Frizzell, *Across the Plains,* 18.

140. Cranston, "Daily Journal"; Fish, "Across the Plaines."

141. DeWitt and DeWitt, *Prairie Schooner Lady,* 139.

142. Lord, *Reminiscences,* 63.

143. Waters, "Account of a Trip," 69.

144. DeWitt and DeWitt, *Prairie Schooner Lady,* 127, 158.

145. Hanna, "Journal."

146. Walker, *Hall Family,* 28.

147. Carpenter, "Diary."

148. Bunyard, "Diary."

149. Mary Maverick, "Memoirs" (1881), Barker Texas History Center, University of Texas, Austin; Parsons, "Women in Sunbonnets."

150. Jean Webster, "The Myth of Hardship on the Oregon Trail," *Reed College Bulletin* 24 (January 1946), 34.

151. Sexton, *Foster Family,* 194–95.

152. Walker, *Hall Family,* 29.

153. Hodgson, "Life of a Pioneer Family"; Hare, "Reminiscences."

154. Capron, "Life in the Army," 367.

155. Hanna, "Journal"; Minnie Lee Cardwell Miller, "The Road to Yesterday" (1937), Bancroft Library, Berkeley, Calif.; Lord, *Reminiscences.*

156. Hopping, "Incidents of Pioneer Life."

157. Miller, "Road to Yesterday."

158. Furness, "From Prairie to Pacific."

159. Belknap, "Reminiscences"; Caples, "Overland Journey"; Olive Gordon Miller, "Pioneer Gordon Family" (n.d.), Bancroft Library, Berkeley, Calif.

160. Other scholars who have also noted that the Plains Indian threat was vastly exaggerated are Munkres, "Plains Indian Threat," 193–221; John D. Unruh, *The Plains Across: The Overland Emigrants and the Trans-Mississippi West, 1840–1860* (Urbana: University of Illinois Press, 1979), 9, 135–36, 156–200, 386, 395–96, 408–9; Elizabeth Hampsten, *Read This Only to Yourself: The Private Writings of Midwestern Women, 1880–1910* (Bloomington, Ind.: Indiana University Press, 1982), 40–42.

161. Chambers, "Reminiscences," 13, 47; Mrs. Edward Dyer, "Diary" (1860), Barker Texas History Center, University of Texas, Austin; Jones, "Recollections"; Karchner, "Diary"; Kaiser and Knuth, "From Ithaca to Clatsop Plains," pt. 1, 282, 363; Dwight G. McCarty, *Stories of Pioneer Life on the Iowa Prairie* (Emmetsburg, Iowa: Emmetsburg Publishing Company, 1974), 20; Valentine McGillycuddy, "Notebook" (1876) and notes kept by his wife, Fanny (1877), Beinecke Collection, Yale University Library, New Haven, Conn.; Norton, "Diary"; Harriet M. Hill Townsend, "Reminiscences" (n.d.), privately held by Frank Kerulis, Waverly, Iowa.

162. Millington, "Journal."

163. Maverick, "Memoirs."

164. Rabb, "Reminiscences."

165. Elizabeth McAnulty Owens, "The Story of Her Life" (1895), Barker Texas History Collection, University of Texas, Austin; Mary Fokes Locklin, "Experience of Abigail McLennan Fokes and Family as Told by Her Daughter" (n.d.), Barker Texas History Center, University of Texas, Austin.

166. Martha V. Webster Simmons, "The Webster Massacre" (1925), Barker Texas History Center, University of Texas, Austin.

167. Rosalie B. Hart Priour, "The Adventures of a Family of Emigrants Who Emigrated to Texas, in 1834; An Autobiography by Rosalie B. Hart Priour" (n.d.), Barker Texas History Center, University of Texas, Austin.

168. Julia Lee Sinks, "Reminiscences of Early Days in Texas" (1896), Barker Texas History Center, University of Texas, Austin.

169. Martha N. McFarlin Gray, "Adventures of John Green McFarlin and an Autobiography" (1931), Barker Texas History Center, University of Texas,

Austin; Eugenie E. Lavender, "Biography" (n.d.), Barker Texas History Center, University of Texas, Austin; Mary A. Baylor, "Reminiscences" (n.d.), Barker Texas History Center, University of Texas, Austin.

170. Jonaphrene S. Faulkner, typescript of novel "Prairie Home" (n.d.), Barker Texas History Center, University of Texas, Austin.

171. Susan P. Newcomb, "Diary" (1865–1869, 1871–1873), Barker Texas History Center, University of Texas, Austin.

172. Ella Bird-Dumont, "True Life Story of Ella Bird-Dumont, Earliest Settler in the East Part of Panhandle, Texas" (n.d.), Barker Texas History Center, University of Texas, Austin.

173. Saunders, "Life Experiences"; Margaret Armstrong Bowie, "Diary of Margaret Armstrong" (1872–1877), Barker Texas History Center, University of Texas, Austin.

174. May Callan Tansill, "Narrative" (n.d.), Barker Texas History Center, University of Texas, Austin.

175. Millie M. Butler, interview 10094, vol. 14, Indian-Pioneer Papers, University of Oklahoma, Norman.

176. Mrs. W. C. Jarhoe, "Papers" (1890–1913), Western History Collections, University of Oklahoma, Norman.

177. Amelia F. Harris, no interview number, vol. 47, Indian-Pioneer Papers, University of Oklahoma, Norman.

178. Adams, "Diary"; Pauline Farseth and Theodore C. C. Blegen, eds., *Frontier Mother: The Letters of Gro Svendsen* (Northfield, Minn.: Norwegian-American Historical Association, 1950), 32.

179. Libbie B. Bradford to John N. Bradford, 1857, Richfield, Minn., in "The Letters of John N. and Libbie B. Bradford, 1862–1864," privately held by John P. Bradford, St. Paul, Minn.; Curt Harnack, "Prelude to Massacre," *The Iowan* 4, no. 3 (February–March 1956), 36–39; Rodney Fox, "Stark Reminder of an Indian Raid," *The Iowan* 9, no. 1 (October–November 1960), 20–21; Hubert E. Moeller, "Iowa's Other Indian Massacre," *The Iowan* 2, no. 4 (April–May 1954), 40; M. A. Roe, "A Pioneer Woman's Letter," in Alice L. Longley Collection, Division of Archives and Historical Museum, Des Moines, Iowa; Elinore Pruitt Stewart, *Letters of a Woman Homesteader* (Lincoln: University of Nebraska Press, 1961), 120–21; Biddle, *Reminiscences;* Lily Klasner, *My Girlhood among Outlaws* (Tucson: University of Arizona Press, 1972), 32–35, 73–78; Budlong, *Memories*, 8–9; Mary Richardson Walker, "Diary" (1848), Huntington Library, San Marino, Calif.; Rachel E. Wright, "The Early Upper Napa Valley" (1928), Bancroft Library, Berkeley, Calif.

180. Mary E. Ackley, *Crossing the Plains and Early Days in California* (San Francisco: Privately printed, 1928), 32; Sarah Davis, "Diary of an Overland Journey from St. Joseph, Missouri to California" (1850), Beinecke Col-

lection, Yale University Library, New Haven, Conn.; Margaret A. Kelley, "Notes on Pioneers" (n.d.), California State Library, Sacramento; Walker, "Crossing the Plains," 3–19.

181. P. A. M. Taylor, "Emigrants' Problems in Crossing the West, 1830–1870," *University of Birmingham History Journal* 5, no. 1 (1955), 88; Schlissel, *Women's Diaries*, 53.

182. Mrs. L. D. Pritchard, interview 8737, vol. 73, Indian-Pioneer Papers, University of Oklahoma, Norman; Lillian Allen, interview 9691, vol. 2, Indian-Pioneer Papers, University of Oklahoma, Norman; Owen P. White, *A Frontier Mother* (New York: Minton, Balch & Co., 1929), 34–35.

183. Walker, "Brief History."

184. Mary Jones, "Papers" (1846–1944), Barker Texas History Center, University of Texas, Austin.

185. Webster, "Myth of Hardship," 33.

186. Unruh, *Plains Across*, 200.

187. Maverick, "Memoirs"; Sinks, "Reminiscences."

188. Martha Lowrence, interview 7884, vol. 56, Indian-Pioneer Papers, University of Oklahoma, Norman.

189. Lois Smith Brown, interview 4496, vol. 12; Lorene Millhollen, interview 8957, vol. 63; Mary Ellen Phillips Wynn, interview 13047, vol. 101; Maud Parshall Norris, interview 9837, vol. 67; and Mabel Sharpe Beavers, interview 6850, vol. 6; all in Indian-Pioneer Papers, University of Oklahoma, Norman.

190. Mary Ellen Williams, interview 6877, vol. 98; and Julia C. Bolen, interview 9113, vol. 9; both in Indian-Pioneer Papers, University of Oklahoma, Norman. Bolen's first husband was a "full blood Comanche," and after his death she said that she married a "full blood Cherokee."

191. Dora B. Parnell, interview 12091, vol. 69; Mary Archibald, interview 12054, vol. 3; and Fannie J. Bell, no interview number, vol. 7; all in Indian-Pioneer Papers, University of Oklahoma, Norman.

192. Mrs. John Wyers, interview 6244, vol. 101; Bertha Brewer Plummer, interview 4833, vol. 72; Ethel Daniel Pfeiffer, interview 1253, vol. 71; Mrs. Arthur Johnson, interview 9025, vol. 48; and Belle M. Yates, interview 12817, vol. 101; all in Indian-Pioneer Papers, University of Oklahoma, Norman.

193. May Johnson, interview 10498, vol. 48, Indian-Pioneer Papers, University of Oklahoma, Norman.

194. Margaret Cring Adams, interview 8499, vol. 1; Lucy J. Auldridge, interview 5776, vol. 3; Mrs. B. M. Austin, interview 9189, vol. 3; Beaulah Smith Young, interview 10436, vol. 101; and Mrs. Andrew J. Wilson, interview 4507, vol. 99; all in Indian-Pioneer Papers, University of Oklahoma, Norman.

195. Samantha Johnson, interview 12027, vol. 48; Mrs. Frances Johnson, interview 8841, vol. 48; and Mary Bell Boothby, interview 4335, vol. 9; all in Indian-Pioneer Papers, University of Oklahoma, Norman.

196. Mrs. Emma Wiltband, interview 4785, vol. 99; Frances Jeannette Wynn, interview 12794, vol. 101; and Bettie Monahan, interview 8566, vol. 64; all in Indian-Pioneer Papers, University of Oklahoma, Norman.

197. Mrs. C. T. Clay, interview 4045, vol. 18, Indian-Pioneer Papers, University of Oklahoma, Norman.

198. Sarah Cothern Molen, interview 9805, vol. 64, Indian-Pioneer Papers, University of Oklahoma, Norman.

199. Fannie Birdwell, interview 8360, vol. 8, Indian-Pioneer Papers, University of Oklahoma, Norman.

200. Webster, "Myth of Hardship," 28; Parsons, "Women in Sunbonnets."

201. Kaiser and Knuth, "From Ithaca to Clatsop Plains," pt. 1, 261.

202. DeWitt and DeWitt, *Prairie Schooner Lady*, 76.

203. Ibid., 144.

204. Love, "Diary."

205. Catherine Jane Bell to Julia, 31 October 1859, Oroville, Calif., Bancroft Library, Berkeley, Calif.

206. Sawyer, "Overland."

207. Hunt, "By Ox Team," 11.

208. Rose, "Diary."

209. Dunham, *Across the Plains*, 4, 7.

210. Strahorn, *Fifteen Thousand Miles by Stage*, 1.

211. Caroline Phelps, "Diary" (1830–1860), Iowa State Historical Society, Iowa City.

212. Hilda Faunce, *Desert Wife* (Lincoln: University of Nebraska Press, 1981), 98–99, 118–19, 158–63, 183–85.

213. Ibid., 195, 279–80.

214. Ibid., 283.

215. Ibid., 291, 304–5.

216. Myres, "Romance and Reality," 411, 413–14.

217. Robert C. and Eleanor R. Carriker, eds., *An Army Wife on the Frontier: The Memoirs of Alice Blackwood Baldwin, 1867–1877* (Salt Lake City: Tanner Trust Fund, University of Utah Library, 1975), 41, 78–79, 99, 109.

218. Vogdes, "Journal."

219. Catherine Jane Bell to Julia, 31 October 1859, Oroville, Calif., Bancroft Library, Berkeley, Calif.; Norton, "Diary."

220. Staples, "Reminiscences"; Budlong, *Memories*, 8, 37–39.

221. Susannah Willeford, "Henry County: On Immigration of Pioneers, 1820–1870," Iowa State Historical Society, Iowa City.

Chapter 5

1. Lillian Schlissel, *Women's Diaries of the Westward Journey* (New York: Schocken Books, 1982), 14.

2. Mary Burrell, "Diary of a Journey Overland from Council Bluffs to Green Valley, California, 1854," Beinecke Collection, Yale University Library, New Haven, Conn.

3. Schlissel, *Women's Diaries*, 15. See also Helen E. Clark, "Diary" (1860), and Cara Whitemore Bell, "Journal, 1872–1876," both in the Denver Public Library, Denver, Colo., and Carol Fairbanks and Sara Brooks Sundberg, *Farm Women on the Prairie Frontier: A Sourcebook for Canada and the United States* (Metuchen, N.J.: The Scarecrow Press, 1983), 47–48.

4. Laura Ingalls Wilder, *The First Four Years* (New York: Harper & Row, 1971), 33; Eliza Ann Egbert, "Diary" (1852), Bancroft Library, Berkeley, Calif.

5. Barbara B. Zimmerman and Vernon Carstensen, eds., "Pioneer Woman in Southwestern Washington Territory: The Recollections of Susanna Maria Slover McFarland Price Ede," *Pacific Northwest Quarterly* 66–67, no. 4 (1976), 143, 147.

6. Bessie L. Lyon, "Hungry Indians," *Palimpsest* 9 (October 1928), 366.

7. Lavinia H. Porter, *By Ox Team to California: A Narrative of Crossing the Plains in 1860* (Oakland, Calif.: Oakland Enquirer Publishing Company, 1910), 56.

8. Burrell, "Diary"; Barsina French, "Journal of a Wagon Trip" (1867), Huntington Library, San Marino, Calif.

9. Christiane Fischer, "A Profile of Women in Arizona in Frontier Days," *Journal of the West* 16, no. 3 (July 1977), 43.

10. Mary Ann Ferrin Davidson, "An Autobiography and a Reminiscence," *Annals of Iowa* 37 (Spring 1964), 256.

11. Susie P. Van de Wiele, "Travels and Experiences in America with Army and Indian Reminiscences," Graff Collection, Newberry Library, Chicago, Ill.

12. Porter, *By Ox Team to California*, 67, 79.

13. Burrell, "Diary"; Porter, *By Ox Team to California*, 34, 67.

14. Schlissel, *Women's Diaries*, 154.

15. Sarah J. Cummins, *Autobiography and Reminiscences* (LaGrande, Oreg.: LaGrande Printing Company, 1914), 42; Mary Saunders, "The Whitman Massacre; A True Story by a Survivor of this Terrible Tragedy which Took Place in Oregon in 1847," Bancroft Library, Berkeley, Calif.; Almira Neff Beam Enos, "Journal" (1858–1866), Bancroft Library, Berkeley, Calif.; Mrs. M. S. Hockensmith, "Diary of a Trip Overland from the Mississippi to California" (1866), Bancroft Library, Berkeley, Calif.; Julia L. Hare, "Rem-

iniscences of Julia L. Hare" (n.d.), California State Library, Sacramento; Mary E. Hopping, "Incidents of Pioneer Life as I Remember and as I Have Been Told" (1962), California State Library, Sacramento; Margaret A. Frink, *Journal of the Adventures of a Party of California Gold-Seekers* (Oakland, Calif.: n.p., 1897), 46; Louisa M. Rahm, "Diary" (1862), Bancroft Library, Berkeley, Calif.; Frances H. Sawyer, "Overland to California" (1852), Bancroft Library, Berkeley, Calif.; Mary Jane Guill, "The Overland Diary of a Journey from Livingston County, Missouri, to Butte County, California" (1860), California State Library, Sacramento; Catherine A. Washburn, "Journal, 1853, from Iowa to Oregon Territory," Huntington Library, San Marino, Calif.; Harriet Bunyard, "Diary of Miss Harriet Bunyard from Texas to California in 1868," in *Annual Publications, Historical Society of Southern California*, no. 13 (Los Angeles: Historical Society of Southern California, 1924), 117, 121; Celinda E. Hines Shipley, "Diary" (1853), Beinecke Collection, Yale University Library, New Haven, Conn.; Elizabeth J. Goltra, "Journal" (1853), Bancroft Library, Berkeley, Calif.; Miriam D. Colt, *Went to Kansas; Being a Thrilling Account of an Ill-Fated Expedition* (Watertown, N.Y.: L. Ingalls & Company, 1862), 125.

16. Colt, *Went to Kansas*, 125.

17. Martha M. Moore, "Journal of a Trip to California in 1860," Beinecke Collection, Yale University Library, New Haven, Conn.

18. Fleming Fraker, Jr., ed., "To Pike's Peak by Ox Wagon: The Harriet A. Smith Day-Book," *Annals of Iowa* 35, no. 2 (Fall 1959), 138; Martha M. Morgan, *A Trip across the Plains in the Year 1849* (San Francisco: Printed at Pioneer Press, 1864), 7, 12, 15–16; Ellen McGowen Biddle, *Reminiscences of a Soldier's Wife* (Philadelphia: J. B. Lippincott Company, 1907), 83; Mrs. Edward Dyer, "Diary" (1860), Barker Texas History Center, University of Texas, Austin.

19. Cynthia J. Capron, "Life in the Army," *Journal of the Illinois State Historical Society* 13, no. 3 (October 1920), 369.

20. Egbert, "Diary."

21. Mrs. B. G. Ferris, *The Mormons at Home* (New York: Dix & Edwards, 1856), 63.

22. Mary A. Hodgson, "The Life of a Pioneer Family" (1922), California State Library, Sacramento; Biddle, *Reminiscences*, 83.

23. Lucy R. Cooke, *Covered Wagon Days: Crossing the Plains in 1852* (Modesto, Calif.: Privately published, 1923), 66.

24. Sandra L. Myres, ed., *Cavalry Wife: The Diary of Eveline M. Alexander, 1866–1867* (College Station: Texas A. & M. University Press, 1977), 38, 102.

25. Ada A. Vogdes, "Journal" (1866–1872), Huntington Library, San Marino, Calif.

26. Catherine M. Haun, "A Woman's Trip across the Plains, from Clinton, Iowa, to Sacramento, California, by Way of Salt Lake City" (1849), Huntington Library, San Marino, Calif.

27. Katherine Dunlap, "Journal" (1864), Bancroft Library, Berkeley, Calif.

28. Frink, *Journal*, 68, 77; Guill, "Overland Diary"; Kate Roberts Pelissier, "Reminiscences of a Pioneer Mother," *North Dakota History* 24 (July 1957), 131; Morgan, *Trip across the Plains*, 15–16; Washburn, "Journal"; Hopping, "Incidents of Pioneer Life"; Edwin Bryant, *What I Saw in California* (Minneapolis: Ross & Haines, 1967), 166; Raymond W. Settle, ed., *The March of the Mounted Riflemen* (Glendale, Calif.: Arthur H. Clark, 1940), 223; James A. Pritchard, *The Overland Diary of James A. Pritchard* (Denver: Old West Publishing Company, 1959), 104; G. T. Byron, "The Overland Emigrant," *Cornhill* 65 (June 1892), 643–44; Elizabeth Page, ed., *Wagons West: A Story of the Oregon Trail* (New York: Farrar & Rinehart, 1930), 115; Dale Morgan, ed., *Overland in 1846: Diaries and Letters of the California-Oregon Trail* (Georgetown, Calif.: Talisman Press, 1963), 96; Thomas D. Clark, *Gold Rush Diary: Being the Journal of Elisha Douglass Perkins on the Overland Trail in the Spring and Summer of 1849* (Lexington: University of Kentucky Press, 1967), 101; Helen S. Giffen, ed., *The Diaries of Peter Decker: Overland to California in 1849 and Life in the Mines, 1850–1851* (Georgetown, Calif.: Talisman Press, 1966), 72; David M. Potter, ed., *Trail to California: The Overland Journal of Vincent Geiger and Wakeman Bryarly* (New Haven, Conn.: Yale University Press, 1945), 138, 152; H. C. Ambler, "West Virginia Forty-Niners," *West Virginia History* 3 (October–July 1941–42), 59–75.

The differences in men's and women's trade interests and patterns can be seen clearly by comparing Jerome Dutton, "Across the Plains in 1850," *Annals of Iowa* 9, no. 3 (October 1910), 468–69; Howard Egan, *Pioneering the West, 1846–1878* (Richmond, Utah: Howard R. Egan Estate, 1917), 47; Pritchard, *Overland Diary*, 104; Reuben G. Thwaites, ed., *Early Western Travels, 1748–1846* (Cleveland, Ohio: A. H. Clark Company, 1906), 145, 149; with Cooke, *Covered Wagon Days*, 66; Guill, "Overland Diary"; Hopping, "Incidents of Pioneer Life"; Rahm, "Diary"; and Vogdes, "Journal."

29. John D. Unruh, *The Plains Across: The Overland Emigrants and the Trans-Mississippi West, 1840–1860* (Urbana: University of Illinois Press, 1979), 166.

30. Schlissel, *Women's Diaries*, 53.

31. Helen Carpenter, "Diary" (1856), Bancroft Library, Berkeley, Calif.; Unruh, *Plains Across*, 157; Frink, *Journal*, 72; Bunyard, "Diary," 121; French, "Journal"; Mrs. Nicholas Harrison Karchner, "Diary" (1862), California State Library, Sacramento.

300

32. Maggie Hall, "The Story of Maggie Hall," Bancroft Library, Berkeley, Calif.; Elizabeth L. Lord, *Reminiscences of Eastern Oregon* (Portland, Oreg.: Irwin-Hodgson Company, 1903), 68–69; Charlotte Stearns Pengra, "Diary" (1853), Huntington Library, San Marino, Calif.; Unruh, *Plains Across*, 157.

33. Abby E. Fulkerth, "Diary of Overland Journey of William L. Fulkerth and Wife from Iowa to California in 1863," Bancroft Library, Berkeley, Calif.; Unruh, *Plains Across*, 159; Lord, *Reminiscences*, 86.

34. Leo M. Kaiser and Priscilla Knuth, eds., "From Ithaca to Clatsop Plains: Miss Ketcham's Journal of Travel," pt. 1, *Oregon Historical Quarterly* 62, no. 3 (1961), 255; Unruh, *Plains Across*, 163; Caroline D. Budlong, *Memories: Pioneer Days in Oregon and Washington Territory* (Eugene, Oreg.: Picture Press Printers, 1949), 4; J. William Barrett, II, ed., *The Overland Journal of Amos Piatt Josselyn* (Baltimore: Gateway Press, 1978), 20.

35. Mary Fetter Hite Sandford, "A Trip across the Plains" (1853), California State Library, Sacramento; French, "Journal"; Unruh, *Plains Across*, 158.

36. Unruh, *Plains Across*, 158.

37. Mary E. Ackley, *Crossing the Plains and Early Days in California* (San Francisco: Privately printed, 1928), 66.

38. Budlong, *Memories*, 38; Nannie T. Alderson, *A Bride Goes West* (Lincoln: University of Nebraska Press, 1969), 186; Fraker, "To Pike's Peak," 137; Hodgson, "Life of a Pioneer Family"; Albert L. Hurtado, "'Hardly a Farmhouse—A Kitchen without Them': Indian and White Households on the California Borderland Frontier in 1860," *Western Historical Quarterly* 14, no. 3 (July 1982), 245–70.

39. Alderson, *Bride Goes West*, 131; Caroline Phelps, "Diary" (1830–1860), Iowa State Historical Society, Iowa City.

40. Sandra L. Myres, ed., "Evy Alexander: The Colonel's Lady at Ft. McDowell," *Montana, The Magazine of Western History* 24 (1974), 32.

41. Ibid., 33.

42. Alderson, *Bride Goes West*, 132, 136.

43. Sarah McAllister Hartman, "Reminiscences of Early Days on Puget Sound, the Friendliness of the Local Indians, and Experiences during the Indian War of 1855" (n.d.), Beinecke Collection, Yale University Library, New Haven, Conn.

44. Phelps, "Diary."

45. Rachel E. Wright, "The Early Upper Napa Valley" (1928), Bancroft Library, Berkeley, Calif.

46. Robert C. and Eleanor R. Carriker, eds., *An Army Wife on the Frontier: The Memoirs of Alice Blackwood Baldwin, 1867–1877* (Salt Lake City: Tanner Trust Fund, University of Utah Library, 1975), 108.

47. Hartman, "Reminiscences."

48. E. Allene Dunham, *Across the Plains in a Covered Wagon* (Milton, Iowa: n.p., ca. 1920s), 7.

49. Mrs. H. T. Clarke, "A Young Woman's Sights on the Emigrant's Trail" (1878), Bancroft Library, Berkeley, Calif.

50. Lodisa Frizzell, *Across the Plains to California in 1852* (New York: New York Public Library, 1915), 25.

51. Malvina V. Manning, "Diary" (1862), Bancroft Library, Berkeley, Calif.

52. Ferris, *Mormons at Home*, 24.

53. Louise S. Gellhorn Boylan, "My Life Story: Reminiscence of German Settlers in Hardin County, 1867–1883," Iowa State Historical Society, Iowa City.

54. Edna Hunt Osborne, interview 7387, vol. 68, Indian-Pioneer Papers, University of Oklahoma, Norman.

55. Carriker, *Army Wife*, 79, 99–100.

56. Eliza R. Snow, "Sketch of My Life" (1885), Bancroft Library, Berkeley, Calif.

57. Mollie Beaver, interview 9409, vol. 6, Indian-Pioneer Papers, University of Oklahoma, Norman.

58. Belle M. Yates, interview 12817, vol. 101, Indian-Pioneer Papers, University of Oklahoma, Norman; Bertha Brewer Plummer, interview 4833, vol. 72, Indian-Pioneer Papers, University of Oklahoma, Norman; Fannie Birdwell, interview 8360, vol. 8, Indian-Pioneer Papers, University of Oklahoma, Norman; Dan McAllister, "Pioneer Woman," *New Mexico Historical Review* 34, no. 3 (July 1959), 162.

59. Jean Webster, "The Myth of Hardship on the Oregon Trail," *Reed College Bulletin* 24 (January 1946), 37; Hodgson, "Life of a Pioneer Family"; Lorene Millhollen, interview 8957, vol. 63, Indian-Pioneer Papers, University of Oklahoma, Norman.

60. Leola Lehman, "Life in the Territories," *Chronicles of Oklahoma* 41 (Fall 1963), 373–75.

61. Emma Brown, interview 8543, vol. 12; Emma Clayton, interview 9672, vol. 18; Matilda Clure, interview 4673, vol. 18; all in Indian-Pioneer Papers, University of Oklahoma, Norman.

62. Mrs. John Barnes, interview 9735, vol. 5; Katherine Provost, interview 1419, vol. 73; Osborne, interview 7387; all in Indian-Pioneer Papers, University of Oklahoma, Norman.

63. Ward G. DeWitt and Florence S. DeWitt, *Prairie Schooner Lady: The Journal of Harriet Sherrill Ward, 1853* (Los Angeles: Westernlore Press, 1959), 78.

64. Hopping, "Incidents of Pioneer Life"; Egbert, "Diary."

65. Barnes, interview 9735.

66. Nancy C. Pruitt, interview 7855, vol. 73, Indian-Pioneer Papers, University of Oklahoma, Norman.

67. Phelps, "Diary."

68. Hartman, "Reminiscences."

69. Alderson, *Bride Goes West*, 91.

70. Phelps, "Diary"; Osborne, interview 7387; Provost, interview 1419; Frances Jeannette Wynen, interview 12798, vol. 101, Indian-Pioneer Papers, University of Oklahoma, Norman; Lucy J. Auldridge, interview 5776, vol. 3, Indian-Pioneer Papers, University of Oklahoma, Norman; Fannie J. Bell, no interview number, vol. 7, Indian-Pioneer Papers, University of Oklahoma, Norman; Plummer, interview 4833.

71. Valentine T. McGillycuddy, "Notebook" (1876), and notes kept by his wife, Fanny (1877), Beinecke Collection, Yale University Library, New Haven, Conn.; Margaret Cring Adams, interview 8499, vol. 1, Indian-Pioneer Papers, University of Oklahoma, Norman; Frances Johnson, interview 6481, vol. 48, Indian-Pioneer Papers, University of Oklahoma, Norman.

72. Mrs. C. C. Clements, interview 9044, vol. 18, Indian-Pioneer Papers, University of Oklahoma, Norman; Lois Smith Brown, interview 4496, vol. 12, Indian-Pioneer Papers, University of Oklahoma, Norman; Loretta C. Morgan, interview 6085, vol. 64, Indian-Pioneer Papers, University of Oklahoma, Norman; Alderson, *Bride Goes West*, 135–36; Phelps, "Diary."

73. Fulkerth, "Diary"; Van de Wiele, "Travels and Experiences," 17.

74. Eliza Spalding Warren, *Memoirs of the West: The Spaldings* (Portland, Oreg.: March Printing Company, 1916), 20–21.

75. Laura W. Johnson, *Eight Hundred Miles in an Ambulance* (Philadelphia: J. B. Lippincott Company, 1889), 61–65.

76. Biddle, *Reminiscences*, 227.

77. Christiane Fischer, ed., *Let Them Speak for Themselves: Women in the American West, 1849–1900* (Hamden, Conn.: Archon Press, 1977), 146.

78. Carpenter, "Diary."

79. Emma Shepard Hill, *A Dangerous Crossing and What Happened on the Other Side: Seven Lean Years* (Denver: Bradford-Robinson Printing Company, 1924), 84.

80. Johnson, *Eight Hundred Miles*, 72, 79.

81. Biddle, *Reminiscences*, 83, 183.

82. Kay Graber, ed., *Sister to the Sioux: The Memoirs of Elaine Goodale Eastman* (Lincoln: University of Nebraska Press, 1978), xi–xii, 172–75.

83. Emily McCowen Horton, *My Scrap-book* (Seattle, Wash.: n.p., 1927), 17.

84. Barnes, interview 9735.

85. Mrs. William N. Moore, interview 7365, vol. 64; Emma Jean Ross Overstreet, interview 7240, vol. 68; Sarah Scott Phillips, interview 6251, vol. 71; Mrs. J. B. Antles, interview 4163, vol. 2; Harriet Gibbons Oakes, interview 12028, vol. 68; all in Indian-Pioneer Papers, University of Oklahoma, Norman.

86. Mrs. Bill Moncrief, interview 4189, vol. 64, Indian-Pioneer Papers, University of Oklahoma, Norman.

87. Sallie Butler, interview 7244, vol. 14, Indian-Pioneer Papers, University of Oklahoma, Norman.

88. Alice Parker, interview 4021, vol. 69, Indian-Pioneer Papers, University of Oklahoma, Norman.

89. Mary Ellen Williams, interview 6877, vol. 98, Indian-Pioneer Papers, University of Oklahoma, Norman.

90. Mrs. B. M. Austin, interview 9189, vol. 3, Indian-Pioneer Papers, University of Oklahoma, Norman.

91. Beaver, interview 9409.

92. Dawn L. Gherman, "From Parlor to Tepee: The White Squaw on the American Frontier" (Ph.D. diss., University of Massachusetts, 1975), 216–19.

93. Kaiser and Knuth, "From Ithaca to Clatsop Plains," pt. 1, 237–87; Kaiser and Knuth, "From Ithaca to Clatsop Plains: Miss Ketcham's Journal of Travel," pts. 2, *Oregon Historical Quarterly* 62, no. 4 (1961), 337–402; Schlissel, *Women's Diaries*, 150–51.

94. James Hewitt, ed., *Eye-Witnesses to Wagon Trains West* (New York: Charles Scribner's Sons, 1973), 10.

95. William Edmundson, "Diary Kept by William Edmundson, of Oskaloosa, while Crossing the Western Plains in 1850," *Annals of Iowa* 8 (October 1908), 516–35.

96. Mary Alice Shutes, "Diary" (1862), Division of Museum and Archives, Des Moines, Iowa.

97. A. W. Harlan, "Journal of A. W. Harlan while Crossing the Plains in 1850," *Annals of Iowa* 11 (April 1913), 39.

98. Harlan, "Journal," 32–62; Ambler, "West Virginia Forty-Niners," 59–75; Giffen, *Diaries of Peter Decker*, 129, 134–35, 183, 187–89; Charles W. Martin, ed., "Joseph Warren Arnold's Journal of His Trip from Montana, 1864–1866," *Nebraska History* 55, no. 4 (1974), 463–552.

99. Schlissel, *Women's Diaries*, 111–14.

100. Kitturah Penton Belknap, "Reminiscences" (1839), Iowa State Historical Society, Iowa City.

101. Harlan, "Journal," 141–62; Ambler, "West Virginia Forty-Niners," 59–75.

102. Carpenter, "Diary."

103. Dutton, "Across the Plains," 466.

104. Ibid., 447–83; Louise Barry, comp., "Charles Robinson—Yankee '49er: His Journey to California," *Kansas Historical Quarterly* 34, no. 2 (1968), 179, 186; Alonzo Delano, *Life on the Plains and among the Diggings* (Ann Arbor, Mich.: University Microfilms, 1966); Harlan, "Journal," 32–62; Georgia W. Read and Ruth Gaines, eds., *Gold Rush: The Journals, Drawings, and Other Papers of J. Goldsborough Bruff, April 2, 1849–June 20, 1851* (New York: Columbia University Press, 1949); Potter, *Trail to California*; Byron N. McKinstry, *The California Gold Rush Overland Diary of Byron N. McKinstry* (Glendale, Calif.: Arthur H. Clark Company, 1975); Pritchard, *Overland Diary*; Charles Glass Gray, "Diary" (1849–1850), Huntington Library, San Marino, Calif.; Howard Stansbury, *An Expedition to the Valley of the Great Salt Lake* (Ann Arbor, Mich.: University Microfilms, 1966); Fancher Stimson, "Overland Journey to California by Platte River Route and South Pass in 1850," *Annals of Iowa* 13, no. 6 (October 1922), 403–40; Milo M. Quaife, ed., *Across the Plains in Forty-Nine* (Chicago: Lakeside Press, 1948); Everett Walter and George B. Strother, eds., "The Gold Rush Diary of Henry Tappan," *Annals of Wyoming* 25 (July 1953), 113–39; Walker D. Wyman, ed., *California Emigrant Letters* (New York: Bookman Association, 1952).

105. John O. Holzhueter, ed., "From Waupun to Sacramento in 1849: The Gold Rush Journal of Edwin Hillyer," *Wisconsin Magazine of History* 49, no. 3 (1966), 222, 228.

106. Andrew F. Rolle, ed., *The Road to Virginia City: The Diary of James Knox Polk Miller* (Norman: University of Oklahoma Press, 1960), 66.

107. Page, *Wagons West*, 114.

108. Stansbury, *Expedition*, 44.

109. Quaife, *Across the Plains*, 105.

110. Walter and Strother, "Gold Rush Diary," 125.

111. Delano, *Life on the Plains*, 64.

112. Clark, *Gold Rush Diary*, 24.

113. Holzhueter, "From Waupun to Sacramento," 223.

114. Andrew J. Rotter, "'Matilda for Gods Sake Write': Women and Families on the Argonaut Mind," *California History* 58 (Summer 1979), 128–34.

115. Alfred M. Doten, "My Adventures in the California Diggins," *Life* 46 (April 1927), 96.

116. Dutton, "Across the Plains," 464.

117. Giffen, *Diaries of Peter Decker*, 73.

118. Dunham, *Across the Plains*, 2, 5, 14; Egbert, "Diary"; Jane Augusta Gould, "Diary" (1862), Iowa State Historical Society, Iowa City; Haun, "Woman's Trip"; Virginia W. Ivins, *Pen Pictures of Early Western Days* (Keokuk, Iowa: n.p., 1905); Sarah Welch Nossaman, "Pioneering at Bona-

parte and near Pella," *Annals of Iowa* 13 (October 1922), 441–53; Phelps, "Diary"; Mary St. John, "Diary" (1858), Iowa State Historical Society, Iowa City. See also John M. Faragher, *Women and Men on the Overland Trail* (New Haven, Conn.: Yale University Press, 1979), 121–33.

119. Belknap, "Reminiscences."

120. Haun, "Woman's Trip."

121. See, for example, the Bourn-Ingalls Family Papers, 1865–1958, Bancroft Library, Berkeley, Calif.; the DeWitt Family Papers, 1848–1867, Bancroft Library, Berkeley, Calif.; the John Kenyon Family Letters, 1856–1865, Iowa State Historical Society, Iowa City; the Alice L. Longley Collection, Division of Museum and Archives, Des Moines, Iowa; and the Parsons Letters, Northampton Historical Society, Northampton, Mass. See also Faragher, *Women and Men*, 103–5, 128–33.

122. Oscar O. Winther, ed., *To Oregon in 1852* (Indianapolis: Indiana Historical Society, 1964), 14.

123. Ellen R. Fenn, "Sweepin' out the Fabled Ghosts," *The Iowan* 14, no. 1 (Fall 1965), 50.

124. Belknap, "Reminiscences."

125. Matilda Peitzke Paul, "Recollections" (1938), Iowa State Historical Society, Iowa City; Shutes, "Diary."

126. Charles R. Berry, ed., "A Prospecting Trip to Idaho: The 1862 Diary of John Green Berry, Jr.," *Idaho Yesterdays* 24 (Fall 1980), 18.

127. Shutes, "Diary"; Haun, "Woman's Trip."

128. Mary Ellis to her mother and sister, 22 February 1857, and Sarah Kenyon to her mother-in-law and sister-in-law, 18 March 1860, Kenyon Family Letters.

129. McKinstry, *California Gold Rush Overland Diary*, 124–25.

130. Read and Gaines, *Gold Rush*, 31.

131. Harlan, "Journal," 45.

132. Hiram W. Studley, "Letter Describing a March to Utah in 1859," *Annals of Iowa* 13 (April 1923), 615.

133. Isaac Jones Wistar, *Autobiography of Isaac Jones Wistar, 1827–1905: Half a Century in War and Peace* (New York: Harper & Brothers, 1937), 57; Francis C. Rosenberger, ed., *Journey to the Gold Fields of California, 1849–1850: The Diary of Zirkle D. Robinson* (Iowa City: Prairie Press, 1966), 5.

134. Merrill J. Mattes and Esley J. Kirk, eds., "From Ohio to California in 1849: The Gold Rush Journal of Elijah Bryan Farnham," *Indiana Magazine of History* 46 (September–December 1950), 307; Holzhueter, "From Waupun to Sacramento," 226; Bryant, *What I Saw in California*, 51; Reverend Samuel Parker, *Journal of an Exploring Tour beyond the Rocky Mountains* (Minneapolis: Ross & Haines, 1967), 53.

135. Truman W. Camp, ed., "The Journal of Joseph Camp, 1859," *Nebraska History* 46, no. 1 (1965), 33.

136. James E. Potter, ed., "The Missouri River Journal of Leonard W. Gilchrist, 1866," *Nebraska History* 58, no. 3 (1977), 275.

137. Owen C. Coy, *The Great Trek* (Los Angeles: Powell Publishing Company, 1931), 250.

138. Studley, "Letter Describing a March," 615.

139. Settle, *March of the Mounted Riflemen*, 83.

140. Richard F. Burton, *The City of Saints and across the Rocky Mountains to California* (New York: Alfred A. Knopf, 1963), 95.

141. Settle, *March of the Mounted Riflemen*, 87.

142. Mattes and Kirk, "From Ohio to California," 308.

143. Nancy B. Parker, ed., "Notes and Documents: Mirabeau B. Lamar's Texas Journal," *Southwestern Historical Quarterly* 84 (January 1981), 326.

144. Niles Searls, *The Diary of a Pioneer and Other Papers* (n.p., 1940), 20; Potter "Missouri River Journal," 287; Holzhueter, "From Waupun to Sacramento," 224; Bryant, *What I Saw in California*, 10, 15.

145. Louise Barry, ed., "Scenes in (and En Route to) Kansas Territory, Autumn, 1854: Five Letters of William H. Hutter," *Kansas Historical Quarterly* 35, no. 3 (1969), 322–23, 327; Irving McKee, ed., *Alonzo Delano's California Correspondence* (Sacramento, Calif.: Sacramento Book Collectors Club, 1952), 70.

146. Wistar, *Autobiography*, 80–81.

147. Barry, comp., "Charles Robinson," 179, 186; Margaret S. Dart, ed., "Letters of a Yankee Forty-Niner," *The Yale Review* 36, no. 4 (June 1947), 657–65; Delano, *Life on the Plains*, 165–70, 203, 211, 218–19, 273; Egan, *Pioneering the West*, 23–24, 29; "Emigration from Iowa to Oregon in 1843," *Iowa Journal of History and Politics* 10 (July 1912), 415–30; Gilbert D. Harlan, ed., "The Diary of Wilson Barber Harlan," pt. 1, *Journal of the West* 3, no. 2 (1964), 148–53, 156–57; Holzhueter, "From Waupun to Sacramento," 219–31; David M. Kiefer, ed., "Over Barren Plains and Rock-Bound Mountains," *Montana, The Magazine of Western History* 22, no. 4 (1972); Martin, "Joseph Warren Arnold's Journal," 530–35; Edward O. Parry, ed., "Observations on the Prairies: 1867," *Montana, The Magazine of Western History* 9, no. 4 (1959), 25–28; Potter, "Missouri River Journal," 282–83, 286–87, 290, 293–94; Pritchard, "Overland Diary," 58, 109; Gary C. Stein, ed., "Overland to California," *American History Illustrated* 12 (May 1977), 26–36.

148. Caspar Weaver Collins to His Mother, 20 September 1862, Collins Letters, Beinecke Collection, Yale University Library, New Haven, Conn.; Randolph B. Marcy, *Thirty Years of Army Life on the Border* (Philadelphia:

J. B. Lippincott & Company, 1963), 3, 13, 18, 25; Thwaites, ed., *Early Western Travels*, 76–77.

149. Burton, *City of Saints*, 64–65.

150. Clark, *Gold Rush Diary*, 44; Page, *Wagons West*, 114.

151. Stein, "Overland," 26–36; Marcy, *Thirty Years*, 3, 18, 25, 47; William E. Wilson, "Hoboing in the West in the 1880's," *Montana, The Magazine of Western History* 18, no. 2 (1968), 42–43, 46–49.

152. Parker, "Notes and Documents," 325.

153. Randolph B. Marcy, *The Prairie Traveler: A Handbook for Overland Expeditions* (New York: Harper & Brothers, 1859), 200, 197.

154. Samuel P. Newcomb, "Diary" (1865), Barker Texas History Center, University of Texas, Austin; Egan, *Pioneering the West*, 174; Thomas D. Clark, *Off at Sunrise: The Overland Journal of Charles Glass Gray* (San Marino, Calif.: Huntington Library, 1976), 78; J. F. Triplett, "The Scout's Story: From the Journal of a Cattleman," *Atlantic Monthly* 135 (April 1925), 493–95; Bryant, *What I Saw in California*, 9; Page, *Wagons West*, 131, 181; Eugene H. Roseboom, ed., "Charles Tinker's Journal: A Trip to California in 1849," *Ohio State Archeological and Historical Quarterly* 61 (January 1952), 80–81.

155. Contrast Dutton, "Across the Plains," 472; Egan, *Pioneering the West*, 174; Harlan, "Journal," 55, 60; Mattes and Kirk (editors), "From Ohio to California," 407–9; Pritchard, *Overland Diary*, 127; Stansbury, *Expedition*, 81, 233, 239; Stimson, "Overland Journey," 403–40; with Mary Jane Caples, "Overland Journal to California" (1911), California State Library, Sacramento; Colt, *Went to Kansas*, 61, 136; Florence Call Cowles, *Early Algona: The Story of Our Pioneers, 1854–1874* (Des Moines, Iowa: The Register and Tribune Company, 1929), 111; Frink, *Journal*, 82; Margret A. Kelley, "Notes on Pioneers" (n.d.), California State Library, Sacramento.

156. Wistar, *Autobiography*, 103.

157. Clarke, "Young Woman's Sights"; Ferris, *Mormons at Home*, 22–24; Frizzell, *Across the Plains*, 25; Hill, *Dangerous Crossing*, 82; Esther Bell Hanna, "Journal" (1852), Bancroft Library, Berkeley, Calif.; Susan S. Magoffin, *Down the Santa Fe Trail and into Mexico: The Diary of Susan Shelby Magoffin, 1846–1847* (New Haven, Conn.: Yale University Press, 1926), 68; Manning, "Diary"; Lucene Pfeiffer Parsons, "The Women in the Sunbonnets" (1850), Stanford University Library, Stanford, Calif.; Juliette Fish Walker, "Crossing the Plains," *Noticas* 16, no. 2 (1970), 4.

158. Mary Stuart Bailey, "A Journal of the Overland Trip from Ohio to California" (1852), Huntington Library, San Marino, Calif.; Carpenter, "Diary"; Mary C. Fish, "Across the Plaines in 1860," Bancroft Library, Berkeley, Calif.; Guill, "Overland Diary"; Helen M. Stewart Love, "Diary" (1853),

Huntington Library, San Marino, Calif.; Ada Millington, "Journal Kept while Crossing the Plains" (1862), Bancroft Library, Berkeley, Calif.; Martha Ann Minto, "Female Pioneering in Oregon" (1849), Bancroft Library, Berkeley, Calif.; Maria J. Norton, "Diary of a Trip across the Plains in '59," Bancroft Library, Berkeley, Calif.; Caroline L. Richardson, "Journal" (1856), Bancroft Library, Berkeley, Calif.; Sandford, "Trip across the Plains."

159. Barry, "Charles Robinson," 179–88; Camp, "Journal," 32–35; Harlan, "Journal, 51; Kiefer, "Over Barren Plains," 18–21; Martin, "Joseph Warren Arnold's Journal," 472–77; Mattes and Kirk, "From Ohio to California," 300–301, 307–8; McKinstry, *California Gold Rush Overland Diary* 223–24; Potter, "Missouri River Journal," 291; Pritchard, *Overland Diary*, 73, 96–98; Settle, *March of the Mounted Riflemen*, 40–43, 56–57, 60–61, 72–73, 82–89, 114–15, 150–53, 160–61, 188–91, 202–5, 210–11, 221–24, 229–33, 236, 240–43, 247–55, 262–65, 280–81, 300–301, 306–15, 320–21, 338–39; Burton J. Williams, ed., "Overland to the Gold Fields of California in 1850: The Journal of Calvin Taylor," *Nebraska History* 50, no. 2 (1969), 142–45.

160. Eleazar S. Ingalls, *Journal of a Trip to California by the Overland Route across the Plains in 1850–51* (Fairfield, Wash.: Ye Galleon Press, 1979), 32; Rolle, *Road to Virginia City*, 21; Shirley Sargent, ed., *Seeking the Elephant: James Mason Hutchings' Journal of His Overland Trek to California* (Glendale, Calif.: Arthur H. Clark Company, 1980), 119; Searls, *Diary of a Pioneer*, 33; Kiefer, "Over Barren Plains," 18; Parker, *Journal of an Exploring Tour*, 35.

161. Rolle, *Road to Virginia City*, 125.

162. Potter, *Trail to California*, 77.

163. Settle, *March of the Mounted Riflemen*, 88.

164. Potter, "Missouri River Journal," 291; Barrett, *Overland Journal*, 55; Pritchard, *Overland Diary*, 73; McKinstry, *California Diary*, 73.

165. Burton, *City of Saints*, 90; McKinstry, *California Gold Rush Overland Diary*, 223–24.

166. John S. Wright, *Letters from the West; or, a Caution to Emigrants* (Ann Arbor, Mich.: University Microfilms, 1966), 29.

167. Delano, *Life on the Plains*, 316.

168. Potter, *Trail to California*, 127.

169. Parker, *Journal of an Exploring Tour*, 53.

170. Barry, "Charles Robinson," 185; Mattes and Kirk, "From Ohio to California," 446; Delano, *Life on the Plains*, 66; Harold F. Taggart, ed., "The Journal of David Jackson Staples," *California Historical Society Quarterly* 22 (June 1943), 124.

171. Potter, "Missouri River Journal," 276.

172. Barry, "Charles Robinson," 34.

173. Parker, *Journal of an Exploring Tour*, 35.

174. Bryant, *What I Saw in California*, 154; Kiefer, "Over Barren Plains," 18.

175. Clark, *Gold Rush Diary*, 184.

176. Caspar Collins to His Mother, 20 September 1862, Collins Letters; Coy, *Great Trek*, 126–27; Bryant, *What I Saw in California*, 52–53; Taggart, "Journal of David Jackson Staples," 119–47.

177. Harlan, "Journal," 57.

178. Lafayette Spencer, "Journal of the Oregon Trail," *Annals of Iowa* 8 (January 1908), 304–10; Mattes and Kirk, "From Ohio to California," 437–68; Parker, "Notes and Documents," 309–30; Wistar, *Autobiography*, 50, 67, 80–81, 101, 219, 221; M. M. Hoffman, "The First Gazetteer on Iowa," *Annals of Iowa* 17 (July 1932), 383–90.

179. Page, *Wagons West*, 128, 165–66, 237.

180. Clark, *Gold Rush Diary*, 44; Bryant, *What I Saw in California*, 107–13; Quaife, *Across the Plains*, 30.

181. Ingalls, *Journal of a Trip*, 50; Giffen, *Diaries of Peter Decker*, 131; Quaife, *Across the Plains*, 119–24.

182. Wistar, *Autobiography*, 67; Clark, *Gold Rush Diary*, 22, 25; Jacob H. Schiel, *Journey through the Rocky Mountains and the Humboldt Mountains to the Pacific Ocean* (Norman: University of Oklahoma Press, 1959), 18–19; W. W. Chapman, "W. W. Chapman's Diary," *Wyoming State Historian Quarterly Bulletin* 1, no. 2 (15 September 1923), 9; Wyman, *California Emigrant Letters*, 103.

183. Delano, *Life on the Plains*, 145.

184. Wyman, *California Emigrant Letters*, 101; Williams, "Overland to the Gold Fields," 143.

185. Thwaites, *Early Western Travels*, 152–53; Sargent, *Seeking the Elephant*, 125; Holzhueter, "From Waupun to Sacramento," 229.

186. Contrast Stansbury, *Expedition*, 154–56; Thwaites, *Early Western Travels*, 152–53; with Dunham, *Across the Plains*, 7; Ferris, *Mormons at Home*, 24.

187. Stansbury, *Expedition*, 254–57.

188. Quaife, *Across the Plains*, 88–89.

189. Although the preponderance of male sources examined showed evidence of a lack of change in male attitudes toward Indians, particularly good examples are Elisha Brooks, *A Pioneer Mother of California* (San Francisco: Harr Wagner Publishing Company, 1922); James Enos, "Recollections" (ca. 1892), Newberry Library, Chicago, Ill.; "Diary of Charles Glass Gray," Huntington Library, San Marino, Calif.; Marcy, *Thirty Years*; Stansbury, *Expedition*; and Quaife, *Across the Plains*. See McKinstry, *California Gold Rush Overland Diary*, 92–94, 96–101, for an example of one of the few male

emigrants who realized that the macho adversary stance of frontiersmen was frequently unnecessary and even humorous. For a useful discussion of predominant American views of American Indians in the nineteenth century, see Alden T. Vaughan, "From White Man to Redskin: Changing Anglo-American Perceptions of the American Indian," *American Historical Review* 87, no. 4 (October 1982), 917–53.

190. Delano, *Life on the Plains*, 309, 319–20.

191. Egan, *Pioneering the West*, 185.

192. Michael J. Brodhead and John D. Unruh, Jr., eds., "Isaiah Harris' Minutes of a Trip to Kansas Territory in 1855," *Kansas Historical Quarterly* 35, no. 4 (1969), 373–85; Barry, "Scenes," 312–36; Parker, *Journal of an Exploring Tour;* LeRoy R. and Ann W. Hafen, eds., *To the Rockies and Oregon, 1839–1842*, vol. 3 (Glendale, Calif.: Arthur H. Clark Company, 1955); Burton, *City of Saints.*

193. Winther, *To Oregon*, 12; Marcy, *Prairie Traveler*, 200, 211; Marcy, *Thirty Years*, 47.

194. Enos, "Recollections."

195. Mary Burrell, "Diary"; Wesley Tonner to His Friend, 10 September 1854, Beinecke Collection, Yale University Library, New Haven, Conn.

196. Winther, *To Oregon*, 12.

197. Parry, "Observations," 27.

198. John T. Dilworth to His Uncles, 30 March 1851, Bringhurst Family Letters, Beinecke Collection, Yale University Library, New Haven, Conn.

199. Although almost two-thirds of the women's sources examined here showed some evidence of favorable changes in female attitudes toward Indians, particularly good examples are Ackley, *Crossing the Plains;* Carriker, *Army Wife;* Cooke, *Covered Wagon Days;* DeWitt and DeWitt, *Prairie Schooner Lady;* Fraker, "To Pike's Peak"; Hare, "Reminiscences"; Hodgson, "Life of a Pioneer Family"; Hopping, "Incidents of Pioneer Life"; Mary Horne, "Migration and Settlement of the Latter Day Saints" (1884), Bancroft Library, Berkeley, Calif.; Ivins, *Pen Pictures;* Rachel C. Rose, "Diary" (1852), California State Library, Sacramento; Van de Wiele, *Travels and Experiences;* Vogdes, "Journal."

200. Gordon W. Allport, *The Nature of Prejudice* (Cambridge, Mass.: Addison-Wesley Publishing Company, 1954), 261–81; Mark Snyder, "Self-Fulfilling Stereotypes," *Psychology Today* 16, no. 7 (July 1982), 60, 65, 67–68.

Chapter 6

1. Allie B. Busby, *Two Summers among the Musquakies* (Vinton, Iowa: Herald Book and Job Rooms, 1886), 19.

2. Lois L. Murray, *Incidents of Frontier Life* (Goshen, Indiana: Evangelical United Mennonite Publishing House, 1880), 92.

3. Susannah Willeford, "Henry County: On Immigration of Pioneers" (ca. 1820–1870), Iowa State Historical Society, Iowa City.

4. Mallie Stafford, *The March of Empire through Three Decades* (San Francisco: George Spaulding & Company, 1884), 118, 171.

5. Frances M. A. Roe, *Army Letters from an Officer's Wife 1871–1888* (New York: D. Appleton & Company, 1909), 10, 96–97.

6. Frances C. Carrington, *My Army Life and the Fort Phil Kearney Massacre* (Freeport, N.Y.: Books for Libraries Press, 1971), 45.

7. Virginia Wilcox, *Pen Pictures of Early Western Days* (Keokuk, Iowa: n.p., ca. 1905), 43–44; Carrie A. Strahorn, *Fifteen Thousand Miles by Stage* (New York: G. P. Putnam's Sons, 1911), 316.

8. Agnes Steward Warner, "Diary" (1853), Huntington Library, San Marino, Calif.

9. Sandra L. Myres, ed., *Cavalry Wife: The Diary of Eveline M. Alexander, 1866–1867* (College Station: Texas A. & M. University Press, 1977), 117.

10. Strahorn, *Fifteen Thousand Miles*, 408.

11. Leo M. Kaiser and Priscilla Knuth, eds., "From Ithaca to Clatsop Plains: Miss Ketcham's Journal of Travel," pt. 2, *Oregon Historical Quarterly* 62, no. 4 (1961), 391; Katherine Dunlap, "Journal" (1864), Bancroft Library, Berkeley, Calif.; Margaret E. Archer Murray, "Memoir of the William Archer Family," pt. 1, *Annals of Iowa* 39 (Summer 1968), 368.

12. Sarah R. Herndon, *Days of the Road: Crossing the Plains in 1865* (New York: Burr Printing House, 1902), 132.

13. Ada A. Vogdes, "Journal" (1866–1872), Huntington Library, San Marino, Calif.

14. Murray, *Incidents of Frontier Life*, 92.

15. Alden T. Vaughan and Daniel K. Richter, "Crossing the Cultural Divide: Indians and New Englanders, 1605–1763," *Proceedings of the American Antiquarian Society* 90, pt. 1 (Worcester, Mass.: American Antiquarian Society, 1980), 55–57.

16. Susan H. Armitage, "Women's Literature and the American Frontier: A New Perspective on the Frontier Myth," in L. L. Lee and Merrill Lewis, eds., *Women, Women Writers, and the West* (Troy, N.Y.: Whitston Publishing Company, 1979), 7.

17. Fanny Wiggins Kelley, "To the Senators and Members of the House of Representatives of Congress" (undated broadside), Graff Collection, Newberry Library, Chicago, Ill.

18. Rosita Rodriges to Her Father, 15 January 1846, Brazos River, Robertson County, Texas, 1846, Barker Texas History Center, University of

Texas, Austin; Emma Polk, "Reminiscence" (n.d.), Iowa State Historical Society, Iowa City; Martha Webster Simmons, "The Webster Massacre" (1925), Barker Texas History Center, University of Texas, Austin.

19. Vaughan and Richter, "Crossing the Cultural Divide," 59, 62.

20. Susan Parrish, "Westward in 1850," Huntington Library, San Marino, Calif.

21. Parrish, "Westward"; Dorothy M. Johnson, "Lost Sister," in Orville Prescott, ed., *Mid-Century, An Anthology of Distinguished Contemporary American Short Stories* (New York: Washington Square Press, 1973), 11–12.

22. Harriet Bunyard, "Diary" (1868), Huntington Library, San Marino, Calif.

23. Ruth S. Thompson, "The Tragedy of Legion Valley," (1928), Bancroft Library, Berkeley, Calif.

24. G. M. Brady, "The Story of Little Silver Hair," *Manuscripts* 28, no. 4 (1976), 294, 299.

25. Wilhelmina B. Carrigan, *Captured by the Indians: Reminiscences of Pioneer Life in Minnesota* (Forest City, S.D.: Forest City Press, 1907), 11, 15–16.

26. Ibid., 3–7.

27. Mary Butler Renville, *A Thrilling Narrative of Indian Captivity* (Minneapolis: Atlas Company's Book and Job Printing Office, 1863), 19, 43–44.

28. Aunt Friendly, *The Children on the Plains* (New York: Robert Carter & Brothers, 1864), 9–10, 101–16.

29. Mrs. J. D. Bell, "A True Story of My Capture by, and Life with the Comanche Indians" (1942), Barker Texas History Center, University of Texas, Austin.

30. Ibid.

31. Sarah J. Cummins, *Autobiography and Reminiscences* (LaGrande, Oreg.: LaGrande Printing Company, 1914), 37, 42; Mary Richardson Walker, "Diary" (1848), Huntington Library, San Marino, Calif.

32. Eliza Spalding Warren, *Memoirs of the West: The Spaldings* (Portland, Oreg.: March Printing Company, 1916), 31; Mary Saunders, "The Whitman Massacre; A True Story by a Survivor of This Terrible Tragedy which Took Place in Oregon in 1847," Bancroft Library, Berkeley, Calif.

33. Polly Purcell, "Autobiography and Reminiscence of a Pioneer," Graff Collection, Newberry Library, Chicago, Ill.; Matilda S. J. Delaney, *A Survivor's Recollections of the Whitman Massacre* (Spokane, Wash.: Esther Reed Chapter, D.A.R., 1920), 5.

34. Abigail Smith to My Dear Friend & Sister in Christ, 7 January 1856, Oregon Territory, Beinecke Collection, Yale University Library, New Haven, Conn.

35. Delaney, *Survivor's Recollections*, 45.

36. Mary Stuart Bailey, "A Journal of the Overland Trip from Ohio to California" (1852), Huntington Library, San Marino, Calif.

37. Murray, "Memoir," pt. 1, 368.

38. Busby, *Two Summers*, 19.

39. Kate McDaniel Furness, "From Prairie to Pacific" (1853), California State Library, Sacramento, Calif.

40. Caroline D. Budlong, *Memories: Pioneer Days in Oregon and Washington Territory* (Eugene, Oreg.: Picture Press Printers, 1949), 39; Miriam D. Colt, *Went to Kansas; Being a Thrilling Account of an Ill-Fated Expedition* (Watertown, N.Y.: L. Ingalls & Company, 1862), 67.

41. Margaret I. Carrington, *Ab-sa-ra-ka, Home of the Crows: Being the Experience of an Officer's Wife on the Plains* (Philadelphia: J. B. Lippincott & Company, 1868), 75.

42. Rachel E. Wright, "The Early Upper Napa Valley" (1928), Bancroft Library, Berkeley, Calif.

43. Christine Bates, interview 5202, vol. 6, Indian-Pioneer Papers, University of Oklahoma, Norman

44. Eleanor Taylor, "Ross Kin: Early Settlers of the West" (1978), Bancroft Library, Berkeley, Calif.

45. Thomas R. Buecker, ed., "Letters of Caroline Frey Winne from Sidney Barracks and Fort McPherson, Nebraska, 1874–1878," *Nebraska History* 62 (April 1981), 25.

46. Busby, *Two Summers*, 76–79.

47. Elizabeth L. Lord, *Reminiscences of Eastern Oregon* (Portland, Oreg.: Irwin-Hodgson Company, 1903), 142.

48. Mary Ann Tatum, "Diary" (1870), Iowa State Historical Society, Iowa City.

49. Renville, *Thrilling Narrative*, 43; Taylor, "Ross Kin"; Mary Ann Rogers, "An Iowa Woman in Wartime," pt. 1, *Annals of Iowa* 35 (Winter 1961), 525; Warren, *Memoirs*, 117.

50. Edith E. Kohl, *Land of the Burnt Thigh* (New York: Funk & Wagnalls Company, 1938), 239.

51. May Callan Tansill, "Narrative" (n.d.), Barker Texas History Center, University of Texas, Austin.

52. Mary Jane Caples, "Overland Journey to California" (1911), California State Library, Sacramento; Annie Argyle, *Cupid's Album* (New York: M. Doolady, 1866), 89.

53. Elisha Brooks, *A Pioneer Mother of California* (San Francisco: Harr Wagner Publishing Company, 1922), 29; Ruth Peterson, comp., "Across the Plains in '57," California State Library, Sacramento; E. Allene Dunham, *Across the Plains in a Covered Wagon* (Milton, Iowa: n.p., ca. 1920s), 11.

54. Dunham, *Across the Plains*, 11.

55. Nancy N. Tracy, "Narrative" (1880), Bancroft Library, Berkeley, Calif.

56. Abigail Smith to My Dear Friend & Sister in Christ, 7 January 1856, Oregon Territory.

57. Alice C. Fletcher, *Historical Sketch of the Omaha Tribe of Indians in Nebraska* (Washington, D.C.: Judd & Detweiler, 1885), 12.

58. Mary E. Arnold and Mabel Reed, *In the Land of the Grasshopper Song* (Lincoln: University of Nebraska Press, 1980), 24.

59. Althea Bass, "Papers" (1847–1955), Western History Collections, University of Oklahoma, Norman.

60. Maria Schrode, "Journal" (1870), Huntington Library, San Marino, Calif.

61. Annie K. Bidwell to Colonel Pratt, 26 April 1904, Chico, Calif., California State Library, Sacramento.

62. Abigail Smith to Beloved Brothers and Sister, 5 May 1840, Oregon Territory.

63. Kay Graber, ed., *Sister to the Sioux: The Memoirs of Elaine Goodale Eastman* (Lincoln: University of Nebraska Press, 1978), 32–34; Thisba H. Morgan, "Reminiscences of My Days in the Land of the Ogallala Sioux," *South Dakota Department of History Report and Historical Collections* 29 (1968), 21–62; Harriet Withers, interview 12066, vol. 99, Indian-Pioneer Papers, University of Oklahoma, Norman

64. Anna Kellough Wyss, interview 5847, vol. 101, Indian-Pioneer Papers, University of Oklahoma, Norman

65. Esther Bell Hanna, "Journal" (1852), Bancroft Library, Berkeley, Calif.

66. Ann Archbold, *A Book for the Married and Single* (East Plainfield, Ohio: Printed at the Office of the "Practical Preacher," 1850), 168–69; Sandra L. Myres, ed., "Evy Alexander: The Colonel's Lady at Ft. McDowell," *Montana, The Magazine of Western History* 24 (1974), 30; Mary Frances Campbell, interview 9068, vol. 15, Indian-Pioneer Papers, University of Oklahoma, Norman.

67. "Narcissa Whitman," in Edward T. James, ed., *Notable American Women* (Cambridge, Mass.: Harvard University Press, Belknap Press, 1971), 595–97.

68. Robert Chandler, "The Failure of Reform: White Attitudes and Indian Response in California during the Civil War Era," *The Pacific Historian* 24, no. 3 (Fall 1980), 292–93.

69. Dunham, *Across the Plains*, 11; Karen Lynn, "Sensational Virtue: Nineteenth-Century Mormon Fiction and American Popular Taste," *Dialogue* 14 (Fall 1981), 101–11; Gary L. Bunker and Davis Britton, *The Mormon Graphic Image, 1834–1914: Cartoons, Caricatures, and Illustrations* (Salt Lake City: University of Utah Press, 1983).

70. *New York Times*, 9 July 1887, and 26 May 1859.

71. Mrs. B. G. Ferris, *The Mormons at Home* (New York: Dix & Edwards, 1856), 70; Helen Carpenter, "Diary" 1856, California State Library, Sacramento.

72. Pauline Wonderly, *Reminiscences of a Pioneer* (Placerville, Calif.: El Dorado County Historical Society, 1965), 7.

73. Lucy Sexton, *The Foster Family, California Pioneers* (Santa Barbara, Calif.: Press of the Schouer Printing Studio, 1925), 193–95.

74. Mary Rockwood Powers, "The Overland Route, Leaves from the Journal of a California Emigrant" (1856), Beinecke Collection, Yale University Library, New Haven, Conn.

75. Peterson, "Across the Plains"; Brooks, *Pioneer Mother*, 14, 29.

76. Emily McCowen Horton, *My Scrap-book* (Seattle, Wash.: n.p., 1927), 27.

77. Ibid.

78. Carpenter, "Diary," Huntington Library, San Marino, Calif.

79. Mrs. Edward Dyer, "Diary" (1860), Barker Texas History Center, University of Texas, Austin; Mary Jane Guill, "The Overland Diary of a Journey from Livingston County, Missouri, to Butte County, California" (1860), California State Library, Sacramento; Ellen Tompkins Adams, "Diary of Ellen Tompkins Adams, Wife of John Smalley Adams, M.D." (1863), Bancroft Library, Berkeley, Calif.; Mary C. Fish, "Across the Plaines in 1860," Bancroft Library, Berkeley, Calif.; Maria J. Norton, "Diary of a Trip across the Plains in '59," Bancroft Library, Berkeley, Calif.

80. Adams, "Diary"; Fish, "Across the Plaines."

81. Catherine M. Haun, "A Woman's Trip across the Plains, from Clinton, Iowa, to Sacramento, California, by Way of Salt Lake City" (1849), Huntington Library, San Marino, Calif.; Stafford, *March of Empire*, 128.

82. Fish, "Across the Plaines." See also Norton, "Diary," for a similar opinion.

83. Mrs. H. T. Clarke, "A Young Woman's Sights on the Emigrant's Trail" (1878), Bancroft Library, Berkeley, Calif.

84. Ward G. DeWitt and Florence S. DeWitt, *Prairie Schooner Lady: The Journal of Harriet Sherrill Ward, 1853* (Los Angeles: Westernlore Press, 1959), 126.

85. Margaret M. Hecox, *California Caravan: The 1846 Overland Trail Memoir of Margaret M. Hecox* (San Jose, Calif.: Harlan-Young Press, 1966), 21–24.

86. Warner, "Diary"; Ada Millington, "Journal Kept while Crossing the Plains" (1862), Bancroft Library, Berkeley, Calif.

87. Horton, *My Scrap-book*, 27.

88. Carpenter, "Diary."

89. Stafford, *March of Empire*, 128–29.

90. Fish, "Across the Plaines."

91. Rachel C. Rose, "Diary" (1852), California State Library, Sacramento.

92. Millington, "Journal."

93. Ibid.; Clarke, "Young Woman's Sights."

94. Millington, "Journal."

95. Mary E. Ackley, *Crossing the Plains and Early Days in California* (San Francisco: Privately printed, 1928), 28; Mary Burrell, "Diary of a Journey Overland from Council Bluffs to Green Valley, California" (1854), Beinecke Collection, Yale University Library, New Haven, Conn.

96. DeWitt and DeWitt, *Prairie Schooner Lady*, 119.

97. Clark, "Young Woman's Sights."

98. Bailey, "Journal."

99. Sexton, *Foster Family*, 135.

100. Jennie Kimball, "Narrative of an Overland Journey from Boston to California and Back Again" (1876), Beinecke Collection, Yale University Library, New Haven, Conn.

101. Sandra L. Myres, *Westering Women and the Frontier Experience, 1800–1915* (Albuquerque: University of New Mexico Press, 1982), 92–93, 96–97; Sarah A. Cooke, "Theatrical and Social Affairs in Utah" (1884), Bancroft Library, Berkeley, Calif.

102. Ferris, *Mormons at Home*, 205.

103. Julie Roy Jeffrey, "Women on the Trans-Mississippi Frontier: A Review Essay," *New Mexico Historical Review* 57, no. 4 (October 1982), 398.

104. Kimball, "Narrative of an Overland Journey."

105. Lucene Pfeiffer Parsons, "The Women in the Sunbonnets" (1850), Stanford University Library, Stanford, Calif.

106. Sexton, *The Foster Family*, 136.

107. DeWitt and DeWitt, *Prairie Schooner Lady*, 119, 126.

108. Herndon, *Days on the Road*, 238.

109. Parsons, "Women in Sunbonnets."

110. Ferris, *Mormons at Home*, 116, 119, 131, 157, 187.

111. Clarke, "Young Woman's Sights."

112. Cooke, "Theatrical and Social Affairs."

113. Mary Rockwood Powers, "A Woman's Overland Journal to California" (1856), California State Library, Sacramento.

114. Myres, *Westering Women*, 93–95.

115. Eliza Roxey Snow, "Sketch of My Life" (1885), Bancroft Library, Berkeley, Calif.

116. Jane Richards, "The Inner Facts of Social Life in Utah" (1880), Ban-

croft Library, Berkeley, Calif.; Phebe W. Woodruff, "Autobiographical Sketch" (1880), Bancroft Library, Berkeley, Calif.; Clara Decker Young, "A Woman's Experience with the Pioneer Band" (1884), Bancroft Library, Berkeley, Calif.

117. Mary Horne, "Migration and Settlement of the Latter Day Saints" (1884), Bancroft Library, Berkeley, Calif.

118. Jane Richards, "Reminiscences" (1880), Bancroft Library, Berkeley, Calif.

119. Helena Erickson Rosbery, "History of Helena Rosbery" (1883), Huntington Library, San Marino, Calif.

120. Mary J. Tanner to Mrs. H. H. Bancroft, 29 October 1880, Salt Lake City, in Utah Miscellany, Bancroft Library, Berkeley, Calif.

121. Martha Brown to Mrs. H. H. Bancroft, 7 August 1880, Ogden City, in Utah Miscellany, Bancroft Library, Berkeley, Calif.; Margaret S. Smoot, "Experience of a Mormon Wife" (1880), Bancroft Library, Berkeley, Calif.

122. Tanner to Bancroft, 29 October 1880; Smoot, "Experience of a Mormon Wife."

123. Smoot, "Experience of a Mormon Wife."

124. Tracy, "Narrative."

125. For a quantitative analysis of Mormon wives involved in plural marriages, see D. Gene Pace, "Wives of Nineteenth-Century Mormon Bishops: A Quantitative Analysis," *Journal of the West* 21, no. 2 (April 1982), 49–57.

126. Marilyn Warenski, *Patriarchs and Politics: The Plight of the Mormon Woman* (New York: McGraw-Hill Book Company, 1978), 3–5, 155–56.

127. Mary E. Cox Lee, "An Inspired Principle and a Remarkable Lady" (1949), Huntington Library, San Marino, Calif.; Constance L. Lieber, "'The Goose Hangs High': Excerpts from the Letters of Martha Hughes Cannon," *Utah Historical Quarterly* 48 (Winter 1980), 37–48; Elinore Pruitt Stewart, *Letters of a Woman Homesteader* (Lincoln: University of Nebraska Press, 1961), 263–68, 273–74.

128. Ibid., 265.

129. Since the objective here is to contrast women's emergent and favorable sympathies toward American Indians with their continuing distrust and dislike of the Latter-Day Saints, a comparison of female and male remarks concerning Mormons is not really germane. It is interesting to discover, however, that men's comments regarding Mormons diverged widely and, in a sense, predictably from women's. Men did mention the Mormons they encountered, sometimes with great regularity, but these references were often nonjudgmental. See Dale Morgan, ed., *Overland in 1846: Diaries and Letters of the California-Oregon Trail* (Georgetown, Calif.: Talisman Press, 1963), 506–7, 514–25, 536–37, 548–52, 558–59, 563, 588–91, 606, 615, 650–55, 658–60; Byron N. McKinstry, *The California Gold Rush Overland Diary of Byron N. McKinstry* (Glendale, Calif.: Arthur H. Clark Company, 1975),

74–75, 80–82, 87–95, 114–19, 146–51, 156–57, 168–69, 180–81, 240–41, 258–59, 292–95, 300–301, 306–7; Eleazar S. Ingalls, *Journal of a Trip to California by the Overland Route across the Plains in 1850–51* (Fairfield, Wash.: Ye Galleon Press, 1979), 40–52, 58–67; Helen S. Giffen, ed., *The Diaries of Peter Decker: Overland to California in 1849 and Life in the Mines, 1850–1851* (Georgetown, Calif.: Talisman Press, 1966), 75, 90–95, 99, 102–3, 110–13, 122–25, 143, 150–51, 162–63.

Unlike women, frontiersmen were rarely negative in their reactions to Latter-Day Saints, usually avoiding such labels as "a poor, deluded people." Reverend Samuel Parker, *Journal of an Exploring Tour beyond the Rocky Mountains* (Minneapolis: Ross & Haines, 1967), 30. Instead, as with other aspects of the trail and new settlements, men emphasized specifics including measurements, soil and land evaluations, armaments, dimensions of buildings, and climate. While frontierswomen, for example, characterized Salt Lake City as a fairyland of white castles, men tended to record its layout, population, and resources. Edwin Bryant, *What I Saw in California* (Minneapolis: Ross & Haines, 1967), 2, 15, 26–27, 163, 276–77; J. William Barrett, II, ed., *The Overland Journal of Amos Piatt Josselyn* (Baltimore: Gateway Press, 1978), 56–59; Andrew F. Rolle, ed., *The Road to Virginia City: The Diary of James Knox Polk Miller* (Norman: University of Oklahoma Press, 1960), 35–45, 53–58; Charles Glass Gray, "Diary" (1849–1850), Huntington Library, San Marino, Calif.; Jacob H. Schiel, *Journey through the Rocky Mountains and the Humboldt Mountains to the Pacific Ocean* (Norman: University of Oklahoma Press, 1959), 70–73, 78–95.

Many men who avoided any assessment of Mormon doctrines, people, and actions did recount the history and theology of the Latter-Day Saints. These accounts sometimes included an explanation of the rationale underlying certain practices, especially polygamy. Max L. Moorhead, ed., *Commerce of the Prairies* (Norman: University of Oklahoma Press, 1954), 218–22; Richard F. Burton, *The City of the Saints and across the Rocky Mountains to California* (New York: Alfred A. Knopf, 1963), 301, 318–21, 326–27, 334–35, 392–95, 402–3, 408–15, 428–29, 432–33, 442–45, 472–73, 476, 483, 494–95, 510–11. On the other hand, some men undertook to defend Mormon leaders, particularly Brigham Young, and Mormon beliefs, especially polygamy. Some of these male observers used words such as cheerful, industrious, intelligent, prudent, sagacious, tolerant, law-abiding, and democratic in their portrayals of Mormons while claiming that they were "ever fair and upright" in their dealings with Gentiles. Howard Stansbury, *An Expedition to the Valley of the Great Salt Lake* (Ann Arbor, Mich.: University Microfilms, 1966), 84–86, 120–50; Burton, *City of the Saints*, 152–53, 182–83, 186–89, 192–95, 198–203, 224–25, 232–33, 248–55, 262–63, 268–69, 274–77, 280–81, 286–87, 290–91, 296–97.

Other men who thought the Latter-Day Saints to be enterprising, energetic, hospitable, and obliging took pleasure in visiting their camps, villages, and cities as well as exchanging gossip, trail news, and route information. Thomas D. Clark, ed., *Gold Rush Diary: Being the Journal of Elisha Douglass Perkins* (Lexington: University of Kentucky Press, 1967), 23, 112–13, 175–80; James Hewitt, ed., *Eye-Witnesses to Wagon Trains West* (New York: Charles Scribner's Sons, 1973), 122–23. After spending some time in Salt Lake City in 1849, one of these men expressed his regret about leaving:

> Tomorrow we leave civilization, pretty girls, and pleasant memories. We have enjoyed ourselves well. Mormons, or Hephites, or Salt Lake Citizens, or whatever name you may call yourselves, I am thankful to you for the kind and courteous attentions manifested to us, and for the many advantages your city in the wilderness offers to the weary emigrant, on his journey overland to California!

Shirley Sargent, ed., *Seeking the Elephant: James Mason Hutchings' Journal of His Overland Trek to California* (Glendale, Calif.: Arthur H. Clark Company, 1980), 156. Another forty-niner who viewed the Mormons as "neighborly fellows ready to share their knowledge of the trail, to carry letters and to give what information they could" explained that "even the Mormons took on a different aspect in this new land." Elizabeth Page, ed., *Wagons West: A Story of the Oregon Trail* (New York: Farrar & Rinehart, 1930), 139.

Despite female fears to the contrary, none of the men surveyed expressed any interest in converting to Mormonism or of adopting the custom of plural marriage in their own lives, nor did they personally accept the Mormon justification for plural marriage. Schiel, *Journey through the Rocky Mountains*, 8–81. Rather, men seemed much more capable than women of seeing both the good and the bad in the Latter-Day Saints and their belief system. Thus, while they could compliment the Saints for religious toleration or a "beautifully written" Constitution, they could also condemn the ignorance of Mormon guides and the misleading tales circulated about the offerings of Salt Lake City. Georgia Willis Read and Ruth Gaines, eds., *Gold Rush: The Journals, Drawings, and Other Papers of J. Goldsborough Bruff, 1851* (New York: Columbia University Press, 1949), 65, 71, 126, 132, 151, 576. Men, charged with the conduct and supply of their parties, responded to Mormons as potential guides, suppliers, and companions in their westward venture. But women, who viewed themselves as cultural conservators, saw Mormons in terms of threats to their own cherished values and beliefs, to say nothing of their own marriages.

130. Donald D. Jackson, *Gold Dust* (New York: Alfred A. Knopf, 1980), 77–82, 121–22; Alex Perez-Venero, *Before the Five Frontiers* (New York: A.M.S. Press, 1978), 79–91.

131. John H. Kemble, *The Panama Route, 1848–1869* (Berkeley: University of California Press, 1943), 149; Oscar Lewis, *Sea Routes to the Gold Fields* (New York: Alfred A. Knopf, 1949), 35, 61.

132. Lewis, *Sea Routes*, 35.

133. Sandra L. Myres, *Ho for California! Women's Overland Diaries from the Huntington Library* (San Marino, Calif.: Huntington Library, 1980), 6.

134. F. N. Otis, *History of the Panama Railroad* (New York: Harper & Brothers, 1867), 46.

135. Joseph W. Gregory, *Gregory's Guide for California Travellers via the Isthmus of Panama* (San Francisco: Reprinted by the Book Club of California, 1949), 9, 11.

136. *New York Times*, 15 August 1887.

137. *Daily Evening Bulletin*, San Francisco, 1 May 1856.

138. Ibid.; *Daily Alta California*, San Francisco, 1 May 1856.

139. Sarah M. Brooks, *Across the Isthmus to California in '52* (San Francisco: C. A. Murdock & Company, Printers, 1894), 31.

140. Ida F. Fitzgerald, "Accounts of Life of Plummer Edward Jefferis including Voyages from New York to California in 1850 and 1854," Huntington Library, San Marino, Calif.

141. Emeline L. S. Benson, "Diary" (1854), California State Library, Sacramento; Margaret DeWitt to Her Parents, no month, no day, 1849; Steamer "Crescent City," Bancroft Library in DeWitt Family Papers, ca. 1848–1867; Mary E. Durant to Her Cousins, 24 December 1853; Steamer "Sierra Nevada," Bancroft Library, Berkeley, Calif.; Angelina Harvey to Her Cousin Mary Ann, 19 November 1863, Jamestown, California, Bancroft Library, Berkeley, Calif.; Taylor, "Ross Kin"; Mrs. E. Van Court, "Reminiscences" (1914), Beinecke Collection, Yale University Library, New Haven, Conn.; Nellie Wetherbee, "Diary" (1860), Bancroft Library, Berkeley, Calif.; Jane McDougal, "Diary" (1849), Huntington Library, San Marino, Calif.; Niles Searles, *The Diary of a Pioneer and Other Papers* (n.p., 1940), 73–77.

142. Brooks, *Across the Isthmus*, 35, 37; Emeline H. Day, "Journal" (1853), Bancroft Library, Berkeley, Calif.; Mary Ann Harris Meredith, "Diary" (1859), California State Library, Sacramento; Sexton, *Foster Family*, 251; Mary Jane Cole Megquier, "California Letters" (1849–1856), Huntington Library, San Marino, Calif.

143. Mrs. D. B. Bates, *Incidents on Land and Water* (Boston: James French and Company, 1857), 283.

144. Megquier, "California Letters."

145. Meredith, "Diary."

146. Day, "Journal"; Julia S. Peck Twist, "Diary" (1861), Bancroft Library, Berkeley, Calif.

147. Mary Bean Simonds Ballou, "Journal" (1851–1852), Beinecke Collection, Yale University Library, New Haven, Conn.; Stafford, *March of Empire*, 18; Mrs. Charles Wood, "Diary" (ca. 1850), Bancroft Library, Berkeley, Calif.

148. Hannah Bourn Ingalls to Her Husband, 5 October 1865, Steamer "New York," Bourn-Ingalls Family Papers, 1865–1958, Bancroft Library, Berkeley, Calif.

149. Mary Pratt Staples, "Reminiscences" (ca. 1886), Bancroft Library, Berkeley, Calif.

150. Twist, "Diary."

151. Megquier, "California Letters."

152. Twist, "Diary."

153. Brooks, *Across the Isthmus*, 35.

154. Stafford, *March of Empire*, 43.

155. Bates, *Incidents of Land and Water*, 284, 288, 308.

156. Megquier, "California Letters."

157. Martha M. Morgan, *A Trip across the Plains in the Year 1849* (San Francisco: Printed at Pioneer Press, 1864), 24.

158. Jessie Benton Fremont, *A Year of American Travel: Narrative of Personal Experience* (San Francisco: Book Club of California, 1960), 27; Meredith, "Diary."

159. Julia L. Hare, "Reminiscences" (n.d.), California State Library, Sacramento; Brooks, *Across the Isthmus*, 37; Wood, "Diary"; Megquier, "California Letters."

160. John Haskell Kemble, "The Gold Rush by Panama, 1848–1851," in John W. Caughey, ed., *Rushing for Gold* (Berkeley: University of California Press, 1949), 55; Mark Snyder, "Self-Fulfilling Stereotypes," *Psychology Today* 16, no. 7 (July 1982), 60, 65, 67–68.

161. Brooks, *Across the Isthmus*, 37.

162. Stafford, *March of Empire*, 8, 20, 23, 25–26, 33–35, 38.

163. Fannie Wallace Reading to Her Grandmother, 4 May 1856, San Francisco, Pierson-Barton Correspondence and Papers, 1841–1868, Bancroft Library, Berkeley, Calif.

164. Hester Harland, "Reminiscences" (1940), California State Library, Sacramento.

165. Sexton, *Foster Family*, 251.

166. As with the overland experience, men's comments on the Panama crossing differed from women's in certain respects. Unhampered by hoop-skirts, children, and nineteenth-century standards of modesty and privacy,

men were much more likely to see the Panama passage as a "pleasant excursion." David Edwards Blaine to Dear Bro. Terry, 5 October 1853, Steamer "Ohio," Letters, 1824–1900, Beinecke Collection, Yale University Library, New Haven, Conn. Men were also much more interested than women in distances, soil and other resources, and business developments. John Xantus, *Letters from North America* (Detroit: Wayne State University Press, 1975), 171–73; William S. Ament, *By Sea to California* (Los Angeles: Powell Publishing Company, 1929), 331–43. Many male emigrants who crossed Panama noted the squalor and nakedness of the natives but argued that Yankee enterprise was rousing them from their "dreamy lethary." Quoted in Myres, *Ho for California!*, 5. Others agreed that the rapid progress of commerce was greatly transforming the country and its people. Myres, *Ho for California!*, 5; Xantus, *Letters*, 171. Thus, unlike women, men tended to see Panama less in terms of its sordid present than of its potentially promising future.

Note on Sources

The major sources for this study are the writings of frontierswomen themselves, especially those who had no particular cause to promote or point of view to advocate in relation to American Indians. These writings include journals, diaries, letters, memoirs, and reminiscences. Such documents are found in state and local libraries and archives ranging from the east to the west coast. Some of the major collections are the Beinecke Collection at Yale University, the Newberry Library in Chicago, the Minnesota Historical Society in Minneapolis, the Museum and Archives in Des Moines, the Denver Public Library, the Western History Collections at the University of Oklahoma in Norman, the Barker Texas History Center at the University of Texas in Austin, the Huntington Library in San Marino, California, the Bancroft Library in Berkeley, California, and the California State Library in Sacramento, California.

Accounts written by frontierswomen can also be found in regional, state, and local historical journals and in book form. The latter are often privately printed and frequently housed in rare book collections. As with those materials in archival collections, these sources represent a cross-section of women including the less-than-literate, the very young and old, the unmarried and widowed, the lower middle class, and those of various ethnic and racial backgrounds. Because diary keeping and letter writing were common activities of nineteenth-century women, we have original accounts from more than just the literate middle-class woman.

Fortunately, there are now a number of finding aids available that are useful in locating the appropriate women's source materials. One of the most comprehensive guides to primary women's sources is Andrea Hinding and Clark Chambers, *Women's History Sources,* 2 volumes (New York, 1979). Other useful resource guides are Lynn Donovan, "Women's History: A Listing of West Coast Archival and Manuscript Sources," *California Historical Quarterly,* 55 (Spring and Summer 1976), 74–83, 170–85; Carol Fairbanks and Sara Brooks Sundberg, *Farm Women on the Prairie Frontier: A Sourcebook for Canada and the United States* (Metuchen, N.J.: Scarecrow Press, 1983); Cynthia E. Harrison, ed., *Women in American History: A Bibliography* (Santa Barbara: Clio Press, Inc., 1979); Joan M. Jensen and Darlis A. Miller, "The Gentle Tamers Revisited: New Approaches to the History of Women in the American West," *Pacific Historical Review,* 49 (May 1980), 173–212; Rayna Green, "Native American Women," *Signs,* 6, no. 2 (Winter 1980), 248–67; Beatrice Medicine, "Bibliography of Native American Women," *The Indian Historian,* 8, no. 3 (1973), 51—53; Sheryll and Gene Patterson-Black, *Western Women: In History and Literature* (Crawford, Nebraska: Cottonwood Press, 1978); and Glenda Riley, "Suggestions for Further Reading," *Journal of the West,* 21, no. 2 (April 1982), 82–88.

Other helpful materials used in this study include prescriptive literature aimed at nineteenth-century women—domestic and other novels, poetry, speeches, sermons, newspaper and journal articles, travelers' commentaries, paintings, drawings, and for the early twentieth century films. Since each of these often supported a particular viewpoint or perspective they must be used cautiously. The didactic literature for women, for example, probably presents a more accurate picture of what many people wished women were doing, than what women actually were doing. Had women already been behaving in the way that these writers outlined, there would have been little need for the scores of guidebooks that appeared throughout the nineteenth century. In addition, travelers' observations often mirrored their own prejudices and expectations more accurately than they did the reality of the western American scene.

The writings of nearly 200 westering men were also employed in this study. As with the women's sources, these male writers ranged from the very literate to those barely so, young to old, single to married, upper to lower class, and were of diverse racial and ethnic stock. The primary difference between the men and the women was that the men frequently moved westward in all-male groups. No similar all-female expeditions existed. The men's documents provide an interesting and enlightening counterpoint to the women's writings. The comparative element is especially significant when men and women migrated in the same family group, as a married couple, or as members of the same wagon train or community.

Finally, the rich and rapidly growing secondary literature on women in the West was incorporated throughout. The past decade has witnessed a veritable burgeoning of scholarly interest in rural and western women. It is hoped that this study not only benefited from that literature, but will generate ideas and hypotheses that will result in even more research in the near future.

Index

Index

Index

Index

Fundamentalism, 2
Furness, Kate, 134, 154, 215–16
Fur trade, 171

Gardner-Sharp, Abbie, 18, 20
Gerodet, 42
Gerstacker, Friedrich, 41, 46, 47, 48, 76
Godey's Lady's Book, 2, 8, 25, 28–29
Goodale, Elaine, 181
Goltra, Elizabeth, 125
Goya, Francisco de, 42
Gray, Martha, 157
Grimke, Angelina, 10
Grund, Francis, 44, 60
Guill, Mary Jane, 129, 136
Guns, 140, 172

Hale, Sarah Josepha, 8–9, 10, 12, 25
Hall, James, 22–23
Hall, Maggie, 99
Hanna, Esther, 128, 139, 153
Hardy, Lady Duffus, 49
Harlan, A. W., 186–87
Haun, Catherine, 99, 134, 172, 189, 191
Hecox, Margaret, 127, 128, 230–31
Hentz, Caroline Lee, 5
Herb remedies, 177
Herndon, Sarah, 129, 235–36
Hill, Emma, 138–39, 180
Hillyer, Edwin, 187–88
Hodgson, Adam, 72, 78
Holmes, Olivia, 99
Holley, Mary Austin, 39
Hope Leslie, 32
Hopping, Mary, 140, 154
Horton, Emily, 90–91, 132
Houston, Samuel, 116

Hurd, Cyrus, 88
Huron Indians, 80

Indians, anti-Indian attitudes, 116; burial customs of, 131, 196–97; childbirth, 139; children, 127, 139; cleanliness of, 128–30; clothing, 126–28, 141, 192–93; crafts, 139; desire for livestock, 158; dietary habits of, 129, 171, 198; differentiation among tribes, 152; dwellings, 138–39, 193–94; families of, 76–77; feared, 83–115, 133; hired by whites, 172–73; in circuses and shows, 20–21; inability to speak English, 130–31; and liquor, 59, 134, 158, 162, 172, 197–98; marriage customs of, 132–33, 197; mating practices, 131; odor of, 130; Oklahoma, 159–60; perceptions of, 30–32, 57–60, 69, 74–77, 124–25, 133–34, 136, 226, 227; sex roles, 77–79; sympathies toward, 140, 142, 151–55, 206–8; trade with, 170–72, 175; viewed by white women, 15–17, 19–20, 121–22; weaponry of, 195; women, 21–24, 32–34, 35, 43–44, 69–72, 74–75, 76–81, 133
Indian Princess, or, La Belle Sauvage, The, 31, 33
Industrialization, 2
Intermarriage, 71–73, 159, 131–32, 174–75, 181–83

Jack Tier, 26
Jackson, Andrew, 17
Jackson, Helen Hunt, 32
Jedlicki, Jerzy, 41
Jefferson, Thomas, 17, 23

331

Index

Index

333

Index